"In breadth of coverage, thoroughness of learning, clarity of analysis and argument and, I think, soundness of judgment, this solid, lucid, pastorally angled treatise has no peer. Evangelicals who research, debate, teach, and counsel on gender, sex, marriage, and family will find it an endlessly useful resource. The easy mastery with which the author threads his way through forty years' special pleadings gives this compendium landmark significance, and I recommend it highly."

—J. I. PACKER
Professor of Theology, Regent College

"A generation ago the most influential book on marriage for me was *God and Marriage* by Geoffrey Bromiley. It was remarkable in being an exposition of the Bible on marriage built around its relation to each member of the Trinity. No stories, just solid meat. I loved it. Now I have been married over 35 years and have sons who are near where I was in their marriages. For them—and for a whole generation under assault on the meaning of marriage and family—I am now looking to Andreas Köstenberger's new and larger *God, Marriage, and Family* to do for this generation what Bromiley's book did for mine. Unlike Bromiley's book, Köstenberger's book takes on the challenges of the present explicitly. That is more necessary now than it was 25 years ago. The special value of this book lies again in its pervasive exposition of Scripture. We are adrift in a sea of speculation without this. I am thankful for the book. I plan to give it to my grown children."

—JOHN PIPER
Pastor for Preaching, Bethlehem Baptist Church, Minneapolis

"This is a superb book—the work of a gifted exegete whose feet are firmly planted in this world. *God, Marriage, and Family* addresses the daunting issues facing today's Christians regarding marriage, divorce, remarriage, sexuality, children, contraception, abortion, singleness, sex roles, and leadership with radical biblical fidelity and practicality. If you want the Bible on these questions, this is the book! As a pastor, I am recommending this book to all my church leaders. The charts and discussion questions make it easy to use and ideal for small groups. What a gift to today's church!"

—R. KENT HUGHES
Pastor, College Church in Wheaton (Illinois)

"Characterized by exemplary exegetical analysis, Köstenberger's book is a refreshing and welcome addition to the current debate on marriage and the family. This outstanding work will help academicians, pastors, counselors and anyone who genuinely seeks to understand God's design from a biblical perspective."

—MARY A. KASSIAN
Author, Edmonton, Alberta

"Anything Andreas Köstenberger publishes is worthy of attention. A New Testament professor with interests both systematic and pastoral is as rare a find as a Warfield or Carson. Köstenberger is such a find. His international education and experience, his teaching career, and his Christian character make him an author to be read with both care and anticipation.

"Growing out of his own teaching, writing, and living, this book is a great addition to any thoughtful Christian's library. If you doubt this, just take a couple of minutes right now and read the preface. If you read the preface, you'll read the book.

"Christians (and pastors) need to think more carefully—this book helps us. You may not agree with all of his conclusions, but you'll be better equipped for living and teaching about God, marriage, and the family. Useful for scholars and ministers, the book's charts and questions make it useful for personal and group studies as well.

"Köstenberger calls his approach 'integrative'—I call it biblical and practical. Sensible, balanced, and biblical, this is a sound and timely summary of the Bible's teaching on some of the most basic and yet controversial topics in today's world. I highly recommend it."
—MARK DEVER
    Senior Pastor, Capitol Hill Baptist Church, Washington, D.C.

"If you are looking for just another collection of saccharine clichés about shiny happy Christian families, then you might want to leave this volume on the bookstore shelf. In this book, a world-renowned biblical scholar joins with a brilliant young ethicist to lay out a vision of where the family fits in the cosmic purposes of God. With clarity, conviction, and straight talk, this book avoids worn-out generalities and tackles head-on issues ranging from singleness to in vitro fertilization to the discipline of children. In an era when too many Christians listen more intently to television therapists than to the Bible on the question of the family, this could be one of the most significant books you ever read."
—RUSSELL D. MOORE
    Dean, School of Theology
    Senior Vice President for Academic Administration,
    The Southern Baptist Theological Seminary

"There has never been a greater need for a comprehensive, well-researched, and thoroughly biblical examination of the interrelated topics of marriage, family, and sexuality. Although not all will agree with each conclusion, Köstenberger has done the church a great service by providing this readable and eminently useful volume, which includes a careful examination of a wide variety of related issues, such as singleness, childlessness, homosexuality, and divorce."
—GORDON P. HUGENBERGER
    Senior Minister, Park Street Church, Boston
    Adjunct Professor of Old Testament,
    Gordon-Conwell Theological Seminary

"It is refreshing to find a book on marriage and the family that is (1) practical and understandable, (2) grounded in the teaching of hundreds of texts taken from the whole Bible, and (3) written by a first-rate New Testament scholar with the help of a widely respected ethics professor. The book is wide-ranging and reflects mature judgment in interpreting Scripture and applying it to life. The author does not avoid controversial issues (such as divorce, homosexuality, contraception, infertility, spanking of children, and male headship, to name a few), but in each case he treats the issues fairly with ample explanation of alternative views. This is an excellent book that deserves to be widely used."

—WAYNE GRUDEM
  Research Professor of Bible and Theology,
  Phoenix Seminary, Scottsdale, Arizona

"Books dealing with biblical perspectives on marriage and the family are readily available today for those interested in pursuing this subject. However, few exhibit the clarity of expression, graciousness of tone, practicality of counsel, and respect for the biblical evidence that is exhibited in this study. This volume should not only be on the shelf of every pastor in this land, but should also be in the syllabus of every course on marriage and the family taught in Christian colleges and seminaries. The author's careful defense of traditional biblical values relating to family life demands a serious reading, especially by those who do not agree with him."

—DANIEL I. BLOCK
  Professor of Old Testament, The Southern Baptist Theological Seminary
  President, Institute of Biblical Research

"*God, Marriage, and Family: Rebuilding the Biblical Foundation* is another welcome volume from the pen of New Testament scholar Andreas Köstenberger, who, with the input of ethicists David W. Jones and Mark Liederbach, has given a definitive volume on the family. Driven by a passion for Scripture and fueled by a sense of urgency borne out of the cultural wars that seek to hide and even destroy the biblical patterns, Köstenberger grapples with salient issues of interest to those who see the family as God's basic unit in his revelation of himself. He does not sidestep difficult issues like homosexuality, adultery, co-habitation, sterility, contraception, and artificial reproductive technologies. We appreciate the author's full and carefully researched treatment of divorce and remarriage and its impact on those in ministry, though here we disagree with his conclusion. Nevertheless, we do warmly commend to women and men—whether single or married—this invaluable resource with extensive exegetical sections, helpful bibliography, personal study questions (as well as the answers to those questions), and a wonderful user-friendly context in which the reader can work and learn."

—PAIGE PATTERSON, President
  DOROTHY KELLEY PATTERSON, Professor of Theology in Women's Studies
  Southwestern Baptist Theological Seminary, Fort Worth, Texas

"With current statistics indicating that the foundations of the family have been eroded just as much among Bible-believing Christians as among the general population, and with marriage itself under full-scale cultural assault, one great need is for clear, sound biblical teaching in the churches. But the issues are knotty and the application is not for the faint-hearted. In this challenging context, Andreas Köstenberger has provided us with a superb exposition of God's Word on these matters. The Christian looking for a brief, understandable, straightforward, intelligent, faithful presentation of what the Bible says about marriage, family, divorce, remarriage, homosexuality, abortion, birth control, infertility, adoption, and singleness need look no further. *God, Marriage, and Family: Restoring the Biblical Foundation* is timely, well-informed, balanced, and pastorally wise. It will educate and encourage Christian shepherds, and challenge and aid the flock in these perilous times. One great advantage of this book is the helpful collection of personal and group study aids accompanying each chapter. This makes the book's solid instruction all the more accessible to teachers, preachers, and congregations, and aids the process of communication and discipleship."

—J. LIGON DUNCAN III
  Senior Minister, First Presbyterian Church, Jackson, Mississippi
  Moderator, General Assembly of the Presbyterian Church in America

"While many popular treatments of marriage and the family are available, very few have explored with care and precision Scripture's own teaching on these crucial subjects. With his extensive background in the interpretation of the New Testament, Dr. Köstenberger has now provided a vital resource for the church. And the timing of this major book could not be better! Köstenberger does not avoid the hard contemporary issues of gender and sexuality but addresses them with sensitivity combined with keen biblical insight. We are indebted to Professor Köstenberger for this invaluable contribution."

—BRUCE A. WARE
  Professor of Christian Theology
  Senior Associate Dean, School of Theology,
  The Southern Baptist Theological Seminary

"With the current attack on marriage and family now raging at a fevered pitch, Köstenberger's book, *God, Marriage, and Family,* is a vital resource that should be in the hands of every evangelical. His approach is rooted in a sound treatment of Scripture, coupled with his own passionate desire to see his culture restored to its Judeo-Christian foundations. Of particular note is the wealth of useful information Köstenberger makes available to his readers, many of whom will subsequently utilize it in their own arenas of life and ministry. This is a book that will often be quoted and that any person concerned about the current debates on marriage and family should have in his library."

—TOM ELLIFF
  Pastor, First Southern Baptist Church, Del City, Oklahoma
  Chairman, Southern Baptist Council on Family Life

"This volume is a treasure trove of biblical wisdom on matters pertaining to marriage, child-rearing, singleness, and sexuality in general. It is understandable for a lay reader, yet informed by a wide range of scholarship. It should find avid readers among individual Christians, but it is also well-suited for use in church or school classroom settings. As Western society struggles to hold on to its social identity, this study reaffirms God's will for self-understanding and family ties. Loving one another in the family is about knowing and reflecting the love of the Father who sent his Son. Readers seeking the whole counsel of God on these matters will find enormous assistance here."

—ROBERT W. YARBROUGH
Professor of New Testament
Chairman of New Testament Department,
Trinity Evangelical Divinity School

"Too often people, even evangelicals, engage in debates about the family or homosexuality or divorce without knowing well what the Scriptures teach. We stand in debt to Köstenberger and Jones for providing a biblically informed discussion on all these issues and more. The book is especially valuable because it is remarkably clear and comprehensible, while at the same time reflecting deep and responsible research. . . . I consistently found the conclusions to be sound and biblically faithful."

—THOMAS R. SCHREINER
Professor of New Testament, The Southern Baptist Theological Seminary

"These days it is important for us to remember that God has something to say about marriage and family. With all of the competing voices insisting on new definitions and unbiblical patterns, Andreas Köstenberger, along with David Jones, has provided the Christian community with an invaluable resource. This book is marked by biblical fidelity, excellent scholarship, readability, and smooth organization, and covers everything from the husband-wife relationship to ethical issues. It will be perfect for the college or seminary classroom, for local church educational programs, and for families trying to conform their lives to the Word of God. I heartily recommend it."

—RANDY STINSON
Executive Director, The Council on Biblical Manhood and Womanhood

"At a time when our society is attempting to redefine the standards and values of marriage and family, Dr. Andreas Köstenberger has brought us back to the biblical foundation. While Dr. Köstenberger does an excellent job in explaining many of the various secular views concerning marriage and family, he shows why God's way is still the better way. He tackles some very difficult and politically sensitive issues in this book. The view of marriage and the family presented in this book may not be the most popular view in our culture today, but it is the biblical view."

—BOB BAKER
Pastor of Pastoral Care
Saddleback Church, Lake Forest, California

"The richness and beauty of God's character and ways are most evident when we observe his entire redemptive story, from creation to final restoration. After all, though parts of a portrait might be interesting, it is the beauty and wonder of the whole that reveals the author. The unique contribution of *God, Marriage, and Family* is Köstenberger's approach: he carefully traces God's unfolding plan for marriage and family from creation through to the end. This holistic approach not only raises intriguing issues generally left unaddressed in a book on marriage, such as the miserable failure of some Old Testament marriages, but more importantly this approach offers a rich and unified biblical theology of the family and marriage.

"Köstenberger tackles difficult topics like divorce, homosexuality, and sexual reproduction within the framework of God's plan for marriage and family as revealed from Genesis to Revelation. Given the complexity of such issues, some will surely disagree with points here and there, but there is no wrangling about his approach. The true beauty of marriage and the family shines most brightly when one looks at these topics as they are developed throughout God's entire story."

—RICHARD W. HOVE
    Campus Crusade for Christ
    Duke University, Durham, North Carolina

GOD, MARRIAGE, *and* FAMILY

REBUILDING THE BIBLICAL FOUNDATION

ANDREAS J. KÖSTENBERGER

WITH DAVID W. JONES

CROSSWAY BOOKS

A DIVISION OF
GOOD NEWS PUBLISHERS
WHEATON, ILLINOIS

Library of Congress Cataloging-in-Publication Data

Köstenberger, Andreas J., 1957-
   God, marriage, and family : rebuilding the biblical foundation / Andreas J. Köstenberger with David W. Jones
     p. cm.
   Includes bibliographical references and index.
   ISBN 1-58134-580-1
   1. Marriage—Biblical teaching. 2. Family—Biblical teaching.
3. Marriage—Religious aspects—Christianity. 4. Family—Religious
aspects—Christianity. I. Title: God, marriage, and family. II. Jones, David
W. (David Wayne), 1973-   . III. Title.
BS680.M35K67   2004
261.8'358—dc22   2004018925

CH		14	13	12	11	10	09	08	07	06	05	04
15	14	13	12	11	10	9	8	7	6	5	4	3	2	1

For my dear wife Margaret and my children
Lauren, Tahlia, David, and Timothy

*"For this reason I bow my knees before the Father,
From whom every family in heaven and on earth is named,
That according to the riches of his glory he may grant you
To be strengthened with power through his Spirit in your inner being,
So that Christ may dwell in your hearts through faith—
That you, being rooted and grounded in love,
May have strength to comprehend with all the saints
What is the breadth and length and height and depth,
And to know the love of Christ that surpasses knowledge,
That you may be filled with all the fullness of God"*
(EPHESIANS 3:14-19)

Andreas J. Köstenberger

For Dawn, Johnathan, and Laura

"As for me and my house, we will serve the Lord"
(JOSHUA 24:15)

David W. Jones

CONTENTS

CHARTS AND LISTS

CHARTS

LISTS

FOREWORD

MARRIAGE AND FAMILY are good gifts from a great God. Unfortunately, in our day the Master's Manual is often neglected and even rejected. Ignorance, apathy, and antagonism abound in our culture when it comes to God's blueprint for the sacred institution of the home. It is out of this context and crisis that I take great pleasure in commending this outstanding work. I am convinced it will become a standard text in the field for many years to come.

In *God, Marriage, and Family,* Andreas Köstenberger (with the help of David Jones) provides a comprehensive and thorough biblical analysis of issues related to marriage and family. The research is first-class, and the bibliography alone is worth the purchase. This book is a gold mine of information as the authors examine the entire breath of Holy Scripture in search of the Bible's teaching on crucial issues related to the life of marriage, family, and the home. The treatment of each subject, in my judgment, is fair, balanced, and judicious. On the few occasions where Bible-believing Christians may legitimately disagree, the authors thoroughly present both sides of the issue while indicating their own preferred view. In their careful scholarship and well reasoned argumentation, the authors provide a model of evenhandedness in dealing with hotly debated issues.

It is rare that you find a book that knits together in such a beautiful tapestry both the theological and the practical. *God, Marriage, and Family* accomplishes this superbly. The book is theocentric and bibliocentric from beginning to end and yet, commonsense observations and spiritual counsel are woven into the fabric of each chapter. Perhaps more books ought to be written by a biblical scholar in collaboration with Christian ethicists who have a special interest in and love for marriage and family.

Having arrived in January 2004 as the new president of Southeastern Baptist Theological Seminary in Wake Forest, N.C., I was immediately impressed by the spirituality and scholarship of its faculty. Drs. Köstenberger and Jones (as well as Dr. Liederbach, who contributed two sections on medical ethics) are among those gems. I love these men and rejoice in this wonderful gift they have presented to the church of the Lord Jesus Christ. I pray that God will give this volume both a wide audience and receptive hearts. *God, Marriage, and Family* calls us to a higher standard, God's standard, when it comes to how we think about marriage and family.

Daniel L. Akin
President
Southeastern Baptist Theological Seminary
Wake Forest, North Carolina

PREFACE

THE VISION FOR THE present volume was born when I (Andreas) was asked to write an essay on marriage and the family in the New Testament for a recent book (*Marriage and Family in the Biblical World;* InterVarsity, 2003). While working on the project, it became clear that while issues related to marriage and the family are integrated in Scripture, there still is no book-length treatment that presents the biblical teaching on these topics in an integrative format. In our own context at Southeastern Seminary, a new course, "Marriage and Family: Foundations," was recently added to the curriculum and is now required of all students, which further underscored the need for this kind of treatment.

Not only are we driven by a passion for God's Word and for teaching what the Bible says on marriage and the family, but recent developments in the general culture further fuel our sense of urgency and concern. Some denominations have found it necessary to add a statement defining marriage as a union between one man and one woman to their official doctrinal base. Episcopalians have appointed an openly practicing homosexual as bishop for the first time in their history. The courts and public officials have ruled, enacted, and spoken out in favor of same-sex marriages. The media, too, tend to be sympathetic to gay rights issues. Others in contemporary government have gone on record as favoring a constitutional amendment defining marriage as between one man and one woman.

On the basis of our conviction that the current cultural crisis with regard to marriage and family is at the root a spiritual crisis, we firmly believe that the only solution is a return to, and rebuilding of, the biblical foundations of these institutions. Once God is removed as the initiator of the institution of marriage and the family, the door is opened to a plethora of human understandings of these terms and concepts, and, in the spirit of postmodernism, no one definition has the right to claim greater legitimacy than any others. The only mechanism to adjudicate between competing definitions, then, is not that of morality but that of public opinion and majority vote.

Continuing down this path of moral decline and corruption would inevitably affect the stability of our civilization. Removed from its Judeo-Christian moorings, our society would instead be built on an ethic whose highest values are no loftier than individual self-fulfillment, personal pleasure, and affluence (as Francis Schaeffer warned decades ago). Hoping that the political process, or reasonable human discussion, will solve the current dilemma of seeking to define or redefine marriage and the family is an illusion. We write this book with the conviction that the only way *forward* is to *return* to Scripture and to put God back at the center of marriage and the family—hence the title of our book, *God, Marriage, and Family*.

In the first chapter, "The Current Cultural Crisis: Rebuilding the Foundation," we seek to make a case for the need for a biblical and integrative treatment of marriage and the family by giving two reasons why such a treatment is vitally important. The following two chapters, "Leaving and Cleaving: Marriage in the Old Testament" and "No Longer Two, but One: Marriage in the New Testament," present the divine institution of marriage in the opening chapters of Genesis, discuss violations of God's plan for marriage in the history of Old Testament Israel, as well as glimpses of the ideal in Old Testament wisdom literature, and derive a Christian theology of marriage, focusing primarily on the teachings of Jesus and Paul. Chapter 4, "The Nature of Marriage: Sacrament, Contract, or Covenant?" is devoted to a discussion of the major views on the nature of marriage and whether marriage is best viewed as a sacrament, contract, or covenant, including a discussion of the implications of the viewpoint adopted in the present work.

Chapters 5 and 6, "The Ties that Bind: Family in the Old Testament" and "The Christian Family: Family in the New Testament," provide an overview of the biblical teaching on the family and discuss topics such as the ancient Israelite conception of family, the importance of teaching children about God, and the need to instill biblical values in young people. We also look at Jesus' encounters with and statements involving children and discuss Paul's teaching on the father's role in the home and in teaching and disciplining his children. Other subjects are the importance of motherhood, the way in which children's obedience is to serve as a vital part of their Christian discipleship, and both good and bad biblical examples of parenting.

Chapters 7 and 8, "To Have or Not to Have Children: Special Issues Related to the Family (Part 1)" and "Requiring the Wisdom of Solomon: Special Issues Related to the Family (Part 2)," deal with a variety of issues related to marriage and the family. Chapter 7 covers childlessness and medical ethics, abortion, contraception, artificial reproductive technologies (ART), and adoption. (The sections on contraception and ART were contributed by our colleague Mark Liederbach.) Chapter 8 is devoted to special issues faced in parenting today, such as single parenting and physical discipline. The chapter concludes with a discussion of spiritual warfare pertaining to marriage and the family. Chapter 9, "Undivided Devotion to the Lord: The Divine Gift of Singleness," surveys singleness in Old and New Testament times (including important statements by Jesus and Paul on the subject) as well as in the early church. The topics of cohabitation and premarital sex as well as courtship and dating are also covered.

The following two chapters deal with the major threats to biblical marriage and the family. Chapter 10, "Abandoning Natural Relations: The Biblical Verdict on Homosexuality," surveys all the major passages on homosexuality (and lesbianism) in Scripture (including those dealing with Sodom and Gomorrah, the Levitical Holiness Code, and the major pronouncements of the apostle Paul on the subject). After a thorough engagement of attempts employed by advocates of homosexuality to prove that Scripture only prohibits certain aberrant forms of homosexuality but not monogamous, faithful same-sex unions, we arrive at a clear, unequivocal conclusion regarding the biblical verdict on homosexuality.

Chapter 11, "Separating What God Has Joined Together: Divorce and Remarriage," deals with the second major threat to biblical marriage and the family. With divorce rates at unprecedented levels, both in the general culture and among Christians, a thorough understanding of the biblical teaching on divorce and remarriage is urgently needed. Unfortunately, this is an area in which there is no consensus even among

Bible-believing Christians. The complexity of the issues involved requires a treatment that is perhaps more technical than that which is provided in the other chapters in order to deal with the different views fairly. We hope that looking at Scripture's teaching on both homosexuality and divorce will prove to reinforce our appreciation for and commitment to building biblical marriages and families.

Family requirements for leaders in the church is the final topic addressed in the book. Chapter 12, "Faithful Husbands: Qualifications for Church Leadership," includes discussions on the meaning of the phrase "husband of one wife" (or "faithful husband") in Paul's Pastoral Epistles; church officers and the issue of divorce; requirements pertaining to church leaders' children; and singleness and church leadership. Chapter 13, "Uniting All Things in Him: Concluding Synthesis," provides a brief summary of our major findings. The final section, "For Further Study: Helpful Resources," identifies materials for those who want to engage in additional research and study.

One word on the title, *God, Marriage, and Family,* may be appropriate as well. While the resemblance to the title of Geoffrey Bromiley's book, *God and Marriage,* is strictly coincidental, it is probably no coincidence that Bromiley's is one of the few more satisfying biblical and thoroughgoing theological treatments on the subject. First written in 1980 (Eerdmans) and reprinted in 2003 (Wipf & Stock), the book retains its usefulness as a survey of the major biblical passages on marriage and their theological ramifications. While Bromiley erects a certain dichotomy between Scripture on the one hand and God on the other (opting for the latter), we would affirm that no such dichotomy exists. Precisely *by studying Scripture* we can know God's will for marriage and the family and rebuild the biblical foundation. Nevertheless, we are honored to build on Bromiley's work in many ways and hope to expand its scope by a more detailed engagement of the relevant biblical texts and a more thorough exploration of related issues. We are well aware that every chapter of the present volume, in turn, could easily be expanded into a still fuller treatment if not an entire monograph.

We trust that the present integrative and biblical treatment of issues related to marriage and the family will prove beneficial not only to seminary students and pastors in local churches but also to a wide variety of other readers. Sunday school classes, home Bible studies, discipleship groups, homeschool families, and others will find this a helpful tool to explore and understand what the Bible teaches about these all-important topics. To this end we have provided a study guide including discussion questions (plus answers) in the back of the volume. Others who are not Christians may want to view this volume simply to see what the Bible teaches on marriage and the family, whether or not they agree with all of our conclusions.

In the interest of full disclosure, David W. Jones wrote initial drafts of chapters 2, 4, 9, and 10, as well as of the introduction and conclusion (chapters 1 and 13). Andreas Köstenberger wrote the remainder of the book and thoroughly revised and added to the initial drafts provided by David Jones. In addition, Mark Liederbach provided the sections on contraception and artificial reproduction technologies in chapter 7, Alan Bandy contributed the discussion of physical punishment in chapter 8 and provided material on single parenting, and Corin Mihaila assisted in preparing the charts and the Personal and Group Study Guide. Special thanks are due Margaret Köstenberger, who thoroughly edited a preliminary version of this book before it was submitted for publication. Dawn Jones read through the manuscript several times and made a number of suggestions for improvement. David and Ann Croteau and Alan Bandy also read through parts or all of an earlier draft of this book (David twice) and provided helpful feedback.

Last but not least, we would like to express our gratitude to our wives and children, who have taught us, and continue to teach us, so much about the true meaning of marriage and the family and give us plenty of opportunity to practice what we preach! Nowhere is it harder to "walk our talk" than in our own homes where our loved ones know our shortcomings as well as (hopefully) our successes. Above all, we are so grateful that, through our Lord Jesus Christ, we have been introduced to a vital relationship with God our heavenly Father, whose loving care and faithfulness we experience every day and without whom we would never have been able to write this book. To God, and to him alone, be the glory.

1

THE CURRENT CULTURAL CRISIS: REBUILDING THE FOUNDATION

FOR THE FIRST TIME in its history, Western civilization is confronted with the need to *define* the meaning of the terms "marriage" and "family." What until now has been considered a "normal" family, made up of a father, a mother, and a number of children, has in recent years increasingly begun to be viewed as one among several options, which can no longer claim to be the only or even superior form of ordering human relationships. The Judeo-Christian view of marriage and the family with its roots in the Hebrew Scriptures has to a significant extent been replaced with a set of values that prizes human rights, self-fulfillment, and pragmatic utility on an individual and societal level. It can rightly be said that marriage and the family are institutions under siege in our world today, and that with marriage and the family, our very civilization is in crisis.

The current cultural crisis, however, is merely symptomatic of a deep-seated *spiritual* crisis that continues to gnaw at the foundations of our once-shared societal values. If God the Creator in fact, as the Bible teaches, instituted marriage and the family, and if there is an evil being called Satan who wages war against God's creative purposes in this world, it should come as no surprise that the divine foundation of these institutions has come under massive attack in recent years. Ultimately, we human beings, whether we realize it or not, are involved in a cosmic spiritual conflict that pits God against Satan, with marriage and the family serving as a key arena in which spiritual and cultural battles are fought. If, then, the *cultural* crisis is symptomatic of an underlying *spiritual* crisis, the solution likewise must be spiritual, not merely cultural.

In *God, Marriage, and Family,* we hope to point the way to this spiritual solution: a return to, and rebuilding of, the biblical foundation of marriage and the family. God's Word is not dependent on man's approval, and the Scriptures are not silent regarding the vital issues facing men and women and families today. In each of the important areas related to marriage and the family, the Bible offers satisfying instructions and wholesome remedies to the maladies afflicting our culture. The Scriptures record the *divine institution* of marriage and present a *Christian theology* of marriage and parenting. They offer insight for decision making regarding abortion, contraception, infertility, and adoption. They offer helpful guidance for those who are single or unmarried and address the major threats to marriage and the family: homosexuality and divorce.

THE CURRENT CONFUSION OVER MARRIAGE AND THE FAMILY

Measured against the biblical teaching on marriage and the family, it seems undeniable that Western culture is decaying. In fact, the past few decades have witnessed nothing less than a major paradigm shift with regard to marriage and the family. The West's Judeo-Christian heritage and foundation have largely been supplanted by a *libertarian ideology* that elevates human freedom and self-determination as the supreme principles for human relationships. In their confusion, many hail the decline of the biblical-traditional model of marriage and the family and its replacement by new competing moralities as major progress. Yet the following list of adverse effects of unbiblical views of marriage and the family upon society demonstrates that replacing the biblical-traditional model of marriage and the family with more "progressive" ones is detrimental even for those who do not view the Bible as authoritative.

One of the negative consequences of the erosion of the biblical-traditional model are skyrocketing *divorce* rates. However, the costs of divorce are troubling, not only for the people involved—especially children—but also for society at large. While children may not show ill effects of the trauma of divorce in the short run, serious negative long-term consequences have been well documented. *Sex outside of marriage*, because it does not occur within the secure environment of an exclusive lifetime commitment, also exerts a heavy price from those who engage in adulterous or otherwise illicit sexual relationships. Teenage pregnancies and abortion are the most glaring examples. While pleasurable in the short run, sex outside of marriage takes a heavy toll both psychologically and spiritually and contributes to the overall insecurity and stress causing the destabilization of our cultural foundation. *Homosexuality* deprives children in households run by same-sex partners of primary role models of both sexes and is unable to fulfill the procreative purposes God intended for the marriage union. *Gender-role confusion*, too, is an increasingly serious issue; many men and women have lost the concept of what it means to be masculine or feminine. This results in a loss of the complete identity of being human as God created us, male and female. Our sex does not merely determine the form of our sex organs but is an integral part of our entire being.

These few examples illustrate the disturbing fact that the price exacted by the world as a result of its abandonment of the biblical foundations for marriage and the family is severe indeed. An integrative, biblical treatment of marriage and the family is essential to clear up moral confusion and to firm up convictions that, if acted upon, have the potential of returning the church and culture back to God's intentions for marriages and families.

The Lack of Biblical, Integrative Christian Literature on Marriage and the Family

It is not only the world that is suffering the consequences of neglecting the Creator's purposes for marriage and the family. The church, too, having lowered itself to the standard of the world in many ways, has become a part of the problem, and is not offering the solutions the world needs. Not that Christians are unaware of their need to be educated about God's plan for marriage and the family. An abundance of resources and activities is available. There are specialized ministries and parachurch organizations. There are marriage seminars and retreats.

There are books on marriage and the family, as well as magazines, video productions, Bible studies, and official statements focusing on marriage and the family. Yet for all the church is doing in this area, the fact remains that in the end there is shockingly little difference between the world and the church. Why is this the case? We believe the reason why all the above-mentioned efforts to build strong Christian marriages and families are ineffective to such a significant extent is found, at least in part, in the *lack of commitment to seriously engage the Bible as a whole*. The result is that much of the available Christian literature on the subject is seriously imbalanced.

Anyone stepping into a Christian or general bookstore will soon discover that while there is a plethora of books available on individual topics, such as marriage, singleness, divorce and remarriage, and homosexuality, there is *very little material* that explores on a deeper, more thoroughgoing level the entire fabric of God's purposes for human relationships. Though there is a place for books focused narrowly on one given topic to address certain specific needs, it is only when we see how the Bible's teaching on human relationships *coheres* and finds its common source in the Creator and his wise and beneficial purposes for men and women that we will have the insight and the strength to rise above our natural limitations and to embrace God's plan for human relationships in their fullness and completeness.

When a couple struggles in their marriage, they often find it helpful to focus on the more superficial remedies, such as improving their communication skills, enriching their sex life, learning better how to meet each other's needs, or similar techniques. Yet often the true cause for marital problems lies deeper. What does it mean for a man to leave his father and mother and to cleave to his wife? What does it mean for a husband and a wife to become "one flesh"? How can they be naked and not ashamed? How can it be that, once married, husband and wife are "no longer two, but one," as Jesus taught, because it is *God* who joined them together? How does sin twist and distort the roles of husband and wife, parent and child? Only if we are seeking to answer some of these deeper, underlying questions will we be adequately equipped to deal with specific challenges we face in our relationships with one another.

Yet the fact remains that many, if not most, of the plethora of popular books written on marriage and the family are theologically weak and not fully adequate in their application of sound principles of biblical interpretation. Many of these authors have Ph.D.s in counseling or psychology but their formal training in the study of Scripture is lacking. Theological and hermeneutical naïveté gives birth to superficial diagnoses, which in turn issue in superficial remedies. It seems that the dynamics and effects of sin are poorly understood in our day. The result is that many Christian self-help books owe more to secular culture than a thoroughgoing Christian worldview. Christian, biblical counselors who take Scripture seriously and believe that diagnoses and remedies must be based on a theologically and hermeneutically accurate understanding of the biblical teaching on marriage and the family find this unhelpful if not positively misleading.

For this reason there remains a need for a volume that does not treat issues related to marriage and the family in isolation from one another but that shows how human fulfillment in these relationships is rooted in the divine revelation found exclusively and sufficiently in Scripture.

THE CONTRIBUTION OF THIS BOOK: BIBLICAL AND INTEGRATIVE

The authors of the present volume believe that a biblical and integrative approach most adequately represents the Bible's teaching on marriage and the family. Within the limited scope of this work, we will attempt to sketch out the contours of a *"biblical theology* of marriage and the family,*"* that is, a presentation of what the Bible *itself* has to say on these vital topics. While we certainly do not claim to have the final word on every issue or to be infallible interpreters of the sacred Word, what we are after is decidedly *not* what *we* think marriage or family should be, based on our own preconceived notions, preferences, or traditional values, but what we believe *Scripture itself* tells us about these institutions. This, of course, requires a humble, submissive stance toward Scripture rather than one that asserts one's own independence from the will of the Creator and insists on inventing one's own rules of conduct.

In such a spirit, and placing ourselves consciously *under,* rather than *above,* Scripture, we will seek to determine in the following chapters what the Bible teaches on the various components of human relationships in an *integrative* manner: the nature of, and special issues related to, marriage and the family, childrearing, singleness, as well as homosexuality and divorce and remarriage. Because the Bible is the Word of God, which is powerful and life-transforming, we know that those who are willing to be seriously engaged by Scripture will increasingly come to know and understand God's will for marriage and the family and be able to appropriate God's power in building strong Christian homes and families. This, in turn, will both increase God's honor and reputation in this world that he has made and provide the seasoning and illumination our world needs at this time of cultural ferment and crisis with regard to marriage and the family.

2

LEAVING AND CLEAVING: MARRIAGE IN THE OLD TESTAMENT

WHAT IS GOD'S PLAN for marriage? As we have seen in the previous chapter, there is considerable confusion on this point in contemporary culture. To address the prevailing cultural crisis and to strengthen Christian convictions on this issue, we must endeavor to rebuild the biblical foundations of this most intimate of human relationships.[1] The treatment on marriage in the Old Testament in the present chapter will proceed along chronological, salvation-historical lines. Our study of the theme of marriage and of the Old Testament teaching on marriage takes its point of departure from the foundational narrative in Genesis 1–3, which roots the institution of marriage firmly in the will of the Creator and describes the consequences of the fall of humanity on the married couple. This is followed by a survey of Israel's subsequent history with regard to the roles of husbands and wives toward each other and traces several ways in which God's creation ideal for marriage was compromised. The last corpus under consideration is the Old Testament wisdom literature, which upholds the divine ideal for marriage in the portrait of the excellent wife in Proverbs 31 and envisions the restoration of the original husband-and-wife relationship in the Song of Solomon.

As we set out to explore the biblical teaching on marriage, it is important to remember that while this is an *important topic* in Scripture, it is not the *primary focus* of divine revelation. Both Testaments center primarily on tracing the provision of salvation by God in and through

Jesus Christ: in the Old Testament *prospectively* by way of promises and anticipatory patterns pointing to the coming of the Messiah, in the New Testament *retrospectively* by way of fulfillment and realization of God's provision of salvation and forgiveness in Jesus Christ. To this end, the Old Testament follows God's promises to Abraham, the giving of the law through Moses, and the Davidic line.

Yet as the history of Israel unfolds, we see various examples of godly and ungodly marriages, as well as Mosaic legislation concerning various aspects of and aberrations from God's pattern for human relationships. While it is therefore salvation history, not marriage, that is the primary focus of divine revelation, the Scriptures were nonetheless "written for our instruction" (1 Cor. 10:11; cf. 2 Tim. 3:16) and therefore provide fruitful material for study.

ROOTED IN CREATION (GENESIS 1–3)

In exploring the biblical teaching on marriage, there is no more important paradigm than God's intended pattern for marriage presented in *Genesis 1–3*.[2] Although the book of Genesis was originally addressed to Israel's wilderness generation in preparation for entering the Promised Land, the early chapters of this book provide the parameters of the Creator's design for marriage in every age. This is reflected in Jesus' and Paul's teaching and applies to our own age as well.[3] Who was this God who had saved Israel from slavery in Egypt and had given the nation the law at Sinai? What are the foundational teachings on the family, societal structures, and sin?

The first three chapters of Genesis provide answers to these questions, initially from the vantage point of ancient Israel, but ultimately for every person who has ever lived.[4] In Genesis 1–3, the God whom Israel had come to know as Redeemer and Lawgiver is revealed as the Creator of the universe, the all-powerful, all-wise, and eternal God who spoke everything there is into being. Marriage is shown to be rooted in God's creative act of making humanity in his image as male and female. Sin is depicted as the result of humanity's rebellion against the Creator at the instigation of Satan, himself a fallen creature, and as becoming so much a part of the human nature that people ever since the Fall are by nature rebelling against their Creator and his plan for their lives.

The depiction of the original creation of man and woman and the subsequent fall of humanity in Genesis 1–3 centers around at least three very important clusters of principles, which will be explored in the following discussion.[5] These are: (1) the man and the woman are created in God's image *to rule the earth for God;* (2) the man is created first and is given *ultimate responsibility for the marriage relationship,* while the woman is placed alongside the man as his "suitable helper"; and (3) the fall of humanity entails *negative consequences* for both the man and the woman. We will treat each of these topics in turn.

Created in God's Image to Rule the Earth for God

The fact that both men and women are *created in the likeness and image of their Creator* invests them with inestimable worth, dignity, and significance. Popular notions of what it means to be created in God's image have often been unduly influenced by Greek concepts of personality.[6] Thus, God's image in the man and the woman has frequently been identified in terms of their possession of intelligence, a will, or emotions.[7] While this may be presupposed or implied to some extent in Genesis 1:27,[8] the immediate context develops the notion of the divine image in the man and the woman in terms of *representative rule* (cf. Ps. 8:6-8).

In light of the original provenance of this text in an ancient Semitic environment, it may be significant that the erecting of a sovereign's image in a given location was tantamount to establishing that person's claim to authority and rule. According to one author,

> It is precisely in his [the man's] function as a ruler that he is God's image. In the ancient East the setting up of the king's statue was the equivalent to the proclamation of his domination over the sphere in which the statue was erected (cf. Dan. 3:1, 5f.). When in the thirteenth century BC the Pharaoh Rameses II had his image hewn out of rock at the mouth of the *nahr el-kelb,* on the Mediterranean north of Beirut, the image meant that he was the ruler of this area. Accordingly, man is set in the midst of creation as God's statue.[9]

By placing his image on the man and the woman and by setting them in a particular environment, therefore, God assigns to them the mandate of *representative rule.* This rule is the joint function of the man and the woman (note the plural pronouns in Gen. 1:28, "God blessed *them*. And God said to *them* . . ."), although the man carries *ultimate responsibility* before God as the head of the woman.[10] While *substantive* elements of the divine image in man (that is, an analogy between the nature of God and characteristics of humans) cannot be ruled out, a *functional* understanding (humans exercising the function of ruling the earth for God) seems to reflect most accurately the emphasis in the biblical record.[11] This appears to be the clear implication from the immediate context of Genesis 1:27, where creation is defined in terms of being fruitful and multiplying and subduing the earth (v. 28). The first man and the first woman were thus charged to exercise representative rule in part by *procreation*.

In this sense, then, human beings are "like God." Just as God rules over a large domain—the whole universe—so humanity is given charge of the entire earth to rule it for God. This also establishes the principle of stewardship: not the man and the woman, but God is ultimately owner of the created realm; the man and the woman are simply the divinely appointed caretakers. Moreover, this stewardship is a *joint* stewardship shared by the man and the woman. *Together* they are to exercise it according to the will and for the glory of God. *Together* they are to multiply and be stewards of the children given to them by God. And *together* they are to subdue the earth by a division of labor that assigns to the man the primary responsibility to provide for his wife and children and to the woman the care for and nurture of her family. The following discussion will continue to unfold God's good design of complementarity.

The Man's Ultimate Responsibility for the Marriage and the Wife's Role as His "Suitable Helper"

The apostle Paul's comments on Genesis 1–3 repeatedly root the man's primary responsibility in the family (as well as in the church) in the fact that he was *created first*. Not only does Paul draw attention to the fact that the man was created first, but he also notes that it is not *the man who was made for the woman, but the woman for the man* (1 Cor. 11:9; cf. Gen. 2:18, 20) and *from the man* (1 Cor. 11:8, 12; cf. Gen. 2:22). Moreover, the man was the one who received the divine command (Gen.

2:16-17), was presented with the woman (2:22), and named the woman with a name derived from his own (2:23; cf. 3:20), which also implies his authority.[12] These facts follow plainly from a reading of the creation narrative in Genesis.

While Genesis 1 simply notes the creation of man as male and female in God's image, Genesis 2 provides further detail on the exact order and orientation of the creation of man and woman. Paul's comments clearly indicate that he considered this account to be historical (rather than mythical or fictional):[13] at the beginning of human history God made the first man, endowed him with life, and placed him in a garden (Gen. 2:7-8, 15). Moreover, God addressed to man certain moral commands (2:16-17). Prior to the creation of the woman, the man had already begun exercising the divine mandate to subdue the earth, naming the animals (2:19-20). In order to supply his need for companionship, God created the woman to be Adam's wife.

God's creation of Eve demonstrates that God's plan for Adam's marriage, as well as for all subsequent marriages, involves a *monogamous heterosexual* relationship. God only made *one* "suitable helper" for Adam, and she was *female*. What is more, it was *God* who perceived Adam's aloneness and hence created the woman. The biblical text gives no indication that Adam himself was even conscious of being alone or discontent in his singleness.[14] Rather, God is shown to take the initiative in fashioning a compatible human companion for the man. For this reason it can truly be said that marriage is *God's* idea and that it was *God* who made the woman of his own sovereign will as a "suitable helper" for the man (Gen. 2:18, 20).

But what is the force of the expression "suitable helper"? A contextual reading of the expression in its original setting suggests that, on the one hand, the woman is *congenial* to the man in a way that none of the animals are (Gen. 2:19-20; she is "bone of [his] bones and flesh of [his] flesh," 2:23), and, on the other hand, that the woman is placed alongside the man as his *associate* or *assistant*. On a personal level, she will provide for the man's need for *companionship* (2:18). In relation to God's mandate for humanity to be fruitful and multiply and to fill the earth and subdue it (1:28), the woman is a suitable partner both in *procreation* (becoming "one flesh" with him [2:24]) and in the earth's *domestication*

(1:28: "And God blessed *them*. And God said to *them* . . ."). Her role is *distinct* from the man's, yet *unique* and exceedingly *significant*. While assigned to the man as his "helper" and thus placed under his overall charge, the woman is his partner in ruling the earth for God.

Those denying female subordination as being rooted in the creative order point to the fact that the term "helper" (Heb. *ezer*) in the Old Testament is repeatedly applied to none less than God himself (Ex. 18:4; Ps. 20:2; 33:20; 70:5; 115:9-11; 121:1-2; 146:5). If God, who is clearly not subordinate to anyone, is called "helper," it is argued, how can it be maintained that the term in and of itself establishes the woman's subordination to the man?[15] Indeed, if the issue were that of *essential* or *ontological* subordination, as to a difference in the nature of a woman's humanity, such would seem to be excluded.

If the question is one of *functional* subordination in terms of *role distinction*, however, the mere application of the expression "helper" to God in the Old Testament does not obviate the woman's subordination to the man in terms of being his "helper."[16] Rather, all that these instances prove is that God, as humanity's "helper," may at times choose to subordinate himself and his own interests to those of human beings by caring for them, providing for them, and so on. This does not affect his divinity, however, just as Jesus' divinity was not diminished by his incarnation.[17] Nor is the Holy Spirit's divinity compromised by his service to and indwelling of flesh-bound human beings.

Moreover, in the case of the woman, Genesis 2 does not teach that she may merely *act* as the man's "helper" *when she so chooses*, but rather that serving as the man's "helper" *sums up her very reason for existence* in relation to the man. Being the man's "helper" is the purpose for which the woman was created, as far as her wifely status is concerned (as a human being, of course, who shares in the image of God, the woman, like the man, is created to bring glory to God and to serve him, but she is to do so within the God-ordained parameters of the husband-and-wife relationship as far as marriage is concerned). Countercultural as that may sound, this is the message of Genesis 2 confirmed by New Testament apostolic interpretation.[18] Also, the woman is described as a "suitable" helper. In context, this distinguishes her from all the other creatures named by the first man, who were all judged unsuitable complements for him. By contrast, the woman is equal to the man in kind, a fellow human being (cf. Gal. 3:28; 1 Pet. 3:7); yet she is also different, the man's "helper" (cf. Eph. 5:22).

That this designation is non-reversible is indicated by the fact that nowhere is the *man* called the *woman's* "helper." Thus equality and distinctness, complementarity and submission/authority must be held in fine balance. The man and the woman are jointly charged with ruling the earth representatively for God, yet they are not to do so androgynously or as "uni-sex" creatures, but each as fulfilling their God-ordained, gender-specific roles. Indeed, since these functional differences are part of the Creator's design, it is only when men and women embrace their God-ordained roles that they will be truly fulfilled and that God's creational wisdom will be fully displayed and exalted.[19]

The Fall of Humanity and Its Consequences

The Fall witnesses a *complete reversal of the roles* assigned by God to the man and the woman. Rather than *God* being in charge, with the *man*, helped by the *woman*, ruling creation for him, a complete reversal takes place: *Satan*, in the form of a serpent, approaches the *woman*, who draws the *man* with her into rebellion against the *Creator*. This does not necessarily imply that the woman is somehow more susceptible to temptation than the man.[20] It does indicate, however, that God's plan for the man and the woman is to have the man, not the woman, assume *ultimate responsibility* for the couple, extending leadership and protection to his female counterpart. Thus the man, by his absence, or at least acquiescence (Gen. 3:6: "her husband with her"; cf. 3:17), shares in the woman's culpability; and she, by failing to consult with her God-given protector and provider, fails to respect the divine pattern of marriage. In the end, it is the *man*, not the woman, who is primarily held responsible for the rebellious act (Gen. 3:9; cf. 3:17; Rom. 5:12-14), though the consequences of the Fall extend to the man and the woman alike, affecting their respective primary spheres.[21]

In the case of the *woman*, recriminations ensue in the realm of childbearing and the relationship with her husband. Regarding childbearing, the woman will experience physical pain. As far as the woman's relationship with her husband is concerned, loving harmony will be replaced by a pattern of struggle in which the woman seeks to exert control over her husband, who responds by asserting his authority—often in an ungodly manner by either passively forcing her into action or actively dominating her (Gen. 3:16; cf. 4:7).[22] The *man,* in turn, will henceforth have trouble in fulfilling God's command to subdue the earth (cf. Gen. 1:28). He must extract the fruit of the land from thorns and thistles and eat his bread by the sweat of his brow (Gen. 3:17-19). In the end, both the man and the woman will die (vv. 19, 22).

In the closing verses of the third chapter of Genesis, God continues to provide for the human couple, clothing them (Gen. 3:21), and, more significantly, predicting a time when the woman's seed—the promised Messiah—will bruise the serpent's offspring on the head (3:15, the so-called *proto-evangelion,* i.e., the good news in seed form of a coming descendent of the woman who would overcome the power of Satan over humanity). In the meantime, however, the couple is expelled from the Garden (3:24) as a sign that their rebellion against the Creator had met with severe sanctions that would cast an ominous shadow on their marriage during their sojourn on earth from that time onwards.

Summary

In our survey of Genesis 1–3 above we have seen how humanity was created in God's image to rule the earth for him (Gen. 1:27-28). We have also learned that God assigned to the man ultimate responsibility for the marriage (which is evident from several references in Genesis 2 and 3) and that he gave the woman to the man as his "suitable helper" (Gen. 2:18, 20). Finally, we observed how the Fall witnessed a complete reversal of the God-ordained pattern of relationships, with abiding, disastrous results overturned only through the coming and the saving death of the Messiah.

As the following investigation will demonstrate, while the Fall changed the marital relationship forever, God's ideal for marriage as articulated in Genesis 1–2 nonetheless continued to set the standard for the responsibilities and roles of husbands and wives toward each other in the subsequent history of humanity. However, although Scripture does attest to a significant number of God-honoring love relationships between men and women in Israel's history, it will be seen that, because of sin, the divine ideal of marriage was frequently subverted through polygamy, divorce, adultery, homosexuality, sterility, and a dilution of gender roles.

DEVELOPMENTS IN THE HISTORY OF ISRAEL (PENTATEUCH, HISTORICAL AND PROPHETIC BOOKS)

In the following discussion, we will first look at the roles and responsibilities of husband and wife toward each other from the vantage point of Old Testament Israel subsequent to the Fall. The importance of the creation narrative in the life of ancient Israel will become apparent in the way in which it continues to set the standard in the *rest of the Pentateuch and the Old Testament historical and prophetic books*. After this, we will discuss several ways in which Old Testament Israel compromised God's ideal for marriage: polygamy, divorce, adultery, homosexuality, sterility, and the erosion of gender distinctions. Hence the state of marriage and the family in much of Old Testament Israel presents itself as in great need of redemption and restoration in the Messiah, which will be discussed in the following chapter.

Marital Roles According to the Old Testament

Even subsequent to the Fall, God's creation design for marriage continues to provide the norm and standard for God's expectations for male-female relationships. Based on the foundational treatment of Genesis 1 and 2, subsequent chapters of the Hebrew Scriptures provide information on the roles and responsibilities of husbands and wives toward each other. While, as will be seen further below, the reality fell often short of the ideal, this does not alter the fact that the standards that were in place for Old Testament couples and believers were grounded in the pre-Fall ideal.

THE ROLE AND RESPONSIBILITIES OF HUSBANDS TOWARD THEIR WIVES

The Old Testament does not contain an explicit "job description" for husbands. Nevertheless, it is possible to infer some of the major responsibilities of husbands toward their wives from various portions of the Hebrew Scriptures. Among these are the following: (1) to love and cherish his wife and to treat her with respect and dignity; (2) to bear primary responsibility for the marriage union and ultimate authority over the family; (3) to provide food, clothing, and other necessities for his wife. We will briefly develop each of these areas of responsibility in the following discussion.

First, then, a man is to *love and cherish his wife and to treat her with respect and dignity.* From Genesis 1 and 2 (which we have already discussed at some length) it is apparent that the woman, like the man, is created in God's image and is charged to fill and subdue the earth together with him (Gen. 1:27-28). As his "suitable helper" and partner in filling the earth and subduing it, and as his complement provided by God, she is worthy of full respect and dignity and is to be cherished as his trusted companion and friend. As the foundational creation narrative stipulates, in order to be united to his wife a man is to leave his father and mother and hold fast to his wife, and they will establish a new family unit (Gen. 2:24). Part of their marital union will be the procreation of offspring (Gen. 1:28).[23]

Second, from the man's creation prior to the woman, later biblical writers (such as Paul, cf. 1 Cor. 11:8-9) rightly infer that his is the *primary responsibility for the marriage union and ultimate authority over his family* including his wife. This is borne out also by several other indicators in the opening chapters of Genesis, including the man's already engaging in his task of subduing the earth by naming the animals prior to the creation of the woman (Gen. 2:19-20); the fact that the man was the recipient of God's command to keep the Garden of Eden and not to eat from the tree of the knowledge of good and evil (2:15-17); and the man's naming of the woman (2:23). It may also be inferred from God calling the man, rather than the woman, to account for humanity's sin, even though it was the woman who sinned first (3:9). While the Fall distorted the way in which men exercised their headship in subsequent generations (3:16b), men were not to avoid their God-given responsibility to be in charge of their marriage and family and all that this entailed. The man's primary responsibility and ultimate authority is consistently seen in the Old Testament pattern of male heads of households, a system which is commonly called "patriarchy" but which is better described as "patricentrism."[24]

Third, a husband was to provide his wife with food, clothing, and other necessities. While the context is that of a man's responsibilities toward concubines or slave wives, the most paradigmatic discussion of the husband's duties in this regard is found in Exodus 21:10, which was the subject of extensive rabbinic discussion and interpretation.[25] This passage stipulates that, "[i]f he [the man] takes another wife to himself, he shall not diminish her *food,* her *clothing,* or her *marital rights.*"[26] According to this passage, the husband's obligations toward his wife (and concubines or slave girls) are delineated as involving the provision of food, clothing, and marital rights respectively.[27] This circumscribes the husband's responsibility to provide his wife with peace, permanence, and security (Ruth 1:9 speaks of "rest").[28]

THE ROLE AND RESPONSIBILITIES OF WIVES
TOWARD THEIR HUSBANDS

Wives' roles and responsibilities toward their husbands were considered to be essentially threefold in *ancient Israel:* (1) presenting her husband with children (especially male ones); (2) managing the household; and (3) providing her husband with companionship.

Regarding the first wifely duty, that of *presenting her husband with children* (particularly sons), people in ancient times married in order to have children. In keeping with the belief that fathers lived on in their children, bearing a child was considered to be an act performed by a wife for her husband.[29] Bearing a son was the noblest contribution a wife could make to her husband and her household. Failure to do so, on the other hand, was viewed as a disgrace. Hence, in the book of Genesis we see that Rachel is desperate that she has not yet borne Jacob any children, and when God later enables her to conceive, she interprets this as God having taken away her reproach (Gen. 30:1, 23).[30]

Second, wives were to *manage their household,* fulfilling the divine mandate of keeping the Garden of Eden prior to the fall of humanity (Gen. 1:28; cf. 2:15). The wife's responsibilities in ancient Israel in this regard included cooking, clothing the family, tending the garden, and harvesting grain (*m. Ketub.* 5:5).[31] Yet while there was a general division of labor along those lines, the boundaries were not rigid, and some of these activities were not limited exclusively to women. Hence,

Abraham (Gen. 18:1-8), Lot (Gen. 19:3), and Esau (Gen. 27:30-31) all are shown to be involved in meal preparations in the Old Testament. Wives also were to supervise household servants involved in domestic chores. We will discuss the example of the Proverbs 31 woman, which features many of these roles and responsibilities, in greater detail below.

Third, in keeping with God's original purpose for creating her (cf. Gen. 2:18), the wife was to *provide companionship* for her husband. While legally his subordinate, ideally the wife served as her husband's confidante and trusted friend (cf. Mal. 2:14). The mutual trust and intimacy characteristic of an ideal marriage is celebrated in the Song of Solomon (e.g., 2:16; 6:3; 7:10) which will be further discussed below.

The Different Ways in Which God's Ideal for Marriage in Genesis 2:24 Was Compromised in the History of Israel

BIBLICAL TERMINOLOGY	CREATION IDEAL	HISTORY OF ISRAEL
"a man . . . his wife"	Monogamy	Polygamy
"hold fast"	Durability Fidelity	Divorce Adultery
"a man . . . his wife . . . become one flesh"	Heterosexuality Fertility Complementarity	Homosexuality Sterility Dilution of gender distinctions

Violations of Various Components of God's Ideal for Marriage in Ancient Israel

We now turn to a discussion of several ways in which God's ideal for marriage as articulated in Genesis 1 and 2 was compromised in the history of Israel. Specifically, we will discuss six such violations of God's ideal for marriage, in each of which a sinful pattern compromised an essential element of the creation paradigm: (1) polygamy (or, more precisely, polygyny) violated God's instituted pattern of marital monogamy; (2) divorce ruptured the durability and permanence of marriage; (3) adultery broke the sacred bond between a man and a woman pledged to marital fidelity; (4) homosexuality developed as an aberrant behavior rebelling against the Creator's design of heterosexual marriage; (5) sterility became a problem which rendered marital relationships devoid of the fertility characteristic of God's original pattern; and (6) the dilution of gender distinctions violated gender complementarity, an essential and foundational aspect of God's plan. We will discuss each of these violations of God's ideal for marriage in the history of Israel in turn.

POLYGAMY

The teaching of Genesis 1–3 that *monogamy* is a foundational part of God's design for marriage notwithstanding, the history of Israel witnesses repeated instances of polygamy.[32] While it certainly was within the Creator's prerogative and power to make more than one wife for the man, God intentionally only made Eve, revealing to Adam his plan with the words, "A man [singular] shall leave his father and his mother and hold fast to his wife [singular], and they shall become one flesh" (Gen. 2:24).[33]

Indeed, one could argue that from a practical standpoint, perhaps God, especially in anticipation of the fall of humanity and the universal death that would ensue, *should* have provided the man with two or more wives. For what would have happened if Eve had died before having children, or had died in childbirth? Would the human race have perished? If God desired for the earth to be populated (Gen. 1:28), does not logic dictate that this could occur faster if Adam were provided with more than one or perhaps even a large number of wives? Yet, in spite of practical arguments such as these in favor of having more than one wife, the Creator's design is simple and clear: one woman for one man. This is the law of marriage established at Creation.

As could be expected, though, after the fall of humanity, God's ideal of monogamy was not consistently upheld.[34] Within six generations, barely after Adam had died, the Bible records that "Lamech took two wives" (Gen. 4:19), perhaps in his presumption seeking to obtain God's primeval blessing (cf. Gen. 1:28) by relying on his own devices—multiplying his wives. While polygamy was *never normative* among the followers of Israel's God, Scripture reveals that it was indeed a recurrent event.[35] In fact, the Old Testament reports that a significant number of individuals in the history of Israel, including many patriarchs and kings, practiced polygamy (or, more precisely, polygyny, marriage to multiple wives),[36] though no instance of polyandry (a wife having more than one husband) is reported. In addition to Lamech, individuals who engaged in polygamy include prominent men such as Abraham (Gen. 16:3), Esau (Gen. 26:34; 28:9), Jacob (Gen. 29:30), Gideon (Judg. 8:30), Elkanah (1 Sam. 1:1-2), David (2 Sam. 3:2-5; 5:13), Solomon (1 Kings 11:3), Ahab (2 Kings 10:1), Jehoiachin (2 Kings 24:15), Ashhur (1 Chron. 4:5), Rehoboam (2 Chron. 11:21), Abijah (2 Chron. 13:21), Jehoram (2 Chron. 21:14), and Joash (2 Chron. 24:1-3).

While it is evident, then, that some very important individuals (both reportedly godly and ungodly) in the history of Israel engaged in polygamy, the Old Testament clearly communicates that the practice of having multiple wives was a departure from God's plan for marriage. This is conveyed not only in Scripture verses that seem univocally to prohibit polygamy (cf. Deut. 17:17; Lev. 18:18),[37] but also from the sin and general disorder that polygamy produced in the lives of those who engaged in the practice. For example, the Old Testament reports disruptive favoritism in the polygamous marriages of Jacob (Gen. 29:30), Elkanah (1 Sam. 1:4-5), and Rehoboam (2 Chron. 11:21). In addition, jealously was a recurrent problem between the competing wives of Abraham (Gen. 21:9-10), Jacob (Gen. 30:14-16), and Elkanah (1 Sam. 1:6). Moreover, Scripture reports that Solomon's foreign "wives turned away his heart after other gods" (1 Kings 11:4), a violation of the first commandment, and David's multiple marriages led to incest and murder among his progeny.

In short, the Bible is clear that individuals in the history of Israel who abandoned God's design of monogamy and participated in polygamy did so contrary to the Creator's plan and ultimately to their own detriment. The sin and disorder produced by polygamy, then, is further testimony to the goodness of God's monogamous design of marriage as first revealed in the marriage of Adam and Eve in the Garden of Eden. Not only is polygamy nowhere in the Old Testament spoken of with approval (though cf. Ex. 21:10-11; Deut 21:15-17), many passages clearly uphold monogamy as the continuing ideal (e.g., Prov. 12:4; 18:22; 19:14; 31:10-31; Ps. 128:3; Ezek. 16:8).[38]

DIVORCE

Another component of God's design for marriage that Old Testament Israel regularly compromised is the *durability* of marriage. Although a later chapter of this volume will explore the topic of divorce in some detail, a few brief comments are in order here. The opening chapters of Genesis make clear that God designed marriage to be *permanent*. This is evident in the paradigmatic description of marriage in Genesis 2:24: "A man shall leave his father and his mother and *hold fast* to his wife, and *they shall become one flesh.*" While there is some debate among scholars regarding the intricacies of what "holding fast" and "becoming one flesh" means, there is no question that God designed marriage to be permanent.[39]

Just as in the case of other elements of the divine design for marriage, however, the Old Testament indicates that many did not respect that God's plan involved the durability of marriage. Indeed, divorce was a serious problem early on in the history of Israel. In the Mosaic code, it was stipulated that a priest could not marry a divorcee (even if she was not the guilty party; Lev. 21:7: "shall not marry . . . a woman divorced from her husband, for the priest is holy to his God"; cf. Lev. 21:14). In an attempt to bridle sins stemming from divorce, Mosaic legislation prohibited a man from remarrying a woman whom he had divorced and who subsequently had married another man (even if her second husband had died, Deut. 24:1-4). The reason for this was that by her second marriage "she has been defiled" (v. 4), perhaps indicating that illegitimate remarriage after divorce amounts to adultery. Moreover, the Old Testament records several examples of divorces and attests to the general practice of divorce among the Hebrews (cf. Ezra 9–10; Neh. 13:23-31; Mal. 2:14-16).

Despite the presence of divorce in the history of Israel, however, the Old Testament confirms that durability continued to be a component of God's design for marriage. This can be seen in the fact that the Mosaic legislation seems specifically to *forbid* divorce if the wife was a virgin at the time the marriage was consummated (cf. Deut. 22:19, 29). In addition, it is evident that God does not approve of divorce, for the Old Testament on several occasions uses the analogy of divorce to describe Israel's spiritual apostasy (cf. Isa. 50:1; Jer. 3:8), and the prophet

Malachi makes clear that God does not approve of divorce motivated by hatred (Mal. 2:16).[40]

ADULTERY

Another way in which God's ideal for marriage was compromised in the history of Israel was the occurrence of adultery. While it could be argued that fidelity was his only option, Adam's lack of an opportunity to commit adultery does not diminish the fact that fidelity is an inherent component of God's pattern for marriage: "A man shall leave his father and his mother and *hold fast* to his wife, and they shall become one flesh" (Gen. 2:24). As with the principle of monogamy discussed above, however, after the fall of humankind the Old Testament reports that numerous individuals struggled with faithfulness to their marriage partners.[41]

Perhaps the best-known incident of adultery recorded in the Old Testament is David's adultery with Bathsheba and the consequent murder of her husband Uriah (2 Samuel 11). Other instances of marital infidelity abound in the history of Israel. In addition to all of the polygamous marriages discussed above (which in effect involved adultery against the first wife), there is Reuben's adultery with Bilhah (Gen. 35:22; cf. 49:3-4), the adultery of the Levite's concubine (Judg. 19:1-2), Hosea's wife Gomer's adultery (Hos. 3:1), and the adultery committed by a host of other unnamed Israelites at which God took offense (Jer. 3:2; 5:7-8; 7:9-10; 23:10; Ezek. 22:11; 33:26; Hos. 4:2; 7:4). Moreover, the Old Testament reports a number of individuals who engaged in sexual sins that likely involved adultery such as Gilead, the father of Jephthah (Judg. 11:1), or Eli's sons Hophni and Phineas (1 Sam. 2:22).

In addition, the book of Genesis records several occasions of near-adultery, which would have been actual adultery had not the Lord providentially intervened, including Abimelech with Sarah (Gen. 20:2-18), Abimelech with Rebekah (26:7-9), and Joseph with Potiphar's wife (39:7-12). All of these accounts communicate the fact that God's ideal of fidelity within marriage was often not upheld in Old Testament times.

Despite these instances of adultery or near-adultery in the history of Israel, however, the Old Testament reiterates in numerous places the fact that God's ideal for marriage is *fidelity*. For instance, the seventh commandment directed God's people in no uncertain terms, "You shall not commit adultery" (Ex. 20:14; Deut. 5:18). The sexual laws in the Holiness Code plainly stipulated, "You shall not lie sexually with your neighbor's wife" (Lev. 18:20), setting the penalty for adultery as death (Lev. 20:10; cf. Num. 5:11-31; Deut 22:22).[42] Moreover, the book of Proverbs repeatedly classifies adultery as both foolish and dangerous (Prov. 2:16-19; 5:3-22; 6:32-33; 7:5-23; 9:13-18; 22:14; 23:27-28; 30:20).

What is more, the Lord frequently used the analogy of physical adultery to depict his displeasure over the spiritual adultery of Israel when they departed from him, their first love, in order to pursue other gods (Jer. 3:8-9; Ezek. 16:32, 38; Hos. 1:1–3:5). In short, then, although many in the history of Israel did not adhere to God's design of fidelity within marriage, the Old Testament is clear that the Lord's standard did not change. God expected his people to be faithful—both to their spouses and to him—and was clearly offended when they were not.[43]

HOMOSEXUALITY

Heterosexuality is an unequivocal component of the Creator's design for marriage. Yet after the fall of humanity, the Old Testament indicates that the principle of heterosexuality was often violated through same-sex relations. Examples include many of the inhabitants of the cities of the plain, Sodom and Gomorrah (Gen. 19:1-29), the Gibeonites in the days of the judges (Judg. 19:1–21:25), as well as numerous other unnamed lawbreakers in the history of Israel (1 Kings 14:24; 15:12; 22:46; 2 Kings 23:7; Job 36:14). In spite of these offenses, however, the Old Testament makes clear that the principle of heterosexuality, established at Creation, continues to be an integral part of God's design for marriage. This is testified to by the severity of the punishment prescribed for homosexuality (death, Lev. 20:13), by the presentation of heterosexuality as normative (Prov. 5:18-19; Eccles. 9:9; Song 1–8), and by the fate of individuals in the history of Israel who engaged in homosexual activity.

Since a later chapter of this book will look at homosexuality in detail, it is not necessary to engage in a full analysis of the topic here. However, a few brief comments are in order. The idea of a homosexual marriage is not only contrary to specific biblical injunctions concerning same-sex intercourse (cf. Lev. 18:22; 20:13; Deut. 23:17), but also runs counter to the Creator's design for marriage. Heterosexuality—not homosexuality—is plainly in view in God's law of marriage: "A *man* [masculine] shall leave his father and his mother and hold fast to his *wife* [feminine], and they shall become one flesh" (Gen. 2:24). What is more, this is the *only* possible arrangement for marriage, as the Creator has commanded and expects married couples to "be fruitful and multiply and fill the earth" (Gen. 1:28).

Since homosexuality involves same-sex intercourse that cannot lead to procreation, it is unnatural and cannot logically entail the possibility of marriage. Indeed, even among the animals, the writer of Genesis repeatedly notes that God made each species male and female, "after its kind," for the express purpose of procreation (Gen. 1:21, 24, 25). Moreover, since an aspect of humanity's representative rule over and subduing of the earth for God is procreation (1:27-28), yet procreation is impossible between two males or two females, homosexuality militates not only against God's design for marriage but against his created order as well.

STERILITY

Fertility is yet another essential part of God's design for marriage of which certain individuals fell short in Old Testament times. Fertility may be implicit in the Lord's description of marriage as a "one flesh" (Gen. 2:24) relationship if one understands there to be sexual overtones in this terminology. Fertility is certainly entailed in God's command to Adam and Eve—incidentally, the first command God ever gave to human beings—to "be fruitful and multiply" (Gen. 1:28). Indeed, in the Bible fruitfulness in marriage is repeatedly described as a virtue to be sought after and is viewed as a blessing once obtained (cf. Ex. 23:26; Deut. 7:14; Ps. 113:9; 127:4-5; 128:3-4).[44] Moreover, certain elements of the Old Testament law appear to be crafted with the intent of furthering the fruitfulness of marriage. Examples include a newlywed soldier being given a year off "to be happy with his wife whom he has taken" (Deut. 24:5) and the institution of levirate marriage that had as its goal the production of offspring for a deceased relative (Deut. 25:5-10). Conversely, the Old Testament views barrenness as a reproach (cf. Gen. 30:1, 22-23; Isa. 4:1; 47:9; 49:21).

Despite the importance placed on fertility in the Hebrew Scriptures, the fact remains that numerous couples in the history of Israel experienced difficulty conceiving children. One important difference between one's lack of fertility and one's failure to implement other components of God's design for marriage is that sterility is not usually a conscious choice. Nevertheless, in the Old Testament sterility is sometimes presented as a curse stemming from personal sin, as in the case of Abimelech's wives (Gen. 20:17-18) and David's first wife, Michal (2 Sam. 6:16-23). On other occasions, sterility is presented as a simple fact of nature, as in the case of the three mothers of the Hebrew race—Sarah (Gen. 11:30), Rebekah (Gen. 25:21), and Rachel (Gen. 30:1)—as well as Manoah's wife (Judg. 13:2), Hannah (1 Sam. 1:2), and the Shunammite who aided Elisha (2 Kings 4:14). While the Bible gives no explicit directives on how to overcome sterility, a common denominator between many of those in Scripture who were at one time fruitless but later became fruitful is prayer. For example, God answered prayers for fertility offered by Abraham (Gen. 15:2-5; 20:17), Isaac (Gen. 25:21), Leah (Gen. 30:17), Rachel (Gen. 30:22), and Hannah (1 Sam. 1:9-20). These answered prayers, as well as the Lord's general multiplication of his people in fulfillment of the Abrahamic covenant, are further testimony to the fact that fertility is an essential component of God's design for marriage, and is possible for those who seek God regarding it.[45]

DILUTION OF GENDER DISTINCTIONS

Complementarity, too, which includes the notion of equal worth but differing roles for the sexes, is an essential and foundational part of God's design of marriage.[46] However, as is evident from the other marital distortions mentioned above, the history of Israel features several instances where the principle of complementarity was not observed. Indeed, individuals who engaged in homosexuality or who purposefully avoided fruitfulness (e.g., Onan, Gen. 38:8-10) cannot be described as having behaved in a manner that is fully consistent with the God-ordained pattern of complementarity.

In addition, the Old Testament features a number of individuals who clearly and specifically abandoned their God-ordained gender roles, some without participating in other marital distortions. For instance, men who failed in the leadership of their home (at least on occasion) include Adam, Eli, David, and Ahaz, and examples of women who (at least at times) were not "suitable helpers" within their families include Eve, Bathsheba, Jezebel, and Athaliah, among others.[47]

Despite these examples of distortion of the Creator's design of gender roles, even after the Fall, the Old Testament repeatedly confirms the fact that complementarity is part of God's plan for marriage. Equal worth of husbands and wives is seen in a number of different spheres: legal parity in regard to parental obedience (Ex. 20:12; 21:15, 17; Lev. 20:9; Deut. 5:16); economic privileges that allowed for daughters and wives to inherit property (Num. 27:1-11; 36:1-9; cf. Prov. 31:13-18, 24); and liberty for both sexes to have personal spiritual encounters (Judg. 13:2-25), experience answered prayer (1 Sam. 1:9-20), engage in public worship (Neh. 8:2), and perhaps even participate in the prophetic office (Ex. 15:20; Judg. 4:4; 2 Kings 22:14; Neh. 6:14).[48]

At the same time, the Lord's design for marriage in the Old Testament includes important functional differences for the sexes as well. In addition to the Lord's specific confirmation of Adam's headship after the fall (Gen. 3:16), complementary gender roles as established at Creation are evident in the Old Testament narratives recounting the marriages of the patriarchs (e.g., Gen. 18:12, where Sarah calls Abraham "my master"; cf. 1 Pet. 3:5-6) and godly kings of Israel (e.g., David: 1 Sam. 25:40-42; 1 Kings 1:16, 31). King Lemuel's description of a virtuous wife as an industrious homemaker under her husband's authority (Prov. 31:10-31) also reflects the complementary pattern instituted in Genesis 2.[49] As with the other components in God's design for marriage, then, it is clear that the history of Israel did not alter the Lord's plan for these institutions.

Summary of Developments in the History of Israel

We have seen that the history of Israel documents several negative patterns that fell short of God's ideal for marriage as articulated in the opening chapters of Genesis, most notably polygamy, divorce, adultery, homosexuality, sterility, and the dilution of gender roles. In each case, these patterns constitute a distortion of the God-ordained institution of marriage. While God designed marriage to be between one man and one woman, polygamy involves marital union with more than one wife. Divorce breaks the sacred bond between husband and wife. In contrast to God's intention for marriage to be a faithful, one-flesh union, adultery entails sexual relations with another person who is not one's spouse. Homosexuality stands against the "one man, one woman" principle involved in biblical marriage. Sterility falls short of the fertility invoked in God's command for the human couple to be fruitful and multiply. The dilution of gender roles militates against God's making humanity as distinctly male *and* female. In all these ways, Old Testament Israel fell short of God's creation ideal for marriage.

What is more, not only can these violations of God's ideal for marriage be demonstrated historically in Israel's history, there are important implications for men and women today as well.

GLIMPSES OF THE IDEAL (WISDOM LITERATURE)

While the Old Testament historical books bear witness to the increasing deterioration of the observance of God's plan for marriage, God's ideal is upheld in the *Old Testament wisdom literature*. The two primary examples are the poem praising the excellent wife in the final chapter of the book of Proverbs and the celebration of married love in the Song of Solomon. These passages provide a refreshing counterpoint to the overall pattern of compromise of God's ideal for marriage presented in the historical and prophetic Old Testament books.

The Excellent Wife (Proverbs 31)

The book of Proverbs concludes with an acrostic poem extolling the virtues of the excellent wife, whose worth to her husband surpasses that of great material wealth. Some have commented that this woman must have been phenomenal, since on the one hand it is said that she rises early in the morning (Prov. 31:15) and on the other that her lamp does not go out at night (31:18)! When did this woman sleep?[50] Indeed, the excellent wife of Proverbs 31 displays many virtues that remain relevant for women aspiring to be godly wives today.

The Proverbs 31 woman:

- is a major asset to her husband (vv. 10, 11);
- is a trusted companion (v. 11);
- is for and not against her husband; she has his well-being and best interests at heart (v. 12);
- is industrious and hardworking (vv. 13, 27);
- procures and prepares food for her entire household (vv. 14, 15);
- rises early (v. 15);
- locates and purchases real estate (v. 16);
- reinvests extra earnings from her home business (v. 16);
- is vigorous and energetic (vv. 17, 25);
- produces clothes for her family and as merchandise (vv. 13, 18-19, 21-22, 24);
- is kind to the poor, reaches out in mercy to the needy (v. 20);
- ensures that she and her children are properly and finely dressed (vv. 21-22);
- contributes to others' respect for her husband and oversees her household so he can devote himself to a role of leadership in the community (vv. 23, 27);
- is ready for the future and prepares for eventualities (vv. 21, 25);
- displays wisdom in speech, and in the teaching of kindness (v. 26);
- is praised by her children and husband (vv. 28-29, 31);
- is God-fearing rather than relying on her physical beauty (v. 30).

While some might find this ideal unattainable, it is a worthy goal to which women today may aspire. Clearly, this kind of woman does not fit the stereotype of a woman who is "confined to the home" or diminished in her personhood.[51] She is a woman of great resourcefulness who is a source of strength and inestimable blessing to her husband and children. Who would not want to have a wife and mother aspiring to such a role model? Fortunately for many of us (including the authors of this book), and by the grace of God, we do.

The Beauty of Sex in Marriage (The Song of Solomon)

In the midst of the deterioration evident during the course of Israel's history, there is one other bright spot in the Hebrew canon: the Song of Solomon. On the basis of the notion that God established marriage,

including the physical union of husband and wife (Gen. 2:18-25, esp.
vv. 24-25: "one flesh . . . both naked and . . . not ashamed"), the Song
of Solomon celebrates the beauty of marital love including its intimate
sexual expression.[52]

The book of Proverbs, too, includes a section extolling sex within
the framework of a faithful, committed marriage relationship and warning against adultery:

> Drink water from your own cistern,
> flowing water from your own well.
> Should your springs be scattered abroad,
> streams of water in the streets?
> Let them be for yourself alone,
> and not for strangers with you.
> Let your fountain be blessed,
> and rejoice in the wife of your youth,
> a lovely deer, a graceful doe.
> Let her breasts fill you at all times with delight;
> be intoxicated always in her love.
> Why should you be intoxicated, my son, with a forbidden woman
> and embrace the bosom of an adulteress? (Prov. 5:15-20)

Together with the repeated injunction in the book of Proverbs for
people to guard their hearts (e.g., Prov. 4:23, NIV) and for men to keep
far away from adulterous women (Prov. 2:16-19; 5; 6:20-35; 7; 22:14;
23:26-28; 31:3), this constitutes a powerful mandate for married couples to build strong spiritual hedges around their relationship and to nurture their marriage commitment with diligence and devotion.[53]

The Song of Solomon, for its part, not only contributes to the
Hebrew (and Christian) canon a collection of love poems celebrating
the strength and passion of married love (including sex) but also antic-
ipates the restoration of the relationship between the first man and the
first woman, Adam and Eve, which was ruptured by the Fall.
Subsequent to the Fall, the judgment pronounced on the woman
included that her desire (*t^ešûqâ*) would be for her husband (Gen. 3:16),
which in all likelihood conveys the woman's sinful desire to manipulate and control her husband rather than to lovingly submit to him.
This is suggested by the close parallel in the following chapter, where

it is said that sin's desire is for Cain, clearly in the sense of a desire for control or mastery (Gen. 4:7).[54]

In the third and only other instance of the term translated "desire" in these passages, Song of Solomon 7:10, the woman exclaims, "I am my beloved's, and his desire is for me." Rather than the woman's desire being illegitimately to control her husband, a restoration of the original state is envisioned in which the husband's desire will be for his wife.[55] Once again, the woman gladly rests in the assurance that she is her husband's, and the husband does not dominate his wife but desires her. Hence, "[l]ove is experienced as a return to paradise."[56] As in the original Garden, the man and the woman will be able to be "both naked and . . . not ashamed" (Gen. 2:25). Importantly, however, this restoration of human love is predicated upon the coming of the messianic king, the greater son of David and Solomon (cf., e.g., Matt. 1:1; 12:42).[57] The parallels in symbolism between the Song of Solomon and Genesis 1–3, the typology involving male-female love, and the messianic thread running through Scripture from Genesis 3:15 to the figure of Solomon, the son of David, in the Song of Solomon, and beyond, and the idealized portrait of love in the Song of Solomon all favor this messianic, end-time orientation of the Song of Solomon.

The Three OT Uses of the Hebrew Word for "Desire" ($t^e\check{s}\hat{u}q\hat{a}$)

SCRIPTURE REFERENCE	TRANSLATION	COMMENTARY
Genesis 3:16	"Your desire shall be for your husband, and he shall rule over you."	Reference to the woman's sinful desire to manipulate and control her husband
Genesis 4:7	". . . sin is crouching at the door. Its desire is for you, but you must rule over it."	Reference to sin's desire to overpower Cain, exhortation for him to master it
Song of Solomon 7:10 (Hebrew 7:11)	"I am my beloved's, and his desire is for me."	Woman's glad assurance that her husband's desire is for her

Contrary to the world's notion that truly exciting love must be outside of the confines of marriage, Scripture makes it clear that it is the very security provided by an exclusive, lifelong marriage relationship that allows for the sexual satisfaction and fulfillment of both the man and the woman. Liberated from the self-centeredness of sin and from the desire to manipulate one's spouse to have one's own needs met, the marriage partners are free to love their spouse in a spirit that is completely self-giving and hence able to love and enjoy the other person without fear of rejection, abuse, or domination. Married love thus turns out to be the fulfillment of every man's and every woman's dream, but it proves elusive to those who have not been renewed and transformed by the Holy Spirit upon repentance and faith in Christ.

INSIGHTS FROM OLD TESTAMENT MARRIAGES

Having examined the theme of marriage and the teaching on marriage in the Old Testament, it is an interesting exercise to now scan the pages of the Old Testament in order to glean insights from specific Old Testament marriages.

Adam and Eve

The first marriage in biblical history, which we have already discussed from the standpoint of important abiding patterns and principles above, was that of *Adam and Eve,* whom God brought together (Gen. 2:23-24) and gave joint stewardship over the earth (Gen. 1:28), which included the mandate of procreation.[58] One assumes that the two, prior to the Fall, enjoyed a season of marital bliss never again experienced in human history (Gen. 2:25: "The man and his wife were both naked and were not ashamed"). Beyond this, Scripture does not provide a record of the marital life of Adam and Eve, other than to indicate that Adam was the one ultimately responsible for the union before God and Eve was to serve as Adam's "suitable helper" (Gen. 2:18, 20).

What is clear is that this divinely intended pattern was subverted at the fall of humanity (Genesis 3), where Eve went beyond her role as Adam's "suitable helper" and acted independently from her husband when yielding to Satan's temptation. The reference to Adam being "with her" (Gen. 3:6) immediately after Eve's forbidden act may indicate that Adam failed in his responsibility to provide responsible leadership in the relationship (see also 3:17: "Because you listened to the voice of your wife . . ."). In any case, life subsequent to the Fall was never the same. The woman's giving of birth to children is now marked by intense pain, and because of her sin nature she will no longer accept her role alongside the man as his "suitable helper" (3:16). The man, for his part, will experience pain in his struggle to subdue the earth (vv. 17-19), and in the end both the man and the woman will die (v. 19).

Abraham and Sarah

Scripture records several interesting incidents in *Abraham and Sarah's* relationship. When Abraham went to Egypt, he concocted a plan to identify his wife as his sister, fearing that the Egyptians would otherwise kill him in order to take Sarah as their own on account of her physical beauty (Gen. 12:10-20; an incident later repeated with Abimelech, Genesis 20). Sarah apparently complied with Abraham's plan and was promptly taken by Pharaoh as one of his wives before the scheme was discovered, suffering the consequences for her husband's cowardice and dishonesty in this instance (even though at many other junctures Abraham was a man of great integrity and courage).[59] Sarah's experience here teaches the lesson to wives that they are under no obligation to follow their husbands into sin but, to the contrary, must make every effort to resist it.

Later, Sarah, who up to that point had borne Abraham no children, sought to remedy the situation by encouraging Abraham to secure offspring through her maidservant Hagar. When the latter conceived and began to despise her mistress, Sarah complained to Abraham and mistreated Hagar (Gen. 16:1-6). After Sarah had given birth to Isaac, she rejoiced, but when Ishmael, Hagar's son, was disdainful toward Isaac, Sarah went to Abraham and told him to get rid of "that slave woman and her son" (Gen. 21:10). In keeping with God's word (v. 12), Abraham complied and sent Hagar and Ishmael away.[60] This series of events illustrates that a couple must not seek to remedy a situation out of unbelief, or the consequences of sin will further complicate their situation.

Isaac and Rebekah, Jacob and Rachel

Both Abraham's son Isaac and his grandson Jacob are scriptural examples of great love for their respective wives. When a wife had been procured for *Isaac*, the biblical record comments at the occasion of his marriage to *Rebekah*: "So she became his wife, and he loved her . . ." (Gen. 24:67). In due course, Isaac and Rebekah's son *Jacob*, in turn, fell in love with *Rachel*, who was "lovely in form, and beautiful" (Gen. 29:17, NIV), and worked to receive her as his wife for fourteen years, evidence of his great love for her.

Despite Jacob's great love for Rachel, marital tensions subsequently arose when Rachel was unable to bear Isaac children. Rachel demanded that Jacob give her children, and he replied, "Am I in the place of God, who has kept you from having children?" (Gen. 30:1-2, NIV). Later, God graciously did enable Rachel to conceive (30:22-24), doubtless reducing the tension that had built up in Jacob's and Rachel's marriage.[61] Their example can teach us that a married couple must face difficulties (such as the wife's infertility) together in prayerful reliance on God rather than being drawn into marital arguments and discord.

Samson and Delilah

Another Old Testament love story, albeit of a less positive overall nature and outcome, is that of *Samson and Delilah* (Judges 16). Unfortunately, Samson serves as an example of someone who did not properly guard his heart and who was seduced by a woman who robbed him of his strength and, eventually, his life. This serves as a warning that even a man as strong, capable, and powerful as Samson is not immune to the lure of a seductive woman and can be brought down by her wiles.

Ruth and Boaz

A much more positive example of a godly love relationship is that of *Ruth and Boaz* as recounted in the book of Ruth. Ruth, a young Moabite widow, who had followed her mother-in-law Naomi back to Judah after the death of her husband, is noticed by Boaz, who shows kindness to her and does not rest until he secures her hand in marriage. Ruth's story (which also has salvation-historical significance in that she was the great-grandmother of King David, Ruth 4:22) is a wonderful example of a (widowed) woman's trust in God in the midst of adverse circumstances.

Hannah and Elkanah

The first book of Samuel opens with an account of the relationship between a man named *Elkanah* and his wife *Hannah,* mother of the prophet Samuel. The dynamic between Hannah, her rival Peninnah, and their husband mirrors the above-told story of Rachel, Leah, and Jacob. Hannah desperately implores the Lord to give her a son, despite her husband's efforts to comfort her: "Don't I mean more to you than ten sons?" (1 Sam. 1:8, NIV).

In her godliness and persistent prayer, Hannah serves an example for future generations of hopeful or expectant mothers. Also exemplary is her initiative in consecrating her son to the Lord. It is apparent that her husband trusts in her, because when she tells him of her plans regarding Samuel, he responds, "Do what seems best to you" (1:23). Hannah's subsequent prayer speaks of deep devotion to God (1 Samuel 2; cf. Mary in Luke 1:46-55).

David and His Wives

The life of *David* holds several lessons regarding marriage. It should be noted at the very outset that David's taking of several wives cannot be condoned and constitutes a violation of God's creation standard of monogamy. Nevertheless, certain lessons can be learned from David's relationships with his wives. David's first wife was Saul's daughter *Michal,* who fell in love with David and was given to him in marriage (1 Sam. 18:20, 27-28). When Saul sought to kill David, Michal warned David and let him down through a window, and he escaped (19:11-12). Later, Michal told Saul's servants who had come to capture David that he was ill (19:14). In these actions, Michal serves as an example of wifely loyalty and solidarity with her husband (without condoning the means—lying—by which she did so), even at the cost of alienating her own father (v. 17).[62]

Later, David married *Abigail,* the beautiful and discerning woman who successfully appeased his wrath after her first husband Nabal had rudely rebuffed David (1 Sam. 25:3, 14-42).[63] Abigail serves as an example of the wife of a great man and leader who treats him in a sensitive and respectful way and is loved by him in return. Her wisdom and humility make her a prime example of the virtues extolled in women in the Old Testament (cf. Prov. 31:10-31).

David's adultery with *Bathsheba* is well-known (2 Samuel 11). The incident ought to warn married men not to compromise their devotion to their wives and cautions married women (such as Bathsheba) to be discreet and modest in their dress and conduct. The importance of this issue in God's eyes is underscored by the fact that two of the ten commandments address it: "You shall not commit adultery" (Ex. 20:14) and "you shall not covet your neighbor's wife" (Ex. 20:17).

Solomon's Foreign Wives

Despite his wisdom, *Solomon's* downfall came when he "loved many *foreign women,*" to whom Solomon "clung . . . in love," despite God's command not to enter into marriage with them, and "his wives turned away his heart." Solomon built high places for all his foreign wives and even joined them in worship of their false gods (1 Kings 11:1-8). This provides a powerful warning for men not to get involved with women who are not believers. It is an illusion to think that we will not be affected by being "unequally yoked" with a non-Christian spouse.[64]

Ahab and Jezebel

King *Ahab's* marriage to *Jezebel* may well rank among the worst in Israel's history. At one point Jezebel helped her husband take over Naboth's vineyard by producing false witnesses against him and having him put to death (1 Kings 21). In the entire story, Jezebel controls and domineers Ahab and tells him what to do, and he complies, in perfect illustration of the verdict pronounced by the Lord on Adam and Eve subsequent to the Fall (Gen. 3:16).

Esther and Ahasuerus

Queen Esther endeared herself to her husband, *King Ahasuerus,* so much that he loved her more than all other women, and she won his grace and favor (Est. 2:17; cf. 5:2). God providentially used Esther's trust relationship with the King to save her people, the Jews, from Haman's sinister plot. Like Ruth, Abigail, and other Old Testament women, Esther serves as an example of wifely wisdom and sensitivity toward her husband, which made him tender toward her and her requests.

Summary

While there may be occasional references to marriages worth investigating in the Old Testament wisdom and prophetic literature, the above
survey is sufficient to illustrate the considerable range of marriages of
salvation-historical significance in ancient Israel. While the Fall forever
affected marriage by introducing sin into spouses' dealings with each
another, there remain many beautiful examples of love and devotion,
such as Isaac and Rebekah, Jacob and Rachel, or Ruth and Boaz. We
also learn how women became the source of temptation and led to the
demise of men like Samson, David, and Solomon. We will continue our
study of marriages in the following chapter on marriage in the New
Testament.

CONCLUSION

We started our survey of the Old Testament teaching on marriage with
a close look at the Genesis creation narrative, which grounds the institution of marriage in the will of God the Creator. We also explored the
consequences of the Fall on this most intimate of human relationships.
This was followed by a survey of Israel's history as presented in the Old
Testament historical and prophetic books. We saw that this history witnessed several ways in which God's creation ideal for marriage was compromised, including instances of polygamy, divorce, adultery,
homosexuality, sterility, and a dilution of gender distinctions. The last
corpus of literature under consideration was the Old Testament wisdom
literature, which presents a refreshing counterpoint to this overall pattern of decline. The book of Proverbs extols the virtuous wife who is
devoted to her husband and family, and the Song of Solomon envisions
a restored love relationship between the man and the woman in and
through the Messiah. In the following chapter, we will seek to complement these insights by a study of the teaching on marriage found in the
New Testament.

3

NO LONGER TWO, BUT ONE: MARRIAGE IN THE NEW TESTAMENT

WE HAVE SEEN THAT marriage was divinely instituted by the Creator. Subsequent to the Fall, sin led to distortions of this divine institution. Marriage turned into a struggle for control in which husbands frequently dominated their wives while wives sought to manipulate their husbands. Divorce broke up marriages even for the most trivial of reasons. Polygamy was practiced (though not widely), and extramarital affairs violated the sacred trust of marital fidelity. Hence, while the divine ideal was set forth clearly and permanently in the creation account, there was a great need for restoration and renewal in the days of Jesus and the early church.

The present chapter, which is devoted to a study of the New Testament teaching on the subject, will attempt to derive a distinctly Christian theology of marriage from the teaching of both Testaments (the Old Testament informed now by the New Testament).[1] After discussing Jesus' view of marriage, we will study Peter's message for husbands and wives as well as Paul's pronouncements on this subject, with special focus on his first letters to the Corinthians and Timothy and his letter to the Ephesians. The chapter concludes with a brief survey of marriages in the New Testament.

No Longer Two, but One: Jesus' High View of Marriage

Jesus' teaching on the requirements of discipleship regularly subordinated one's kinship ties to the obligations of the kingdom.[2] However, while our Lord had much to say about people's need to give first priority to Jesus' call to discipleship, he provided comparatively little instruction on marriage. Doubtless the major reason for this is that Jesus, as did his contemporaries, assumed the validity of the divine pattern for marriage set forth in the opening chapters of Genesis.[3] For this reason it would be fallacious to assume that, because Jesus emphasized people's higher spiritual calling and requirements for Christian discipleship, he held a low view of marriage or now viewed this divine institution as dispensable or superseded by a higher, nobler calling, perhaps involving singleness in light of the imminent end of the age.[4]

Quite to the contrary. When questioned about divorce, Jesus affirmed the permanent nature of marriage in no uncertain terms. Adducing both foundational Old Testament texts, Genesis 1:27 and 2:24, he asserted, "So they [husband and wife] are no longer two, but one. Therefore what God has joined together, let man not separate" (Matt. 19:6, NIV).[5] This makes clear that Jesus considered marriage to be *a sacred bond between a man and a woman, established by and entered into before God*. As John Stott aptly notes, "The marriage bond *is more than a human contract:* it is a divine yoke. And the way in which God lays this yoke upon a married couple is not by creating a kind of mystical union but by declaring his purpose in his Word."[6]

While Jesus held a very high view of marriage, however, as mentioned above and as will be discussed more fully in the following chapter, his teaching on natural family ties provides important parameters for its overall significance and places it within the larger context of God's kingdom.[7] The culmination of this development will be reached in the eternal state, where people will no longer marry but will be like the angels (Matt. 22:30 par.). Thus, Jesus lays the groundwork for Paul's teaching that "from now on those who have wives should live as if they had none . . . for this world in its present form is passing away" (1 Cor. 7:29, 31, NIV). While *remaining the foundational divine institution* for humanity, which should be nurtured, cared for, and protected, marriage should not be viewed as an end in itself, but should be *subordinated to God's larger salvation purposes.*[8] We will deal with this at greater length in our discussion of Paul's teaching on the nature of marriage in Ephesians.

SUBMISSION AND SENSITIVITY: PETER'S MESSAGE TO HUSBANDS AND WIVES (1 PETER 3:1-7)

Peter's comments on the marriage relationship are penned in the context of believers suffering at the hands of unbelievers, in the present instance believing wives called to live with unbelieving husbands. Peter's general rule of conduct is submission "for the Lord's sake to every human institution" (1 Pet. 2:13), including government (vv. 13-17), authorities at work (v. 18) and at home (3:1). In the case of work relationships, submission is urged not only to superiors who are "good and gentle but also to the unjust" (2:18). Wives "likewise" are to be submissive to unbelieving husbands (3:1).[9]

In all of this, Christ has set the example (1 Pet. 2:21), all the way to the cross (2:24). Marriage, as well as other human relationships, is thus set in the larger framework of a believer's Christian testimony in the surrounding unbelieving world. While there is no guarantee (cf. 1 Cor. 7:16), believing wives are to work and pray that their husbands "may be won without a word by the conduct of their wives—when they see your respectful and pure conduct" (1 Pet. 3:1-2; cf. 1 Cor. 7:12-14). Such wives are to cultivate inner, spiritual beauty (described by Peter in 1 Pet. 3:4 as "adorning . . . the hidden person of the heart with the imperishable beauty of a gentle and quiet spirit"), being submissive to their husbands as Sarah was to Abraham, even when their directives are not informed by a regenerate mind and heart, as long as this does not involve sin (1 Pet. 3:3-6; cf., e.g., Genesis 20).[10]

The general principle issuing from Peter's counsel is that leading unbelievers to Christ is a greater cause than insisting on justice in human relationships. Believers are to defer their craving for justice until the last day, trusting God as Jesus did (1 Pet. 2:23). While Paul enjoins believing wives in his letters to the Ephesians and Colossians to submit to their believing husbands, here Peter raises the bar further still. Wifely submission to an unbelieving husband—and any resulting suffering—is beautiful in the sight of God if borne reverently and with hope in God.[11]

In the context of the third chapter of Peter's first letter, there seems to be an almost imperceptible shift of focus from marriages between a believer and an unbeliever to those between believers. While verses 1-4 appear to apply primarily to the former, verses 5-6 evoke "the holy women" of the past, including Sarah, whose husband Abraham, while occasionally sinning against Sarah, is hardly the prototype of the unbelieving husband. Thus Peter, like Paul, envisions marital relationships between believers that are characterized by wifely submission ("wives, be subject to your own husbands," 1 Pet. 3:1) and husbands' considerate treatment of their wives ("husbands, live with your wives in an understanding way, showing honor to the woman . . . , since they are heirs with you of the grace of life," 3:7).

In the sole verse addressed to husbands, Peter admirably balances the recognition of distinctions between the marital partners and the notion of their equality in Christ. On the one hand, wives are called "the weaker vessel" with whom husbands are to live in an understanding way.[12] Yet on the other hand, wives are called "heirs with you" together with their husbands of the gracious gift of life (1 Pet. 3:7). The reference to removing any obstacles for joint marital prayer likewise presupposes that the initial focus on marriages between a believer and an unbeliever has now given way to those between believers.

ALL THINGS UNDER ONE HEAD: PAUL'S VISION FOR MARRIAGE

Of the New Testament writers, it is Paul who provides the most thorough treatment of marriage. We will first look at the apostle's teaching in 1 Corinthians 7 and 1 Timothy before turning to Paul's most extended discussion of marriage in his letter to the Ephesians.[13]

Fulfilling One's Marital Obligations (1 Corinthians 7:2-5)

Paul's pronouncements on marriage in his first letter to the Corinthians are part of his response to a letter sent to him by the Corinthians, in which they had requested that the apostle rule on several controversial issues (1 Cor. 16:17; cf. 1 Cor. 7:1: "Now concerning the matters about which you wrote"). In the first instance, Paul takes a strong stand against a false *asceticism* that values singleness as more spiritual than marriage (7:1). Suppressing their physical functions for the sake of spiritual advancement, the proponents of this teaching called on those who were married to refrain from sexual intercourse with their spouse or even encouraged them to divorce their spouses in order to pursue an allegedly higher, sexless spirituality.

While 1 Corinthians 7 is often discussed in the context of Paul's high valuation of singleness, it is worthy of note that the same chapter also contains a very strong affirmation of marriage. According to Paul,

> . . . each man should have his own wife, and each woman her own husband. The husband should fulfill his marital duty to his wife, and likewise the wife to her husband. The wife's body does not belong to her alone but also to her husband. In the same way, the husband's body does not belong to him alone but also to his wife. Do not deprive each other except by mutual consent and for a time, so that you may devote yourselves to prayer. Then come together again so that Satan will not tempt you because of your lack of self-control (1 Cor. 7:2-5, NIV).

Paul's concern in the present passage, then, is that the husband and wife not withdraw from normal marital sexual relations but that they fulfill their sexual obligations toward their marriage partner.[14] This reveals Paul's respect for and high view of marriage and contradicts both the misguided spirituality promoted by some in the original Corinthian context and the later asceticism and imbalanced accentuation of virginity in the patristic period.

Marriage an Honorable State (1 Timothy 2:15; 4:1-4)

Similar to 1 Corinthians, 1 Timothy contains a very strong reaffirmation of the centrality of marriage in the age of Christ. As in Corinth, there were some in the Ephesian context (to which 1 Timothy is addressed) who taught that Christians ought to abstain from marriage. Paul counters this teaching with extremely strong language, contending that those "who forbid marriage" (1 Tim. 4:3) were "devoting themselves to deceitful spirits and teachings of demons" (4:1). In contrast, he maintains that "everything created by God [including marriage] is good, and nothing is to be rejected if it is received with thanksgiving" (4:4).

Earlier in the letter, Paul affirms "childbearing" (i.e., a woman's devotion to her domestic and familial duties, including childrearing) as a vital part of women's life of faith (1 Tim. 2:15) and calls candidates for both overseer and deacon to be faithful to their wives (1 Tim. 3:2, 12; cf. Titus 1:6) and to manage their households well, keeping their children submissive (1 Tim. 3:4; cf. Titus 1:6). In the former passage, Paul adduces both the Genesis Creation and Fall narratives (cf. 1 Tim. 2:13-14), which indicates that he views marriage as a divine creation ordinance, which has been affected by the Fall but is in no way superseded in the age of Christ.

The Roles of Husband and Wife (Ephesians 5:21-33)

The most detailed Pauline treatment of marriage is found in his letter to the Ephesians.[15] It will be important to study the passage on marriage (Eph. 5:21-33) in the *context of the entire letter.* We will see that marriage is set within the larger context of God's end-time restoration of all things under the headship of Christ, which includes the bringing together of all things, including believing Jews and Gentiles, in the body of Christ, the church. Christ's relationship with the church, in turn, provides the pattern for a Christian marriage, in which the husband is appointed as the head (as Christ is the head of the church) and the wife is called to submit to her husband (as the church is to Christ). We will explore this at some length in our discussion of Ephesians 5:21-33 below.

At the very outset Paul affirms God's overarching purpose for humanity (including married couples) in the age of Christ: "to bring all things in heaven and on earth together under one head (*anakephalaiōsasthai*) even Christ" (Eph. 1:10, NIV). This establishes *Christ* as the focal point of God's end-time program, and more particularly, Christ *as head* (Eph. 1:22), not only over the church (v. 22), but over every authority, in the present as well as the coming age (v. 21). Clearly, Christ's headship here conveys the notion of supreme authority, not merely that of provision or nurture, as is sometimes alleged.[16] As the exalted Lord, Christ is the head (*kephalē*), and all things are subjected to him (*hypotassō*; cf. Phil. 2:9-11).

The first important lesson for marriage from Paul's teaching in Ephesians is therefore that *the marriage relationship must be seen within the compass of God's larger salvation-historical, end-time purposes, that is, the bringing of "all things in heaven and on earth together under one head, even Christ"* (Eph. 1:10, NIV). This includes spiritual powers who will be fully submitted to Christ (1:21); the bringing together of Jews and Gentiles in one salvation-historical, end-time entity, the church (2:11-22; 3:6-13); the restoration of creation (cf. Rom. 8:18-25), which men, as divine image bearers, are currently working to subdue (Gen. 1:28); and, most relevant for our present purposes, *the restoration of the male-female marriage relationship as realized by Spirit-filled, committed Christian believers, who overcome the cursed struggle of manipulation and dominance (cf. Gen. 3:16)*[17] *in the power of Christ, and relate to each other in proper submission and Christ-like love.* While God's purposes therefore are greater than marriage or male-female roles, they significantly include this relationship (see 1 Pet. 3:1-7).

Paul continues to develop these important truths in the following chapters of his letter. In Ephesians 2, he affirms that believers (and hence also Christian husbands and wives) were once in the realm of Satan, but now they have been made alive in Christ, by grace (Eph. 2:5). They have been raised and exalted *with him,* participating in his victory over Satan (2:6). God's end-time plan to bring together all things in and under Christ is nowhere more evident than in his inclusion of the Gentiles in the community of believers together with believing Jews (2:11-22; 3:6).[18] This is termed by Paul a salvation-historical "mystery," hidden in the past in God's own purposes, but now brought into the open and unpacked by the apostle himself.[19]

At the close of his discussion of believers' spiritual blessings in Christ, Paul prays for all believers that Christ would live in their hearts by faith and that, rooted and established in love, they would know the love of Christ in their lives (Eph. 3:17, 19). The fact that Paul begins his prayer with a reference to God as "the Father from whom every family in heaven and on earth is named" (3:14-15) underscores the relevance of Paul's prayer not only for believers in general but *for married couples and families in particular.* By Paul's calling God the Father from whom every family *on earth* is named, the Creator is identified as the one who both established marriage and has rightful jurisdiction over it. By Paul's linking God's rule over families *in heaven and on earth,* his end-time purposes of uniting all things under Christ's headship are shown to encompass earthly families as well as heavenly realities. And since Christ is shown to have supreme authority over all supernatural as well as earthly beings, the husband's headship (affirmed in Eph. 5:23 below) by analogy is seen as connoting the exercise of authority over his wife as well.

The second half of the letter is given to an exposition of the new life in Christ that believers are to enjoy in the unity of the "body of Christ," the church. They are to walk in a manner worthy of their calling, give preference to one another in love, and preserve spiritual unity in peace (Eph. 4:1-3; cf. 4:4-6). God has given spiritual gifts and instituted various ministries in the church to equip believers for ministry of their own. In all this, his goal is the "perfect man" (*andra teleion,* Eph. 4:13, NKJV) who speaks the truth in love and in all things grows into Christ, who is the head (4:13-16). Paul then contrasts the old self, with its independence, lack of submission to authority, rebelliousness, and bondage to passions and lusts, with the new self, which is characterized by proper submission, a respectful attitude toward authority, and love. Becoming a Christian is like putting off old clothes and putting on new ones (Eph. 4:22, 24; cf. Col. 3:9-10): there must be a marked, noticeable change in spirit and behavior—including behavior enacted in the context of marriage and the family.

In the context immediately preceding Paul's teaching on marital roles, he exhorts believers to live lives of love in keeping with the love of Christ, who gave his life as a sacrifice for them (Eph. 5:1-2; cf. 5:25). Conversely, there must be no sexual immorality (*porneia;* 5:3; cf. 1 Cor. 6:15-16). As God's end-time community, the church (and hence every believer) ought to be filled with the Spirit (5:18) in correspondence to God's filling of the Old Testament sanctuary with his spiritual presence.[20] In the first instance, this Spirit-filling refers to congregational worship (and is thus corporate, rather than merely individualistic, in import; 5:19-20).[21] Still continuing the same sentence in the original Greek, Paul then relates Spirit-filling also to the marriage relationship (5:21-24). *Being properly submitted* (*hypotassō,* 5:21, 22) is thus a mark of Spirit-

filling, in contrast to believers' previous lifestyle, which was characterized by rebellion toward authority.

The second important lesson for married couples, then, is that the
instructions for wives and husbands (as well as those for parents/chil-
dren and slaves/masters later on) are *directed to Spirit-filled believers
rather than to those outside of Christ*. It should therefore surprise no one
that Paul's words are foolishness to those who do not follow the path
of Christian discipleship. This does not mean, however, that Ephesians
5:21-33 contains instructions on male-female relationships that are
merely private in nature. Rather, these injunctions set forth the Creator's
divine ideal and abiding will for *all* married men and women, rather
than merely believers in Jesus Christ.

In the following verses, Paul, using the format of the ancient household code, cites models for both wives and husbands to emulate: for
wives, the church in her submission to Christ (Eph. 5:24); for husbands,
Christ's sacrificial love for the church, resulting in her cleansing, holiness, and purity (5:25-28). Later, Paul will add a second, commonsense
analogy from the nature of things, appealing to self-interest: everyone
loves one's own body; therefore, in light of the one-flesh union between
husbands and wives, if husbands love their wives, this is tantamount to
husbands loving themselves (5:29-30).

On the basis of Ephesians 5:21 ("submitting *to one another* out of
reverence for Christ"), some argue that Paul does not teach the submission of wives to their husbands *only* but *also* that of husbands to their
wives in "mutual submission."[22] Admittedly, this is what Ephesians
5:21, read by itself, might suggest, but we must not stop reading at 5:21
but glean from the following verses what is Paul's definition of "submitting to one another." It is clear that the answer is (our third important principle on marriage from Paul's letter to the Ephesians) that *wives
are to submit to their husbands* who are called the "head" of their wives
as Christ is the head of the church (Eph. 5:22-24) while *husbands are to
love their wives with the sacrificial love of Christ* (vv. 25-30). This runs
counter to the notion of "mutual submission" within the context of
identity of gender roles.[23] As a noted commentator contends, "mutual
submission coexists with a hierarchy of roles within the [Christian]
household. . . . there is a general sense in which husbands are to have a

submissive attitude to wives, putting their wives' interests before their own. But this does not eliminate the more specific [role] in which wives are to submit to husbands."[24]

A comparison with Ephesians 1:22 and 4:15 further supports the notion, fourth, that *"headship" entails, not merely nurture* (though it does that, see Eph. 5:29), *but also a position of authority.* This author-itative position of the man is a function, not of intrinsic merit or worth on his part, but of God's sovereign creative will (and is perhaps reflec-tive of God's authority in light of his revelation of himself as Father). Hence the husband's leadership, as well as the wife's submission, is to be exercised within the orbit of grace rather than legalism or coercion. It should also be noted that the abbreviated Colossian parallel, "Wives, submit to your husbands, as is fitting in the Lord" (Col. 3:18) sums up the entirety of Paul's counsel to Christian wives with regard to their mar-ital disposition (no word about "mutual submission" here).[25]

The fact that wives are called to recognize and respect proper authority over them is not unique to them. Men, too, must submit to Christ, local church leadership and discipline, the civil authorities, and their employers. Nevertheless, as mentioned, this does not alter the fact that there is a sense in which wives are called to submit to their husbands in a way that is *non-reciprocal* (cf. 1 Pet. 3:1-6 in the context of 2:13, 18). Husbands' exercise of authority, in turn, must not be an arbitrary or abusive one, but should be motivated by love.[26] Again, Peter's teach-ing is found to cohere with that of Paul: "Husbands, in the same way be considerate as you live with your wives, and treat them with respect as the weaker partner and as heirs with you of the gracious gift of life" (1 Pet. 3:7, NIV).

It must also be pointed out, fifth, that it is thus manifestly *not* true that wifely submission is *merely a result of the Fall* as is at times erro-neously claimed.[27] To the contrary, as we have seen in chapter 2 above, Genesis 2 contains several indications that headship and submission were part of God's original creation: God created the man first (Gen. 2:7; noted by Paul in 1 Cor. 11:8 and 1 Tim. 2:13) and laid on him a dual charge (Gen. 2:15-17); and God made the woman from the man and for the man (2:21-22; cf. 1 Cor. 11:8-9) as his suitable helper (Gen. 2:18, 20). God's post-Fall judgment in Genesis 3:16 does not alter the fact that male headship is part of his design of the husband-and-wife relationship prior to the Fall; it merely addresses the negative consequences of sin on the way in which husband and wife now relate to each other.[28] That wifely submission is not merely a result of the Fall is further supported by the present passage, where it is *Christian* women, that is, those who have been redeemed and regenerated in Christ, who are nonetheless enjoined to submit to their husbands (Eph. 5:22). As mentioned, this is consistent with Paul's message elsewhere, where he stresses, with reference to Genesis 2:18, 20, that it is not the man who was made for woman, but the woman for the man (1 Cor. 11:9), so that "the head of every man is Christ, and the head of the woman is man" (1 Cor. 11:3, NIV).

For this reason it must be concluded that the understanding that the restored pattern for marriage in Christ *transcends* that of submission and authority is not borne out by the New Testament, be it here or elsewhere. Notably, Paul refutes as heretical the understanding (as advocated by some in his day) that "the resurrection has already taken place" (2 Tim. 2:18), that is, that the future has so invaded the present that believers' present lives no longer need to heed principles built into the fabric of creation by the Creator. Contrary to the false teachers, God's created order continues to provide the framework for human relationships (cf. 1 Tim. 4:3). While subverted by the Fall, this order is not to be set aside by Christians. Rather, it is God's redemptive purpose in Christ to counteract the effects of sin in human relationships (and other spheres) by believers' new life in the Spirit. Only in heaven will people no longer be given in marriage but be like angels (Matt. 22:30 and parallels). Currently, they still marry, have children, and are to fulfill the cultural mandate of subduing and cultivating the earth in keeping with the male-female roles established at Creation.

Paul rounds out his discussion with a familiar allusion to Scripture: ". . . and the two will become one flesh" (Eph. 5:31; cf. Gen. 2:24: "they"). Some believe that this reference to the creation narrative draws a connection between the marriage union and Christ's relationship with the church by way of typology, that is, a "typical" correspondence along salvation-historical lines, with Adam prefiguring Christ, Eve foreshadowing the church, and Adam and Eve's relationship typifying the union of Christ and the church.[29] This is possible, though it is important to note that Paul's focus here lies on the union of Christ and the church (cf. Eph. 5:30-32) and no longer on marriage (which dominated the discussion in Eph. 5:21-29).[30] Hence Paul's appropriation of Genesis 2:24 may be best described as an analogy or illustration (whereby the marital "one-flesh" union illustrates the union between Christ and the church) rather than typology.

In any case, Paul's major point seems to be that marriage has the honor of embodying the "one-flesh" principle that later in salvation history became true spiritually also for the union of the exalted Christ with the church, which is described by Paul in terms of "head," "members," and "body." This, too, like the inclusion of Gentiles in God's salvific plan, is a *mystērion:* it was hidden in the divine wisdom in ages past but now has been given to Paul to reveal. Marriage is thus shown to be part and parcel of God's overarching salvation-historical purpose of "bringing all things together under one head, even Christ" (Eph. 1:10, NIV). The lesson to be drawn from this is that marriage in Christian teaching, rather than being an end in itself, is to be subsumed under Christ's rule. Just as Christ must rule over all heavenly powers (Eph. 1:21-22) and over the church (4:15), he must also rule over the marital relationship (5:21-33), the family (6:1-4), and the workplace (6:5-9). A married couple is part of the church (understood as family of families, cf. 1 Tim. 3:15), and it, too, is part of that spiritual warfare that resolutely resists evil (Eph. 6:10-14) and seeks to promote God's purposes in this world (foremost the preaching of the gospel, 6:15, 19-20).[31] Thus the marriage relationship should also be viewed in the context of Christian witness in an unbelieving environment, both directly by the husband's and the wife's living out God's purposes for the Christian couple, and indirectly by being part of a biblical church that actively propagates the gospel message.

Finally, not only is marriage part of *God's end-time purposes in Christ* (Eph. 1:10) and part of the *Spirit's operation* (5:18), it is also part of one other important larger reality that is often overlooked, namely that of *spiritual warfare* (6:10-18).[32] This means that marriage ought not to be viewed merely on a horizontal, human plane but understood as involving spiritual attacks that require husbands and wives to "put on the full armor of God" in order to withstand those attacks. Since spiritual warfare pertains not merely to the marriage relationship but to family life at large (cf. 6:1-4), we will return to this issue more fully under the heading "Marriage and the Family and Spiritual Warfare" in chapter 8, where we will discuss several important issues related to marriage and the family.

Principles of Marriage from Paul's Letter to the Ephesians

PRINCIPLES OF MARRIAGE	SCRIPTURE REFERENCE
Marriage is part of God's larger purposes in Christ	Eph. 1:10
Paul's instructions are directed to Spirit-filled believers	Eph. 5:18
Wives are called to submit, men to love (not "mutual submission")	Eph. 5:21-33
Headship entails authority (not merely nurture)	Eph. 5:23-24 (cf. Eph. 1:22; 4:15)
Submission is still required of Christian women (not merely a result of the Fall)	Eph. 5:22; Col. 3:18 (cf. Gen. 2:18, 20; 1 Cor. 11:3, 9)
To teach that Christian marriage no longer involves submission is to exaggerate the redemptive scope of Christ's work in this life	Eph. 5:22 (cf. Matt. 22:30 par.; 1 Tim. 1:3; 2 Tim. 2:18)
Marriage involves spiritual warfare, which requires that husbands and wives put on the "full armor of God"	Eph. 6:10-18

Summary and Application

We close our discussion of Paul's teaching on marriage in Ephesians with several points of application. First, while some may view submitting to one's husband's authority as something negative, a more accurate way of looking at marital roles is to understand that wives are called to *follow their husband's loving leadership* in their marriage. This leadership and submission is to take place in the context of a true partnership, in which the husband genuinely values his wife's companionship and counsel and the wife sincerely values her husband's leadership. It is one of the unfortunate legacies of radical feminism that many tend to view male-female relationships in adversarial terms. This is contrary to God's desire and design and to the biblical message.

Second, there is a *difference between traditional and biblical marriage*. Traditional marriage may be understood as the type of division of labor by which women are responsible for cooking, cleaning, doing the laundry, and so on, while men are at work earning the family income. While Scripture does specify work outside the home as men's primary sphere and the home as the center of women's activity (e.g., Gen. 3:16-19; Prov. 31:10-31 [though the woman's reach is not *limited* to the home]; 1 Tim. 2:15; 5:10, 14), the Bible is not a law book and does not seek to legislate the exact division of labor husband and wife ought to observe.[33] Hence within the biblical parameters outlined above, there remains room for the individual couple to work out their own distinctive and specific arrangement. This may vary from couple to couple and ought to be considered a part of Christian freedom. For example, some women may be more gifted in the area of finances than men. In certain families it may be advantageous for the woman to keep the family finances if the couple is agreed as long as the husband maintains ultimate responsibility over this area. Conversely, some men may be better at cooking than their wives. Again, there seems to be no good reason why in certain families men could not contribute in this way as long as the couple is agreed. Problems may arise only if the pattern were to be so completely reversed that a given husband is focusing primarily or exclusively on the domestic sphere while the wife is part of the labor force. However, even this may not be problematic if for a *limited* time a couple, say, while the husband is pursuing an education, agrees on this type of arrangement.[34] There will also be exceptional cases where the wife needs to assume the role of primary provider on a *permanent* basis (such as when a husband's physical disability does not allow him to maintain gainful employment). Nevertheless, such couples should also strive prayerfully to emulate the biblical pattern of headship and submission, to the extent that this is possible. Even these unusual circumstances do not alter the pattern in Scripture for husbands and wives in general.

Third and last, *improper caricatures* of the biblical teaching of wifely submission and the husband's loving leadership (which includes the proper exercise of authority) must be *rejected* as either deliberate or unwitting attempts to discredit such a model as unworthy of a woman's human dignity or our modern, "enlightened" times. The kind of submission Scripture is talking about is not akin to *slavery* where one person owns another. It is not *subservience* where one person is doing the bidding of another without intelligent input or interaction. It is not even truly *hierarchical,* since this conjures up notions of a military-style, top-down chain of command in which the soldier is asked to obey, no-questions-asked, the orders of his superior. None of these labels constitute an accurate description of Scripture with regard to the roles of men and women nor do they fairly represent the understanding of gender roles set forth in the pages of this book.

Rather, the biblical model for marriage is that of loving complementarity, where the husband and the wife are partners who value and respect each other and where the husband's loving leadership is met with the wife's intelligent response. If Christ chooses to submit to God the Father while being equal in worth and personhood, there seems to be no good reason why God could not have designed the husband-and-wife relationship in such a way that the wife is called to submit to the man while likewise being equal in worth and personhood. As Paul writes to the Corinthians, "But I want you to understand that the head of every man is Christ, the head of a wife is her husband, and the head of Christ is God" (1 Cor. 11:3).

Analogous to the previous chapter, we will seek to glean insights from several specific examples of marriages before concluding our discussion of marriage in the New Testament.

INSIGHTS FROM NEW TESTAMENT MARRIAGES

Compared with the Old Testament, the New Testament provides less material on examples of marriages.

The Gospels

Little information is given about the marriage of Mary, the mother of Jesus, and Joseph (the accounts of the virgin birth precede their marriage union). The Gospels focus mostly on Jesus' call to discipleship and contain few examples pertaining to the marital relationship of particular couples. Many of Jesus' followers are featured as individuals who have benefited from his ministry and have been called by him to a spiritual commitment. Some of his most devoted followers, such as Mary of Bethany, were apparently unmarried. If they were married, little or no information about their marriage is given.

The Book of Acts

The New Testament provides a bit more information regarding marriages in the early church. As in the case of the Gospel evidence, some followers of Christ in the book of Acts either are unmarried (such as Lydia; Acts 16:11-15) or little specific information is given about their marriage relationship (such as the Philippian jailer, who believed with his entire household, 16:25-34). Beyond this, the book of Acts features a handful of examples of marriages, both positive and negative. We will briefly discuss one negative and then one positive example.

ANANIAS AND SAPPHIRA

A negative example is provided by Ananias and Sapphira, who conspire to lie to the apostles about their giving and are both judged severely for their dishonesty (Acts 5:1-11). The lesson from this is that even if one marriage partner chooses to sin, the other ought to make his or her own decision and do what is right, regardless of the consequences. God does not expect one marriage partner to follow the other into sin.[35]

AQUILA AND PRISCILLA

A very positive example of a marriage committed to Christian ministry, even missionary service, is provided through the account of Aquila and Priscilla. Paul first meets this couple in Corinth and works alongside them as a tentmaker (Acts 18:2-3). Later, they join Paul on his journey to Ephesus (18:18-19), where they are left by the apostle while he continues his travels. Sometime after this they hear the gifted preacher Apollos in the synagogue and, observing his need for further instruction, take him and explain to him the way of God more accurately (18:26). The two are mentioned again in Romans 16:3, where both are called Paul's "fellow workers in Christ Jesus" who risked their lives for him. Apparently, Priscilla and Aquila had returned to Rome by that time (cf. Acts 18:2, which refers to the original expulsion of all Jews from Rome by Claudius). The final reference to this couple is found in 2 Timothy 4:19, where Paul sends greetings to the couple (back in Ephesus?) from his Roman prison.[36] This noted missionary couple was among Paul's most strategic allies in his Gentile mission (cf. Rom. 16:4), playing important roles in such major centers as Ephesus, Corinth, and Rome. Together they hosted house churches wherever they went, instructed others such as Apollos, and even "risked their necks" for Paul.

One delicate aspect of the New Testament's portrayal of this couple is that Priscilla seems to have had a leading role in their relationship. This is borne out by the fact that in four of the six instances where she is mentioned in the New Testament, Priscilla's name appears before that of her husband (Acts 18:18-19, 26; Rom. 16:3; 2 Tim. 4:19; Aquila is mentioned first in Acts 18:2 and 1 Cor. 16:19). Scholars have speculated that the reason for this is that Priscilla was converted before her husband, perhaps having led him to faith in Christ, or that she played a more prominent part in the life and work of the church than her husband.[37] Alternatively, it has been conjectured that "Prisca [the shortened form of her name] was the more dominant of the two or of higher social status, and she may either have provided the financial resources for the business or have been the brains behind it."[38] Regardless of the reasons (none of which are specifically stated in the biblical texts), we observe that here is perhaps one of the most outstanding New Testament examples of a married couple fully committed to serving Christ together in the cause of Christian mission.

The Rest of the New Testament and Conclusion

Neither the epistolary nor the apocalyptic genre easily lends itself to a more detailed portrayal of marital relationships, so that the New Testament letters and the book of Revelation do not provide significant material in this regard. However, together with our survey of marriages in the Old Testament above and our discussion of examples of parenting in both Testaments below, the above-mentioned instances in the book of Acts (not to speak of didactic material on marriage and the family in Scripture) add up to a significant resource for the study and application of God's will in these areas.

CONCLUSION

The above survey of the New Testament teaching on marriage showed that marriage is uniformly affirmed as the foundational, divinely appointed institution for humanity in the age of Christ.

Jesus' major pronouncement on the subject was made when he was asked by some Pharisees about his views on divorce (Matt. 19:3). This became an occasion for our Lord to reaffirm God's ideal of *monogamous, lifelong, and heterosexual marriage,* with reference to both foundational Old Testament texts on the subject (Matt. 19:4-6; cf. Gen. 1:27; 2:24). According to Jesus, "what God has joined together, let man not separate" (Matt. 19:6, NIV, par. Mark 10:9). This makes clear that Jesus did not view marriage as a mere social institution or convention. Rather, according to Jesus, marriage is a sacred bond between a man and a woman instituted by and entered into before God.

Apart from this major marriage-affirming pronouncement, many of Jesus' statements address the critical importance of following him in *discipleship.* While discipleship in Jesus' teaching is not set in *contrast* with valuing marriage, it is presented as the *indispensable requirement* for any true, committed follower of Christ, transcending and encompassing even his or her familial obligations. The fact that Jesus considered singleness to be a kingdom gift for the select few (Matt. 19:11-12) indicates that he clearly assumed marriage as the norm in this life (though not in the life to come, Matt. 22:30).

Among the New Testament writers, Peter, in his first letter, teaches wifely submission even to unbelieving husbands (1 Pet. 3:1-7). As models, he holds up the "holy women of the past" such as Sarah, who treated her husband Abraham with respect (even though he was not always the perfect husband, as the book of Genesis attests).

Paul, too, his positive comments regarding singleness notwithstanding, strongly affirmed marriages and sought to strengthen them. When writing to Corinth, he defended marriage against those who elevated singleness as a superior state that allowed for greater spirituality (1 Cor. 7:2-5). When writing to Timothy in Ephesus, likewise, he defended marriage against those "who forbid marriage" (1 Tim. 4:3), which he denounced as "teachings of demons" (4:1). For women, Paul affirmed the central role of "childbearing," that is, their domestic and familial duties (2:15), and for men who would lead the church, he required marital fidelity and diligent parental discipline of children.

Paul's teaching on marriage is given its fullest expression in the letter to the Ephesians. At the very outset, he set marriage within the larger framework of God's plan of bringing "all things in heaven and on earth together under one head, even Christ" (Eph. 1:10, NIV). Just as Christ has been made head over every human and heavenly authority (1:21), so the husband was put in charge over his wife (5:22-24). This was done by "the Father from whom every family in heaven and on earth is named" (3:14-15). According to Paul, this *headship* implies both the *wife's submission to her husband's authority* and the *husband's loving, sacrificial devotion to his wife*. Paul also teaches that it is an indispensable prerequisite for a Christian marriage that both spouses are *believers* and that they are *Spirit-filled* as they fulfill their marital roles and obligations.

Hence the New Testament builds on and further elaborates on the Old Testament teaching on marriage while cohering with the divine ideal of marriage presented in the book of Genesis.

4

THE NATURE OF MARRIAGE: SACRAMENT, CONTRACT, OR COVENANT?

NOW THAT WE HAVE concluded our study of the biblical teaching on marriage, we are in a position to evaluate the three most commonly held views on the nature of marriage. There are three basic views on the nature of marriage: (1) marriage as a sacrament; (2) marriage as a contract; and (3) marriage as a covenant. We will look at each of these definitions in turn.[1]

MARRIAGE AS A SACRAMENT

The view of marriage as a sacrament, while harking back to Scripture, is largely a product of church tradition. *Sacramentum* is the Latin term used by Jerome in the fourth-century Vulgate to translate the Greek expression *mystērion* ("mystery"), which describes the analogy between marriage and the union of Christ and the church in Ephesians 5:32.[2] The *sacramental model* of marriage has its roots in the writings of the influential church father Augustine, who in his text *De bono conjugali* ("On the Good of Marriage"), as well as in his later writings, noted three main benefits of marriage: offspring, fidelity, and the sacramental bond.[3] A survey of his works reveals that in using the phrase "sacramental bond" (*sacramentum*) Augustine was trying to communicate that marriage creates a holy, permanent bond between a man and a women, which depicts Christ's union with the church.

However, as the Roman Catholic Church (which built much of its theology on Augustine's writings) developed its full-fledged sacramental theology including the seven sacraments dispensed by the church (baptism, first communion, confirmation, the Eucharist, marriage, holy orders, and anointing the sick), Augustine's concept of marriage was *recast*. In its reconceived manifestation, officially codified at the Council of Trent (1545–1563), the Roman Catholic Church defined marriage (using Augustinian terminology) as a *sacrament*.[4]

According to the sacramental model of marriage, it is by participating in this ecclesiastical rite that grace is accrued for the married couple on the basis of the supposition that God dispenses grace through the church and participation in its sacraments. Not only are sacraments "signs that point to the presence of God among his people," "they are also *efficacious* signs, that is, they *bring about or effect what they signify*. Catholics believe that God wills to make himself present and to *confer his grace* upon us in a particular way *whenever a sacrament is properly enacted within the church*."[5] To this end people must approach the sacrament with reverence and faith.[6]

While this view of marriage has proved attractive to some,[7] it is deficient biblically for several reasons. First and foremost, there is nothing in the institution of marriage itself that "mystically" dispenses divine grace.[8] It is not the case, as the Roman Catholic Church maintains, that when marriage is entered into under the auspices of the Church, it is in itself an institution where Christ is "personally present" in a mystical way. There is no intrinsic power in the marriage vows themselves. The prerequisite for a Christian marriage is not the "sacramental blessing" of the institutionalized church, but becoming "new creatures" in Christ (cf. 2 Cor. 5:17; Eph. 4:23-24), by being regenerated, "born again" in him (cf. Titus 3:5).

Second, this approach to marriage does not cohere with the thrust of the biblical teaching on marriage as a whole, according to which the Creator designed marriage as the vehicle for *creating new physical life,* not as a *mechanism for attaining spiritual life*. In other words, the life imparted through marriage operates through procreation and is extended to a married couple's physical offspring (cf. Gen. 1:27-28; 2:23-24) rather than being channeled to the couple by virtue of participating in a sacramental or "mystical" ecclesiastical rite in which grace is dispensed by the sheer working of the institution itself (*ex opere operato*).[9]

A third problem with this model of marriage is that it subjects the husband-wife relationship to the control of the church. There is no biblical injunction supporting this notion. Christ himself is said to be the head of the church and the Lord and Savior of both husband and wife (Eph. 5:23-27; cf. 1 Cor. 11:3). For these and other reasons[10] we conclude that the sacramental model is not borne out by scriptural teaching but is largely a product of patristic and medieval mystical thought that goes beyond and in fact counter to the biblical conception of marriage. Rightly understood, marriage may be viewed as "sacramental" in the Augustinian sense of constituting a sacred, permanent bond between a man and a woman, but it is not a "sacrament" in the way Roman Catholic theology has defined it.

MARRIAGE AS A CONTRACT

A second model of marriage is the *contractual* model. The contractual model constitutes the prevailing secular view of marriage in Western culture.[11] While in Old Testament times there is no major discernible distinction between contracts and covenants,[12] because people regularly invoked God as a witness when entering into mutual agreements, there is a sharp disjunction between (secular) contracts and (sacred) covenants in modern secular society.

In contrast to the sacramental model (which takes Scripture at least as its point of departure) and the covenantal view (which roots marriage in the biblical teaching on the subject), the contractual approach does not necessarily (or typically) seek to invoke Scripture as its source or grounds of authority. Rather, proponents of this approach view marriage as a bilateral contract that is voluntarily formed, maintained, and dissolved by two individuals. Gary Chapman lists five general characteristics of contracts:

(1) they are typically made for a limited period of time;
(2) they most often deal with specific actions;
(3) they are conditional upon the continued performance of contractual obligations by the other partner;
(4) they are entered into for one's own benefit; and
(5) they are sometimes unspoken and implicit.[13]

The contractual model, which harkens back to the medieval ecclesiastical courts and the writings of the Enlightenment era thinkers,[14] roots marriage in civil law. According to this view, the state is charged with overseeing the institution of marriage and has authority to grant both marriage licenses and certificates of divorce. Christians who hold to this model may "Christianize" their marriage by injecting Christian terminology into their vows and by formally commencing their marriage in a church, yet such Christianization is really only a thin veneer, for in such cases the officiating minister ultimately only has power to marry couples by the authority vested in him by the state.

Although this is the prevailing model of marriage in Western culture (including Western Christianity), we see limitations on several grounds. First, this teaching is reductionistic and not found anywhere within the pages of Scripture to describe marriage as a whole. An aspect of marriage is that an agreement is made between a man and a woman, but this does not cover the whole of what marriage is.[15] In fact, the contractual model did not exist as a developed model of marriage until the seventeenth century at the earliest. As Paul Palmer notes, the Latin term from which the word "contract" was derived (*contractus*) "was never used in classical Latin *even for pagan marriage*, and . . . until the High Scholastic period [ca. 1250–1350] the preferred word for Christian marriage was *foedus* or covenant."[16] It seems unlikely that it would take the church well over a millennium to discover the true nature of marriage.

A second objection to this view is that, given the central place of marriage in God's created order, the contractual model does not cohere. It is deficient in that it provides an extremely weak basis for the permanence of marriage. In essence, the contractual model of marriage bases the security and stability of marriage on the ability of people not to sin. If one spouse commits a grievous enough sin to break the contract, the other partner is free to dissolve the union. In light of humanity's (including Christians') universal sinfulness, this renders marriage a highly precarious and unstable institution. This, however, does not accord with Scripture's pervasive emphasis on the permanence and sacred nature of marriage before God (Matt. 19:4-6, esp. v. 6, and parallels; cf. Gen. 2:24).

Third, and finally, this model of marriage is inadequate because, by rooting matrimony in civil law, it opens the door (at least in principle) to a variety of marital arrangements that Scripture clearly prohibits. To cite but a few of the more egregious examples, it would only require an amendment of civil law in order to allow for "legal" same-sex marriage, polygamy, incestuous marriage, or bestiality, and so on. As demonstrated below, however, Scripture consistently and unequivocally disallows these forms of marriage (e.g., Gen. 1:27-28; 2:23-24; Lev. 18; 20:10-21). For this reason any model of marriage that substitutes human laws for divine revelation as the basis for understanding the nature of this vital relationship falls short of the scriptural teaching concerning marriage and ought therefore be considered inadequate and unacceptable for Bible-believing and committed Christians.

None of this is to say that marriages entered into before a public official but not in a church wedding ceremony are invalid or that such couples are not really married. They are. Our point here is simply that those who hold to a contractual view of marriage, while truly married, fall short of what Scripture itself depicts as the nature of the marital bond. If such a couple converts to Christ, therefore, there is obviously no need to get married again, but simply for that couple to commit themselves to this fuller, more adequate understanding of what it means to be married according to Scripture—which is best described as a covenant or as a creation ordinance with covenantal features, as the following section will seek to demonstrate.

Marriage as a Covenant

A third approach to the nature of marriage is the *covenantal* model.[17] This position defines marriage as a *sacred bond between a man and a woman instituted by and publicly entered into before God (whether or not this is acknowledged by the married couple), normally consummated by sexual intercourse.*[18] Although this view has taken on various nuances in the writings of different authors (and ultimately will be shaped by one's general understanding of biblical covenants),[19] its essence is that marriage is conceived, not merely as a *bilateral contract* between two individuals, but as a *sacred bond* both between husband and wife and between the couple and God.[20]

Unlike the sacramental view, which roots marriage in the standards of *church law* (that is, the church's own understanding of itself and the nature of marriage), and the contractual view, which roots marriage in the standards of *civil law* (that is, human stipulations regulating people's common life in society), the covenantal view roots marriage in the standards of *divine law* (that is, the authoritative divine revelation found in Scripture itself). In keeping with Stott's definition of marriage on the basis of Genesis 2:24, the covenantal view therefore holds that "[m]arriage is an exclusive heterosexual *covenant between one man and one woman, ordained and sealed by God,* preceded by a public leaving of parents, consummated in sexual union, issuing in a permanent mutually supportive partnership, and normally crowned by the gift of children."[21]

While there are various types of covenants established in Old Testament times, the term "covenant" (Heb. *bᵉrît,* less frequently *ʾēšed;* LXX: *diathēkē*) in general conveys "the idea of a solemn commitment, guaranteeing promises or obligations undertaken by one or both covenanting parties."[22] The expression is frequently used for commitments between God and human beings (e.g., the Noahic, Abrahamic, Mosaic, Davidic, and new covenants), yet it also refers to a variety of agreements between humans (e.g., Gen. 21:22-24; 1 Sam. 18:3; 1 Kings 5:1-12; 2 Kings 11:17), including marriage (Prov. 2:17; Ezek. 16:8; Mal. 2:14).[23] It is therefore important not to commit what linguists call "illegitimate totality transfer" and to import all the features of a divine-human covenant into a given human covenant relationship (such as marriage). For instance, the analogy between marriage and the Christ-church relationship (involving the new covenant) in Ephesians 5:21-33 should not be taken to imply that these are equivalent in every respect. The new covenant, for its part, is eternal, while marriage, according to Jesus, is limited to this life only (Matt. 22:30).[24]

In addition, it should be recognized that the biblical notion of marriage as a covenant at the very least incorporates contractual features. As Instone-Brewer points out, the Hebrew word (*bᵉrît*) is the same for both contract and covenant, and the theological meaning of "covenant" is "an agreement that a faithful person would not break even if the partner to whom that person is in covenant breaks the stipulations of the covenant."[25] The later prophets (esp. Jeremiah 31; cf. Ezekiel 36–37), however, spoke of a "new covenant" that God would promise to keep whether or not his people would. According to Instone-Brewer, this irrevocable covenant is unlike any other Old Testament covenant, and it is the irrevocable nature of the new covenant that makes it so special and unique.

Advocates of the covenantal model of marriage support this view primarily with reference to two clusters of passages: (1) covenantal language in the Genesis 2 narrative recounting the divine institution of marriage between the first man and the first woman (see esp. Gen. 2:24); (2) passages of Scripture that explicitly refer to marriage as a "covenant" (esp. Prov. 2:16-17; Mal. 2:14) and biblical analogies and passages in which marriage is implicitly treated in covenantal terms.[26] We will briefly survey the contribution of these two clusters of passages and then suggest five ways in which the covenantal nature of marriage ought to inform contemporary marriages.

Covenantal language (that is, terms that convey the concept of covenant) in the foundational Genesis narrative may include the reference to the "one flesh" union between husband and wife in Genesis 2:24. The consummation of marriage through sexual intercourse may serve as the equivalent to the oath in other Old Testament covenants.[27] Adam's naming of Eve in Genesis 2:23 is consistent with God changing the names of Abram and Jacob upon entering into a covenant relationship with them (Gen. 17:5; 35:10).

Explicit biblical terminology referring to marriage as a "covenant" includes the reference to the adulterous woman forgetting "the *covenant of her God*" in Proverbs 2:16-17. This most likely refers to the (written or oral) marriage agreement between the woman and her husband before God,[28] as is suggested by a similar reference in the book of Malachi: "The Lord was witness between you and the wife of your youth, to whom you have been faithless, though she is your companion and your wife by *covenant*" (*bᵉrît*; Mal. 2:14; cf. Ezek. 16:8).[29]

In closing, several *concerns* that have been raised regarding a covenant view of marriage should be briefly addressed. First, some have observed that marriage is *not explicitly referred to as a covenant* in the New Testament (note the absence of explicit covenant terminology in the major New Testament passage on marriage, Ephesians 5:21-33). Though this is true, the concept is still present in the New Testament (cf. Matt. 19:6 par. Mark 10:9). It is also true that "covenant" is not the *only* biblical concept applied to marriage, though it is the *major* one. Other biblical models of the nature of marriage, such as *the analogy of Christ and the church,* are true reflections of the New Testament teaching on marriage as well (Eph. 5:21-33, though historically no view of marriage has been developed around this analogy, which is one reason why it seems legitimate to incorporate it into the covenant view).

Three Models of the Nature of Marriage

	SACRAMENTAL	CONTRACTUAL	COVENANTAL
Definition of Model	Marriage as a means of obtaining grace	Marriage as a bilateral contract that is voluntarily formed, maintained, and dissolved by two individuals	Marriage as a sacred bond between a man and a woman instituted by and entered into before God
Roots of Model	Church law	Civil law	Divine law
Source of Model	Augustine and Council of Trent 1545-1563	Medieval ecclesiastical courts and Enlightenment thinking	Covenantal language in Genesis 2; Proverbs 2:16-17; and Malachi 2:14; other biblical analogies and allusions
Weaknesses or Concerns Raised Regarding Model	Nothing in nature of marriage that "mystically" dispenses divine grace	Reductionistic; not found in Scripture to describe marriage as a whole	Marriage not explicitly referred to as covenant in NT
	Does not cohere with thrust of biblical teaching on marriage as a whole; marriage a wellspring of new physical life, not a mechanism for attaining spiritual life	It provides an extremely weak basis for the permanence of marriage—the ability of people not to sin	Marriage transcends notion of covenant; part of God's created order
	It subordinates the husband-wife relationship to the control of the church	Opens the door to a variety of marital arrangements prohibited in Scripture	No demonstrable distinction between contract and covenant in OT terminology

Second, others have noted that marriage *transcends the notion of covenant,* since it is rooted in God's created order, which precedes the establishment of covenant relationships later in biblical history. This should not minimize the importance of considering marriage as a covenant, though it does mean that marriage as conceived at Creation is even more than a covenant. It is *a creation ordinance with covenantal features.*[30]

Third, as mentioned, Instone-Brewer and others contend that, in its ancient Near Eastern context, there is *no clear demonstrable distinction between marriage as a contract and marriage as a covenant,* so that Old Testament references to marriage as a "covenant" should be understood in contractual rather than covenantal terms. Indeed, this is an important piece of evidence, which should caution us from importing notions derived from divine-human agreements in Old Testament times and even more so from the "new covenant" inaugurated by Jesus Christ. That covenant must remain primary, and marriage should be conducted according to the pattern of Christ's loving headship and the church's willing submission. With these qualifications, however, it does seem proper to approach marriage as a covenant.[31]

IMPLICATIONS OF A COVENANT VIEW OF MARRIAGE

In light of the above observations, what does it mean for a couple to embrace the view of marriage as a covenant? If the marriage covenant is defined as *a sacred bond instituted by and publicly entered into before God (whether or not this is acknowledged by the married couple), normally consummated by sexual intercourse,* we submit that embracing the "marriage covenant" concept means a couple must understand and commit itself to at least the following five things:

(1) *The permanence of marriage:* Marriage is intended to be permanent, since it was established by God (Matt. 19:6 par. Mark 10:9). Marriage constitutes a serious commitment that should not be entered into lightly or unadvisedly. It involves a solemn promise or pledge, not merely to one's marriage partner, but before God. Divorce is not permitted except in certain biblically prescribed circumstances.[32]

(2) *The sacredness of marriage:* Marriage is not merely a human agreement between two consenting individuals (a "civil union"); it is a relationship before and under God (Gen. 2:22;

hence a "same-sex" marriage is an oxymoron; since Scripture universally condemns homosexual relationships, God would never sanction a sacred marital bond between two members of the same sex). While sacred, however, marriage is not therefore a "sacrament." It is not a mystical union under the church's auspices serving as a vehicle for securing or sustaining one's salvation.

(3) *The intimacy of marriage:* Marriage is the most intimate of all human relationships, uniting a man and a woman in a "one flesh" bond (Gen. 2:23-25). Marriage involves "leaving" one's family of origin and "cleaving" to one's spouse, which signifies the establishment of a new family unit distinct from the two originating families. While "one flesh" suggests sexual intercourse and normally procreation, at its very heart the concept entails the establishment of a new kinship relationship between two previously unrelated individuals by the most intimate of human bonds.

(4) *The mutuality of marriage:* Marriage is a relationship of free self-giving of one human being to another (Eph. 5:25-30). The marriage partners are to be first and foremost concerned about the well-being of the other person and to be committed to each other in steadfast love and devotion. This involves the need for forgiveness and restoration of the relationship in the case of sin. "Mutuality," however, does not mean "sameness in role." Scripture is clear that wives are submit to their husbands and to be their "suitable helpers," while husbands bear the ultimate responsibility for the marriage before God (Eph. 5:22-24 par. Col. 3:18; Gen. 2:18, 20).

(5) *The exclusiveness of marriage:* Marriage is not only permanent, sacred, intimate, and mutual; it is also exclusive (Gen. 2:22-25; 1 Cor. 7:2-5). This means that no other human relationship must interfere with the marriage commitment between husband and wife. For this reason our Lord treated sexual immorality of a married person (Matt. 19:9; including even a husband's lustful thoughts, Matt. 5:28) with utmost seriousness. For this reason, too, premarital sex is illegitimate, since it violates the exclusive claims of one's future spouse. As the Song of Solomon makes clear, only in the secure context of an exclusive marital bond can free and complete giving of oneself in marriage take place.

CONCLUSION

In the present chapter, we have investigated the three major models of marriage that describe marriage as a sacrament, as a contract, or as a covenant. We have concluded that the biblical concept of marriage is best described as a covenant (or a creation ordinance with covenantal features), *a sacred bond between a man and a woman, instituted by and publicly entered into before God (whether or not this is acknowledged by the married couple), normally consummated by sexual intercourse.* Rather than being merely a contract that is made for a limited period of time, conditional upon the continued performance of contractual obligations by the other partner, and entered into primarily or even exclusively for one's own benefit, marriage is a sacred bond that is characterized by permanence, sacredness, intimacy, mutuality, and exclusiveness.

For both the husband and the wife, living out their proper, God-willed roles, fully aware of the larger salvation-historical and cosmic implications of their relationship, becomes therefore an important part of their discipleship. What is more, it is an integral part of their one-flesh union that they produce not merely *physical* offspring, but that they pursue the nurture and facilitate the growth of *spiritual* offspring—that is, aid the Spirit's work in the lives of their children in conviction of sin, conversion, regeneration, and sanctification. But this is to anticipate the following chapter.

5

THE TIES THAT BIND: FAMILY IN THE OLD TESTAMENT

NOW THAT WE HAVE studied God's plan for marriage, it is time to turn to an investigation of the biblical teaching on the family.[1]

What is a family? Building on our definition of marriage in the previous chapter as a sacred bond between a man and a woman, instituted by and publicly entered into before God (whether or not this is acknowledged by the married couple), normally consummated by sexual intercourse, we may define "family" as, *primarily, one man and one woman united in matrimony (barring death of a spouse) plus (normally) natural or adopted children and, secondarily, any other persons related by blood.*[2] As will be seen below, in biblical times extended families lived together in larger households, while in modern Western culture the family unit is usually comprised of the nuclear family (father, mother, and children) living in the same household.[3]

In the following survey, we will first investigate the ancient Israelite conception of family and explore the Old Testament teaching on the roles and responsibilities of fathers, mothers, and children. After this, we will discuss the importance placed in the Hebrew Scriptures on parental instruction of children about God. Insights can also be gleaned from Old Testament family relationships, which will be presented at the end of the present chapter.

THE ANCIENT ISRAELITE CONCEPTION OF FAMILY

Because of their descent from a common ancestor, the Israelites perceived themselves as a large extended kinship group.[4] The Old

Testament features four major terms related to family: (1) ʿam ("people"); (2) šēbeṭ maṭṭeh ("tribe"); (3) mišpāḥâ ("clan"); and (4) bêt ʾāb ("house of a father").[5] While ʿam ("people") typically has the nation of Israel as a referent and šēbeṭ maṭṭeh ("tribe") reflects the people's tribal structure as descendants of the twelve sons of Jacob, mišpāḥâ ("clan") usually designates a subgroup smaller than the tribe but larger than the family.

The most relevant expression for our present purposes is the fourth one, bêt ʾāb, the Hebrew term for "family" (lit., "father's house"; cf., e.g., Judges 17–18). Unlike the modern Western notion of a nuclear family consisting of husband, wife, and children, ancient Israelite households were comprised of large extended families, also including a couple's married children's families, any as of yet unmarried sons and daughters, and male and female hired servants and slaves along with their families.

THE ROLE AND RESPONSIBILITIES OF FATHERS

As Daniel Block notes, like most ancient Near Eastern cultures, Israelite families were *patrilineal* (i.e., official descent was traced through the father's line), *patrilocal* (i.e., married women became a part of their husband's household), and *patriarchal* (the father was in charge of the household).[6] While most identify the ancient Israelite family structure by the term "patriarchy" ("rule of the father"), Block contends that the expression "patricentrism" ("centered around the father") may be better suited for this type of arrangement, since, first, feminism has permanently discredited patriarchy even in its nonabusive forms by giving it a negative connotation and, second, "patricentrism" better reflects the "normative biblical disposition toward the role of the head of a household in Israel."[7] Like the spokes of a wheel, family life radiated outward from the father as its center. The community was built around the father and bore his stamp in every respect.[8] Also, third, while the father indisputably ruled his household, the Old Testament rarely focuses on his power (Gen. 3:16 speaks of a subversion of the man's proper exercise of authority). Rather than functioning as a despot or dictator, in healthy households the father and husband usually inspired the trust and security of its members (cf. Job 29:12-17; Ps. 68:5-6).[9]

Hence, it was not primarily the power and privileges associated with the father's position but rather the responsibilities associated with his headship that were emphasized.

Block lists the following nine primary responsibilities of the father in ancient Israel:[10]

- personally modeling strict personal fidelity to Yahweh;[11]
- leading the family in the national festivals, nurturing the memory of Israel's salvation;[12]
- instructing the family in the traditions of the exodus and the Scriptures;[13]
- managing the land in accordance with the law (Leviticus 25);
- providing for the family's basic needs for food, shelter, clothing, and rest;
- defending the household against outside threats (e.g., Judg. 18:21-25);
- serving as elder and representing the household in the official assembly of citizens (Ruth 4:1-11);
- maintaining family members' well-being and the harmonious operation of the family unit; and
- implementing decisions made at the clan or tribal level.

Apart from their responsibilities toward their wife (or wives),[14] fathers also had obligations toward their children. As Block points out, lists such as the following demonstrate the inadequacy of labeling the father's role in ancient Israel "patriarchal" with the predominant or even exclusive emphasis being placed on his exercise (or even abusive exercise) of authority.[15] Fathers' responsibilities toward their sons included the following:[16]

- naming their children (together with their wives);[17]
- consecrating their firstborn sons to God;[18]
- circumcising their sons on the eighth day (Gen. 17:12; 21:4; Lev. 12:3);
- delighting in, having compassion on, and loving their sons;[19]
- nurturing their sons' spiritual development, modeling before them their own deep personal commitment to God and the Scriptures, instructing them in the Scriptures and the traditions

of salvation and covenant, and giving public witness to their spiritual commitment;[20]

- guarding their own ethical conduct so as not to involve their sons in their sin (Ex. 20:5; Deut. 5:9);
- instructing their sons in the way of wisdom, developing their character and skills for life and vocation, and teaching them to follow in their father's steps (Proverbs 1–9);
- disciplining their sons when they erred and presenting them to the communal leaders for discipline when the sons refused to be corrected;[21]
- judiciously managing their household affairs, especially with regard to inheritance, so as to ensure a smooth transition to the subsequent generation;
- arranging for their sons' marriage to suitable wives (Genesis 24; Judges 14);
- pronouncing blessings on their sons prior to their death (Genesis 27; 48–49).

The list of fathers' obligations toward their daughters is shorter, given the generally male-oriented perspective of the Old Testament:[22]

- protecting his daughter from male "predators" so she would marry as a virgin, thus bringing honor to his name and purity to her husband (cf. Ex. 22:16-17; Deut. 22:13-21);
- arranging for his daughter's marriage by finding a suitable husband and making proper arrangements;[23]
- ensuring a measure of security for his daughter by providing a dowry (cf. Gen. 29:24, 29);
- protecting his daughter from rash vows (Num. 30:2-15);
- providing security for his daughter in case the marriage failed;[24] and perhaps also
- instructing his daughters in the Scriptures.[25]

THE ROLE AND RESPONSIBILITIES OF MOTHERS

The Old Testament contains many indications of an elevated status of the wife and mother in ancient Israel. (1) In Genesis 1 and 2, the woman, like the man, is said to have been created by God in his likeness (Gen.

1:27); (2) the man and the woman are said to have joint responsibility for subduing the earth and cultivating it (1:28); (3) the woman is placed alongside the man as his "suitable helper," not as his servant or slave (2:18, 20); (4) the woman's creation from the man's rib may also convey the notion that she is close and dear to his heart (2:22); (5) the woman's name in the Hebrew designates her as the man's counterpart (2:23); and (6) the one-flesh union between husband and wife also accentuates their closeness and intimacy (2:24-25). At the same time, it is clear that the wife and mother was functionally subordinated to her husband and male head of the household.[26]

Block provides the following evidence for the dignity of the wife and mother and her influence within the household in ancient Israel:[27]

- men and women related to each other on a complementary level in both courtship and, once married, in lovemaking (Song of Solomon);
- wives and mothers often named their children;[28]
- the fifth commandment stipulates that children honor their fathers *and mothers;*[29]
- both father and mother rose to their daughter's defense if her virginity at the time of her wedding was called into question;
- Old Testament wisdom literature often sets a mother's wisdom in instruction in parallelism to that of a father (Prov. 1:8; 6:20);[30]
- the excellent wife in Proverbs 31 exudes initiative, creativity, and energy; while subordinate to her husband, she is not subservient to him;
- women often exercised great influence over their husbands, both positive and negative;[31]
- although excluded from official leadership roles in the community, they were occasionally appointed in *ad hoc* prophetic roles and participated in religious affairs.[32]

Major threats to women's security in ancient Israel were polygamy, divorce, and widowhood.[33] While it is commonly argued that women in ancient Israel had no legal status and were treated as their fathers' and then husbands' legal property, Daniel Block argues persuasively that this was not in fact the case. After thorough investigation, he concludes that

... to view women in ancient Israel as chattel of their husbands and fathers is to commit a fundamental fallacy: the failure to distinguish between authority and ownership, legal dependence and servitude, functional subordination and possession. The consistent and unequivocally patricentric worldview of biblical authors cannot be denied, but this does not mean that those under the authority of males were deemed their property. To the contrary, in keeping with the radical biblical ideal of servant leadership as a whole, husbands and fathers were to exercise authority with the well-being of their households in mind.[34]

The mother's responsibilities to her children are well summarized in Proverbs 31: providing food, clothing, and shelter.[35] At a child's birth, mothers would cut the umbilical cord, bathe the child, and wrap it in a cloth (cf. Ezek. 16:3-4). During the first decade of the child's life, he or she was the special concern of his or her mother. Since in ancient Israel the home was the primary place for education, the mother's example and instruction were vital. Once children reached adolescence, they would increasingly spend more time with their fathers, though this does not mean that the mothers' influence was no longer felt. Mothers would also train their daughters for their future roles as wives and mothers. This was even more important since daughters upon marriage would leave their paternal household and join that of their husband. Nevertheless, mothers would continue to follow the course of their daughters' lives, and being able to witness the birth of grandchildren was considered to be a special blessing and delight (e.g., Ruth 4:14-16). Mothers also bore responsibilities toward domestic servants and slaves.[36]

PROCREATION

Procreation was considered to be an integral part of God's plan for marriage.[37] As the Creator had told the first human couple in the beginning, "Be fruitful and multiply and fill the earth" (Gen. 1:28; cf. 9:1, 7; 35:11). Though originally two individual persons, husband and wife become "one flesh" (2:24) in their marital union, which is given visible expression by the children resulting from that union. Consequently, barrenness was regularly seen in Old Testament times as the result of divine disfavor (e.g., Gen. 29:31), while children were regarded as a gift and bless-

ing from God (e.g., 13:16; 15:1-6; Ex. 23:25-26; Ps. 127:3-5; 128:3-6).[38]
Rachel's outcry to Jacob is symptomatic, "Give me children, or I shall
die!" (Gen. 30:1; cf. 30:22-23; see also the plight of Sarah in Genesis 16;
21:1-7; Hannah in 1 Samuel 1; and Elizabeth in Luke 1:25; cf. Luke 1:6-
7). The removal of barrenness amounts to the lifting of divine reproach
and is tantamount to being "remembered" by the Lord (Gen. 30:23; 1
Sam. 1:19-20). Without discriminating against childless couples, in the
Old Testament the general expectation for man and woman created by
God is therefore to be married and to have children.[39]

THE ROLE AND RESPONSIBILITIES OF CHILDREN

The most common terms for children in the Old Testament are *bēn*
("son"), *bat* ("daughter"), *yeled* ("fetus, male child, youth"), *yaldâ*
("female child"), and *zeraʿ* ("seed"). The Hebrew Scriptures also feature
a considerable variety of terms for the different stages of childhood
(including words for unborn children, newborns, infants, nursing and
weaned children), and young adulthood (including terms for adolescents
as well as young women of childbearing age and young men, the latter
especially in the book of Proverbs).[40] Childhood was considered to
extend from one month to five years and youth from five to twenty years
(Lev. 27:1-7).[41]

The esteem in which children were held in ancient Israel (which is
reflected in the breadth of vocabulary used for children and youth) can
be attributed to several factors and convictions:[42] (1) the belief that every
human being is created in the image of God (Gen. 1:27; Psalm 8); (2)
the view that children ensure the perpetuation of humanity and the fulfillment of the divine mandate to subdue and cultivate the earth (Gen.
1:26; 5; 9:18-19); (3) the notion that the conception of children was ultimately a product of divine action and hence a sign of God's favor (with
the corollary that barrenness was viewed as a sign of divine disfavor);[43]
(4) the valuing of children as an important economic asset; (5) the belief
that in a sense parents live on in and through their children (hence one's
worst fate was for one's "seed" to be cut off and one's "name" to be
blotted out; cf. 1 Sam. 24:21; 2 Sam. 14:7; Ps. 37:28; Isa. 14:20-21).

The firstborn (*bĕkōr*) was held in particularly high esteem as the
privileged heir.[44] Firstborn sons were acknowledged as belonging to God

and consecrated to him in a special ceremony. Circumcision was another exceedingly important religious rite, serving as a mark of the covenant. It was carried out on male infants on the eighth day after birth (Genesis 17). Otherwise, there were no uniform ceremonies to mark events in the lives of young people in ancient Israel. The book of Proverbs provides a fascinating glimpse into the training of young men in wisdom and discretion and will be the subject of a separate section below.

The first and foremost responsibility of children and young people was respect for parents. The importance of this obligation was highlighted in numerous ways:[45]

- words denoting respect for parents are elsewhere used with reference to reverence for God himself;[46]
- respect for parents is the constitutive principle of the nation, being the first of the horizontal covenant principles mentioned in the Ten Commandments (Ex. 20:12; Deut. 5:16);
- the command to honor one's parents entails respect for both father and mother;[47]
- the command has no qualification, limitation, or termination;
- respect for parents carries with it the promise of divine blessing and a long life (cf. Eph. 6:1-3);
- in the Levitical Holiness Code, the command to honor one's parents is paramount;
- later legislation labels treatment of one's parents with contempt as an offense punishable by death;
- Ezekiel cites disrespect for one's parents as one of the reasons for the fall of Jerusalem and the destruction of the temple in 586 B.C.

A second area of responsibility for children in ancient Israel was helping in and around the parental home in a variety of ways once they were old enough to do so. Block provides a good sketch of the ways in which these activities typically unfolded:

Five- and six-year-old boys and girls would begin to pick vegetables, gather fuel and clean up after a meal. The household would organize tasks according to gender by the time they reached adolescence, assigning the males labor that required greater strength and danger (hunting, handling domesticated livestock, and butchering cattle and sheep) and training females in the special skills needed to run a house-hold (harvesting vegetables, preparing food, spinning yarn, knitting garments and caring for babies; cf. Prov 31:10-31).[48]

Once the children were older, other responsibilities included guarding the genealogical integrity of a family through "levirate marriage," a marriage between a widow whose husband had died without having left a male offspring and the brother of the deceased (i.e., the brother of a deceased man was expected to marry his widow; Deut. 25:5-10). In addition, children were responsible to provide for their parents in their old age, which is one reason why childlessness caused considerable anxiety. Beyond this, children were to show respect for older people other than their parents or grandparents as well.[49]

THE IMPORTANCE OF TEACHING CHILDREN ABOUT GOD

Passing on the Message (Pentateuch, Historical Books, and Psalms)

Prior to entering the Promised Land, the Israelites were reminded of God's revelation to them after they had left Egypt and had embarked on their exodus. This reminder encompassed the law (Deut. 4:1-14, esp. v. 9), including the Ten Commandments (Deut. 5:6-21); the Shema ("Hear, O Israel: Our God is the LORD, the LORD alone!" Deut. 6:4); and the greatest commandment: "You shall love the LORD your God with all your heart and with all your soul and with all your might" (Deut. 6:5).[50] Then the Israelites were given the following charge:

> And these words that I command you today shall be on your heart. You shall teach them diligently to your children, and shall talk of them when you sit in your house, and when you walk by the way, and when you lie down, and when you rise. You shall bind them as a sign on your hand, and they shall be as frontlets between your eyes. You shall write them on the doorposts of your house and on your gates. (Deut. 6:6-9; cf. 4:9)

Once in the Promised Land, the Israelites were not to forget the Lord who had delivered them from bondage in Egypt. They were not to put God to the test and were to diligently keep his commandments and "do what is right and good in the sight of the LORD, that it may go well with" them (Deut. 6:12, 16-18). Moreover, "When your son asks you in time to come, 'What is the meaning of the testimonies and the statutes and the rules that the LORD our God has commanded you?'" the Israelites were to testify to God's deliverance and revelation (Deut. 6:20-25). This echoes Moses' earlier instruction subsequent to the institution of the Passover during the exodus, where the Israelites are told to impart the message of God's deliverance of the nation to their offspring (Ex. 13:14). After the crossing of the Red Sea, Joshua is similarly concerned that the significance of God's redemptive acts is passed on to succeeding generations: "When your children ask in time to come, 'What do those stones mean to you?' then you shall tell them that the waters of the Jordan were cut off before the ark of the covenant of the LORD. When it passed over the Jordan, the waters of the Jordan were cut off. So these stones shall be to the people of Israel a memorial forever" (Josh. 4:6-7; cf. 4:21-22).

The psalmist, too, underscores the importance of teaching one's children about God. He pledges that he will not hide what God has done in ages past from his children "but tell to the coming generation the glorious deeds of the LORD, and his might, and the wonders that he has done" (Ps. 78:4). He will speak to them about the law, which God "commanded our fathers to teach to their children, that the next generation might know them, the children yet unborn, and arise and tell them to their children, so that they should set their hope in God and not forget the works of God, but keep his commandments; and that they should not be like their fathers, a stubborn and rebellious generation . . ." (Ps. 78:5-8). Thus, from generation to generation, God's ways and will are to be passed on for children to learn from the sins of their fathers and for God to be known as mighty and glorious.

The Pentateuch, the Old Testament historical books, and the book of Psalms are pervaded by the consciousness that parents (and especially fathers) must pass on their religious heritage to their children. God's express will for his people Israel is still his will for God's people in the church today. Christian parents have the mandate and serious obligation to instill their religious heritage in their children.[51] This heritage centers on the personal experience of God's deliverance from sin and his revelation in the Lord Jesus Christ and his death for us on the cross. Christian parents ought to take every opportunity to speak about these all-important matters with their children and to express and impart to their children personal gratitude for what God has done. While there may be Christian Sunday school teachers and other significant teachers in a child's life, parents must never go back on their God-given responsibility to be the primary source of religious instruction for their children.[52]

Train Up a Child (the Book of Proverbs)

The teaching of the book of Proverbs on childrearing is perhaps best encapsulated by the familiar verse, "Train up a child in the way he should go; even when he is old he will not depart from it" (Prov. 22:6). While this should not be considered a divine promise, it is the product of keen and solid observation of what usually occurs in life, and this should be taken seriously.[53] In the end, however, children do make their own decision as to which way they want to go. Most likely, once grown, children will tend to follow in the path they were shown when still a child. This is why parental discipline and instruction are so important, and why obedience and respect for authority must be infused in a child during his or her formative years.[54]

According to the book of Proverbs, the *purpose* of biblical parental instruction is to *inculcate wisdom and the fear of the LORD* (which is the beginning of wisdom, Prov. 1:7) into sons and daughters.[55] Wise children bring great gladness and joy to parents (Prov. 23:24-25; 29:3, 17), while foolish ones bring grief (10:1), shame (28:7), and, in some cases, ruin to parents (19:13). Essentially, young people must choose between two ways: the way of wisdom or the way of folly. By their very nature, children are *simple* and in need of instruction (1:22). They lack sense and are naïve and gullible (14:15), which makes them vulnerable to the wrong influences if not trained in character (9:16). Unless corrected, what starts out as naïve simplicity leads to full-grown folly (14:18), which can be avoided through proper instruction in biblical wisdom.

The *value of wisdom* is manifold, and to instruct children in this wisdom is life-giving. Wisdom rescues young men from the wiles of the adulteress (Prov. 2:16-19; 5; 6:20-35; 7; 22:14; 23:26-28; 31:3). Wisdom also leads young people to submit to parental discipline and correction (3:11-12, quoted in Heb. 12:5-6; Prov. 15:32; 23:13-14). In fact, wisdom, which is part of the very fabric of creation (Prov. 8:22-31), is their very life (4:13); that is, wisdom is not merely a state of mind but provides real protection from danger or even death. Essentially, what young people must be taught by their parents, therefore, is to trust the Lord with all their heart and to acknowledge him in all their ways, rather than being self-reliant or following the wrong kinds of role models or influences (3:5-6).

By example and explicit instruction, parents are to teach their children and youth a wide array of positive attributes:[56]

- diligence and industriousness (Prov. 6:6-11; 11:27; 12:24; 13:4; 15:19; 18:9; 19:24; 20:4, 13; 21:5; 22:13; 26:13-16);
- justice (11:1; 16:11; 17:23; 20:10, 23; 31:8-9);
- kindness (11:17);
- generosity (11:24; 19:6);
- self-control, particularly of speech (12:18; 13:3; 21:23) and temper (14:17, 29; 15:18; 16:32; 19:11; see also 25:28);
- righteousness (12:21, 28; 14:34);
- truthfulness and honesty (12:22; 16:13; 24:26);
- discretion in choosing friends (13:20; 18:24), particularly a spouse (18:22; 31:10-31);
- caution and prudence (14:16; 27:12);
- gentleness (15:1, 4);
- contentment (15:16-17; 16:8; 17:1);
- integrity of character (15:27; 28:18);
- humility (16:19; 18:12; 22:4);
- graciousness (16:24);
- forthrightness (rather than duplicity; 16:30; 17:20);
- restraint (17:14, 27-28; 18:6-7; 29:20);
- faithfulness in friendship (17:17) and otherwise (28:20);
- purity (20:9; 22:11);
- vigorous pursuit of what is good and right (20:29);
- skillfulness in work (22:29);
- patience (25:15).

Negatively, parents are to teach their children to refrain from a pleasure-seeking lifestyle (Prov. 21:17), particularly from engaging in partying, and gluttonous eating and drinking (23:20-21; 28:7). Children and youth should be taught not to be arrogant or vain (21:24). To this end, parents are to administer proper *discipline,* to which children ought to submit: "My son, do not despise the LORD's discipline or be weary of his reproof, for the LORD reproves him whom he loves, as a father the son in whom he delights" (3:11-12; cf. 13:1). This includes physical discipline: "Whoever spares the rod hates his son, but he who loves him is diligent to discipline him" (13:24; cf. 22:15; 23:13-14). If a child is left to his or her own devices, the only predictable result is shame (29:15). Some today find physical discipline "deeply troubling" (if not "poisonous pedagogy").[57] Yet the inspired biblical book of Proverbs presents discipline (including physical discipline) as part of wisdom, and thus the appropriate use of it should not be ruled out for Christian parents today.[58]

INSIGHTS FROM OLD TESTAMENT FAMILY RELATIONSHIPS

As mentioned, Scripture is replete with examples of good as well as bad parenting. These things, too, "took place as examples for us" to learn from them (cf. 1 Cor. 10:6). One thinks of Rebekah, Isaac's wife, who favored her second-born, Jacob, over her firstborn, Esau, and ensured that the former, rather than the latter, received the patriarchal blessing (Genesis 27). One thinks of Hannah, mother of Samuel the prophet, who asked God for a son, and, once her prayer was answered, consecrated him to the Lord (1 Samuel 1). Hannah's prayer of exultation (1 Sam. 2:1-10) serves as the salvation-historical antecedent of Mary's *Magnificat,* uttered prior to the births of John the Baptist and Jesus (Luke 1:46-56).

In the immediately following context, Hannah's godliness and Samuel's service to the Lord with Eli the priest are contrasted with Eli's wicked sons who "treated the offering of the LORD with contempt" (1 Sam. 2:17), leading to God's rejection of Eli's household. Eli's attempt at confronting his sons is pathetically tepid: "And he said to them, 'Why do you do such things? For I hear of your evil dealings from all the people. No, my sons; it is no good report that I hear the people of the LORD spreading abroad. . . .'" (2:23-24). As the inspired text continues, "But they would not listen to the voice of their father, for it was the will of the LORD to put them to death" (2:25b). Samuel, on the other hand, in another typological anticipation of Jesus, "grew in the presence of the LORD" 2:21; cf. Luke 2:52: Jesus "increased . . . in favor with God and man").

The opposing truth that bad parents can sometimes have great children is borne out by Saul's son Jonathan, who loved David as his own brother, even though his father, Saul, repeatedly attempted to kill David out of jealousy (1 Samuel 20).

David, for his part, had plenty of grief with his sons. Amnon raped his half-sister Tamar (2 Sam. 13:1-22). Absalom, another of David's sons, murdered his half-brother Amnon (13:23-33) and led a conspiracy against his father, so that David had to flee Jerusalem (2 Samuel 15). In due course, Absalom was killed, and despite the grief Absalom caused him, David was disconsolate upon hearing of his son's death: "O my son Absalom, my son, my son Absalom! Would I had died instead of you, O Absalom, my son, my son!" (2 Sam. 18:33).

Later, another of David's sons, Adonijah, attempts to usurp the throne, and the sacred writer adds the following devastating verdict: "His father [David] had never interfered with him by asking, 'Why do you behave as you do?'" (1 Kings 1:6a, NIV). David, busy with his regal affairs and doing "God's work," had failed to keep his sons accountable and to discipline them properly. No wonder they did not know their limits when they got older and rebelled against authority! If children are simply left to do as they please, this will come back to haunt their neglectful parents. It may take some time for parenting failures to become apparent, but here, too, the principle is valid that people reap what they sow (Gal. 6:7). The pattern continued in Solomon's son Rehoboam, who foolishly listened to the advice of his peers rather than the elders and gave a harsh response to the people of Israel, which promptly issued in his loss of rule over ten of the tribes (1 Kings 12:1-24).

CONCLUSION

In the present chapter we have taken a closer look at children and parenthood in the Old Testament. First, we learned about the ancient Israelite conception of family and about the roles and responsibilities of fathers, mothers, and children. After this, our attention focused on Old

Testament passages such as Deuteronomy 6:4-9 that underscore the importance of teaching children about God. The book of Proverbs was found to be an indispensable resource for training children in the ways of God, which includes administering discipline. Our final survey of Old Testament family relationships yielded several important insights, including those from the lives of Hannah, David, and Solomon.

6

THE CHRISTIAN FAMILY:
FAMILY IN THE
NEW TESTAMENT

AS WE HAVE SEEN in the previous chapter, the ancient Israelite conception of family placed an exceedingly great value on one's kinship ties. We learned about the Old Testament teaching on the roles and responsibilities of fathers, mothers, and children, and on the importance of teaching children about God. We also discussed examples of good and bad parents in the Old Testament. In the present chapter, we will endeavor to build on these foundations and learn about the New Testament teaching on children, parenting, and the home. As will be seen, both Jesus and Paul provide a significant amount of instruction on this vital topic. The chapter concludes with insights from New Testament family relationships.

THE EXAMPLE AND TEACHING OF JESUS

First-century Palestine and Jesus' Example

In Jesus' day, the extended family lived together (e.g., Mark 1:30), typically sharing a three or four-room home. Like their mother, daughters were to take a domestic role (Matt. 10:35; Luke 12:53),[1] and boys were to emulate their father's example according to the ancient Israelite maxim "like father, like son."[2] Jesus himself learned his father's trade as a craftsman (Matt. 13:55; Mark 6:3).[3] The variety of terms used in the New Testament for "child" by Jesus and others—such as *brephos* (baby, infant, fetus), *nēpios* (small child, 3 or 4 years of age), *teknon* and *teknion* (child, offspring in general), *paidion* and *paidarion* (small child, normally below age of puberty), *pais* (young person, normally below age of puberty)—indicate an awareness of the child in its social setting and stages of development.[4] Jesus himself modeled obedience in relation to his earthly parents (Luke 2:51: "And he went down with them and came to Nazareth and was submissive to them") and supremely toward his heavenly Father (e.g., Mark 14:36; cf. Heb. 5:8).

Jesus' Teaching on the Family and Discipleship

While Jesus affirmed marriage and blessed children, he conceived of the community of believers in familial terms transcending those of people's natural relations.[5] This, as has been mentioned several times before, is one of the most striking, distinctive, and central aspects of Jesus' call to discipleship.[6] In Jesus' own words, "If anyone comes to me and does not hate his own father and mother and wife and children and brothers and sisters, yes, and even his own life, he cannot be my disciple."[7] In keeping with Old Testament prediction, Jesus came, not to bring peace, but a sword, "to set a man against his father, and a daughter against her mother, and a daughter-in-law against her mother-in-law. And a person's enemies will be those of his own household" (Matt. 10:34-36).

In his own personal experience, Jesus knew spiritual rejection even within his natural family (Mark 3:21; 6:1-6a; John 7:1-9) and asserted that his primary loyalty and that of his followers must be to God the Father (Luke 2:49; Mark 3:31-35). Leaving one's natural family behind, even literally, was regularly expected of Jesus' first followers, at least for the duration of Jesus' three-year earthly ministry (though it appears that subsequently the disciples resumed normal family relations, 1 Cor. 9:5). This is made clear by what is perhaps the earliest account of Jesus' calling of his disciples in Mark's Gospel, where Jesus calls Simon, his brother Andrew, and the sons of Zebedee, and these fishermen leave their natural vocation and family contexts in order to follow Jesus (Mark 1:16-20 = Matt. 4:18-22; cf. Luke 5:2-11).

Those who resist Jesus' call to discipleship frequently are unwilling to forsake their natural ties in favor of total allegiance to Jesus.[7] Luke records a series of three such memorable instances, where would-be disciples of Jesus are unwilling to follow him unconditionally and are turned back, being told, respectively, that "Foxes have holes and birds of the air have nests, but the Son of Man has no place to lay his head"; "Let the dead bury their own dead, but you go and proclaim the kingdom of God"; and "No one who puts his hand to the plow and looks back is fit for service in the kingdom of God" (Luke 9:58, 60, 62 NIV; cf. Matt. 8:19-22).

All three of the Synoptic Gospels also record a rich young man's unwillingness to part with his wealth in order to follow Jesus, setting his refusal in contrast to the disciples' unconditional commitment to their Master (Mark 10:17-31 = Matt. 19:16-30 = Luke 18:18-30). Upon Peter's remark that he and his fellow disciples have left everything to follow him, Jesus responds with the promise that there is "no one who has left house or brothers or sisters or mother or father or children or lands, for my sake and for the gospel, who will not receive a hundredfold now in this time, houses and brothers and sisters and mothers and children and lands, with persecutions, and in the age to come eternal life" (Mark 10:29-31 and parallels).

Jesus himself set the example by repeatedly renouncing his own natural family ties where they potentially stood in conflict with higher spiritual loyalties.[8] Thus, the twelve-year-old Jesus responded to his parents' anguished concern, "Why were you looking for me? Did you not know that I must be in my Father's house?" (Luke 2:49). Later, Jesus rebukes, first his mother, and then his brothers for failing to understand the divine timing underlying his ministry (John 2:4; 7:6-8).

Again, he refused to be drawn back into the confines of his natural relations when his concerned family went to take charge of him, fearing that the strains of his busy ministry had caused him to lose his mind. When told that his family was waiting for him outside, he queried in a dramatic gesture, "Who are my mother and my brothers?" Answering his own question, he looked at those seated in a circle around him and issued the weighty pronouncement, "Here are my mother and my brothers! Whoever does the will of God, he is my brother and sister and mother" (Mark 3:31-35 and parallels; see also 3:20-21). In due course, it appears that Jesus' mother and (at least some of) his brothers indeed acknowledged that they, too, must subordinate their familial claims to allegiance to Jesus as their Savior and Lord (e.g., Acts 1:14; but see already Luke 1:46-47).[9]

Examples could be multiplied (cf. Luke 11:27-28; John 19:26-27), but the implications of Jesus' teaching on discipleship are clear. Rather than preaching a gospel urging believers to make marriage and family[10] their ultimate priority—though obviously these have a vital place in God's purposes for humanity—Jesus placed natural kinship ties in the larger context of the kingdom of God.[11] Thus, while Jesus affirmed natural relations, such as the divine institution of marriage and the need to honor one's parents (Mark 10:8-9, 19 par.), he acknowledged the higher calling of discipleship. One's commitment to truth may lead to division, not peace, in one's natural family (Matt. 10:34), and in this case following Jesus must take precedence (Luke 9:57-62).[12]

While Jesus placed people's obligations within the larger framework of God's kingdom,[13] however, this should not be taken to imply that Christians are to neglect their family responsibilities. As Paul would later write, "But if anyone does not provide for his relatives, and especially for members of his household, he has denied the faith and is worse than an unbeliever" (1 Tim. 5:8). Clearly, Jesus' physical presence on this earth and his three-year public ministry necessitated unconditional physical following of the Master in a unique way. At the same time, the spiritual principle that following Jesus ought to be every Christian's first priority continues to apply, and where this brings an individual into conflict with his or her natural family obligations, he or she must first seek God's kingdom and his righteousness (Matt. 6:33).

Children in the Ministry of Jesus

Jesus did not deal with children merely on the level of what they should do or think but on the level of who they were in God's eyes. Studying how Jesus understood children can help us know how we should view and relate to our own and other children. Jesus' earthly ministry intersected with children on a number of occasions.[14] As mentioned, Jesus more than once *restored children to their parents by way of miraculous healing.*[15] In one instance, Jesus put a child in the disciples' midst as an example of the *nature of discipleship,* asserting that, "Whoever receives one such child in my name receives me, and whoever receives me, receives not me but him who sent me" (Mark 9:36-37 and parallels). This must have been startling for Jesus' audience, since in his day it would have been uncommon for adults to think they could learn anything from a child. At another juncture, children were brought to Jesus to receive a blessing from him (Mark 10:13-16 and parallels).[16]

The climactic pronouncement, "I tell you the truth, anyone who will not receive the kingdom of God like a little child will never enter it" (Mark 10:15, NIV), ties together the earlier-recorded instances of Jesus' receptivity toward children with an important characteristic of the kingdom, a humble lack of regard for one's own supposed status (cf. Luke 22:26, NIV: "Instead, the greatest among you should be like the youngest"). For Jesus, there is no better way to illustrate God's free, unmerited grace than pointing to a child.[17] For unlike many adults, children are generally entirely unpretentious about receiving a gift. Moreover, "little ones," that is, the least, regardless of age, are a repeated focus in Jesus' teaching on discipleship (Matt. 18:5; Luke 9:48).[18] Indeed, God's kingdom must be entered in a childlike spirit, a lesson that was yet to be learned by Jesus' followers.

In sayings preserved by Matthew, Jesus focuses even more specifically on the sense of dependency and trust that are characteristic of children and that are traits essential for those who would enter his kingdom. In Matthew 11:25-26, Jesus praises the Father for concealing his truth from the self-proclaimed wise and understanding and revealing it to little children. This statement turns out to be prophetic when in Matthew 21:15 the children are shouting in the temple, "Hosanna to the Son of David!" while the chief priests and the teachers of the law are indignant at the sight of the children's praise of Jesus and of "the wonderful things he did."

According to Jesus, the quality in children that is most emblematic of kingdom virtues is their *low status*. Unless an individual therefore turns and becomes like a child, he will never enter the kingdom of heaven (Matt. 18:3). While children may not necessarily be humble in a spiritual sense—much less "innocent"—their lack of status, their unpretentiousness, and their dependence on others make them suitable illustrations of the need for would-be candidates for Jesus' kingdom to "become nothing" and be stripped of their earthly status (cf. Phil. 2:6-

7). Hence they embody Jesus' radical call for discipleship and his requirement for his followers to "take up their cross" in total self-abandonment (e.g., Mark 8:34-38 and parallels).

There are several other ways in which children came to *typify desirable attitudes* in believers in the early church: as an image representing the needy, the "little ones" who are members of the church (Mark 9:42; Matt. 18:6-14; cf. Acts 20:35); as a "metaphor for learning in expressing the relationship of pupil to teacher as child to parent" (Mark 10:24b; 2 Cor. 12:14; 1 Tim. 1:2; 1 John 2:1); and as a symbol of hope and new beginning (Isa. 9:6 cf. Luke 2:12-14) in association with imagery of birthing as a new creation, be it in elaboration of the pupil-teacher relationship (Gal. 4:19) or with reference to the birth pangs of the messianic age (John 16:21; Rom. 8:22; 1 Thess. 5:3; Rev. 12:2; cf. Isa. 26:16-19; 66:7-14).[19]

Overall, then, we learn from Jesus that we should not look down on children because they are not fully grown and hence are of lower social status than adults. Like Jesus, we should treat children with respect and dignity, as unique and precious creatures made by God and valuable in his sight. What is more, contrary to our natural inclination that may tell us that we can learn nothing from children and that the relationship is strictly one-way from parent or adult to child, we should look at children also from the vantage point of desirable kingdom traits they may exemplify in a more pronounced way than we do ourselves. This is one way in which God defies the wisdom of those who are wise in their own eyes, and the pride of those who think they are something in and of themselves (Matt. 11:25-27; cf. 1 Cor. 1:27-29).

Ministry to children, therefore, should be conducted in a humble spirit of service rather than in a patronizing manner, and should be viewed as a privilege rather than as an undesirable chore left to those who are unable to attain to a higher calling. While children have much to learn, they also have much to teach us, if we are humble enough to listen to them and to observe them. Their simple faith that takes God at his word, their believing prayer trusting God to do what they ask, their willingness to explore new things and to follow the lead of another—these are but a few examples of qualities in children that adults will find inspiring and worth emulating. By repeatedly pointing to children as models of kingdom values and attitudes, Jesus elevated those who are lowly in this world and humbled those with status, power, and position.

PAUL'S TEACHING ON THE ROLE OF FATHERS, MOTHERS, AND CHILDREN

The Ancient Household and "Household Codes"

In order to arrive at a deeper understanding of the New Testament teaching on the various roles and responsibilities of the respective members of a family, it will be instructive to look briefly at the ancient household and the genre of the "household code." Unlike the modern household, ancient households included not only a married couple and children but other dependents, such as slaves, as well, with the head of the household in a position of authority to which wife, children, and slaves were to submit. The New Testament features several adaptations of the Greco-Roman "household code" (esp. Eph. 5:21–6:9; Col. 3:18–4:1), a literary device or kind of list that addresses the various members of the household as to their duties, usually progressing from the "lesser" (i.e., the one under authority) to the "greater" (i.e., the one in a position of authority).[20] The underlying assumption of this code is that order in the household will promote order on a larger societal scale as well. Believers' conformance to the ethical standards of such a code would render Christianity respectable in the surrounding culture (1 Tim. 3:7; 6:1; Titus 2:5, 8, 10; 3:8; 1 Pet. 2:12) and aid in the church's evangelistic mission (1 Thess. 4:12).[21] In keeping with the Pauline pattern, we will comment first on the subordinate group, i.e., children, and then proceed to discuss parents, both fathers and mothers.[22]

Children in Paul's Teaching

Before turning our attention to Paul's teaching on children, it will be helpful to set this topic in its larger biblical and cultural context.[23] As mentioned, in the Old Testament, honoring one's parents is mandated, while rebellion against one's parents is tantamount to disrespect toward God himself. Disobedience toward one's parents is put on the same level as treason and idol worship (see, e.g., Ex. 21:15, 17; Lev. 19:3; 20:9; Deut. 21:18-21; 27:16).[24] First-century Jews (as well as the Greco-

Roman world at large), too, prized obedience in children.[25] It was recognized, however, that such obedience could not be assumed to arise
naturally but must be inculcated from childhood. Ultimately, the standing and honor of the entire family was at stake. What is more, the hand
of divine blessing could be withdrawn if God's commandment to honor
one's parents and his injunction for parents to raise their children in the
nurture and admonition of the Lord were disregarded. Hence, the man
of God must see to it "that his children obey him with proper respect"
(1 Tim. 3:4, NIV; cf. Titus 1:6). In the New Testament, disobedience to
parents is viewed as a phenomenon characteristic of the end times (Mark
13:12; 2 Tim. 3:1-2; cf. 1 Tim. 1:9) that would draw divine judgment
(Rom. 1:30, 32).[26]

The apostle Paul considered children's obedience to be vital. The
major Pauline injunction pertaining to children is found as part of the
"household code" in Ephesians 6:1-3: "Children, obey your parents in
the Lord, for this is right[:] 'Honor your father and mother' (this is the
first commandment with a promise), 'that it may go well with you and
that you may live long in the land.'"[27] While the commandment to
honor one's parents is cited five other times in the New Testament (Matt.
15:4; 19:19; Mark 7:10; 10:19; Luke 18:20), the attached promise is
cited only in Ephesians. Paul's words in Colossians 3:20-21 are similar:
"Children, obey your parents in everything, for this pleases the Lord.
Fathers, do not provoke your children, lest they become discouraged"
(NET: "disheartened").

In the more extensive passage in Ephesians, Paul indicates that children's submission to their parents is a result of Spirit-filling (Eph. 6:1;
cf. 5:18: "be filled with the Spirit . . ."), which suggests that only regenerate children can consistently live out this pattern of relationship, in the
power of the Holy Spirit.[28] Why ought children to obey their parents?
By the forward-pointing phrase "this is right" in Ephesians 6:1, Paul
roots children's obligation to obey their parents in the Old Testament
Decalogue (Ex. 20:12, LXX; cf. Deut. 5:16).[29] Interestingly, the command
to honor one's parents follows immediately after the first four commandments (which have to do with God's holiness) as the first commandment that relates to right relationships between human beings on
a horizontal level. In the present passage, Paul treats children as respon-

sible members of the congregation whose obedience to their parents "is all of a piece with their submission to Christ."[30] The phrase "in the Lord" in Ephesians 6:1 is equivalent to "as to the Lord" or "as to Christ" (cf. Eph. 5:22; 6:5) and indicates that children's obedience is part of their Christian discipleship. Obedience means honor, respect, and, properly understood, "fear" of one's parents (Lev. 19:3; cf. Lev. 19:14). In the context of the present passage, children's obedience to their parents epitomizes a submission that arises from a godly fear of Christ himself (Eph. 5:21).

The promise that it would go well with children who honor their parents referred in the original context to long life in the (promised) land of Israel (Ex. 20:12: "that your days may be long *in the land that the LORD your God is giving you*"). Paul universalizes the promise and thus indicates its continued relevance and applicability. No longer is the promise limited geographically; obedient children are promised a long life on earth wherever they may live. Ephesians 6:1-3 appears to be addressed primarily to children "who are in the process of learning and growing up" or at least are old enough that they could be "provoked to anger" (cf. Eph. 6:4).[31] However, while children's responsibilities toward their parents change once they establish their own family, they do not therefore cease. In a later letter, Paul notes that children's responsibility to honor their parents also entails caring for them in their old age (1 Tim. 5:8),[32] which is viewed as proper repayment for having been reared by them (5:4).

By way of implication, it is critical that parents teach children the importance of obedience. Parents who neglect to hold their children accountable for rendering obedience fail them in that they do not help them along the path of Christian discipleship, of which obedience is a central component. Hence the primary importance of obedience is not for parents to receive their children's obedience, but for parents to help children to *learn to exercise obedience* ultimately *in their relationship with God*. The fact that proper obedience is possible, for children as well as for adults, ultimately only as a result of a faith commitment to Jesus Christ and in the power of the Holy Spirit suggests that introducing the child to a personal relationship with God in Christ ought to be a burning fire in the heart of every Christian parent (primarily because of their concern for their child's salvation). Nevertheless, obedience should be demanded, and disobedience punished, even in (as of yet) non-Christian children.

Fathers and the Importance of Fatherhood in Paul's Teaching

In Ephesians 6:4, Paul writes, "Fathers, do not provoke your children to anger, but bring them up in the discipline and instruction of the Lord." The Colossian parallel reads, "Fathers, do not provoke your children, lest they become discouraged" (Col. 3:21).[33] While children ought to obey both parents (Eph. 6:1; Col. 3:20), fathers bear special responsibility for disciplining their children and are specifically singled out by Paul in the present passage.[34] Although mothers may actually spend more time with them, the father is given the primary responsibility for disciplining his children. The apostle's exhortation to fathers not to exasperate (Eph. 6:4, NIV) their children echoes his earlier concern about anger in Ephesians 4:26-27, 31, while the positive injunction to bring up children in the training and admonition of the Lord recalls the earlier emphasis on learning Christian teaching in Ephesians 4:20-21.[35]

It is important that fathers not provoke their children to anger (cf. Eph. 4:26-27, 31). If anger is prolonged, Satan will seek to exploit the familial discord to further his own ends. Fathers are therefore to avoid any attitudes, words, or actions that have the effect of provoking anger in their children, including "excessively severe discipline, unreasonably harsh demands, abuse of authority, arbitrariness, unfairness, constant nagging and condemnation, subjecting a child to humiliation, and all forms of gross insensitivity to a child's needs and sensibilities."[36] Children are persons with dignity in their own right. They are not slaves owned by their parents, but are entrusted to them by God as a sacred stewardship. In the Colossian passage, Paul notes that as a result of improper treatment, children may become discouraged (Col. 3:21). Indeed, few things are more heartbreaking than a child who has "lost heart" because of poor parenting.

Positively, fathers are to bring up their children "in the discipline and instruction of the Lord." The term "bring up" or "nourish," used in Ephesians 5:29 for Christ's nurture of his church, conveys the sense of rearing children to maturity, which includes, but is not limited to, providing for their physical and psychological needs. "Discipline" (*paideia*) and "instruction" (*nouthesia*) are closely related, but probably not synonymous. In its New Testament usage, the term translated "discipline" (*paideia*) or the related verb *paideuō* may refer to education or training in general (Acts 7:22; 22:3; 2 Tim. 3:16; Titus 2:12) or specifically to chastisement for wrongdoing (1 Cor. 11:32; 2 Cor. 6:9; Heb. 12:5, 7, 8, 11). In Ephesians 6:4, the reference is in all likelihood to training in general, while encompassing discipline for wrongdoing as well. The phrase "in the Lord" (Eph. 6:4) implies that fathers themselves must be Christian disciples, so that they can raise their children and administer discipline in a way that is truly and thoroughly Christian.

Moving beyond our discussion of Ephesians 6:4 and looking at other relevant New Testament references, we observe that fathers' primary role is to provide for their children and to ensure proper nurture and discipline. This involves formal as well as informal education and entails the exercise of various forms of discipline, including physical discipline (Prov. 13:24; 22:15; 23:13-14; Heb. 12:6; Rev. 3:19; cf. Sir. 3:23; 30:1-3, 12).[37] As in the Greco-Roman world where the father's authority (*patria potestas*) held unrivaled sway in his household, in both Jewish culture and biblical teaching the father ought to command great respect. As mentioned, however, fathers are not to use their position of authority to exasperate their children, but to treat them with gentleness (1 Cor. 4:15, 21; 1 Thess. 2:11; Col. 3:21; Eph. 6:4).[38] Also, it is interesting to note that the skills required to manage one's private household are the same as those necessary for governing in a public setting (1 Tim. 3:4-5).[39]

By way of implication, fathers (and mothers) must strike a balance between proper discipline and loving nurture and support. Neither the "encouraging parent" who neglects to discipline his child nor the strict disciplinarian fulfills the biblical ideal of parenting. Paul sought to strike just such a balance when he wrote to the Thessalonian believers that he and his associates had sought to be "gentle among you, like a mother caring for her little children" (1 Thess. 2:7, NIV), dealing "with each of you as a father deals with his own children, encouraging, comforting and urging you to live lives worthy of God" (vv. 11-12, NIV). Ultimately, fathers ought to realize that their fatherhood derives from the "one God and Father of all" "from whom every family in heaven and on earth is named" (Eph. 4:6; 3:15) and who cares and provides faithfully for all his children and acts as a perfect Father toward them all (Heb. 12:5-10).[40]

Mothers and the Importance of Motherhood in Paul's Teaching

The apostle Paul taught that one of the primary roles of women is that of "childbearing," that is, not only the act of giving birth but their domestic role related to the upbringing of children and managing of the home (1 Tim. 2:15; cf. 5:14).[41] Thus, motherhood is not disparaged in biblical teaching; contrary to many in modern society, it is held up as the woman's highest calling and privilege. In fact, in his first letter to Timothy, the apostle intimates that, for women, straying from the home is yielding to the devil's temptation in a similar way to Eve overstepping her bounds at the original Fall (1 Tim. 2:14-15).[42] This exposes the unbiblical nature of a feminism that promotes gender equality understood as sameness and encourages women to forsake their calling in the home for the sake of finding self-fulfillment in a career outside the home.[43]

In fact, 1 Timothy 2:15 speaks a powerful message to our culture "where many are seeking to 'liberate' women from all encumbrances of family responsibilities in order to unleash them on a quest for self-fulfillment apart from such functions." To the contrary, "it is precisely by participating in her role pertaining to the family that women fulfill their central calling."[44] This is not a matter of seeking to restrict women to the home, but of determining the essence of women's calling from God and of encouraging them to live it out. This will result not only in greater blessing and fulfillment for women themselves, but also for their husbands and families, and it will bring honor to the God who created us male and female.

The Importance of Older Women Mentoring Younger Women

In his letter to Titus, Paul delineates the duties of both older and younger Christian women.

OLDER WOMEN

Older women must be treated with respect (1 Tim. 5:1-2), and they have the important obligation to mentor younger women with regard to their family responsibilities (Titus 2:3-5). Older women are to exemplify the following four characteristics: (1) to be reverent in the way they live; (2) not to be slanderers;[45] (3) not to be addicted (literally, "bound" or "enslaved") to much wine;[46] and (4) to be "teachers of the good." Older women who avoided slander and wine were sure to stand out in their immoral Cretan surroundings (the destination of Titus). The restricted movement often brought about by advanced age makes older people (then as today) particularly susceptible to fill their days with pastimes such as drinking or gossiping; this calls for godliness and self-control.

Older women are to cultivate virtue, yet not as an end in itself, but for the purpose of training young women.[47] Nevertheless, it is impossible to train others in qualities oneself does not possess. There is a great need in the contemporary church for older women who are godly and who obey the biblical command to train young women in the faith. Many younger women long for more mature women to take them under their wings and to teach them how to live the Christian life, especially since many of them lack such godly models in their own family or live at a great distance from their own family. Notably, such training—usually involving private rather than public instruction—is to focus squarely on the domestic sphere.[48]

YOUNGER WOMEN

Paul groups instructions for younger women in three pairs plus one final general injunction, starting and ending with their relationship to their husbands (Titus 2:4-5). First, they are to be *certain kinds of wives and mothers:* lovers of their husbands and lovers of their children (Titus 2:4). Second, they are to be *cultivating Christian character:* self-controlled and pure (Titus 2:5; cf. 1 Tim. 5:22; 2 Cor. 11:2; Phil. 4:8; 1 Pet. 3:2; 1 John 3:3). Third, they are to be engaged in activities with the *right kind of attitude:* workers at home (Titus 2:5; cf. 1 Tim. 5:14) and kind (literally "good"; cf. 1 Thess. 5:15; Eph. 4:28). Finally, they are to be *subject to their own husbands* (cf. Eph. 5:24; Col. 3:18; 1 Pet. 3:1, 5).

What can we learn from Paul's teaching here as it relates to parenting? Perhaps the following observations will prove helpful.

(1) While marriages should be strong, young women need *other significant relationships*. They need to be mentored by older women endowed with life experience and the skill and wisdom that come from years of practicing Christian virtues.

(2) *Love of husbands* comes before *love of children* (note the sequence "love their husbands and children" in Titus 2:4). Both qualities were admired in wives in both Jewish and Greco-Roman culture. Putting love for husband first is important, since it allows parents to model a healthy and biblical marriage relationship before their children (cf. Prov. 14:26). Also, if a couple's marriage relationship is neglected, their parenting and the entire family will likely suffer as a result as well.

(3) Wives are called both to *love* and to *submit to* their husbands.[49] Their submission is not to be grudging or perfunctory but loving and willing. The Greek word for "submit," *hypotassō*, conveys the notion of "placing oneself under" another person's authority, which implies that this is done voluntarily rather than under compulsion. Ephesians 5:21-33 links wives' submission with *respect* for their husband (5:22, 33). This respect ought to be freely given. Respect does not mean uncritical adoration, just as submission does not mean subservience.

(4) Women need *self-control* in dealing with their husbands and children. As wives, they are to exhibit sexual fidelity. As mothers, they must maintain a loving disposition toward their children rather than grow irritable, resisting the temptation to view them as burdens rather than blessings from God.

(5) Women's hearts are to be *pure* and their attitude toward others in the home to be *kind* rather than antagonistic or hostile.

(6) Women are to be *devoted first and foremost to the home*, "supervis[ing] their households with discretion and industry."[50]

(7) To an age when devotion to married life and childrearing is often disparaged (in contrast to antiquity, when such was a highly lauded virtue), Paul speaks of the *blessing* God has in store for women who defy secular stereotypes and focus on their God-given calling related to family and the home.

(8) The desired *result* of proper wifely submission and diligent

homemaking will be that *no one will revile the word of God* (cf. 1 Pet. 3:16). In other words, wives who live by these principles will make it harder for unbelievers to have bad things to say about Christianity, and perhaps this will open the door to communicating the gospel to them.

The Roles and Responsibilities in a Household According to Scripture

ROLES	RESPONSIBILITIES	TEXTS
Fathers	Provide for family, children	2 Cor. 12:14
	Ensure proper nurture and discipline	Eph. 6:4; Col. 3:21; Heb. 12:6
Mothers	Raising of children, motherhood	1 Tim. 2:15
	Managing the home	1 Tim. 5:14
Children	Obedience to parents	Eph. 6:1-3; Col. 3:20
	Care for parents in old age	1 Tim. 5:8

INSIGHTS FROM NEW TESTAMENT FAMILY RELATIONSHIPS

The New Testament includes a good number of examples of both good and bad parenting. On the positive side, one thinks of Mary, the mother of Jesus, and her godly response to the angel's announcement (Luke 1:38). When Jesus was twelve years old, Mary and Joseph lost track of him for several days (!), and when they found him in the temple, expressed typical parental concern: "Son, why have you treated us so? Behold, your father and I have been searching for you in great distress" (2:48). They did not understand Jesus' response that he must be in his Father's house. Then Jesus returned with them to Nazareth "and was submissive to them. And his mother treasured up all these things in her heart" (2:51). Hence, Jesus models filial obedience, and Mary is exemplary as a godly, caring mother who has a deep concern for the well-being of her child.

While later, during his public ministry, Jesus finds it necessary occasionally to draw a line between his natural relations and the requirements of discipleship (e.g., John 2:4; Matt. 12:46-50 and parallels; Mark 3:20-21, 31-35; Luke 11:27-28), he provides for his mother (John 19:26-27) and doubtless maintains a close filial bond. In keeping with Simeon's prophecy that "a sword will pierce through your own soul also" (Luke 2:35), Mary had to watch helplessly as her son was crucified (John 19:25 and parallels). The last time she is mentioned in the New Testament, Mary "the mother of Jesus" is found in the upper room praying together with Jesus' brothers, the apostles, and other godly women (Acts 1:14).

The New Testament also features many caring and distraught parents who bring their children to Jesus for him to heal them. The widow's son at Nain (Luke 7:11-15) and the daughter of the synagogue ruler Jairus (Mark 5:21-43; Luke 8:40-56) come to mind, both of whom are raised by Jesus from the dead. Others include the Gentile Syrophoenician woman who exercises unusual faith and from whose daughter Jesus exorcises a demon (Matt. 15:21-28; Mark 7:24-30). Another man brings his son who suffers from epilepsy, and the boy is healed instantly (Matt. 17:14-18 and parallels). A Capernaum official travels to Cana to plead with Jesus to heal his son, and Jesus obliges by performing a "long-distance" miraculous healing (John 4:46-54).

Mothers' relationships with their sons were often particularly close, as in the case of Mary and Jesus (Luke 2:48-51; John 2:1-5; 19:25-27) or the widow's son, "the only son of his mother" (Luke 7:12). That sometimes mothers can be a bit overzealous on behalf of their children is illustrated by the request of the mother of the sons of Zebedee, who boldly asks Jesus to grant her sons places of preeminence in his kingdom (Matt. 20:20-21). Jesus' gracious but firm response makes it clear that in this case motherly zeal and ambition on behalf of her sons were misplaced (20:22-28).

IMPLICATIONS

On the basis of our survey of the biblical teaching on the family, including the roles of father, mother, and children, in both Old and New Testaments, we draw the following implications for Christian, biblical parenting.[51]

Fundamentally, children, like all people, ought to be considered spiritual individuals who are uniquely created by God and yet are fallen sinners, so that the task of parenting is not merely that of behavioral conditioning but spiritual nurture and training. The use of one particular methodology in the exercise of external discipline has some value but is limited in its usefulness. An engagement of the root cause of all unrighteous human behavior, sin, should be the goal (Rom. 3:23; 6:23). In reality, only those children and young people who experience personal regeneration through faith in Christ and receive the indwelling Holy Spirit can truly and permanently live a life pleasing to God and benefit as their parents guide them toward greater wisdom. This, however, does not do away with the need for parental discipline and training prior to a child's conversion. It does mean, though, that parental efforts can only go so far unless aided by the internal, supernatural enablement in the response of the child. Thus the child's conversion is truly an important aspect of parental guidance.

For this reason also parents ought not to be surprised or shocked when their children disobey. *Of course* children will disobey—they are sinners! Parents rather should be expecting their children to sin, even after they have come to faith in Christ. Such an expectation is realistic and enables the parent to deal with each infraction calmly and deliberately, administering discipline with fairness, justice, and consistency (cf. Eph. 6:4; Col. 3:21). Whether or not they are believers (yet), children need their parents to set and enforce standards for right or wrong behavior. This is how children learn to assume responsibility for their actions and come to realize that there are consequences for obedience as well as for disobedience. Hence the parents' role is both positive and negative, similar to the effect of Scripture in a person's life—they must teach and train their children in righteousness, but they must also discipline and correct (2 Tim. 3:16-17).

The role of the parent in the life of a child who is converted is not that of a substitute for the Holy Spirit (though prior to a child's conversion, the parent may have a more direct role in convicting the child of sin). Nor can parents make moral choices *for* their children. Parents ought to consider themselves entrusted with the (temporary) responsibility and stewardship of nurturing and cultivating a child's heart and mind in light of the Scriptures and on behalf of God (Ps. 127:3; 128:3-4). This also entails respect for the child's individuality and unique creation in the eyes of God (Ps. 139:13-14; Prov. 22:6). Every child is different and unique, and parental techniques that may work well with one child may not work as well with another.[52]

In all these cases, therefore, there is no substitute for the Holy Spirit's leading in each individual situation. Parents should prayerfully search the Scriptures, team up with other families if living nearby, and with other Christian parents in their church. Talking to each other in order to arrive at a joint parenting philosophy is also essential for a married couple, so that they are unified in their approach and are pulling together rather than moving in different directions. In addition, parents should make the necessary adjustments in their approach to parenting along the way.

To be sure, no human parent is adequate to this task without divine help, nor are children able to pursue these characteristics apart from divine enablement. Parents occasionally may need to ask forgiveness from their children, which may help the children to understand that their parents are sinners, too. Parents should model a prayerful attitude of dependence on God in all things, so that children come to realize that even their parents and other adults have limitations and need God's help. Finally, joint worship, both as part of a local congregation and as a family at home, is a vital part of knitting a family together as brothers and sisters in Christ.[53]

CONCLUSION

Our survey of children and parenting in the New Testament in this chapter took its point of departure from Jesus' own example and from his teaching on and encounters with children during his earthly ministry. From this we turned our attention to ancient "household codes" and Paul's teaching on children and parenthood. On children and fathers, the special focus was Ephesians 6:1-4. With regard to motherhood and older women mentoring younger women, 1 Timothy 2:15 and Titus 2 proved to be particularly relevant.

At the end of our study of the biblical teaching on marriage and the family, we will do well to remember that these institutions are not ends in themselves nor do they exist primarily for our own good, but God has created both institutions for *his* greater glory. As the German theologian Dietrich Bonhoeffer wrote,

> [T]hrough marriage men are brought into being for the glorification and service of Jesus Christ and for the increase of his kingdom. This means that marriage is not only a matter of producing children, but

also of educating them to be obedient to Jesus Christ. . . . [I]n marriage it is for the service of Jesus Christ that new men are created.[54]

This is why a Christian marriage and family must be committed and subjected to Jesus Christ. This is also why marriage and the family must not be viewed in any way as an obstacle to true personal holiness, purity, and sanctification, but as an important key to the development of these and other virtues. In godly homes, husband and wife sharpen one another as "iron sharpens iron" (Prov. 27:17), and their children are drawn into the communal life of the family and into the path of discipleship pursued and modeled by their parents, which fulfills the Lord's desire for godly offspring (Mal. 2:15).

This, too, is part of obeying the risen Christ's commission for his followers to "go . . . and make disciples" (Matt. 28:18-20). What is more, in the case of one's own children, too, discipleship entails baptism in the name of the Father, Son, and Holy Spirit, and being taught to obey everything Jesus commanded his followers (cf. v. 19). Baptism and committed instruction, formal (such as by way of catechism, Sunday school, or programs like Awana in a church context or as part of a deliberate, intentional plan of instruction in the home) as well as informal (as opportunities arise), are not optional, but form an essential part of life in God's integrated design of marriage and the family.

Not only are children to be taught the Christian faith and helped to pursue the path of discipleship, they are to be included in ministry performed in the context of the family and the church. What God desires is happy, secure, and fulfilled families where the needs of individual family members are met but where this fulfillment is not an end in itself but becomes a vehicle for ministry to others. In this way God uses families to bring glory to himself and to further his kingdom, showing the world what he is like—by the love and unity expressed in a family, by the husband's respect for his wife, the wife's submission to her husband, and the children's obedience (even if imperfect). What is more, the husband-wife relationship also expresses how God through Christ relates to his people the church. Thus it can be truly said that families have a vital part to play in God's plan to "bring all things in heaven and on earth together under one head, even Christ," "for the praise of his glory" (Eph. 1:10, 12, NIV).

To Have or Not to Have Children: Special Issues Related to the Family (Part 1)

EXCEPT FOR THOSE WHO are called by God to a life of singleness, God's ideal is that of a monogamous, lifelong marriage crowned with the gift of children. In part because of the presence of sin in this fallen world, however, many complicating factors and issues have arisen that we shall deal with in the present chapter.[1] In the present and the following chapter, we will look at childlessness and modern medical ethics, abortion, contraception, artificial reproductive technologies, adoption, and some contemporary issues in Christian parenting, such as single parenting, physical punishment, fostering masculinity and femininity, and principles of parental discipline. In contrast to the other chapters in this book, these two chapters take their starting point from relevant contemporary issues related to marriage and the family rather than from the biblical material directly. Nevertheless, we will adduce scriptural teaching and/or principles on the subject under consideration wherever possible.

CHILDLESSNESS AND RELATED MEDICAL ISSUES

There is perhaps no one who can better appreciate the value of children today than a woman who is unable to conceive and who desperately wants to have children of her own. Not that childless couples or single persons are not in the will of God or cannot make significant contributions to the kingdom; physical fruitfulness is but a part of God's overall desire for humans to be fruitful, which includes spiritual fruitfulness as well. As Jesus told his followers, "This is to my Father's glory, that you bear much fruit, showing yourselves to be my disciples. . . . I chose you and appointed you to go and bear fruit—fruit that will last" (John 15:8, 16, NIV). This applies to single persons and childless couples as well as to married people.

Nevertheless, the bearing and raising of children remains a vital part of the divine design for men and women today. God's overarching plan for humanity to "be fruitful and multiply" has numerous contemporary implications covering a wide range of issues, such as abortion, contraception, infertility, and adoption. With the advances of modern medicine, childless couples have a much wider array of options than used to be the case. This, in turn, raises for believers questions regarding the appropriateness of procedures such as in vitro fertilization, surrogate parenting, and artificial insemination.[2] In the following pages we will treat each of these topics in turn.

ABORTION

Abortion is not a practice condoned by Scripture, both on account of its general teaching regarding the value of human life and on the basis of specific passages.[3] Both Testaments teach that children are a blessing from God (Ps. 127:3-5; Mark 10:13-16 pars.) and regard the killing of children with particular horror (e.g., Ex. 1:16-17, 22; Lev. 18:21; Jer. 7:31-32; Ezek. 16:20-21; Mic. 6:7; Matt. 2:16-18; Acts 7:19). God is shown to be active in the creation of human beings from the time of conception (Old Testament examples include births to Sarah [Gen. 17:15-22; 21:1-7], Leah, Rachel [Gen. 30:1-24], Ruth [Ruth 4:13-17], and Hannah [1 Sam. 1:19-20]; in the New Testament, see especially Elizabeth in Luke 1:24-25, 39-44), so that human procreation in fact represents "a co-creative process involving man, woman and God."[4] The psalmist provides a particularly moving tribute to God's involvement in creating a human being even in the mother's womb:

> For you formed my inward parts;
>   you knitted me together in my mother's womb.

I praise you, for I am fearfully and wonderfully made.
Wonderful are your works;
    my soul knows it very well.
My frame was not hidden from you,
when I was being made in secret,
    intricately woven in the depths of the earth.
Your eyes saw my unformed substance;
in your book were written, every one of them,
    the days that were formed for me,
      when as yet there were none of them (Ps. 139:13-16).

Another biblical passage makes clear that God forms the fetus in the womb and that in fact he has personal knowledge of the unborn child: "Before I *formed you* in the womb I *knew you,* and before you were born I *consecrated you*; I *appointed you a prophet* to the nations" (Jer. 1:5, emphasis added; see also Job 10:9-12; 31:15; Ps. 119:73; Eccles. 11:5). While the Old Testament does not provide any theoretical discussion as to whether or not a fetus is a "person," it does "depict the fetus as the work of God and the object of his knowledge, love, and care, and hence its destruction must be considered contrary to the will of God."[5]

The Old Testament's "profound respect for life in the prenatal stage"[6] is also revealed by the Mosaic stipulation that the one who harms an unborn child in his or her mother's womb must be punished "life for life, eye for eye, tooth for tooth, hand for hand, foot for foot, burn for burn, wound for wound, stripe for stripe" (Ex. 21:22-25).[7] All of these passages clearly imply that Scripture views human life as beginning at conception and that there is no such thing as a "human right" to take the life of an unborn child. This is in keeping with the biblical affirmation that God is a God of life and that everything he created (especially human beings) is precious and worth preserving (e.g., Psalm 8). In this regard, Scripture differs markedly from ancient pagan cultures.

While abortion was often attempted in the ancient world, more common was the exposure of a newborn child after birth.[8] One of the main reasons why abortion was not as common is that mothers would likely have died as a result. Also, boys were valued more highly than girls, so that people waited until after the birth to see whether the child was a boy or a girl. If it was the latter, the choice was often to expose the poor infant, as is illustrated by a pre-Christian non-literary papyrus from Egypt written by a man named Hilarion from Alexandria to his wife Alis at home in the interior: "I beg and entreat you, take care of the little one, and as soon as we receive our pay I will send it up to you. If by chance you bear a child, if it is a boy, let it be, if it is a girl, expose it" (*P. Oxyrhynchus* 744).[9] Such an exposed child was left to die on a trash heap or in some isolated location. Sadly, at times slave traders would take a child to have it reared in slavery or, if a girl, for a life of prostitution (Justin, *Apology* 1.27). In the Greco-Roman world, exposure was not considered infanticide, but refusal to admit to society, which did not carry negative moral implications.

This stood in marked contrast to Jewish law which, on the basis of Exodus 21:22-25, prohibited abortion (Josephus, *Against Apion* 2.25 §202; *Pseudo-Phocylides* 184-185; b. Sanhedrin 57b) and exposure (Philo, *Special Laws* 3.110-119; *Virtues* 131–133; *Sibylline Oracles* 3:765-766; Tacitus, *Histories* 5.5). The above-cited passage in Exodus stipulates that anyone who hits a pregnant woman and causes harm should be punished "life for life, eye for eye, tooth for tooth, hand for hand, foot for foot," etc. (the *lex talionis*), which was taken by Jewish law to imply the recognition that preborn life is of equal value to life after birth. The first-century Jewish writer Philo, in the just-cited portion in *Special Laws,* distinguished between early- and late-term abortions and spoke out against the latter (*Special Laws* 3.110-119).[10]

The early Christians, following the lead of the Jews, likewise condemned abortion and exposure. In the *Didache,* an ancient manual of church instruction, we read: "'You shall not commit murder . . .': you shall not procure abortion, nor commit infanticide" (*Did.* 2:2). The *Epistle of Barnabas* states similarly, "Thou shalt not procure abortion, thou shalt not commit infanticide" (*Ep. Barn.* 19:5). Justin writes in his *First Apology* that, "But as for us, we have been taught that to expose newly-born children is the part of wicked men . . . , first, because we see that almost all so exposed . . . are brought up to prostitution . . ." (*Apol.* 1.27). The *Epistle to Diognetus* describes Christians as follows: "They marry as all men, they bear children, but they do not expose their offspring" (*Ep. Diogn.* 5:6; see also Athenagoras, *Plea* 35; Minucius Felix, *Octavius* 30–31).[11]

It is not our purpose here to address the contemporary debate regarding abortion directly.[12] As the above-cited biblical and extrabiblical passages make clear, however, the ancient world witnessed a marked difference between the pagan world and Judeo-Christian teaching on the subject. While certain aspects of complexity have been introduced into the modern discussion, many of the pertinent issues were already addressed in the first centuries of the Christian era (and even prior to this period). As the preceding survey has shown, the view that life begins at conception has been the traditional Judeo-Christian view, and this view alone seems to do justice to the teaching of Scripture and the life and practice of the early church. For this reason abortion must be considered the unauthorized taking of a preborn human life, which is contrary to God's will.[13]

CONTRACEPTION (BY MARK LIEDERBACH)

Scripture does not speak directly to the question of whether or not it is biblically appropriate to use contraceptive measures. There is no explicit biblical passage that mentions the term "contraception," nor are there any plain texts that specifically address the issue of whether or not it might be appropriate to use contraceptive measures. This said, however, one should not assume that Scripture is completely silent on the matter.

The Question of the Legitimacy of Contraception in General

As noted above, Genesis 1:28 identifies procreation as a primary end of the marital union, while Psalm 127 describes children as a blessing from God. Thus, when considering the question of whether or not to use contraception, one must start from the perspective that having children is the expected norm for marriages and should be understood as a good gift from a loving heavenly Father. In the words of Albert Mohler, "We must start with a rejection of the contraceptive mentality that sees pregnancy and children as impositions to be avoided rather than as gifts to be received, loved, and nurtured. This contraceptive mentality is an insidious attack upon God's glory in creation, and the Creator's gift of procreation to the married couple."[14]

Having recognized the important connection between sexual expression and childbearing, however, does it follow that every act of sexual intercourse must "be open" to conception? Those who answer this question in the affirmative will often cite the Genesis 38:6-10 account of Onan and Tamar in support of their position. In this passage, God takes the life of Er, the oldest son of Judah, because he was "evil in the sight of the LORD" (NASB) leaving his wife Tamar a widow. The Hebrew custom known as levirate marriage (Deut. 25:5-10) stipulated that when a married man died without leaving offspring, his widow should marry the dead man's next closest male relative. The first child from that subsequent marriage would then take on the name of the older brother and become his heir so that the name of the first husband "will not be blotted out from Israel" (Deut. 25:6, NIV).

In the present instance, Onan, as Er's next oldest brother, therefore was to take on the responsibility of providing Tamar with a child. According to Genesis 38:9, however, while Onan did indeed have sexual intercourse with Tamar, he prevented her from conceiving a child by withdrawing from her prior to ejaculation. Instead of providing her with an heir for her first husband, Scripture indicates that he "wasted his seed on the ground" (NASB). As a result, his action was "displeasing in the sight of the LORD," and God took his life as well (v. 10, NASB).

Roman Catholics typically cite this passage to suggest that what particularly displeased the Lord was the interruption of the sexual process for the purpose of preventing procreation. Every act of sexual intercourse, it is argued, ought to be open to procreation. Thus, the interruption by Onan, as well as any form of interruption or use of artificial means to prevent conception during sexual intercourse, is morally reprehensible. In their view, all means of contraception that interrupt the natural process of procreation are contrary to God's will.[15]

Upon closer scrutiny, however, it appears that the Lord's displeasure in Genesis 38:10 ought not to be equated with the prevention of pregnancy per se but with the particularly exploitive, abusive, and wasteful way in which Onan carried out his sexual relations with Tamar.[16] Deuteronomy 25:5-10 indicates that if the brother refuses to complete his "duty" to provide an offspring, the penalty is not death but shaming (vv. 9-10). It would appear, then, that the severity of the punishment indicates that reasons beside the refusal to provide an offspring for his deceased brother prompted God to take Onan's life.

How, then, ought one reason biblically with regard to contraception? Scripture indicates that, in addition to procreation, God created marriage to meet other ends as well. Companionship through the development of a sacred marital bond (Gen. 2:18, 24), sexual pleasure (Prov. 5:15-23, Song of Songs), and fidelity (1 Cor. 7:1-9), to name but a few, are all biblically appropriate purposes for which God created the marital sexual union. Therefore, while it seems clear that over the course of their marriage a couple ought to seek to have children (perhaps even many, see Ps. 127:5), it does not follow that *in every particular sexual encounter* the couple need to refrain from the use of contraception. The sexual encounter in marriage retains a high value for the purposes of union, pleasure, fidelity, and so on, even in the event that a couple uses contraception as a part of their family planning. Indeed, "[t]he focus on 'each and every act' of sexual intercourse within a faithful marriage that is open to the gift of children goes beyond the biblical demand."[17]

Morally Permissible and Impermissible Forms of Contraception

Concluding that the use of contraception is morally permissible *in general*, however, does not mean that *any and every* particular form of birth control is morally acceptable. Indeed, because passages like Exodus 20:13 specifically prohibit the taking of innocent life, the "profound respect for life in the prenatal stage" found in the Judeo-Christian ethic must also influence one's perspective on which forms of birth control are biblically permissible.[18]

ACCEPTABLE FORMS OF BIRTH CONTROL

Which forms of birth control are morally acceptable? In short, the answer is that it is *only those that are contraceptive in nature, that is, those that exclusively prohibit conception*. Resting on this foundational principle, one can then fairly easily evaluate which forms of family planning are appropriate and which are not.

Acceptable forms include natural methods such as *abstinence* (the only biblically legitimate option for those who are not married) and the *rhythm* or *calendar method* (in its various forms such as relying on body temperature cycles or timing of ovulation and fertility periods).[19]

In addition, artificial methods that exclusively seek to prevent conception are also morally acceptable. These include *"barrier methods"* such as a diaphragm, a cervical cap, and condoms and spermicides such as foams, creams, sponges, or vaginal suppositories.

UNACCEPTABLE FORMS OF BIRTH CONTROL

Unacceptable forms of family planning include all forms of induced *abortion*. Thus, the *intrauterine device or "IUD"* is an unacceptable method, because its primary function is to create an unstable environment for the fertilized egg to implant in the uterine wall by depleting the endometrial lining, making it incapable of supporting the life of the child.

RU-486 or the so-called *"abortion"* or *"morning after"* pill is likewise morally unacceptable since its primary function is to prevent the implantation of a new fetus in the uterine wall. The drug works to directly prohibit the establishment and continuation of the pregnancy by blocking the body's natural secretion of progesterone, the vital hormone that prepares the uterus to receive a fertilized egg and to help maintain the pregnancy once it occurs.

METHODS REQUIRING SPECIAL MENTION AND EXTRA CARE

Special mention needs to be made at this point about two forms of birth control widely practiced by Christians and non-Christians alike: sterilization and the use of "the pill."

Sterilization as a means of contraception involves a surgical procedure designed to permanently terminate a person's fertility. For the male, a vasectomy blocks the *vas deferens* (ejaculatory duct) and thus prevents the sperm from leaving the body during ejaculation. For the female, "tubal occlusion" is the procedure that effectively blocks a woman's fallopian tubes in order to prevent sperm from coming into contact with the woman's eggs, thereby preventing fertilization.

There are several important considerations with sterilization that may caution us against its use. For instance, it is an elective procedure that involves the intentional and permanent setting aside or inactivation of a bodily function. The permanence of the procedure makes it a different case from the use of a condom or other temporary measures. In addition, we might ask whether it is ever right to remove a part of one's body (cf. Lev. 21:20; Deut. 23:1; 1 Cor. 6:19) simply for convenience's sake,[20] and whether this is the proper way to treat the body as the "temple of the Holy Spirit" (1 Cor. 6:19).

In both Old and New Testaments, Scripture indicates that while care for the physical body is not to be of primary concern, it should be treated with honor and respect (cf., e.g., Gen. 2:7; Ex. 21:22-25; 1 Cor. 6:12-20). As ethicist John Jefferson Davis contends,

> The apostle's point is that the believer does not have the right to exercise unlimited dominion over his or her body but should view the body as a trust from the Lord, to be cared for in ways that are glorifying to God. And surgical operation—such as sterilization—is not merely a personal "choice," but a decision that needs to be seen within the biblical framework of stewardship of the human body. Given the fact that our human bodies are a trust from God, and in light of the positive valuation placed on human procreative powers and large families in the Old Testament, these powers should not be rejected or surgically destroyed without compelling justification.[21]

While the subject has yet to receive adequate attention among evangelicals,[22] some might respond that the same reasoning adduced above regarding the appropriateness of using certain forms of contraception applies here as well. God has given us intelligence and powers of judgment to fulfill his command to "be fruitful and multiply" in our individual personal circumstances in keeping with scriptural commands and principles (such as the sacredness of human life). In light of our conclusion that it is fallacious to interpret this command to mean that every act of marital sexual intercourse must be open to procreation, it would seem appropriate that a given couple could determine that they have reached the point where they believe God would not have them conceive any more children. The question, then, becomes whether or not sterilization is a legitimate means of ensuring that no additional children are conceived. Indeed, while not every Christian would agree that sterilization involves an improper violation of one's body as the temple of the

Holy Spirit,[23] it is vital that believers submit their personal desires to a prayerful consideration of what is scripturally permissible.

While arguments can be made both against and in favor of sterilization as a form of birth control for Christians, therefore, since Scripture does not directly address the various forms of modern sterilization practices, it seems appropriate to refrain from dogmatism in this area. Where Scripture does not directly address a given matter, biblically informed principles must be applied to specific issues with wisdom and care. We have known godly couples who assured us that they pursued sterilization in an attitude of prayer and trusting the Lord. We have also known other, equally godly, couples who later regretted having followed through with this procedure and sought to reverse it in order to have more children. Both cases suggest that it is imperative that a couple who would use a given method honestly search their hearts and motives during the process of making such a decision and be certain that pragmatic considerations and personal desires do not override scriptural principles or unduly shape what they perceive to be the leading of the Holy Spirit.

Another birth control method requiring special mention and extra care is what is popularly known as *"the pill."* Because of its wide acceptance in the culture, some Christians may be surprised to learn that the moral acceptability of "the pill" (and the many various applications of the same basic chemical products) is under question by Christian ethicists. Yet, while the convenience and effectiveness of this form of birth control have certainly commended it to many, there are serious moral questions that must be addressed before a decision is made as to whether or not "the pill" qualifies as an acceptable form of contraception.

There are two basic categories of hormonally based chemical contraceptives: combined and progestin-only contraceptives. *Combined contraceptives* (containing both estrogen and progestin) come in both an oral form (usually referred to as COCs—combination oral contraceptives—such as Ortho Cyclen or Ortho-trycyclen) and an injectable form (CICs—combined injectable contraceptives—such as Cyclofem and Mesigyna). *Progestin-only contraceptives* likewise are produced in oral and injectable form. Progestin-only pills (POPs) contain the hormone progestin and are taken daily, while progestin-only injectable contraceptives (PICs) such as Depro-Prevara and Noristerat require an injection roughly once every two to three months. Norplant is another version of progestin-based birth control involving a surgical procedure to insert small tubules containing progestin under the skin. This method is said to be effective for years.[24]

According to the *Physician's Desk Reference,* all of these versions of both combined contraceptives and progestin-only contraceptives work by employing the same three basic mechanisms of action. The first of these is to prevent ovulation (a contraceptive mechanism). The second is to alter the cervical mucus buildup which increases the difficulty of the sperm entering the uterus and thereby fertilizing the egg (a contraceptive mechanism). The third mechanism—in all forms of both combined contraceptives and progestin-only contraceptives—whether intended or not, is to inhibit the *endometrium* (uterine lining), thereby making it incapable of supporting the life of the newly conceived child should fertilization take place. This third mechanism, then, is not a contraceptive measure but an *abortifacient,* that is, the mechanism works as a "fail safe" means to control birth if the other two mechanisms do not prevent conception.[25]

PDRHealth.com, a web service provider which bases its information on material from the *Physician's Desk Reference,* describes these three mechanisms in the following manner:

> Suppression of ovulation is the main mode by which OCs, Depo-Provera, and Lunelle prevent pregnancy; the implant system *causes ovulation suppression about 50 percent of the time.* However, throughout each pill cycle, and continuously with Norplant implants and Depo-Provera, the mucous covering the cervix—the site where sperm enters the uterus—stays thick and sticky, making it very difficult for sperm to get through. This gooey impediment also acts on the sperm cell itself. It prevents fertilization by interfering with chemical changes inside the sperm that allow it to penetrate an egg's outer coating.
>
> *Even if ovulation and fertilization do take place, hormonal methods provide another measure of protection: changes to the uterine lining.* Normally, estrogen initiates the thickening of the lining of the uterus in the first part of the cycle, while progesterone kicks in later to help the lining mature. Since both hormones are present throughout the pill cycle, and progestin is supplied continuously by implants

and the shot, *the usual hormonal variations are masked and the lining rarely has a chance to develop enough to nurture a fertilized egg.*[26]

To summarize, with regard to both the combined contraceptives
and progestin-only contraceptives the main moral problem occurs when
the first and second mechanisms of action fail (prevention of ovulation
and of fertilization due to mucus buildup) and fertilization of an egg
takes place. At this point these methods cease to be contraceptive in
nature and function as abortifacients. While the chances of the first two
methods failing are admittedly low (more so with combined contraceptives), given the fact that so many women are using these forms of birth
control there is no question that for some "the pill" or its equivalents
are functioning at least at times to terminate the life of a conceived
child.[27] Indeed, if the "profound respect for life in the prenatal stages"
of a child's development discussed earlier holds the moral authority it
ought to, then perhaps it is right to reevaluate whether a low chance of
aborting one's child is worth the risk at all.[28]

Finally, due to the somewhat enigmatic use of terminology relating
to this subject, those who wisely seek advice from a primary care physician and/or OB/GYN ought to ask questions with precision and care.
For example, a young couple may ask their doctor whether or not a particular form of oral or chemical contraceptive runs the risk of causing
an abortion. Depending on how that doctor defines "abortion" and
"pregnancy," the answer may vary. For some the word "abortion" is
understood to mean the termination of a pregnancy. The term "pregnancy," however, may be understood to mean that the fertilized egg *has
already implanted in the uterine wall.* If this is how the doctor defines
pregnancy, he or she may indicate that combined contraceptives and
progestin-only contraceptives do not cause abortion because they do not
terminate the growth of a fertilized egg once it has become embedded in
the uterine wall. What is left unclear to that couple, however, is that "the
pill" may indeed function to terminate the life of a newly conceived child
by preventing the fertilized egg from implanting in the uterine wall
where the "pregnancy" would otherwise begin.

For this reason, then, instead of inquiring as to whether or not a certain form of combined contraceptives and progestin-only contraceptives
"can function to cause an abortion," the wise couple will seek to deter-

mine whether or not the combined contraceptive or progestin-only contraceptive functions to inhibit the growth of the endometrial lining. If so, it could then prevent a fertilized egg from implanting in the uterine wall and thereby cause the death of a newly conceived child. Other points of clarification that might prove helpful when discussing this issue with one's physician or OB/GYN are: (1) whether or not the method of birth control prevents fertilization of the egg 100 percent of the time; (2) whether or not there are *any* products on the market that have been proven by clear documentation to prevent fertilization of the egg 100 percent of the time; and (3) whether or not there are any forms of combined contraceptives or progestin-only contraceptives that do not change the *endometrium* (the lining of the uterine wall) so that it cannot sustain a fertilized egg that might otherwise implant and grow toward birth.[29] To date, this author has not been able to substantiate an affirmative answer to any of these questions.[30]

Acceptable and Unacceptable Forms of Birth Control

ACCEPTABLE FORMS OF BIRTH CONTROL	UNACCEPTABLE FORMS OF BIRTH CONTROL	METHODS NEEDING SPECIAL CONSIDERATION
General principle: Methods that are contraceptive in nature, i.e., exclusively prohibit conception	*General principle:* All forms of induced abortion	*General principle:* Methods requiring special mention and extra care
Abstinence	Abortion	Sterilization (vasectomy, tubal occlusion)
"Rhythm or calendar method"	IUD (intrauterine device)	"The pill" and its many applications (combined and progestin-only contraceptives)
"Barrier methods" (diaphragm, cervical cap, condoms, and spermicides)	RU-486 ("abortion" or "morning after" pill)	*Issues involved:* treatment of body as temple of the Holy Spirit (sterilization), serious questions regarding the sanctity of life ("the pill")

By way of conclusion, with regard to sterilization it is important to reiterate the need to take great care in avoiding dogmatism on matters that Scripture either does not prohibit or does not directly address. It is the principle of honoring "the temple of the Holy Spirit" that one must seriously consider before deciding whether or not to employ such a method. With regard to use of "the pill," moral justification for its use is much more tenuous due to the simple fact that the principle of the sanctity of life directly applies. In both cases, however, it would seem that the consideration of scriptural principles ought to lead one away from employing sterilization or "the pill" with its many variations as a means of family planning.

ARTIFICIAL REPRODUCTIVE TECHNOLOGIES (ART) (BY MARK LIEDERBACH)

The Challenge of Infertility

In light of the clear scriptural mandate for couples to "be fruitful and multiply" (Gen. 1:28), one of the more difficult trials a married couple can face is the inability to have children. The Old Testament records the agonizing emotions and experiences of both Sarah (Genesis 15–17) and Hannah (1 Sam. 1:1-11) as they struggled with their own experiences of infertility. The New Testament, likewise, indicates that Elizabeth remained childless well into her old age (Luke 1:7). In each of these cases, God was gracious and allowed these women to conceive and bear children who would in due course play major roles in his redemptive plan. Arguably, however, God does not always act through miraculous means to overcome a couple's infertility.

In recent years, advances in modern reproductive technology have paved the way for otherwise infertile couples to give birth to children of their own. In light of these advances, how should Christians respond? Is it appropriate to take advantage of these new technologies? There are those who would argue that prayer and faith alone are the proper response of Christians in the face of infertility.[31] Most Christians, however, relying on the fact that God created human beings with the ability to reason and gave them dominion over the earth (Gen. 1:28-31), do not reject the use of medical intervention as long as the type of intervention does not violate other clear principles of Scripture (i.e., the sanctity of human life).[32]

As a result of the progress of modern medicine, those who in previous generations would have had no hope of giving birth to a child of their own now have available many and varied options. These medical advances include something as simple and non-technical as encouraging a man to increase his sperm count simply by changing the form of underwear he is wearing, to the heavily technologically dependent procedures of artificial insemination, in vitro fertilization or even cloning for reproductive purposes.[33] While all of the available reproductive technologies require at least some level of ethical evaluation, the more complicated and technologically dependent ones also tend to be more ethically complicated.

In what follows we will first provide a brief description of each of the major artificial reproductive technologies and then discuss the various ethical issues involved by using four important guiding principles.

Description of Methods

The following is a brief explanation of five of the more frequently employed forms of reproductive technologies.

Intrauterine insemination (IUI), which is also known as *artificial insemination* (AI), is usually the first option chosen by infertile couples when the problem of infertility resides chiefly in the male. The usual problem is either low sperm count or, for whatever reason, defective sperm. Relatively simple in nature, this procedure involves the collection and accumulation of male sperm and then the injection of that sperm (usually with a needle-less syringe) into the female uterus during the most fertile part of a woman's cycle. The hope, then, is that the reproductive process would proceed from that point along "natural" lines. This procedure can take place with either the husband's sperm (AIH; artificial insemination husband) or a donor's sperm (AID; artificial insemination donor). Ethically speaking, there are far fewer problems with AIH than AID (see discussion below).

Gamete intrafallopian transfer (GIFT) is the procedure by which female eggs are harvested through the use of super-ovulatory hormonal drugs stimulating the maturation and release of several eggs. These eggs are then harvested by means of a minor surgical procedure utilizing ultrasound guidance in the vagina. The male semen that is also collected is treated to make it less viscous, facilitating the conception process. These gametes are then placed together in a single catheter, separated only by a tiny air bubble, and placed together in the woman's fallopian tubes. The procedure facilitates the reproductive process by assuring contact between egg and sperm and thus raising the probability that conception will occur and pregnancy begin.

In vitro fertilization (IVF) is very similar to GIFT in technical procedure but has one major distinction. While in the GIFT procedure fertilization and conception take place within a woman's body, in the case of IVF fertilization takes place in an artificial environment ("in vitro" literally means "in glass," referring to the test tube or petri dish where conception occurs). As with GIFT, the woman receives hormonal treatments in order to stimulate the release of multiple eggs which are then harvested for use in the procedure. Male sperm is also collected, and these gametes (eggs and sperm) are then placed in the same petri dish in hopes that as many conceptions as possible will take place. The reproductive technician will then screen the newly formed embryos and, via embryo transfer (ET), will attempt to implant as many as four of the embryos into the woman's uterus in hopes that she will become pregnant with at least one. The remaining embryos will then be either destroyed or frozen for use in future birthing attempts. Studies indicate that roughly 25 percent of these frozen embryos will not survive the freeze and thawing process prior to the next attempt.[34]

Surrogacy or *surrogate motherhood* refers to the procedure in which the gestation and birth of a baby occur in a woman who is either not the child's biological mother or who is willing to donate her egg and carry a child but relinquishes parenting rights to those contracting with her to carry the child. Thus "genetic surrogacy" results from an IUI procedure where the husband of a given couple donates his sperm in order for the surrogate to conceive, carry the child through gestation, and then to give birth. While genetically related to the surrogate mother, this baby "belongs" to the couple that contracted with her to carry and birth the child. "Gestational surrogacy" differs from genetic surrogacy in that the conception of the child takes place via GIFT or IVF and the embryo is then placed by way of ET into the surrogate mother. The role of the surrogate in this case is to carry and give birth to the child, not to conceive or donate her egg. In both forms of surrogacy, the surrogate mother, in exchange for a fee, typically contracts to release all rights to parent the child once it is born.[35]

Principles for Evaluation

As in the case of contraception, it is important to recognize that simply because a technology is available, this does not necessarily mean that it is ethically permissible to employ it. Rather, it is imperative to explore the available options with regard to how they align with biblical principles that ought to guide the decision making process. In the matter of reproductive technologies, there are four principles that are particularly germane.

First, as in the case of contraception, *respect for the sanctity of human life* directly relates to the issue of reproductive technologies, for the following reasons. Some forms of reproductive technology, such as cloning, pose a direct threat to the life of the child due to the inexact nature and development of the technology. Other forms of reproductive technology may not directly threaten life, but the manner in which they are employed does. For example, it is common practice in certain methods of artificial insemination or in vitro fertilization to fertilize 5 or 6 ova at a time. Each of the resulting conceptions is a child waiting to be placed in a woman's uterus in order to grow toward birth. Unfortunately, it is also common practice for the doctors to select only 1 or 2 of these eggs for implantation, leaving the others to be "destroyed."

Another way a reproductive technology threatens the sanctity of life is when the technique used (such as artificial insemination or the use of fertility drugs) results in a multi-child pregnancy. In such cases, a woman may now be carrying four or five children in her womb. Because there is greater risk of miscarrying under these conditions, it is often the case that reproductive specialists will recommend a procedure known as "selective reduction." While often described as a means to increase the chances that some of the babies may be born alive, the term "selective reduction" is in reality nothing more than a form of abortion in which one or more of the children are killed in order to increase the odds of the others proceeding to live birth.

Thus, in such procedures (artificial insemination, in vitro fertilization) a couple must be willing to have all the conceptions implanted and carried to full term in order for this technology to meet the biblical standards with regard to the sanctity of life (with the possible exception of instances where the life of the mother is at stake). As John Van Regenmorter advises, *"Do not allow more embryos to be formed than the number of children you are willing to parent."*[36] Likewise, those using fertility drugs must recognize ahead of time that a multiple child birth is a possibility and "selective reduction" is not a biblically legitimate option.

A second biblical principle that must be considered is that of *respect for all human beings as image bearers*. Because all humans bear the image of God (Gen. 1:27), it is wrong to use or treat another as a means to an end only, or purposely to put them in harm's way when they have not incurred guilt and there is no other reason than convenience for such a choice. Once again, in the case of some forms of reproductive technologies it is common practice to fertilize several eggs and then freeze these children for an indefinite amount of time only to be used or discarded if the parents opt to forgo having any more children. Such practices are both inherently disrespectful and use these children merely as a means to the parents' chosen goals and must therefore be discarded as inappropriate avenues for Christians to pursue.

A third guiding principle for determining the moral value of a given reproductive technology is *respect for the fidelity of the marital bond*. Genesis 2:24 states that a man is to "leave his father and his mother and hold fast to his wife, and they shall become one flesh." It is within the context of this one-flesh relationship of husband and wife that God gave the command to be fruitful and multiply. Likewise, Scripture elsewhere not only condemns adulterous relationships (Ex. 20:14; Deut. 5:18; Rom. 13:9) but also affirms the exclusive nature of the marital bond (Matt. 19:5; 1 Corinthians 6–7; Eph. 5:28-31). This biblical emphasis on the unity and exclusivity of the marital bond has direct implications on the use of reproductive technologies, particularly those methods that utilize the genetic material (donor egg, donor sperm, donor DNA) from someone other than the husband or wife. Because the use of donor egg or sperm introduces into the marriage (specifically the sexually related area) sexually related genetic material of a third person, there is considerable doubt with regard to the morality of such a practice.

While one would be hard pressed to place this in the exact category of what society has historically understood to be adultery, one could easily argue that using donor egg or sperm is tantamount to adultery or at the very least an inappropriate intrusion upon the exclusive nature of marital fidelity and sexuality.[37] As Scott Rae rightly points out, "the weight of biblical teaching suggests that third-party contributors are not the norm for procreation. Scripture looks skeptically on any reproductive intervention that goes outside the married couple for genetic material. That would mean that technologies such as donor insemination, egg donation, and surrogate motherhood are morally problematic."[38]

A fourth and final principle that ought to guide the evaluation of whether or not to use reproductive technologies relates not so much to the *form of technology* but the *heart of the one wanting to use it*. While the desire to have and raise genetically related children is grounded in the created norms and cemented in God's imperative for us to "be fruitful and multiply," it is nonetheless important not to place one's hope or sense of worth too greatly on one's ability to have children. The final hope of the Christian does not lie in the ability to manipulate human reproductive systems, nor in the ability to have children at all. Whether it be through direct miraculous intervention (as in Hannah's case) or through the technological advancements made possible through the minds God has given us, children are a gift from God. Beyond this, Scripture indicates that our ultimate hope lies not in our ability to have children but rather in our Savior Jesus Christ.

In conclusion, then, while the use of reproductive technology may be *generally* permissible, one should not make the further assumption that *every form* of reproductive technology is therefore biblically and morally acceptable. Concerns for the respect for human life, human dignity, and fidelity to the marital bond need to govern one's evaluation of any particular form of reproductive technology. Indeed, once one considers the rather large ethical uncertainty and "gray areas" regarding many of these technologies (not to mention the financial costs), perhaps wisdom would suggest limiting one's efforts in this direction in favor of pursuing adoption. This may certainly be the path of wisdom when one considers the explicit and positive biblical depiction of adoption, the subject to be discussed next.

Artificial Reproductive Technologies (ART) and Potential Problems

REPRODUCTIVE METHOD	PRINCIPLE OF EVALUATION	AREAS OF RELEVANCE
Intrauterine insemination (IUI) or Artificial insemination (AI)	#1 Respect for the sanctity of human life	Artificial insemination, in vitro fertilization
Gamete intrafallopian transfer (GIFT)	#2 Respect for all human beings as image bearers	Fertilization, freezing, then forgoing of offspring
In vitro fertilization (IVF)	#3 Respect for the fidelity of the marriage bond	Donor insemination, egg donation, surrogate motherhood
Surrogacy or surrogate motherhood	#4 Heart of the one wanting to use a given method	General principle for the use of modern artificial reproductive technologies

ADOPTION

There are several instances of actual adoption in both Testaments.[39] In the Old Testament, Dan and Naphtali, and later Ephraim and Manasseh, were adopted by Jacob (Gen. 30:1-13; 48:5); Moses was adopted by Pharaoh's daughter (Ex. 2:10); and Esther was adopted by Mordecai (Est. 2:7) In what follows we will discuss each of these Old Testament instances of adoption in some more detail.[40]

As far as adoptions through Jacob are concerned, Dan and Naphtali were Jacob's and Rachel's sons through Rachel's maidservant Bilhah, whom Rachel gave to Jacob as a wife since she had borne him no sons (Gen. 30:1-8). Analogously, Jacob adopted Gad and Asher, his sons with Leah through her maidservant Zilpah (Gen. 30:9-13), officially taking them into his family. Later, Jacob also adopted Joseph's sons, Manasseh and Ephraim (Gen. 48:5), and blessed them (vv. 8-22), and possibly also his great-grandsons, the sons of Machir, Manasseh's son (50:23). Jacob's adopted sons were given rights to inheritance equal to his biological sons through Leah and Rachel.[41]

Moses was born to his Jewish parents, Amram and Jochebed, at a time when all baby boys were to be killed by the edict of Pharaoh king of Egypt. In order to save Moses' life, his mother devised a plan that resulted in none other than Pharaoh's daughter adopting Moses as her son. Once grown, however, Moses "refused to be called the son of Pharaoh's daughter" (Heb. 11:24), returning to his birth family and meeting with his birth brother Aaron. Moses' adoption as well as his return to his birth family was part of God's plan of salvation, which involved Moses' leading his people Israel out of their bondage in Egypt into the Promised Land. Moses' mother's plan to save her child's life is a wonderful example of a birth mother's love for her child.

Esther, an orphan, was adopted by her cousin Mordecai. Their story is a wonderful testimony to the close relationship between an adoptive father and his child (though some Christian parents today may find it hard to see the wisdom of letting Esther participate in a beauty pageant). The Old Testament book of Esther recounts how "every day Mordecai walked in front of the court of the harem to learn how Esther was and what was happening to her" (Est. 2:11). Esther, in turn, followed her adoptive father's instructions and "had not made known her kindred or her people, as Mordecai had commanded her, for Esther obeyed Mordecai just as when she was brought up by him" (Est. 2:20). In the end, Esther is used providentially by God to save the Jewish nation.

In the New Testament, the most prominent example is Jesus' adoption by Joseph, who served as his earthly father, participating in his naming (Matt. 1:25), presenting him in the temple (Luke 2:22-24), protecting him from danger by taking him and his mother to Egypt (Matt. 2:13-15), and by teaching him a trade (Matt. 13:55; Mark 6:3). These biblical examples may serve as encouraging evidence for some married couples that the practice of adoption has honorable biblical precedent. Together with the metaphoric use of adoption in the New Testament, which will be discussed below, these passages show that adopted children are to be taken into the loving, intimate, and permanent context of a biblical marriage and family.[42]

In a spiritual sense, Paul teaches that believers are adopted into God's family as his sons and daughters (Rom. 8:15, 23; 9:4; Gal. 4:5; Eph. 1:5).[43] Rather than draw on the notion of divine adoption in Greco-Roman mythology or the Roman ceremony of *adoptio* (in which a minor was transferred from the authority of his natural to that of his adoptive father), the apostle develops this concept by appropriating Old

Testament exodus typology and the messianic adoption formula in 2 Samuel 7:14 ("I will be a father to him, and he will be a son to Me," NASB; cf. 2 Cor. 6:18; see also Ps. 2:7; 89:26-27) within the context of new covenant theology. Just as Israel was redeemed and received her covenant privileges at the exodus (Ex. 4:22; Deut. 1:31; Hos. 11:1), so New Testament believers were redeemed from their slavery to sin in and through Christ, receiving their adoption as God's children (cf. 2 Cor. 6:18 citing 2 Sam. 7:14).[44] Significantly, this will be fully realized only in the future at the final resurrection (Rom. 8:23).

While in Old Testament times certain ethnic constraints applied, believers are now "all sons of God through faith in Christ Jesus" (Gal. 3:26, NIV). If anyone belongs to Christ, he is Abraham's descendant and included in the promise (v. 28). This is an end-time, salvation-historical event of first-rate import: through adoption, believers are introduced into the filial relationship between Jesus the Son and God his Father, sharing together in the new family of God.[45] While the distinction between Jesus as the unique Son of God and believers as sons and daughters of God in Christ is not obliterated (e.g., John 20:17), believers nonetheless become in a real, spiritual sense brothers and sisters of Jesus as well as of one another. "Both the one who makes men holy and those who are made holy are of the same family. So Jesus is not ashamed to call them brothers" (Heb. 2:11, NIV). Even fruitfulness is to some extent transformed from physical childbearing to the harmonious, productive operation of the various members of the body of Christ according to the spiritual gifts supplied by God the Spirit.[46]

CONCLUSION

Today's world presents us with a considerable amount of issues related to reproduction, some of the most important of which were discussed in the present chapter. Our first topic was that of abortion. We concluded that the view that life begins at conception has strong scriptural support and therefore rightly has been the traditional Judeo-Christian view. For this reason abortion cannot be biblically justified.

The next subject was contraception. After determining that contraception is a legitimate Christian option in principle, we discussed morally acceptable and unacceptable forms of birth control. Special attention was given to sterilization and the birth control pill, which call for extra care and discernment. While Christians may use contraception, they ought to refrain from using methods of birth control that are actually abortion.

Our treatment of artificial reproductive technologies, likewise, sought to wade through the difficult ethical issues raised by the variety of new procedures, and to adjudicate what are and are not ethically permissible options for Christians today.

Our final topic of discussion was that of adoption. We found a considerable body of material in Scripture dealing with this issue, both in literal and in figurative terms. This adds up to strong biblical precedent for adoption as an honored Christian avenue for glorifying God and building a Christian family, especially for couples having difficulty conceiving children of their own.

REQUIRING THE
WISDOM OF SOLOMON:
SPECIAL ISSUES RELATED TO
THE FAMILY (PART 2)

THE CHALLENGE OF PARENTING raises a host of issues, some of the most pertinent of which will be discussed in the treatment below. One fundamental question is which method or childrearing philosophy parents will choose. Single parents are confronted with many challenges unique to their particular situation. Another controversial topic is the legitimacy or illegitimacy of physical discipline, which will be covered as well. Other subjects discussed include the task of cultivating masculinity and femininity in children, basic principles of parental discipline, and spiritual warfare as it pertains to marriage and the family.

PARENTING IN TODAY'S WORLD
Which Method?

Many popular parenting books are seeking to impart a given method, often focused on the proper administration of discipline.[1] There are several advantages to this focus on method. First, following a particular method increases the confidence of parents that they have a plan and a purpose in their parenting. Second, focusing on method provides for predictability and consistency. It may be that certain kinds of behavior result in certain rewards or punishment. This enhances success in conditioning, since, all things being equal, children will tend to seek to avoid negative consequences and to strive for positive rewards. Third, adopting a method binds parents together with other parents who use the same method. Support groups of like-minded parents provide a forum for discussion and help with difficulties that may arise.

A focus on method also has several downsides. First, parental confidence may in fact give them a false security that all is well when, at least in the long run, it may not be. Short- or medium-term behavioral conditioning may well be successful, yet in the long run young people may rebel against rigid parenting. Second, a focus on method may place the emphasis on an abstract set of principles rather than on people. Parenting cannot be reduced to an exact science, for it deals with people and relationships. Third, on a related note, a focus on method tends to give inadequate weight to the individuality and uniqueness of each child. While every child needs to be disciplined when there is disobedience, *the way this discipline is administered* may need to be adjusted in order to do justice to the personal characteristics of each individual child.

In the end, therefore, a proper approach to parenting needs to leave adequate room for the *relational* component in parenting. Christian parenting should be undergirded by *wisdom derived from meditation on Scripture,* the *filling of the Holy Spirit, advice from others* (this is where quality literature on parenting can be very helpful if it is balanced and based on biblical principles), and *relational experience* with the child. Ultimately, we should be careful not to rely on any one human method that, no matter how biblical it may claim to be, is always one step removed from the Bible. Our supreme trust should be in God and in his Word, and we must humbly acknowledge that our understanding of Scripture is not to be equated with the teaching of Scripture itself.

In this relationship of parenting, there must be a balance of unconditional love, spiritual nurture, and discipline (Eph. 6:4) in a context of discipleship and Christian growth (2 Pet. 3:18). Biblical parenting requires that parents understand that their children are not merely disobedient, they are also sinful, and they are disobedient *because* they are sinful. Hence, children ultimately need salvation, not merely parental discipline. Moreover, as mentioned in a previous chapter, children are also "simple" (in the scriptural meaning of that term—see Prov. 1:22), which requires parental instruction, training, and constant cultivation, much like a garden needs to be tended continually and consistently.

Parents, too, are sinners, and so must guard against putting their own interests above those of their children. Are they concerned that their children disobey in public simply because this causes them embarrassment? Do they want them to do well in school simply because this brings prestige and recognition for them as parents? Do they want them to choose a particular career or to choose a particular mate because this renders them socially more acceptable or desirable? Do they make decisions regarding their children's education primarily on the basis of their own convenience (daycare, babysitters, grandparents, etc.) rather than on the basis of what is best for their children?[2]

Advantages and Weaknesses of a "Method" Approach to Parenting

ADVANTAGES	WEAKNESSES
Increases the confidence of parents that they have a plan and purpose in their parenting	Parental confidence may in fact give them a false security that all is well when at least in the long run it may not be
Provides for predictability and consistency	Places the emphasis on an abstract set of principles rather than on people
Brings parents together with other parents who use the same method	Tends to give inadequate weight to the individuality and uniqueness of each child
	Tends to lose sight of the various stages of development in a child and young person's life, which requires flexibility and constant adjustment

Single Parenting

Single parenting was not part of God's intended purpose in the beginning. For this reason biblical teaching on single parenting is elusive. Some affinity may exist between issues related to single parenting and scriptural passages pertaining to orphans and the fatherless on the one hand and to widows on the other, though there are obvious differences. In those instances where single parenthood is a result of divorce, the term "single parent" does not fully reflect reality in that the child still has both parents, even though they are no longer married. In those cases, "single parent" more accurately refers to the spouse who is given custody of the child or children of a broken marriage, so that a distinction may be made between a child's "custodial" and "non-custodial" parent.

Single parenthood as a result of divorce entails several difficulties for the custodial and the non-custodial spouse and for the children involved. First, children may (and frequently do) end up emotionally torn between the parents as a result of the marital breakup and its aftermath.[3] This will in all likelihood have a negative effect on the psychological development of the child or children of divorce. Not infrequently do those children feel guilt as if they were responsible for the failure of their parents' marriage.

What is more, in most cases such children grow up in a bi-polar environment, relating to both the mother and the father. While the payment of alimony or child support is a legal requirement for children up to age 18, for single mothers employment tends to be a virtual necessity in order to provide adequately for their child or children. Thus not only does one person have to fill the role of both mother and father, that person also needs to act as provider. Discipline, too, becomes the sole responsibility of the single parent.[4]

Just as God is the God of the orphans and the widows, God's heart goes out in a special way to single parents who shoulder the load of being both father and mother to a child or several children. The Bible portrays God as the defender of the fatherless (Deut. 10:18; 27:19; Ps. 10:18; 82:3), as their sustainer and helper (Ps. 10:14; 146:9), and as their father (Ps. 68:5).[5] Because God himself serves as the protector and provider for the fatherless (as well as of widows and aliens), he commands his covenant people to do likewise.

The Israelites were enjoined to provide the fatherless with food and other material needs (Deut. 14:29; 24:19-21; 26:12-13), and they were to defend the cause of the fatherless by protecting them from injustice.[6] The prophets warned of severe consequences if God's people were to fail in this regard.[7] In the New Testament, James echoes these commands when he writes that "Religion that God our Father accepts as pure and faultless is this: to look after orphans and widows in their distress and to keep oneself from being polluted by the world" (James 1:27, NIV).

The church today can help alleviate the burden faced by single parents in a variety of ways.[8] To begin with, single parents should not be singled out as a "ministry project" but should be treated on a normal level as fellow believers in Christ. With sensitivity and empathy, individual believers and the church as a whole will have no difficulty identifying several areas of need typically faced by single parents in which they can offer assistance, be it filling the void left by the absence of the other parent, financial support, or meeting social and other needs.[9]

Physical Discipline

A debate exists also over the use of physical punishment (spanking) as a valid or appropriate means for parents to discipline their children.[10] The point of departure for the present discussion is the references in the book of Proverbs to the "rod" of correction, which is presented as serving three primary purposes: (1) as a means of disciplining a child based on parental love (Prov. 13:24); (2) as a way to remove folly and to impart wisdom (22:15; 29:15); and (3) as a possible aid to the child's salvation (23:13-14). The "rod" is mentioned in Proverbs also as a means of correcting or punishing fools (10:13; 14:3; 22:8; 26:3).

At the time of writing, spanking is already outlawed in Austria, Croatia, Latvia, and all the Scandinavian countries, and nations considering a ban include Canada, England, Germany, Italy, Belgium, Bulgaria, and the Republic of Ireland. The United Nations Committee on the Rights of the Child is increasingly pressuring countries to outlaw physical punishment of children or face censure and public criticism.[11] The use of physical punishment in childrearing has been challenged in three major ways: (1) spanking a child is tantamount to physical abuse; (2) spanking is archaic and psychologically damaging; and (3) a discontinuity exists between the Old and New Testament views on children and discipline and that the New Testament supersedes the Old Testament injunctions on physical discipline.

The charge that spanking is *tantamount to abuse* stems from a heightened sensitivity to the traumatizing effects of child abuse. The question of children's rights came to the forefront of discussion when 1979 was declared the "International Year of the Child."[12] One such right stated was "freedom from fear or physical harm and abuse."[13]

Subsequently, Sweden enacted anti-spanking laws.[14] Although legislators in Germany, as recently as 1997, expressly conceded the parents' right to physical correction, many Americans and Europeans agree that the law should ban spanking.[15]

The distinction between spanking and physical abuse is further blurred as a result of the rhetoric frequently employed by anti-spanking advocates. Words like "beat," "hit," and "brutalize" replace "spanking" or "paddling."[16] In addition, Oosterhuis quotes Van Leeuwen to point out that "although eighty percent of sexual abuse and family violence occurs in alcoholic families, the next highest incidence of both abuses takes place in intact, highly religious homes."[17] This language, coupled with instances of actual abuse, conveys the idea that corporal discipline is equivalent to physical abuse.[18]

Second, physical discipline has been deemed *archaic and psychologically damaging* for children. Oosterhuis argues that ancient societies considered children as property, thereby rendering the child as no different from a slave. Hence, disobedient children and slaves are accorded the same punishment. She posits, "Because ancient laws implemented severe physical punishments for infractions, physical pain was freely used by parents and masters to correct misbehavior."[19] Therefore, she maintains that as society now has a higher regard for children, spanking represents an invalid form of discipline.[20]

Another writer, Alice Miller, argues that physical punishment causes serious psychological trauma. She cites the findings by neurobiologists who "have established that traumatized and neglected children display severe lesions affecting up to 30 percent of those areas of the brain that control our emotions"[21] and suggests that Hitler and his Nazi followers were the byproduct of physical discipline as children.[22] She also implies that spanking will cause children to become delinquent adults, noting that 90 percent of Americans in jail were abused as children.[23] Therefore, while historically parents may have beaten their children, modern society has since learned that physical punishment severely traumatizes them.

The final charge avers that a discontinuity exists between the Old and New Testament views on children and discipline, and that *the New Testament supersedes the Old Testament injunctions on physical discipline*.[24] Both Gillogly and Oosterhuis refer to the loving and accepting way in which Jesus handled children as setting forth a new paradigm for viewing children.[25] Rather than children being considered as property to be managed, "Christ's children were to be given rights of personhood with independence and responsibilities."[26] Not only did Christ elevate the status of children, he also abolished the notion of physical discipline.[27] Therefore, parents must recognize the historical developments of God's creative work.[28]

Should parents exercise physical disciplining? The modern criticisms against spanking typically employ overstatement and inflammatory rhetoric.[29] Appealing to *excessive* cases that involve abuse does not justify abandoning spanking as a form of discipline.[30] Children need to learn the consequences of wrong behavior, and spanking can be a useful means to convey that lesson.[31] However, parents should take their child's unique personality and temperament into account[32] and be aware that some children may respond better to alternative forms of positive or negative consequences and reinforcement (i.e., timeout, rewards, loss of privileges).[33]

Cultivating Masculinity and Femininity

Another parenting issue of great contemporary relevance is that of cultivating *masculinity and femininity* in our children. While the subject is vast and cannot be fully treated here, a few comments may be helpful. As mentioned in the opening chapter, the world today is characterized by a growing degree of gender confusion. At least in part, this is one of the not-so-positive results of the feminist revolution. James Dobson, in his book *Bringing Up Boys,* bears eloquent witness to the fact that boys are in a state of crisis in our culture because they have often lost a sense of what it means for them to be a man.[34] Robert Lewis shares the same burden in his book *Raising a Modern-Day Knight: A Father's Role in Guiding His Son to Authentic Manhood.*[35]

The conviction that sex and gender are not merely biological and sociological functions but that they define us as who we are as men and women in a more thoroughgoing way is rooted in the biblical creation account. In Genesis 1:27, we read that God created man in his own image as male and female. Yet while both the man and the woman were made in God's image, they were not therefore made the same. As

Genesis 2 makes clear, God first made the man and subsequently the woman as the man's "suitable helper" (Gen. 2:18, 20). Their union is presented, not as same-sex marriage, but as a partnership of a man and a woman, individuals who are distinct in their gender identity and who thus complement one another.[36]

Nurturing boys' and girls' distinctive masculine and feminine identities is an important part of Christian parenting. With regard to young people moving toward marriage, and in courtship, it seems in keeping with the distinctive roles assigned by God to the man and the woman (see chapter 2 above) that men take the initiative and women respond to men's leadership. While there may be exceptions, in principle this is not merely a matter of traditional role division but an implication of the fact—attested by Scripture—that God put men in charge of both the home and the church and assigned to them the ultimate responsibility and authority for these institutions.

If there is confusion in this regard during courtship, this does not bode well for the couple subsequent to marriage. How much better it is if proper biblical roles are practiced already prior to marriage during the courtship period. For this reason we encourage those readers who are as of yet unmarried but who envision marriage in the future to read the preceding chapters on marriage, and here especially the sustained treatment of Ephesians 5:21-33 in chapter 3, and to resolve to put this pattern of relating with members of the opposite sex into practice even while they are still single.

Principles of Parental Discipline

On a practical note, as we come to the end of our section on special issues in parenting today, we would like to adduce several biblical principles of disciplining children. While parenting cannot be reduced to a formula (despite many how-to books on the subject), Scripture does offer important instructions and guidelines for administering discipline.

First, to be effective, discipline must be *consistent*. Children should know what constitutes right and wrong behavior, and they should know that wrong behavior will be punished (and right behavior rewarded), and that this will be done in a predictable and equitable rather than an arbitrary manner.

Second, discipline ought to be *age-appropriate* (cf. Luke 2:51-52). An obvious example is that spanking may not work effectively with older children. The older the child, the more important it will be to reason with him or her about why a given kind of behavior is unacceptable and to explain why a certain form of punishment is chosen.

Third, discipline must adhere to the universal biblical principles of *fairness* and *justice*. One entailment of this is that *the punishment should fit the offense*. Practical wisdom suggests that an unduly harsh sanction will likely embitter the child and fail to have its remedial consequences. Conversely, an unduly lenient punishment will likely send the message that the parent is not serious about discipline. Fairness also means that parents should give children an opportunity to present their view of the situation before deciding on a specific punishment. Otherwise, it may be that a child will not accept the discipline as fair and will grow discouraged and bitter over time (Col. 3:21).

Fourth, discipline should be *child-specific* (a function of the individuality and unique creation of each child by God; see above). The purpose of discipline is to help children avoid wrong behavior and attitudes in the future and to encourage right attitudes and conduct. To that end, what will work well with one child may not work as well with another. A child who does not enjoy reading will not perceive a limitation on reading time as a real punishment. Every child is different.

Fifth, discipline should be administered in *love* and *not anger* (cf. Eph. 6:4; Col. 3:21). Parents should not take a child's disobedience personally but should act with their children's best interests at heart. They are God's instruments to help children learn obedience, which is one of the principles God has built into this universe.

Sixth, discipline should be *future-oriented* and *forward-looking*. The primary purpose should not be immediate compliance (though this is desirable), but a child's long-term development into a mature and responsible Christian adult. We are to "train up a child in the way he should go," so that "when he is old he will not depart from it" (Prov. 22:6). "For the moment all discipline seems painful rather than pleasant, but later it yields the peaceful fruit of righteousness to those who have been trained by it" (Heb. 12:11).

Seventh and last (though we could continue), discipline must be part of a *relationship* between parent and child that is larger and more permanent than any temporary form of discipline. Limiting discipline to behavioral modification by a system of rewards and punishments may be effective in the short term, but may well lead to rebellion in the end. Children are not laboratory rats that can be conditioned by stimuli to behave in a certain way—they are precious and unique creatures of God, who has invested them with personal worth and dignity. If we respect and embrace this larger relational context, we stand a much better chance of reaping a relationship with our child that continues far beyond the childhood and growing-up years.

Conclusion

These are issues that can only be briefly touched upon here in passing, but they are issues that illustrate the complexity and (at times almost overwhelming) responsibility of being a parent in today's world. Clearly, Scripture is sufficient to provide the parameters for parenting. Rather than relying unduly on the surrounding culture and conforming to cultural values, norms, and expectations, Christian parents must take their cue from Scripture, and only from Scripture. At the same time, however, Scripture does not address every conceivable issue with which a parent may be confronted. There is therefore no substitute for wisdom, consultation with other Christian parents, the Holy Spirit's guidance, and cultivating the mind of Christ.

Children are a blessing from the Lord and a reward from him. Investing in our children is worth our very best efforts. If we sow faithfully the seeds of Scripture and Christlikeness into our children's lives, very likely we will one day reap a harvest of blessing. Yet there is even more at stake. The very Creator who told the first man and the first woman to be fruitful and multiply and fill the earth will receive glory if we live out his creation design in our marriages and families. Hence, it is for our own good as well as for the glory of God that we ought to strive to be the best parents we can possibly be—with God's help.

MARRIAGE AND THE FAMILY AND SPIRITUAL WARFARE

Marriage and the family are not exempt from the cosmic conflict that is raging between God and his angels on the one hand and Satan and his demons on the other. Because marriage and the family are not merely a human convention or cultural custom but a divine institution, it should be expected that Satan, who seeks to rob God of his glory, would attack marriage. For this reason, too, we must treat marriage and the family not merely in the context of the current cultural crisis (see chapter 1) but also within the framework of the perennial cosmic conflict that requires a spiritual perspective and skilled engagement of the enemy in spiritual warfare.

Clearly, spiritual warfare surrounding marriage and the family is a reality, and awareness of this conflict as well as skill in engaging in it are imperative. Yet while there is a plethora of materials on marriage and the family, as well as a considerable body of literature on spiritual warfare,[37] rarely are those issues treated jointly. We are aware of no current volume on marriage and the family that provides even the most cursory treatment of spiritual warfare.[38] Regularly, the focus is on fulfilling one's partner's needs in marriage, improving one's communication skills, or resolving marital conflict. From reading any of these books, one would never know that spiritual warfare is a vital issue in marriage and the family. Yet, in fact, spiritual warfare is an all-encompassing reality.

A Struggle from the Beginning

Spiritual warfare has been a part of married life and childrearing from the beginning. The foundational biblical narrative in Genesis 3 recounts how the tempter, Satan, prevailed upon the first woman to violate God's commandment and how her husband followed her into sin. Ever since, marriage has resembled more a struggle for control and conscious and unconscious efforts at mutual manipulation than an Edenic paradise. The first known instance of sibling rivalry issued in Cain killing his brother Abel out of envy and jealousy. The rest of the Old Testament chronicles a whole series of ways in which sin has affected marital and family relationships ever since the Fall.[39]

The message of the New Testament is no different. Arguably the most important treatment of spiritual warfare, Ephesians 6:10-20, is preceded by extended treatments of marriage (5:21-33) and child-rearing (6:1-4). These passages, in turn, are preceded by sections on believers' spiritual blessings in Christ (1:3-14), on their having been made alive in Christ (2:1-10) and now being one in Christ with other believers (2:11-22; 4:1-16), and on living as children of light, putting off the old sin nature and putting on the new nature, "created to be like God in true righteousness and holiness" (4:17–5:20, esp. 4:20-24; passage quoted is 4:24, NIV). Unfortunately, these sections are regularly compartmentalized. In Paul's thinking, however, it is precisely in people's relationships with one another, be it at work or at home, among Christians or between believers and unbelievers, that spiritual warfare manifests itself and conscious dealing with it becomes a necessity.

In fact, Ephesians 6:10-20 is "a crucial element to which the rest of the letter has been pointing."[40] In the structure of the entire letter, the practical teaching in chapters 4–6 is predicated upon the doctrinal instruction in chapters 1–3. For this reason every believer must have a thorough grasp of what it means to be chosen in Christ to be holy and blameless (1:4, 11); to have been predestined to be adopted as God's son or daughter in Christ by God's pleasure and for the praise of his glorious grace (1:5-6, 11); to have redemption through his blood and the forgiveness of sins (1:7); and to have been sealed with the Holy Spirit as a deposit guaranteeing our inheritance in Christ (1:13-14). Believers must understand that their conversion entails turning away from sin, so that they no longer carry out the bidding of their sinful nature, and turning to God and serving him in the power of the Holy Spirit (2:1-10). They must understand their unity in Christ with other believers (2:11-22; 4:1-16) and confront sin in their own lives as they count their old sinful nature dead in Christ and themselves alive in their risen Lord (4:17–5:20).

In the more immediate context of Ephesians 6:10-18, the main command governing Paul's treatment of marriage and the family in 5:21–6:4 is "Be filled with the Spirit" (5:18).[41] The warfare passage in 6:10-18 then seamlessly picks up where 5:18 left off, calling on believers to take up the sword of the Spirit (6:17) and to pray in the Spirit (6:18), always remembering that their "struggle is not against flesh and blood, but against the rulers, against the authorities, against the powers of this dark world and against the spiritual forces of evil in the heavenly realms" (6:12, NIV).[42] Hence it is vital to look at the biblical teaching on marriage and the family on the one hand and on spiritual warfare on the other in an integrated way. In living out their Christian faith in their marriages and families, believers must recognize that their sinful nature will lead them to rebel against God's plan unless aided by the Holy Spirit, and that the devil will seek to use their sinful tendencies and inclinations to lead them astray.

A Battle for the Mind

What is the key element in spiritual warfare? According to Scripture, it is human minds. "But I am afraid that just as Eve was deceived by the serpent's cunning, your *mind*s may somehow be led astray from your sincere and pure devotion to Christ" (2 Cor. 11:3, NIV). "For though we live in the world, we do not wage war as the world does. The weapons we fight with are not the weapons of the world. On the contrary, they have divine power to demolish strongholds. We demolish arguments and every pretension that sets itself up against the knowledge of God, and we take captive every *thought* to make it obedient to Christ" (10:3-5, NIV). Just as Satan reasoned with Eve as to why she should disobey God in the Garden, it is people's thought life that is the arena in which our spiritual battles are won or lost.[43]

For this reason believers ought to saturate their minds with scriptural teaching regarding their new position in Christ. To go no further than the book of Ephesians, which contains the primary passage on marriage and the family, Ephesians 5:21–6:4, we learn that Christians have been blessed with every spiritual blessing in Christ (Eph. 1:3): they were chosen in Christ to be holy and blameless (1:4, 11); were predestined to be adopted as his sons and daughters in Christ (1:5, 11); were redeemed and received forgiveness of sins through his blood (1:7); and were given the Holy Spirit as a deposit guaranteeing their inheritance (1:13-14). While they used to gratify the cravings of their sinful nature prior to their conversion to Christ (2:3), they were raised up with Christ and seated with him in the heavenly realms (2:6). They have been saved by grace through faith (2:8). On the basis of this understanding of their new position in Christ, believers will be able to deal effectively with the various temptations and struggles with which they are confronted in their marriages and families.

*The Devil's Toolbox: Sexual Temptation, Anger,
and Insensitivity*

Several New Testament passages teach that the devil's efforts to destroy marriages and to subvert family life did not stop at the Fall but continue to this very day. While three particular infractions are singled out, doubtless others could be added. A first area of vulnerability Satan will seek to attack is susceptibility to *sexual temptation*.[44] In 1 Corinthians 7:5, Paul counsels married believers not to abstain from sexual relations, "except by mutual consent and for a time" for the purpose of prayer, but then to come together again, so that Satan may not tempt them because of their lack of self-control. This would seem to indicate that the sexual component of the marriage relationship is very much a regular target of Satan's attack and must be carefully guarded by the married couple.[45]

A second area of weakness that Satan will target is *unresolved anger*. As Paul writes in Ephesians 4:26-27, "Do not let the sun go down while you are still angry, and do not give the devil a foothold" (NIV). While not limited to marriage, this pronouncement certainly includes the marriage relationship, cautioning believers not to allow broken relationships to render them vulnerable to the devil. Related injunctions pertaining to childrearing are found in Paul's letters to the Ephesians and Colossians, where fathers are enjoined not to provoke their children to anger lest they become discouraged (Eph. 6:4; Col. 3:21).

Thirdly, Satan will seek to disrupt marriages by sowing the seeds of *marital conflict* through the *husband's insensitivity* to his wife. The apostle Paul tells husbands to love their wives and not to be harsh with them (Col. 3:19). Peter writes similarly, "Husbands, in the same way be considerate as you live with your wives, and treat them with respect as the weaker partner and as heirs with you of the gracious gift of life, so that nothing will hinder your prayers" (1 Pet. 3:7, NIV). According to Peter, the husband's insensitivity toward his wife may cause spiritual disruption in marriage; and marital discord, in turn, becomes a hindrance to united, answerable prayer.[46]

Whether it is the couple's sex life, unresolved conflict, inconsiderateness toward one's wife, or some other area, the New Testament makes clear that all are part of spiritual warfare, and that husbands and wives must take the necessary precautions in order not to lose in the spiritual war that rages concerning their marriage. What is more, it is important to realize that the enemy is not only an external one (i.e., the devil), but that our first ancestors allowed the enemy inside, as it were, by succumbing to the devil's lure and rebelling against the Creator. Thus the devil is now able to use the world at large which is separated from God as well as our inborn, innate sinful nature to reinforce sin's power over us (1 John 2:15-17). The only way this power can be consistently and effectively overcome is for a believer to recognize himself or herself as a new creature in Christ and to live under the direction and guidance of the Holy Spirit (1 John 4:4).

How to Fight the Battle: Three Important Lessons

How, then, are we to fight in the spiritual war in which we are engaged? At least three important lessons emerge from the biblical teaching on spiritual warfare. First, an *awareness of the fact that there is a battle* is imperative for success. Anyone who, in the case of war, fails to realize that he is engaged in conflict will no doubt be an early casualty because of his failure to properly protect himself. It is the same in the realm of marriage. Arguably, divorce rates are skyrocketing, not primarily because of the lack of good intentions, the unavailability of resources and instruction on how to conduct a strong biblical marriage, or even the lack of love, but because many, unbelievers and believers alike, inadequately recognize that spiritual warfare is a certain reality that calls for a concerted, deliberately planned response.

Second, it is essential to *know one's spiritual enemy*. This enemy is not one's marriage partner. Nor is it one's children. It is Satan, the enemy of our souls, who employs a variety of strategies, methods, and schemes (cf. 2 Cor. 10:4; Eph. 6:11; 1 Pet. 5:8-9), including that of exploiting and inciting our sin nature and the sinful aspects of the godless world around us. While the devil is highly intelligent, he nonetheless remains a creature. Thus he is neither omniscient nor omnipresent; God and Satan are not evenly matched. The devil can, and in fact does, miscalculate—the most striking instance being the cross, when what Satan thought would be his greatest triumph was turned into his final defeat as Jesus rose from the dead. Satan specifically targets people's areas of weakness and greatest vulnerability, and every individual must be pre-pared for this in order not to be caught off guard. Yet as with Paul, believers today will find that God's grace is more than sufficient for every challenge they face in the power of Christ, as long as they are diligent to "put on the full armor of God" (see below).

Third and finally, *spiritual battles must be fought by the use of proper weapons.* As mentioned, some lose a spiritual conflict in which they are engaged because they fail to realize that a battle is in fact rag-ing and that their involvement is not optional but essential. Yet others may realize they are in a war but may fail to use proper spiritual weapons (or protective gear, as it were). Once again, such persons will soon become casualties. In the context of Christian marriages, as well as in parenting, it is imperative that believers, in order to overcome a spiritual enemy—be it their own sinfulness or evil supernatural opposi-tion—put on the "full armor of God" (Eph. 6:10-18):

- *truth:* like all believers, spouses must "put off falsehood and speak truthfully" to one another (Eph. 4:25, NIV), yet they must speak "the truth *in love*" and hence "in all things grow up into him who is the Head, that is, Christ" (4:15, NIV); in their speech they must make every effort to "not let any unwholesome talk" come out of their mouths, "but only what is helpful" for *building each other up* "according to their needs" (4:29, NIV);

- *righteousness:* righteousness is both one's right standing with God in and through Christ (e.g., Rom. 5:1, 9; 2 Cor. 5:21) and one's dealings with God and one's fellow human beings with integrity (e.g., Psalm 15); for this reason it is only mar-riages where both spouses are *Christians* that can truly and consistently live out God's will for marriage (Eph. 5:18; cf. Rom. 8:9);

- *peace:* as believers, the husband and the wife have been given the peace of Christ in the Holy Spirit (John 14:27; 16:33); they know that they have been eternally forgiven and that they are sons and daughters of God (John 1:12; 1 John 3:1); being at peace with God (Rom. 5:1), they can be at peace with each other and act as peacemakers in the world around them (Matt. 5:9; 2 Cor. 5:17-18);

- *faith:* as is true for all believers, husband and wife must follow the Lord Jesus Christ in discipleship and learn to trust him to meet all their needs and overcome all challenges and adversity; their overriding concern should not be material needs but the extension of God's rule in the world (Matt. 6:25-34); faith in God also entails trusting God with one's husband or wife, and trusting God the Holy Spirit's continued transforming work in their lives;

- *salvation:* because a married couple is secure in their assurance of salvation and eternal destiny, they can truly love each other unconditionally and selflessly; the husband can provide responsible, loving leadership without abusing his authority, and the wife can trust and submit graciously to God's leading of her through her husband (Eph. 5:21-33);

- *the Word of God:* because there is no lasting foundation for our lives other than God's Word (cf. Matt. 7:24-27; Heb. 4:12-13; 1 Pet. 1:23-25), a married couple must be committed to "remain in God's word" (John 8:31; 15:4, 7) through regular personal and joint study of Scripture and faithful attendance of and participation in a local church where the Word of God is preached (2 Tim. 4:2);

- *prayer:* regular joint prayer is essential for marriage partners at all times to "keep the unity of the Spirit through the bond of peace" (Eph. 4:3, NIV); husband and wife ought to make a habit of bringing their thanksgiving and requests before God and trust him to act on their behalf (Phil. 4:6-7; 1 Pet. 5:7); in exceptional circumstances a couple may even choose to refrain from sexual relations for a time for the purpose of concerted prayer (1 Cor. 7:5).

What is more, while it is the responsibility of every individual believer, couple, and family to wage spiritual warfare in keeping with biblical principles, one must not forget the larger context of the local church, which entails the principle of accountability on this larger scale and, if necessary, even church discipline.

Implications

As Christians are engaged in spiritual conflict, they must embrace the truth that there is in fact a spiritual battle raging; they must strive to know their enemy, the devil, who incites human sin nature to resist God;

and they must fight using proper, spiritual weapons. As the apostle Paul writes, "Our struggle is not against flesh and blood. . . . Therefore put on the full armor of God, so that when the day of evil comes, you may be able to stand your ground, and after you have done everything, to stand" (Eph. 6:12-13, NIV).

Spiritual Warfare and Marriage and the Family

THREE AREAS OF WEAKNESS TARGETED BY SATAN	THREE LESSONS ON SPIRITUAL WARFARE
Sexual temptation (1 Cor. 7:5)	Awareness of the fact that there is a battle
Unresolved anger (Eph. 4:26-27; 6:4)	Knowledge of one's spiritual enemy
Husband's inconsiderateness (Col. 3:19; 1 Pet. 3:7)	Waging warfare with proper spiritual weapons

Spiritual warfare is the all-encompassing, ruling reality for the marital relationship. Those who ignore it do so at their own peril. Just as the devil attacks those with potential for church leadership, he seeks to subvert human marriages, because they have the greatest potential for displaying to the world the nature of the relationship between Christ and his church (Eph. 5:31-32).

If believers want to have a part in showing the world by their marriages what a glorious and good God they have, they must, for God's sake as well as their own, engage in spiritual warfare, and they must do so using spiritual weapons. Then, and only then, will Christian marriages reflect the image and design of the Creator. For in the end, it is God's glory, not merely human fulfillment and satisfaction, that is the proper goal of Christian marriages.[47]

FAMILY WAYS

We close with a few suggestions on how to protect our Christian marriages and families and build strong positive Christian family traditions. Those of us who did not grow up in Christian homes in particular are faced with the challenge and opportunity of building cohesiveness and a sense of identity in our families by establishing distinctive family ways.

One important practice is that of *family worship, devotions, or Bible study.*[48] While it is helpful for our children to be taught the Bible in Sunday school, Awana, or other similar programs, Christian parents must never abdicate or delegate to others the responsibility of teaching their children the Bible. As the head of the home, the father ought to assume responsibility for leading his children to Christ and of encouraging them on the path of Christian discipleship. This includes reading and studying Scripture together, singing and praying together, and facing challenges and adversity (as well as successes and triumphs) together as a family in a spirit of faith and trust in Christ.

Another important way in which we can strengthen our families is by instituting distinctive *family traditions.*[49] This includes how we celebrate major holidays, be it religious holidays such as Christmas or Easter or national holidays such as Thanksgiving or Memorial Day. It will be advisable in each case to filter out secular or pagan accretions and to focus on the Christian content or essence of these holidays. All of this is part of inculcating in children a sense of their religious and national heritage similar to the way in which Israelites were told to teach their children the meaning of the Passover or the exodus.

Also, we will want to encourage *wholesome activities,* such as reading, outdoor activities, and spending time with other children who can serve as positive role models. This will make it easier to limit unwholesome activities, such as excessive TV watching, compulsive web surfing, or an addiction to computer games. It is also important to teach our children the value of friendship, how to select their friends wisely, and how to be good friends to others.

Finally, we should heed the principles of *spiritual warfare* discussed above. This will be important especially when resolving conflict. For, ultimately, our enemy is not flesh and blood—each other—but the devil and the evil supernatural. Hence we should cultivate mutual respect and others-centeredness in the spirit of Christ (Phil. 2:1-11).

In all these things, may our families be wholly submitted to the Lordship of Christ, may they be characterized by both love and faith, and may they bring glory, rather than dishonor, to our Lord and Savior Jesus Christ.

CONCLUSION

In this chapter we have discussed a variety of contemporary issues in Christian parenting, such as single parenting, physical discipline, cultivating masculinity and femininity, and principles of parental discipline. At the outset, we highlighted dangers of approaches that focus on method to the detriment of cultivating a relationship with the child and stressed the importance of relying on the Spirit's guidance in parenting. In our treatment of single parenting, we adduced biblical teaching on God's concern for the fatherless and discussed some of the ways in which the church can assist single parents. The debate concerning physical punishment was surveyed as well, and while the biblical teaching prevents us from disallowing this form of discipline, important cautions were registered in this regard. Fostering masculinity and femininity was identified as of utmost importance in our culture that is increasingly reaping the fruit of radical feminism's anti-male bias. We also identified several biblical principles of parental discipline that may be used as a general framework for holding children accountable for their actions, and we discussed the important topic of spiritual warfare pertaining to marriage and the family. In closing, we suggested ways in which believers can institute family worship and cultivate distinctive Christian family traditions.

We are aware that there are many other issues that might have merited inclusion in this chapter, but hope that the issues we chose to cover illustrate the need to ground application in biblical teaching, and that they will serve as case studies for issues we were not able to address. This concludes our focus on the biblical teaching on marriage and the family. We move now to a discussion of various specific issues related to marriage and the family, such as singleness (chapter 9), as well as the distortions of the biblical model for marriage and the family in homosexuality (chapter 10) and divorce (chapter 11).

Undivided Devotion to the Lord: The Divine Gift of Singleness

POST-ADOLESCENT SINGLES are probably the most overlooked social group in the contemporary Western church. While larger congregations typically do have "college and career" ministries (some of which seem to operate at least in part as church-sponsored dating services), and while the topic of singleness occasionally engenders a brief chapter in a book on marriage and the family (witness the current example), for the most part singles have been marginalized within the modern church.[1] To most Western Christians it appears self-evident that *marriage is the normal state*. Therefore, when a post-adolescent single is found within the body of Christ, many well-meaning believers view it as their Christian duty to locate a compatible mate for that individual.

Moreover, when someone does remain single well into his or her twenties and thirties, either by choice or by circumstances, many people begin to try to diagnose the problem (be it sexual orientation, physical appearance, intellectual ability, social ineptitude, unduly high standards, or other factors) that has trapped the single person in the unnatural and undesirable condition of being unmarried. It is probably no exaggeration to say that the thought that singleness could be an acceptable permanent state has not even occurred to many people in our churches today. What is more, the only call of God that Western

Christians fear more than the call to missions is the call to a life of celibacy.

Given the fact that 46 percent of the U.S. population over the age of 15 was single at the beginning of the twenty-first century,[2] the neglect and distortion of the state of singleness by the Western church is anything but justified. Although most will eventually marry, statistics indicate that a growing number will never do so, and many who do will find themselves single once again because of divorce or the death of a spouse. For these reasons, and in light of the fact that many of the heroes of the Christian faith have been single (including Jesus)[3]—not to mention the scriptural teaching that singleness can be a gracious gift of God (Matt. 19:11-12; 1 Cor. 7:7)—the contemporary church stands in urgent need of reappraising its stance on the issue of singleness.

SINGLENESS IN THE OLD TESTAMENT

In Old Testament times, singleness was rare among individuals old enough to marry, which was usually age 12 or 13 for females and age 15 or 16 for males.[4] In fact, due largely to God's command to procreate (Gen. 1:28), people in Old Testament culture lacked the concept of anything akin to the contemporary notion of adolescence or the equivalent of an extended period of adult maturity without a spouse and children.[5] Being single was viewed by the majority of people as living contrary to creation. Indeed, if someone was single in the Old Testament era, they generally fell into one of the following categories.

The first category of singles in the Old Testament era is that of *widows*.[6] In short, like today, widowhood was not a desirable position in ancient times. Widows often faced financial struggles (cf. 2 Kings 4:1) and were certainly among the most helpless in ancient society (Deut. 10:18; Isa. 54:4).[7] History reveals that because singleness was viewed as so unnatural, most widows sought to remarry as soon as possible, and many did remarry (e.g., Ruth 3–4).[8] Yet, for widows who did not or could not remarry, the Lord did make certain special provisions, such as the institution of levirate marriage (Deut. 25:5-6)[9] and the concession that childless widows from priestly families could return to their father's household and partake of the priestly food (Lev. 22:13). In addition, God frequently reminded his people of their sacred duty to care for needy widows,[10] and the Lord repeatedly described himself as a defender of widows.[11] Nevertheless, widowhood was an unenviable position in Old Testament times that was largely looked upon as a reproach (Isa. 4:1). The concept of widowhood was even occasionally used by the Lord as a threatened punishment for Israel's spiritual disobedience (Isa. 47:8-9).

A second category of singles in the Old Testament era is that of *eunuchs*. Like those who found themselves widows, being a eunuch was not an enviable position in ancient times. Although eunuchs were part of many oriental royal courts, serving in positions such as keepers of virgins or concubines (Est. 2:3, 14-15), queens' attendants (4:5), confidants (1:12), overseers (Dan. 1:7), and even leaders in the military community (2 Kings 25:19; Jer. 52:25), for ancient Jews, being a eunuch would have been a detestable position, for it precluded one from the congregation of worshipers of the Lord (Deut. 23:1), as well as from participation in the priesthood (Lev. 21:20). Moreover, while several eunuchs in Old Testament times are presented in a "favorable" light, such as the three eunuchs that cast Jezebel out of her window to her death (2 Kings 9:32-33) and the sons mentioned by Isaiah who would serve in the palace of the king of Babylon (Isa. 39:7), eunuchs generally were looked upon with disdain. Becoming a eunuch was occasionally included in the threatened divine judgment for turning from the Lord (2 Kings 20:18; Isa. 39:7), and Isaiah notes that the Lord will remedy the unnatural state of eunuchs in the end times (Isa. 56:3-5).

A third category of singles in the Old Testament era was comprised of *those who could not marry* due to disease (e.g., leprosy) or severe economic difficulties.[12]

Fourth, there were those who did not marry because of some type of *divine call*. Perhaps the greatest example of an individual remaining single, at least for a time, because of a divine call is the prophet Jeremiah (though the command may have been due to the lack of suitable women "in this place"). In Jeremiah 16:1-4 the prophet writes,

> The word of the LORD came to me: *"You shall not take a wife,* nor shall you have sons or daughters in this place. For thus says the LORD concerning the sons and daughters who are born in this place, and concerning the mothers who bore them and the fathers who fathered them in this land: They shall die of deadly diseases. They shall not be

lamented, nor shall they be buried. They shall be as dung on the surface of the ground. They shall perish by the sword and by famine, and
their dead bodies shall be food for the birds of the air and for the
beasts of the earth."

A divine call to or even a conscious choice of a lifetime of singleness,
however, was rare in ancient times,[13] as this is the only such example of
an explicit divine call to singleness in the Old Testament.[14]

A fifth category of singles in Old Testament times were the
divorced.[15] Divorces were almost always initiated by the husband (Deut.
24:1-4; but see Judg. 19:1-2). Deuteronomic legislation sought to protect the divorced woman by requiring her husband to issue a certificate
of divorce as legal proof of the dissolution of marriage. Similar to the
death of a woman's spouse, divorce would put her in a very vulnerable
economic position. Like a widow or orphan, the divorced woman
would be left without male provision and protection. If unable to
remarry, she would likely be economically destitute and in dire need of
help from others.

The sixth and final category of singles in ancient Israel were *unmarried young men and women*. Fathers typically arranged for the marriage
of their children to suitable partners (Genesis 24; Judges 14). They
sought to protect their daughters from male predators to ensure that
they would marry as virgins (cf. Ex. 22:16-17; Deut. 22:13-21) and provided their daughters with a dowry, which would be returned to the
daughters if the marriage failed. As mentioned, in ancient Israel daughters tended to marry at the onset of puberty, at about thirteen years of
age, while sons would marry a couple of years later.[16] For this reason
there was hardly any interim between childhood and the married state
that might meaningfully be termed "singleness."

SINGLENESS IN THE NEW TESTAMENT

As in Old Testament times, in the New Testament era singleness was not
as clearly defined a concept as it is in the Western world today. Indeed,
during the time of Christ, if a person was "single," he or she more likely
than not was in transition, whether that person was too young to marry,
the death of a spouse had left the person widowed, or for some other rea-

son. In short, in New Testament times, singleness as a settled state and a conscious lifestyle choice was uncommon, and marriage was the norm.[17]

This said, however, John the Baptist, Jesus, and the apostle Paul were single,[18] and despite the fact that there is comparatively little information on singleness in the New Testament, both Jesus and Paul mention that there is such a thing as celibacy, the "gift from God" (1 Cor. 7:7),[19] or, as Jesus put it, being "eunuchs for the sake of the kingdom of heaven" (Matt. 19:12). Both Jesus and Paul indicate that such a call to singleness allows unmarried persons to devote greater and more undistracted attention to religious service.[20] As Paul comments in his major treatment on the subject,

> I want you to be free from anxieties. The unmarried man is anxious about the things of the Lord, how to please the Lord. But the married man is anxious about worldly things, how to please his wife, and his interests are divided. . . . I say this for your own benefit, not to lay any restraint upon you, but to promote good order and to secure your *undivided devotion to the Lord* (1 Cor. 7:32-35).

A survey of Jesus' and Paul's comments on singleness engenders two observations. First, in contrast to the traditional Jewish interpretation of the Old Testament (though not necessarily the Old Testament itself), in the teachings of Jesus and Paul singleness is a *positive* concept. Whereas in the Old Testament era singleness tended to be viewed negatively—if not completely contrary to nature—both Jesus and Paul assert, as well as model, the idea that singleness is acceptable, though not the norm (cf. 1 Cor. 7:9; 1 Tim. 4:1-3). What is more, singleness is viewed as a *gift* bestowed by God. This must have been a revolutionary teaching for first-century listeners steeped in Old Testament traditions.

Moreover, in the book of Revelation, the seer praises celibacy, at least metaphorically, as he describes the 144,000 apocalyptic Jewish evangelists as those "who have not defiled themselves with women . . . *they are virgins*. It is these who follow the Lamb wherever he goes. These have been redeemed from mankind as firstfruits for God and the Lamb, and in their mouth no lie was found, for they are blameless" (Rev. 14:4-5). Interestingly, the impetus for the celibacy of the 144,000 evangelists is the same as that mentioned by Jesus and Paul—that is, greater devotion to the Lord, or in the words of the seer, to "follow the Lamb wherever he goes." Overall, then, singleness is viewed positively throughout the New Testament from the Gospels to Revelation.

A second observation that arises from a reading of Jesus' and Paul's statements on singleness is that not only is celibacy a divine *gift*, it is also a divine calling that is both limited to the select *few* and freely *chosen* rather than foisted upon the individual by his or her circumstances or condition. To quote Jesus' remarks introducing and concluding his pronouncement on being a eunuch for the kingdom of heaven, "Not everyone can receive this saying, but only those to whom it is given. . . . Let the one who is able to receive this receive it" (Matt. 19:11-12). Jesus' words seem to indicate that it takes special grace from God for individuals called to singleness for the sake of God's kingdom to recognize this calling.

The apostle Paul, writing to the Corinthians, casts the issue as follows: "But because of the temptation to sexual immorality, each man should have his own wife and each woman her own husband. . . . *But if they cannot exercise self-control,* they should marry. For it is better to marry than to be aflame with passion. . . . But if you do marry, you have not sinned . . ." (1 Cor. 7:2, 9, 28). Clearly, then, while singleness is a positive condition in which Christians are free to remain if they are unmarried, especially if they are so gifted, it is wrong to expect someone to adopt a life of singleness against their will.[21] Indeed, as Paul later wrote to Timothy, forbidding marriage is one of the "teachings of demons" (cf. 1 Tim. 4:1-3).

SINGLENESS IN THE EARLY CHURCH

It is a remarkable fact that some of the most important protagonists of early Christianity (including possibly the apostle Paul) were single.[22] While it is reasonably clear that Paul was celibate throughout most, if not all, of his apostolic career (see esp. 1 Cor. 7:8: "unmarried, as I am"),[23] some have suggested that he may have been widowed[24] or abandoned by his (unbelieving) wife after his conversion to Christianity.[25] However, the evidence for a former marriage of Paul is entirely circumstantial. Paul himself does not address this subject, and in the end we must confess that "[w]e simply do not know."[26] In any case, Paul's unmarried state during most, if not all, of his apostolic career enabled this strategically called man to spearhead the Gentile mission in a way that a married man probably never could have. His frequent travels and imprisonments also would have put great strains on a marriage. By contrast, many of the other apostles had wives (cf. 1 Cor. 9:5, where Paul, too, asserts in principle the right to have a wife).

Singleness in the Old and the New Testament

	OLD TESTAMENT	NEW TESTAMENT
VIEW ON SINGLENESS	In light of Gen. 2:24, marriage is treated as the norm; singleness is generally viewed as undesirable	Marriage is still considered the norm, but in view of kingdom concerns singleness is presented as an advantageous state for those who are called to it
CATEGORIES OF SINGLENESS	Widow	A gift given by God; not required of all (1 Cor. 7:7)
	Eunuch	
	Those who could not marry for reasons of disease or economic difficulty	
	Divine call	A calling extended by God and accepted by those so called (Matt. 19:11-12)
	Divorcee	
	Young men and women prior to marriage	

In keeping with contemporary Jewish custom, married men, with their wives' permission, could leave home to study with a rabbi, as Jesus' disciples did (Mark 1:18-20; 10:28-29 par.). Paul also recognizes that spouses may temporarily refrain from sexual relations "by mutual consent and for a time" for the purpose of extended prayer (1 Cor. 7:5, NIV)—undoubtedly a seldom invoked exception in most Christian marriages.[27] However, Paul urges marriage partners to resume sexual relations after this brief period of abstinence so that Satan will not tempt them because of their lack of self-control. Demonstrably, however, as mentioned, celibacy was not the norm for the apostles (1 Cor. 9:5).[28]

As with the apostles, in the early centuries of the church singleness was the exception, not the rule. Although there were some notable proponents of celibacy, such as the third-century Alexandrian theologian

Origen,[29] most of the leaders in the early church were married, and they frequently taught on the goodness of marriage. However, due to a convergence of factors—including Gnostic Greek philosophy that exalted the spirit over the body, the ascetic doctrine of certain quasi-Christian groups such as the Manicheans, and the Roman church's growing desire to centralize its power base—celibacy was gradually accepted and subsequently exalted by the church.[30] Indeed, as early as the end of the fourth century, many local church councils began to request and then to require that clergy remain single, and celibacy was mandated for all church leadership at the First Lateran Council in 1123.

This slide toward the idealization of singleness (or, as the Roman Catholic Church would put it, "being married to the Church") can be seen in the growth of the institutions of monasticism and nunnery throughout the first millennium of church history, as well as in the evolving writings of some of the most prominent theologians of the church. The fifth-century church father Augustine, for example, when writing on sexual intercourse in marriage, noted that marriage is good and that "a man and his wife could play their active and passive roles in the drama of conception without the lecherous promptings of lust."[31] While Augustine believed that lust often taints intercourse, and that procreation must be the aim of sex, he asserted that the act itself is nonetheless good within the sanctified bonds of marriage. Augustine even appealed to the sexual intercourse between Adam and Eve in the Garden of Eden as a paradigm for Christian marriage partners to emulate.

By the twelfth century, however, when writing about sexual intercourse in marriage, Thomas Aquinas noted, "Even married sex, adorned with all the honorableness of marriage, carries with it a certain shame. . . . Now virginity is defined by a moral integrity. . . . Without a doubt then the state of virginity is preferable."[32] While Aquinas believed marriage to be honorable, in accord with then-contemporary church doctrine he considered singleness to be the more desirable state. However, Aquinas's belief that married sex "carries with it a certain shame" stands in direct conflict with Scripture, which says that "everything created by God is good, and nothing is to be rejected if it is received with thanksgiving" (1 Tim. 4:4). According to Genesis 1:31, God viewed the creation of humanity as male and female as "very good," and in 2:18, God is shown to consider the man's condition without a woman to be "not good."

SUMMARY

Before discussing various issues related to singleness, it may be helpful to summarize the major findings of our survey of singleness in the Old and New Testament and in the early church. Our study of the Old Testament teaching on singleness surfaced six categories of single people: (1) widows or widowers; (2) eunuchs; (3) those who could not marry because of disease or economic difficulty; (4) those who remained unmarried because of a divine call; (5) the divorced; and (6) young men and women prior to marriage.

Virtually all of these categories continue in the New Testament era.[33] Yet while singleness in Old Testament times seems to have been uncommon and often involuntary, the New Testament features statements by both Jesus and Paul commending the advantages of singleness for kingdom service. Jesus says that some are "eunuchs for the sake of the kingdom of heaven" (Matt. 19:12), while Paul calls celibacy a "gift from God" (1 Cor. 7:7) and proceeds to elaborate on ways in which singleness may promote "undivided devotion to the Lord" (vv. 32-35, NIV).

As in Old and New Testament times, marriage continued to be the norm in the early church (e.g., 1 Cor. 9:5), with the notable exception of the apostle Paul, who was unmarried at least throughout most (if not all) of his apostolic ministry. A few centuries subsequent to the Christian era, however, a convergence of factors—such as Gnostic Greek dualism elevating the spirit over the body, or the asceticism of quasi-Christian groups such as the Manicheans—led to the gradual exaltation of singleness as spiritually superior to marriage.

Although church leaders such as Augustine affirmed that marriage is honorable and sex is good within the bonds of marriage, the late patristic and medieval periods witnessed a trend toward exalting singleness. By the twelfth century A.D. celibacy was mandated for all church leadership, and Thomas Aquinas went on record as believing that even sex within marriage carries with it a certain shame, while virginity conveys moral integrity and is thus preferable. We move now to a discussion of issues related to singleness in our day, followed by a study of biblical teaching on singleness addressed to various groups.

ISSUES RELATED TO SINGLENESS

Singleness and Ministry

In contrast to the Roman Catholic Church, which requires celibacy of all its priests (ostensibly because Jesus himself was unmarried), evangelicals do not view celibacy as a ministerial requirement. Since in their view church leaders do not embody Christ in a sacramental sense (administering mass following the pattern of Old Testament priestly service), there is correspondingly no need for them to refrain from sexual relations in order to remain ritually pure. Thus, singleness is considered to be a gift given by God to the select few, rather than a requirement for all ministers.[34]

Applied to the contemporary context, singleness should be recognized as a gift for the select few that holds significant *advantages for ministry,* but is neither *intrinsically superior* nor *inferior* to the institution of marriage. While Paul assumes that church officers as a rule will be married (1 Tim. 3:2, 12; Titus 1:6) and considers marriage and the family to be a training and proving ground for prospective church leaders (1 Tim. 3:4-5; cf. 1 Tim. 3:15), this should not be construed as a requirement.[35] The church needs both its single and its married members. While in most churches married couples with children make up the fabric of the congregation, married people should treat single people as full and rightful members of their congregation.

This is imperative all the more as singles are privileged to devote themselves more fully to kingdom service, including studying the Scriptures, praying for others' needs, and serving in a variety of strategic roles (including that of missionaries). Socially, married people should include singles in their activities and gathering as part of Christian love and brotherhood. Single individuals, for their part, ought to find their sufficiency in Christ and in serving him. Nevertheless, unless a single person feels satisfied in this state, it is likely that God will eventually lead that person to get married, which is the primary divinely instituted pattern of human relationships in the Old Testament and is reaffirmed in the New.

Cohabitation and Premarital Sex

Apart from loneliness, one of the greatest temptations that singles face is the temptation to illegitimate sexual intercourse. Doubtless this is one of the reasons why the last several decades have seen a marked rise in cohabitation without marriage as well as in the practice of premarital sex.[36] It clearly follows from biblical teaching, however, that both cohabitation and premarital sex are violations of God's design for male-female relationships.[37] In fact, in biblical times, Jews regarded a woman's premarital sexual activity as tantamount to prostitution, the penalty for consensual sex with a person to whom one was not married frequently being death[38] or divorce.[39]

As we have argued, Scripture presents marriage as a sacred, inviolable, and exclusive relationship between one man and one woman, properly entered into by the mutual pledge of lifelong marital faithfulness and consummated by sexual relations, which constitutes the marriage as a "one-flesh" union (Gen. 2:23-24). According to Jesus, the marital union constitutes the man and the woman as no longer two but one, having been joined together by none other than God (Matt. 19:6; Mark 10:8-9). Paul maintains that even sexual intercourse with a prostitute results in a one-flesh union, albeit an illegitimate one (1 Cor. 6:15-17, referring to Gen. 2:24; cf. Eph. 5:31).[40] The same is true for any form of sexual intercourse outside of a monogamous marriage relationship.[41]

Some may argue that the situation is different for engaged couples, because in this case a couple is planning to be united in marriage in the future. What harm is done, it may be argued, if a future husband and wife engage in sexual activity with each other prior to marriage, since they have every intention to pledge mutual loyalty to one another in any case? Yet apart from the fact that there are no guarantees and the engagement may end up being broken, engaging in premarital sex even to one's future marriage partner is not fully responsible. As one writer aptly characterizes it, premarital sex amounts to *a futile attempt to act as if married while taking more and offering less than married love requires* in terms of "the degree of responsibility and the kind of love and trust and fidelity" husband and wife are called to have for one another.[42]

While it is inevitable that those in the larger culture who are not committed to observing biblical teaching in this area persist in cohabitation or engage in illicit sex, there can be no doubt that this is not an option for believers. *Sexual abstinence prior to marriage* and *sexual faithfulness in marriage* are the biblical expectations, and it is evident that the practice of the former constitutes the best preparation for the observance of the latter.[43] Not only should singles refrain from sexual activity prior to marriage, they should also avoid anything that could potentially lead to it, striving for purity in speech and thought.[44] Women are to display modesty in appearance, and both women and men are called to exercise self-control.[45]

What, then, are the implications for Christians who engage in cohabitation and premarital sex, be it out of ignorance regarding the biblical teaching on this issue or in deliberate, conscious violation of Scripture? And what are the implications for unbelievers who live together without being married and/or practice premarital or extra-marital sex? In the case of genuine believers, if they are members of a local church, those in leadership ought to instruct the young people that Scripture does not permit cohabitation and premarital sex and exhort them to stop sinning against the Lord in this way. If the exhortation goes unheeded, church discipline ought to be exercised.

In the case of unbelievers, their primary need is turning away from their sin and trusting Christ as their Lord and Savior, which transcends the issue of cohabitation and premarital sex. Nevertheless, God may desire to use this particular sin in these people's lives to call them to repentance and faith, and, where possible, believers whose relationship with the couple permits this ought to take the opportunity to address the issue with this non-Christian couple, "in the hope that God will grant them repentance leading them to a knowledge of the truth, and that they will come to their senses and escape from the trap of the devil, who has taken them captive to do his will" (2 Tim. 2:25-26, NIV).

Courtship and Dating

In ancient Israel, the betrothal between a young man and a young woman was viewed as akin to marriage (except for sexual intercourse, which was reserved for the latter) and hence breaking the betrothal required the issuing of a formal divorce.[46] With regard to the selection of a mate and specific betrothal and wedding customs, in biblical times marriages were often negotiated by the parents of a future couple. The pre-marital arrangements included the provision of a dowry or bride price,[47] but not courtship or dating in the modern sense. Hence, the primary role in making proper arrangements for a young couple's marriage fell to the parents, while the young people's involvement was much more limited.[48]

In contemporary Western culture the pendulum has swung to the other extreme. Often parents have virtually no say in whom their son or daughter chooses to marry (though parents are often still expected to pay for their daughter's wedding). The fact that today many delay entering into the state of marriage in order to pursue a course of education results in a prolonged time period during which young people are neither a close part of their original family nor yet part of a new family which they may one day establish. This places them in a position of independence and lack of accountability that can have disastrous consequences especially if they are inadequately prepared for the exercise of this freedom. Also, since premarital sex and cohabitation are widely practiced,[49] modern wedding ceremonies often tend to be anticlimactic.

One of the key issues in this area is what constitutes true love. Young people often say that they cannot help with whom they "fall in love," and Hollywood has done its fair share to perpetuate the stereotype that love has a pull or power over people that is impossible or futile to resist. If this were true, of course, it would excuse any number of actions, including premarital sex, adultery, divorce, and perhaps even homosexuality or rape.[50] In each of these cases, if the call to love is irresistible and excuses irresponsible actions, love (so defined) becomes the supreme ethical principle that overrules all other moral considerations.

Over against this travesty of love, Scripture sets the ideal of human love that is other-centered, self-sacrificial, and focused on the true inner person rather than on changing external characteristics (see esp. 1 Corinthians 13; cf. Prov. 31:30). This is the love husbands are called to exercise toward their wives, a love that is patterned after Christ's love for the church (Eph. 5:25-30). Not only does the pursuit and exercise of this kind of love make a difference in what one will look for in a mate, it will also make all the difference in one's marriage relationship. True love will wait to have sex until marriage and will seek to uphold the dignity of the other person.

The book of Proverbs makes clear that finding a God-fearing wife is a special blessing from the Lord (Prov. 18:22). What young men ought to look for in a prospective wife is not so much beauty as godly character and a gentle and quiet spirit (1 Pet. 3:3-4). The apostle Paul teaches that Christians should be careful not to enter into close relationships with persons of the opposite sex who are not believers (cf. 1 Cor. 7:39; 2 Cor. 6:14). To be sure, we have all heard stories of people who ended up leading their future spouses to the Lord, but to presume upon the Lord's will in this regard would be to put the Lord to the test (Matt. 4:7 par. Luke 4:12, citing Deut. 6:16), which is not a godly thing to do.

We have no direct biblical command dealing with the question (often asked by Christians today) whether or not dating is appropriate for Christians and, if so, at what age.[51] Young men and women certainly should respect their parents' wisdom in setting reasonable parameters in this regard and trust the Lord that in his good time, if he wants them to marry, he will bring their future spouse across their path. Older singles would be wise to spend their time in ministry and service and in the company of other mature singles and couples in groups to avoid the challenges that more intimate settings might present. If God cares for us and is intimately involved in every facet of our lives—and he is—will he not also actively guide us in this very important area? Many of us can gratefully attest to the fact that he does.

BIBLICAL TEACHING ON SINGLENESS ADDRESSED TO PARTICULAR GROUPS

While Scripture at times addresses the issue of singleness in general, there are other times when it has a specific message to a particular group of single people. Under the present heading we will survey, in turn, biblical injunctions focused on the following groups: young men; young women; widows or widowers; single parents; and divorcees.

Young Men

The Scriptures have much to say to young (and often unmarried) men. In the Old Testament young men are addressed throughout the book of Proverbs. As mentioned in the previous chapter, young men are warned against falling into the trap of the adulterous woman and exhorted to guard their hearts in all purity. Examples of fine and godly young single men include Joseph, Samuel, David, Solomon, and Daniel and his friends, to name but a few.

God-fearing Joseph eluded the grasp of Potiphar's wife when she made sexual advances (Gen. 39:12). Young Samuel assisted Eli the priest and was "ministering before the LORD" at Shiloh (1 Sam. 2:18), and "the young man Samuel grew in the presence of the LORD" (1 Sam. 2:21; cf. 2:26). David faithfully tended his father's flock (1 Sam. 16:11) even after he had been anointed by Samuel as the future king of Israel (v. 19) and rendered devoted service to king Saul (16:21-23) even though Saul later sought to kill him (18:10-11). One of Saul's servants described David as one "who is skillful in playing, a man of valor, a man of war, prudent in speech, and a man of good presence, and the LORD is with him" (16:18). Solomon, David's son, ruled wisely, was used by the Lord, and established his kingdom even in his younger years (1 Kings 2:12, 27, 46).

Daniel and his friends were among the "youths without blemish, of good appearance and skillful in all wisdom, endowed with knowledge, understanding learning, and competent to stand in the king's palace" (Dan. 1:4). In his wisdom and understanding, as well as in his integrity and diplomacy, young Daniel was without peer (1:8-21). Among the numerous negative examples of ungodly young men are Joseph's brothers (who in their jealousy sold him into slavery, Gen. 37:12-36), Eli's sons (who had sexual relations with women serving at the entrance to the tent of meeting and ignored their father's words, 1 Sam. 2:22-25) and king Rehoboam's peers (who foolishly counseled him to respond harshly to people's request to lighten their load, 1 Kings 12:8-11).

In the New Testament, Jesus' training of the twelve (though they were not necessarily single, such as Peter; cf. Matt. 8:14 and parallels) offers ample lessons for young men who may be given to impetuousness (Peter, e.g., Matt. 16:22; 17:4), overzealousness (James and John; cf. Luke 9:54), cynicism or skepticism (Thomas; cf. John 11:16; 20:25), or competitiveness (endemic among the twelve; e.g., Matt. 20:20-24 par. Mark 10:35-41). In Paul's writings, Timothy (who admittedly was probably not single, though the New Testament is silent in this regard) is instructed not to let anyone look down on his youth but to set an example in speech, conduct, love, faith, and purity (1 Tim. 4:12). Paul's foremost disciple is to cleanse himself from anything dishonorable and to be set apart and useful to his Master, ready for every good work (2 Tim. 2:21). To this end he must "flee youthful passions and pursue righteousness, faith, love, and peace, along with those who call on the Lord from a pure heart" (2 Tim. 2:22).

Paul also issues repeated warnings against appointing new converts to positions of church leadership (1 Tim. 3:6; 5:22). If appointed prematurely, such a person may "become puffed up with conceit and fall into the condemnation of the devil" (3:6; young men's need for humility and submissiveness to older men is emphasized also by the apostle Peter: see 1 Pet. 5:5). This highlights the spiritual dimension of a young man's life and his potential for service in the church. Young men hold particular promise and potential for good in the kingdom, but they also have pronounced points of vulnerability, which Satan will seek to attack in order to render them ineffective.

As mentioned previously, one of the primary areas of vulnerability for young men (especially those who are single) is that of *sexual temptation*. While young Christian women are enjoined in Scripture to dress modestly (see below), the fact is that, both in the larger culture and also in the church, this is often not the case. The media display a deluge of lascivious and sexually tempting material, and in the age of the internet pornography it is only a few mouse clicks away.[52] Many young men also struggle with masturbation.[53] It is essential that they are not only committed to maintaining purity in thought and conduct but that they have a plan to guard themselves against succumbing to sexual temptation. Such a plan may include (but not be limited to) the following steps.

First, they would be wise to *pray and trust God* (rather than themselves) to deliver them from temptation (Matt. 6:13; Luke 11:4; Matt. 26:36, 40-41 and parallels). The Psalms are replete with the desperate cry of the righteous: "Lord, deliver me!" As did the disciples in the Garden of Gethsemane, young men must realize that while the spirit is willing, the flesh is weak (Matt. 26:41). They will not be able to resist temptation in their own strength; they must look to God and appropriate his power to strengthen them in their hour of temptation. For God is faithful:

Therefore let anyone who thinks that he stands take heed lest he fall. No temptation has overtaken you that is not common to man. God is faithful, and he will not let you be tempted beyond your ability, but with the temptation he will also provide the way of escape, that you may be able to endure it (1 Cor. 10:12-13).

Not only is God faithful, Jesus Christ our Lord can help us when we are tempted: "For because he himself has suffered when tempted, he is able to help those who are being tempted" (Heb. 2:18). Nevertheless, it is important to be proactive and to pray ahead of time before being faced with temptation so that "having done all," we may be able to stand (Eph. 6:13). If caught unprepared, resisting temptation may be too difficult.

Second, young men should aspire to *grow strong in the Lord and the knowledge of his Word.* In this way they will develop the true confidence that they are strong, that God's Word lives in them, and that, in Christ, they have overcome the evil one (1 John 2:12, 14; cf. Prov. 20:29). When faced with temptation, Jesus showed himself to be one who was intimately acquainted with God's Word and who was able to use it effectively to counter Satan's schemes (Matt. 4:1-11; Luke 4:1-13).

Third, young men must make every effort to *cultivate the virtues of self-control* (Titus 2:6; cf. 1 Tim. 3:2; Titus 1:8) and *purity of heart* (1 Tim. 4:12; 2 Tim. 2:22). Self-control (much-praised in the book of Proverbs) is a trait of spiritual maturity and a result of years of practice. As the writer of Hebrews points out, "solid food is for the mature, for those who have their powers of discernment trained by constant practice to distinguish good from evil" (Heb. 5:14). Purity of heart is commended by our Lord as the kingdom quality by which we will see God (Matt. 5:8). This means that we must not love the world or the things in the world— the desires of the flesh and the desires of the eyes and pride in possessions—for the world with its desires is passing away (1 John 2:15-17).

Fourth, young men should *seek the company and accountability of other, like-minded male believers* in this critical area. Paul tells Timothy to flee youthful passions and to pursue Christian virtues "along with those who call on the Lord from a pure heart" (2 Tim. 2:22). If we want to successfully guard against sexual temptation, we must live in accountable relationships with other like-minded men in the church.

Fifth, if young men understand that the *temptation is not the sin,* then they can more appropriately prepare for temptation and will less likely be overcome by it when it occurs. As the writer of Hebrews reminds us, even Jesus "in every respect has been tempted as we are, yet without sin" (Heb. 4:15). This makes clear that it is not sin to be confronted with temptation, but only to succumb to it. All of us will be tempted many times in a day, and sexual temptation (especially for young men) will be among the most potent challenges we face. According to the apostle Peter, the devil is prowling around like a roaring lion, seeking whom he may devour (1 Pet. 5:8). Yet we are called to resist him, firm in our faith (1 Pet. 5:9).

Sixth, *when we do sin,* we should realize that *God stands ready to forgive* (1 John 1:9; 2:1). Rather than being immobilized by guilt, we ought to confess our sins and experience God's cleansing and renewal and move on in full assurance that forgiveness is always available in Christ. "Let us then with confidence draw near to the throne of grace, that we may receive mercy and find grace to help in time of need" (Heb. 4:16). Obviously, this does not mean we should presume on God's grace. As Paul wrote, "Are we to continue in sin that grace may abound [as he was accused of teaching]? By no means! How can we who died to sin still live in it?" (Rom. 6:2). Now that we have been set free from sin, we ought to present the members of our body as instruments of righteousness (vv. 15-23).

Seventh, being on guard against sexual temptation does *not* mean young men should be *paranoid* toward young women or avoid them (as first-century Jewish rabbis taught and practiced). This would be rude and disrespectful. To the contrary, Timothy (a young man) is told by the apostle to treat older women like mothers and *younger women like sisters, "in all purity"* (1 Tim. 5:2). Hence, younger men are not to shun younger women but to love them as their sisters in the Lord.

Eighth and finally, *do not overestimate your ability to resist temptation nor underestimate the power of the temptation and the tempter himself.* If your power is too small and the temptation too great, do what Joseph did when approached by Potiphar's wife (Genesis 39)—take flight while you can!

This list is certainly not exhaustive, but it illustrates young men's need to develop a concerted strategy in dealing with sexual temptation. Satan is out to destroy our witness and to inflict damage on our ability to advance God's kingdom. Unless we take proper steps to march together in this area, we are bound to become one of the many casualties and will prove ineffective rather than being "set apart as holy" and "useful to the master . . . , ready for every good work" (2 Tim. 2:21).

We close this section with a pertinent quote from Paul's letter to the Romans:

> The night is far gone; the day is at hand. So then let us cast off the works of darkness and put on the armor of light. Let us walk properly as in the daytime, not in orgies and drunkenness, not in sexual immorality and sensuality, not in quarreling and jealousy. But put on the Lord Jesus Christ, and *make no provision for the flesh, to gratify its desires* (Rom. 13:12-14).

Young Women

Most of the biblical material relating to women is addressed to married women. We have already provided a fairly extensive discussion of Paul's instructions to both older and younger married women in the chapter on the Christian family (chapter 6) above. Especially since women in biblical times usually got married at an early age, and because girls typically moved directly from their father's jurisdiction and household to that of her new husband, there was comparatively less of a need for New Testament authors to provide explicit instructions for young women prior to marriage. This explains why the present section is considerably shorter than that dealing with younger men above.

While the biblical passages addressed specifically to young men focus on the need for self-control and on guarding against sexual temptation, Scripture's primary emphasis with regard to women (including those who are young) is that of *modesty in appearance* (1 Tim. 2:9-10; 1 Pet. 3:3-6; though self-control is repeatedly mentioned as well: see 1 Tim. 2:9, 15; Titus 2:3, 5).[54] According to the apostle Paul, "women should adorn themselves in respectable apparel, with modesty and self-control, not with braided hair and gold or pearls or costly attire, but with what is proper for women who profess godliness—with good works" (1 Tim. 2:9-10). This does not mean that women must not wear any jewelry or cannot ever braid their hair. Rather, their focus ought to be on developing spiritual virtues and on devoting themselves to good works.

The apostle Peter echoes the spirit of Paul's instructions when he writes, "Do not let your adorning be external—the braiding of hair, the wearing of gold, or the putting on of clothing—but let your adorning be the hidden person of the heart with the imperishable beauty of a gentle and quiet spirit, which in God's sight is very precious" (1 Pet. 3:3-4). As the "excellent wife" of Proverbs 31 is well aware, "Charm is deceitful, and beauty is vain, but a woman who fears the LORD is to be praised" (Prov. 31:30). Prominent biblical examples of modest, God-fearing women are Ruth (Ruth 2:10, 13; 3:7, 14) and Jesus' mother Mary (Luke 1:34, 38).

Modesty is not limited to the issue of what kinds of clothes women wear. It extends also to non-verbal cues, mannerisms, suggestive behavior, and acting aggressively and taking improper initiative. Modesty does not mean wearing only dull, unfashionable clothes, shunning makeup or perfume, or remaining silent in the company of the opposite sex. Just as wealth is not bad in itself (but only the *love* of money, 1 Tim. 6:10; cf. Matt. 6:24), so physical beauty is not bad—it is the gift of God. Yet, like wealth, beauty should be viewed as a stewardship from God and should be accompanied by wisdom and discretion (Prov. 11:22).

Widows or Widowers

Another group of unmarried men and women that receives special treatment in Scripture is widows and widowers.[55] "Widowhood could be a severe test in the Greco-Roman world, since women were usually not the direct heirs of their husband's wills. Rather, the widow had her dowry as well as any stipulation which the testator made for her care to his heirs. . . . If the son or sons did not care for their mother (or often, their step-mother), the woman could be in a dire condition if her dowry was not substantial."[56] According to James, pure religion is therefore this: "to look after orphans and widows in their distress" (James 1:27, NIV).[57]

Widows were vulnerable to those who would prey on them and exploit their situation for financial gain. Jesus denounced the Jewish religious leaders for "devouring widows' houses" (Mark 12:40 par. Luke 20:47). One of the best-known widows in Scripture is the unnamed woman who threw her widow's mite into the temple treasury and was praised by Jesus for her devotion (Mark 12:41-44 par. Luke 21:1-4). Of the evangelists, it is Luke who shows a particular interest in widows. He features Anna, a widow who prophesied regarding the infant Jesus (Luke 2:36-38); preserves Jesus' reference to the widow in Zarephath in Elijah's day (4:25-26; cf. 1 Kings 17:8-24); records the story of the raising of a widow's son (Luke 7:12); and includes the parable of the persistent widow (18:1-8). Jesus cared for widows, and so should his followers.

Care for widows was also an important part of the ministry of the early church. Seven mature men from among the congregation were appointed in order to ensure that the Greek-speaking widows were not neglected in the daily distribution of food (Acts 6:1-6). Widows were a recognized group of people among the first Christians (9:39, 41). The apostle Paul addresses the church's responsibility to provide for "true" widows (1 Timothy 5:3-16, which includes guidelines on identifying widows worthy of support). "Honoring" such widows is presented as an application of the fifth commandment (cited by Paul in Eph. 6:2) and does not merely involve the paying of respect but also has a material dimension. The widows Timothy is instructed to honor are, literally, "widows who are truly widows" (1 Tim. 5:5, 16), that is, widows who meet the following qualifications.

First, such a widow has *no relatives to care for her,* be it children, grandchildren, or other descendants (1 Tim. 5:4). If she does, they are to support her. This is how they are to learn to put their religion into practice: by (literally) "returning payments" to their parents and grandparents (cf. 2 Tim. 1:3). Caring for one's kin is pleasing to God—as a practical outworking of the fifth commandment to honor one's father and mother—as is living peaceful and quiet lives in all godliness and holiness (cf. 1 Tim. 2:3). It is all too easy to relinquish to the church this responsibility of caring for family members. Yet church funds ought to be reserved for the most needy and those who have no natural relations to assist them materially.

Second, a "true widow" who is "left alone"—that is, without relatives to care for her—in order to prove herself worthy of the church's support, *puts her hope in God* (1 Tim. 5:5; cf. 4:10; 6:17). She does so by continuing in entreaties and prayers (cf. 1 Tim. 5:5) "night and day."[58] Conversely, the "true widow" does *not indulge in a pleasure-seeking lifestyle* (1 Tim. 5:6; cf. James 5:5), as some of the younger widows seem to have done (1 Tim. 5:13). Those widows are spiritually "dead" even while still alive physically (1 Tim 5:6; contrast Rom. 8:10; John 11:25).

In addition to the above requirements, third, Paul also establishes an *age limit:* in order to be eligible for church support, widows must be at least sixty years old (1 Tim. 5:9), presumably because at that age remarriage was unlikely and/or because women under sixty were considered capable of working. This kept the list reasonably short, especially since life expectancy was limited (today, in the age of retirement benefits and social security [see further below], the age limit may correspondingly be set higher). Younger widows should remarry (1 Tim. 5:11-15; cf. 1 Cor. 7:8-9).

Not only is such a widow to live in prayerful dependence on God (1 Tim. 5:5), she must, fourth, have been *"faithful to her [deceased] husband"* (5:9, NIV; cf. 3:2, 12; Titus 1:6; contra most other versions, which have some variation of "having been the wife of one man"). Also, fifth, a widow must be *well-known for her good deeds,* of which five are singled out explicitly (1 Tim. 5:10):

(1) bringing up children (cf. 1 Tim. 2:15);
(2) showing hospitality (cf. Rom. 12:13; Heb. 13:2; 1 Pet. 4:9), presumably opening her home to traveling believers, particularly teachers (3 John 5-8);
(3) "washing the feet of the saints" (an idiom for humble service, based on Jesus' literal washing of his disciples feet; see John 13; cf. Phil. 2:1-11);
(4) helping those in trouble (*thlibō*, denoting various kinds of distress; e.g., 2 Cor. 1:6; 4:8); and
(5) devoting herself to all kinds of good deeds, a catch-all category frequently used in Paul (2 Cor. 9:8; Col. 1:10; 2 Thess. 2:17; 1 Tim. 2:10; 6:18; 2 Tim. 2:21; 3:17; Titus 1:16; 3:1).

These standards for widows, most of which relate to the domestic sphere, are very high, in some ways even reminiscent of the requirements for church leaders (cf. 1 Tim. 3:1-13). By adhering to this rule, Timothy will ensure that the church assists only women worthy of support and that available funds are used for those who have no other means of support and who meet criteria of Christian maturity.

Younger widows, for their part, ought not to be held to a pledge of singleness which they may not be able to keep—and thus incur judgment—when their sensual desires overcome their devotion to Christ (1 Tim. 5:11-12). As Paul states elsewhere, it is better to marry than to burn (1 Cor. 7:9). Moreover, unmarried younger widows may get into the habit of being idle (1 Tim. 5:13; cf. Titus 1:12) and going about from house to house, turning into gossips (cf. 3 John 10) and busybodies (cf. 2 Thess. 3:11), saying things they ought not to (like the false teachers: cf. Titus 1:11).

Thus Paul's advice to younger widows is to remarry, care for their children, manage their homes—filling out what is referred to merely as "childbearing" in 1 Timothy 2:15—and to give the enemy no opportunity for slander (1 Tim. 5:14; cf. 2 Cor. 5:12). He ominously concludes that some have already turned away to follow Satan (1 Tim. 5:15), making explicit what is only intimated in 1 Timothy 2:15, that is, they have fallen prey to false teaching.

Paul concludes his instructions concerning widows with an exhortation to believing women to care for widows in their family in order to relieve the church (1 Tim. 5:16). This way the congregation can help those widows who are "true widows," that is, those who meet the qualifications set forth by Paul. Paul's treatment of this question provides a helpful case study of how to deal with a particular issue in the church. While in the age of social security, life insurance, and retirement benefits the landscape has changed considerably, the church must continue to properly care for those widows who have no other means of support. Caring for widows and other needy individuals is one important way in which the church can reflect the gracious heart of God and the compassion and mercy of the Lord Jesus Christ.

Single Parents

Single parents may be those who had one or several children without marrying their partner, divorcees, or widows/widowers.[59] This group is faced with several challenges: (1) a need to provide for their child or children materially while being available to nurture them emotionally and spiritually as a parent; (2) the lack of a spouse, which leaves the child or children without a primary role model of one sex, be it male or female; and (3) a variety of other needs and challenges.

Paul's above-cited advice to younger widows would seem to apply also to single parents at large, namely that, if possible, they ought to remarry in order to lighten their load both materially and with regard to their parenting task.[60] As with singles who are not parents, the church should include single parents in its social gatherings to help alleviate the gap opened up by the absence of one parent in this family. If no other family members are able to offer financial assistance, the church may also need to provide material help and other support.

Divorcees

Divorcees are yet another group that makes up the amorphous category of "singles." We will discuss the question of possible biblical exceptions for divorce in chapter 11 below. In chapter 12 we will deal with the issue of whether or not divorced men are eligible to serve as church leaders in cases of biblically legitimate divorces (if, indeed, we find that there are such cases).

Believers should come alongside divorcees and offer support and encouragement. The costs of divorce are high, and divorces leave many scars that require healing, both for the divorced person and for any children of divorce.[61] Divorce is not the unpardonable sin, and forgiveness is always available in Christ, even though there will still be consequences with which the divorced person will have to cope.

If the way in which Jesus dealt with the adulterous woman is any indication, our Lord would have us deal even with the guilty party of a divorce with compassion, grace, and mercy rather than a judgmental attitude. There are many ministries open to divorced people in the church, and divorcees should serve as an integral part of the body of Christ. As in many other areas, the church ought to set the example in dealing with divorcees in a redemptive manner.[62]

PRACTICAL IMPLICATIONS

What, then, are some of the practical implications of singleness?[63] First, singles (as well as married people) need to keep in mind the fact that *the married state is not the final destiny of anyone* (Matt. 22:30; cf. Rom. 7:3; 1 Cor. 7:39). Rather, when we arrive in God's presence, like the angels who are currently before the throne in heaven, we will worship God for all eternity free from the bonds of human marriage. This is because as members of the body of Christ, all believers are ultimately betrothed to the Lamb to be with him and to glorify him forever (Isa. 43:7; 1 Cor. 10:31; 2 Cor. 11:2).

Second, in view of our ultimate destiny and our current betrothal to Christ, *it is imperative that singles remain content,* for as the apostle Paul wrote, "There is great gain in godliness with contentment" (1 Tim. 6:6; cf. Phil. 4:11). Or, in other words, when singles display habitual discontentment with their present marital status, they communicate to a watching world that Jesus is insufficient for them or that perhaps he is incapable of meeting their desires (or unaware of them). This ever-present duty to cultivate contentment is one of the reasons why Paul could write to the Corinthians, "I think that in view of the present distress it is good for a person to remain as he is. Are you bound to a wife? Do not seek to be free. Are you free from a wife? Do not seek a wife. But if you do marry, you have not sinned, and if a betrothed woman marries, she has not sinned. Yet those who marry will have worldly troubles, and I would spare you that" (1 Cor. 7:26-28).

Third, single people ought to keep in mind the fact that all who forsake marriage and family in the present world for the sake of God are in this life *rewarded with new family in the Body of Christ,* as well as with an eternal family in the kingdom of heaven (cf. Luke 18:28-30). As Isaiah wrote, "Let not the eunuch say, 'Behold, I am a dry tree.' For thus says the LORD, 'To the eunuchs who keep my Sabbaths, who choose the things that please me and hold fast my covenant, I will give in my house and within my walls a monument and a name better than sons and daughters; I will give them an everlasting name that shall not be cut off'" (Isa. 56:3-5).

CONCLUSION

In the present chapter we have investigated singleness in the Old and New Testament and in the early church. We have also explored issues related to singleness, such as singleness and ministry, cohabitation and premarital sex, and courtship and dating; we have studied biblical teaching on singleness addressed to particular groups, such as young men, young women, widows or widowers, single parents, and divorcees; and we have drawn some practical implications.

Our survey of the Old Testament teaching on singleness surfaced six categories: widows or widowers; eunuchs; those who could not marry because of disease or economic difficulty; those who remained unmarried because of a divine call; the divorced; and young men and women prior to marriage. Virtually all of those categories continue in the New Testament era (though Jesus uses "eunuchs" in a figurative rather than literal sense in Matt. 19:12). Nevertheless, an interesting dynamic can be observed throughout Scripture. While singleness was *not in view at God's creation of humanity,* and was *somewhat uncommon and often undesirable in Old Testament times, in the New Testament both Jesus and Paul speak positively of the advantages for Christian ministry afforded by singleness,* and *according to Jesus' teaching there will be no marriage in heaven.* Hence we notice a progression from *no singleness* (creation) to *singleness as an uncommon and often undesirable phenomenon* (Old Testament times) to *singleness as an advantageous state for ministry* (New Testament) to *universal singleness* (the final state). How can we account for this development?

A Biblical Theology of Singleness: From Creation to the Final State

	CREATION	OLD TESTAMENT	NEW TESTAMENT	FINAL STATE
SINGLENESS	Non-existent	Uncommon and generally undesirable	Advantageous for kingdom ministry	Universal
MARRIAGE	The norm	The norm	The norm	No marriage, but "like the angels"

First of all, it should be noted that while this progression may be surprising, there is no actual conflict between the Old and the New Testament or between Jesus and Paul. Underlying the entire biblical record is the notion that, in this life, marriage is the general expectation, while singleness is the exception. Also, as the above biblical survey shows, many of the categories of singleness—widows/widowers, divorced, young men and women prior to marriage, divine call/gift—span both Testaments. If singleness is viewed more positively in the New Testament, this may be at least in part due to the fact that the marriage-less final state casts its shadow forward (the future invading the present, as it were), so that already at the present time what will be the universal state of human beings for eternity has certain advantages for citizens of God's kingdom.[64]

10

ABANDONING NATURAL RELATIONS: THE BIBLICAL VERDICT ON HOMOSEXUALITY

IN PREVIOUS CHAPTERS we surveyed the Creator's plan for marriage and the family, observed the integrated nature of God's design for these institutions, and traced various perversions of the biblical model in the history of Israel. One of the most serious distortions of God's plan for marriage and the family, it was noted, is homosexuality. This sin was a persistent problem in ancient Israel (e.g., Sodom and Gomorrah, the Gibeonites during the time of the judges, the recurring appearance of homosexuals during the reign of ungodly kings, and so on), was manifest in the New Testament world (Rom. 1:24-28; 1 Cor. 6:9-11; 1 Tim. 1:9-10), and continues to be a challenge in twenty-first century society.

As was noted in the opening chapter, homosexuality is an increasing phenomenon in contemporary *culture*. The move toward the official acceptance of homosexuality in modern American society started in 1973, when the American Psychological Association removed homosexuality from its list of psychological diseases in the *Diagnostic and Statistical Manual of Mental Disorders*.[1] In the wake of this decision, homosexuality has gradually gained ground in secular culture to the extent that currently several states are moving toward the recognition of same-sex marriages (or "civil unions"). This trend is cause for concern given that throughout history even non-Christian societies have typically rejected homosexuality.[2]

Not only is secular culture increasingly embracing homosexuality as an alternative lifestyle, however, even many in the church are softening their stance.[3] Some pastors have revealed their homosexual orientation, many of the mainline denominations are vigorously discussing the moral legitimacy of homosexuality, and at least one denomination has elected a practicing homosexual as one of its leaders.[4] Even some of the more conservative evangelical groups are faced with issues related to homosexuality on the local church level.[5] In some cases, they have excluded homosexual-endorsing churches from their fellowships. In other instances, they have produced official statements dealing with this issue.

HOMOSEXUALITY AND THE INTEGRATED NATURE OF MARRIAGE AND THE FAMILY

When compared with the *biblical* pattern of marriage and the family set forth in the opening chapters of Genesis, homosexuality falls short on numerous fronts. First, as the antithesis of *heterosexuality*, homosexuality is at odds with God's design for marriage and the family at its most foundational level. This is made clear by the words of Genesis 2:24, which conceive of marriage in heterosexual rather than homosexual terms: "A *man* [masculine] shall leave his father and his mother and hold fast to his *wife* [feminine], and they [the man and the woman] shall become one flesh."[6]

A second component of the biblical model of marriage that homosexuality violates is its *complementary* nature.[7] According to Genesis 2 and 3—where the man is given charge of his wife, while the woman is placed alongside him as his "suitable helper"—differences in gender role are an essential part of the Creator's design for marriage. These roles were assigned by God at Creation (Gen. 2:18, 20) and were reaffirmed both after the Fall (Gen. 3:16-19) and in New Testament teaching (Eph. 5:22-33; 1 Pet. 3:1-7). Since these marital roles are tied inherently and unalterably to gender, same-sex partners cannot participate in this aspect of biblical marriage.[8]

A third integrated component of God's design for marriage and the family that homosexuality does not fulfill is the *duty to procreate*.[9] As mentioned, procreation is a central element of marriage and undeniably part of the Creator's plan for this vital social institution. This can be seen in the very first commandment ever given by God to the human couple, "Be fruitful and multiply and fill the earth" (Gen. 1:28).[10] By nature, however, homosexuality falls short of this essential component of the biblical/traditional model of marriage and the family, since it precludes reproduction.[11]

Not only does homosexuality fall short of the biblical pattern of marriage with regard to *heterosexuality, complementarity,* and *fertility,* homosexual couples also often do not uphold other aspects of biblical marriage such as *monogamy, fidelity,* and *durability*.[12] The extent of homosexuality's departure from the biblical model of marriage and the family may be one of the reasons why this sin is so severely chastised in Scripture. Indeed, homosexuality does not merely misrepresent or misunderstand God's design for marriage and the family at just *one* point; it rather skews the Creator's model at *almost every* point.[13]

Not surprisingly, therefore, severe punishment is both stipulated for and experienced by homosexual offenders in Scripture. When writing to the Romans, Paul lists homosexuality as one of the undesirable moral consequences of the sin of rejecting God. Not only does Paul reiterate the Old Testament teaching that homosexuality is wrong, he also notes that homosexuality is so "contrary to nature" (Rom. 1:26) that its participants cannot help but be aware of the fact that their actions are incompatible with the Creator's design for marriage and the family—and that this willful rebellion against God renders them ultimately deserving of death.[14]

HOMOSEXUALITY IN THE OLD TESTAMENT[15]

While Scripture alludes or explicitly refers to homosexuality at least two dozen times,[16] the three main sections of Scripture dealing with homosexuality are the account of the destruction of Sodom and Gomorrah in Genesis 18–19; the sexual laws of the Holiness Code in Leviticus 18 and 20; and the apostle Paul's remarks on homosexuality in his letter to the Romans and in his first letters to the Corinthians and to Timothy. As will be seen, each of these biblical passages clearly condemn homosexuality, and it is only by a radical reinterpretation that the scriptural message regarding homosexuality is turned into a positive and accepting stance toward this practice.[17]

Sodom and Gomorrah

The account of the destruction of Sodom and Gomorrah (Gen. 18:17–19:29) is probably the best-known episode in Scripture revealing God's opposition to homosexuality. The account is particularly significant for at least the following three reasons: (1) it is both the first and the most detailed account of God's confrontation of homosexuality; (2) it is the only pre-Mosaic mention of homosexuality in Scripture; and (3) the sin and destruction of Sodom and Gomorrah are frequently cited in Scripture[18]—often clearly in the context of sexual sin—and the account of the Israelite civil war with the tribe of Benjamin, sparked by the homosexual sin of the Gibeonites (Judges 19–21), seems to be structured in such a way as to parallel the events that transpired at Sodom and Gomorrah. It is therefore no wonder that homosexual advocates have devoted considerable attention to this account, for if they can convincingly demonstrate that the transgression that precipitated the ruin of these two cities was not homosexuality, they will have overturned a very important portion of the biblical witness against it.[19]

In the attempt to revise the traditional understanding of the sin of Sodom and Gomorrah, two major new interpretations have been proposed. First, some scholars have suggested that the sin that led to the ruin of these two cities was not homosexuality but rather *gang rape*. Although he was not the first to offer this interpretation, arguably the most influential proponent of this view has been Walter Barnett. In his short yet widely circulated booklet *Homosexuality and the Bible: An Interpretation,* Barnett writes, "The sin of Sodom does not necessarily lie in homosexuality or homosexual behavior. Rather, this wicked thing that Lot enjoins the townspeople not to do is rape, pure and simple, and gang rape at that."[20] Barnett believes that this event, along with the companion account of the Israelite civil war with the Benjamites over the sexual sin of the Gibeonites, may not even have entailed *homosexual* gang rape, but rather *heterosexual* gang rape. He asserts, "Even if the original intent of both the townsmen of Sodom and Gibeah was homosexual rape, obviously both stories are about heterosexual males who indulge in it as sport."[21]

Barnett's view has been very influential and appears in the writings of many other pro-homosexual writers. For example, this interpretation is found in the volume *Is the Homosexual My Neighbor? Another Christian View,* by Letha Scanzoni and Virginia Ramey Mollenkott, who contend, "The Sodom story seems to be focusing on . . . violent gang rape. . . . Violence—forcing sexual activity upon another—is the real point of the story. To put it another way: even if the angels had taken on the form of women for their earthly visitation, the desire of the men of Sodom to rape them would have been every bit as evil in the sight of God."[22] This interpretation, then, teaches that God destroyed Sodom and Gomorrah not because of homosexuality per se, but because of gang rape.

In response, the element of truth in this view should be plainly acknowledged in that the sin of Sodom and Gomorrah did indeed involve the *intent to rape.* These interpreters err, however, in attempting to limit the transgression of these two cities *exclusively* to gang rape and in trying to redefine the intended sin as a form of *heterosexual*-oriented rape. Indeed, identifying the sin that led to the destruction of Sodom and Gomorrah as heterosexual rape seems tenuous at best in light of Jude's statement that the inhabitants of "Sodom and Gomorrah . . . indulged in sexual immorality and *pursued unnatural desire . . . defil[ing] the flesh*" (Jude 6-8; cf. 2 Pet. 2:4-10). In other words, the offenders at Sodom and Gomorrah did not just have *uncontrollable* sexual desires, but *unnatural* sexual desires. Moreover, limiting the definition of the sin of these two cities exclusively to gang rape—be it heterosexual or homosexual—seems problematic in light of the fact that the intended rape never actually occurred. Yet God still destroyed both Sodom and Gomorrah. Therefore, if the sin of the men gathered around Lot's house is identified as, and limited to, gang rape, God turns out to be unjust, since he destroyed Sodom (both men and women!) for a sin they never actually committed, and killed the inhabitants of Gomorrah for a sin in which they had no part whatsoever, not even unintentionally. For these reasons, this interpretation of the sin that led to the destruction of Sodom and Gomorrah is highly implausible.

A second, even more influential, attempt at revising the traditional understanding of the sin of Sodom and Gomorrah holds that it was not homosexuality, but rather *inhospitality*. Doubtless the most influential proponent of this view has been D. Sherwin Bailey, who is widely recognized as the first scholar to have suggested this interpretation, in his landmark study *Homosexuality and the Western Christian Tradition*. In short, this view rests upon the definition of the Hebrew word *yāda'* which is translated as "know" in Genesis 19:5. According to this interpretation, since in the vast majority of the 943 uses of this word in the Old Testament it means "to get acquainted with," this ought to be its connotation in the account of Sodom and Gomorrah. Therefore, when the men of Sodom surrounded Lot's house and inquired, "Where are the men who came to you tonight? Bring them out to us, that we may *know* them" (Gen. 19:5), they were simply asking to be *introduced* to the angelic visitors on account of the fact that Lot had failed to acquaint them properly with the townspeople. Or, in the words of Bailey, "Since *yāda'* commonly means 'get acquainted with,' the demand to 'know' the visitors whom Lot had entertained may well have implied some serious breach of the rules of hospitality."[23]

This interpretation has been adopted and repeated by almost every pro-homosexual Bible exegete who has dealt with this passage. Harry A. Woggon wrote, "The sin of Sodom and Gomorrah was seen in the Old Testament to be a violation of the sacred obligation of hospitality toward strangers."[24] John J. McNeill labeled the inhospitality purportedly displayed at Sodom as "the crime that cries out to God for vengeance."[25] John Boswell claimed that "the original moral impact of the [Sodom and Gomorrah] passage had to do with hospitality."[26] James B. Nelson asserted, "Contemporary biblical studies persuasively indicate that the major theme of the story [of Sodom and Gomorrah] and concern of the writer were not homosexual activity as such, but rather the breach of ancient Hebrew hospitality norms."[27] What all of these interpreters have in common, then, is their view that the sin of Sodom and Gomorrah was lack of hospitality rather than homosexuality.

While this interpretation is creative and obviously persuasive to some, a brief review of the facts surrounding the destruction of Sodom and Gomorrah reveals that this view, too, is untenable. Concerning the Hebrew word *yāda*ʾ it must be noted that while this term usually does mean "to get acquainted with," it can also refer to sexual relations, as it clearly does in Genesis 4:1, 17, 25; 24:16; 38:26. The decisive factor in determining the definition of this word (or any term with multiple possible meanings) necessarily must be the context. Following this principle, in the context of the Sodom and Gomorrah passage *yāda*ʾ must have a sexual connotation when it occurs in Genesis 19:5, for when the term recurs three verses later the sexual meaning is the only one that makes sense. Otherwise, Lot would be saying that his daughters, who were engaged to two of the inhabitants of Sodom, had never actually been acquainted with a man! Moreover, Lot's offering of his two daughters to the men of Sodom makes absolutely no sense if the men knocking at his door were merely asking to be introduced to his house guests. Why not just introduce the angels to the inquisitive townspeople, if that was all that was requested of him?

Another problem with this interpretation is that, if Lot was the one who sinned by breaking the local hospitality codes, then why was his life spared by the angelic visitors while the law-abiding townspeople were destroyed by the divine judgment? What is more, considering that Lot was a resident of Sodom, why were the inhabitants of Gomorrah killed for a sin in which they had no part? And if the residents of Sodom were so peaceable and honest that they came to Lot's house late at night to enact the local hospitality codes, then why could God not find ten righteous people in the whole city (Gen. 18:32)? Nor can this interpretation explain why Lot seems to have felt threatened by the appearance of the townspeople (19:6) or why the mob declared their intent to harm both Lot and his visitors without provocation (v. 9). It should also be noted that this interpretation is at odds with every interpretation of this passage prior to the middle of the twentieth century, as well as with the aforementioned verse in Jude 7 (cf. Luke 17:26-29; 2 Pet. 2:6-7, 10). In summary, therefore, this view is invalid, in fact, untenable, on numerous counts.

Despite the attempts of many, then, it seems clear that the sin that led to the destruction of Sodom and Gomorrah was not heterosexual gang rape, inhospitality, or some other sin unrelated to homosexuality (or an errant subset of it).[28] Rather, as already indicated in our critique of pro-homosexual interpretations of the account, it is highly likely that the sin that brought God's judgment on these people was that of homosexuality, for the following reasons.

First, the reference to the sin of Sodom and Gomorrah in Jude 6-7 (cf. 2 Pet. 2:4-10) speaks of people who "indulged in sexual immorality and *pursued unnatural desire . . . defil[ing] the flesh.*" "Unnatural desire," both in its New Testament context (cf. Rom. 1:26-27) and in its ancient cultural environment (see below), almost certainly indicates that the sin in view is homosexuality.

Second, the sin in view in the Sodom and Gomorrah incident is clearly sexual (the highly probable meaning of the word *yāda'* in Gen. 19:5, 8),[29] and in context refers not merely to illicit sexual intercourse but to intercourse that is perverse and condemned by God.

Third, the sin of homosexuality best accounts for God's terrible judgment on Sodom and Gomorrah. It is highly unlikely that the judgment for inhospitality or merely intended gang rape (be it heterosexual or homosexual) would have been as severe.

Hence, the sin of Sodom and Gomorrah was that of homosexuality.

The Levitical Holiness Code

A second section of Scripture for which pro-homosexual exegetes have proposed different interpretations is the sexual laws of the Holiness Code in the book of Leviticus.[30] There are two laws in the Holiness Code that specifically address homosexuality. These are Leviticus 18:22 ("You shall not lie with a male as with a woman; it is an abomination") and 20:13 ("If a man lies with a male as with a woman, both of them have committed an abomination; they shall surely be put to death; their blood is upon them"). Indeed, these laws constitute a significant portion of the biblical witness against homosexuality, for they both explicitly address homosexual relations in a casuistic manner and prescribe the death penalty for homosexual offenders (which God had previously enacted at Sodom and Gomorrah). Clearly, then, these two verses would need to be radically reinterpreted in order for one to make the claim that the Bible does not prohibit the practice of homosexuality.

Advocates of homosexuality who have dealt with these verses have generally adopted an occasional, culturally relative approach—that is, they claim that these verses are culture-bound temporal directives given to the Israelites, not eternally binding moral absolutes meant for the elect throughout the ages. While individual exegetes have made this argument in different forms with various nuances, the foundational argument that supports this view is usually the same (at least for those who believe in the continuity between the Testaments).[31] In short, this view centers on the use of the Hebrew word *tōʿēbāh,* which is translated "abomination" in both of these verses. According to proponents of this position, when the term *tōʿēbāh,* is used in Scripture, it usually refers to some type of ritual impurity connected to idol worship. Therefore, when God prohibited homosexuality in Leviticus 18:22 and 20:13, he was not addressing homosexuality per se, but rather, in the context of this portion of the Holiness Code, prohibited *homosexual acts performed by Canaanite temple prostitutes as part of the worship of false gods.*

To quote Walter Barnett, "The whole context of these injunctions [in Leviticus 18:22 and 20:13] is a polemic against the Israelites imitating the defiling practices of the Canaanites whom they displaced in Palestine. Thus again, the prohibition is probably directed against the practice of ritual homosexual prostitution as found in the Canaanite fertility cult. In any event the intent cannot be to condemn all homosexuality and homosexual behavior."[32] Similarly, John Boswell writes, "The Levitical enactments [in Lev. 18:22 and 20:13] against homosexual behavior characterize it unequivocally as ceremonially unclean rather than inherently evil."[33] Scanzoni and Mollenkott assert similarly, "The reasons given for these proscriptions [in Lev. 18:22 and 20:13] involve several factors [such as] separation from other nations . . . avoidance of idolatry . . . and ceremonial uncleanness. . . . [Homosexual] practices were part of the fertility religions."[34] This view, then, attempts to limit both the interpretation and the application of Leviticus 18:22 and 20:13 to homosexual acts committed in the worship of idols.

In response to this interpretation, it must be noted that while the Hebrew word *tōʿēbāh,* can refer to some type of ritual impurity connected to idol worship (cf. 2 Kings 16:3; Isa. 44:19; Jer. 16:18; Ezek. 7:20), it frequently does not have this connotation (cf. Gen. 43:32; Ps. 88:8; Prov. 6:16-19; 28:9). Indeed, sometimes *tōʿēbāh,* refers to activities that are morally offensive to God, such as homosexuality. In the context of this passage in the Holiness Code, it is interesting to note that activities other than homosexuality are also labeled as *tō'ēbāh* (cf. Lev. 18:26), including incest (18:6-18), adultery (18:20), and bestiality (18:23). If we were to apply a consistent hermeneutic throughout this passage, we would be forced to conclude that these other activities are likewise only prohibited within the context of idol worship. Of course, such an interpretation would be irresponsible in light of the fact that these other activities are consistently condemned throughout Scripture, as is homosexuality.[35]

Moreover, even if it could be proven that the laws in the Holiness Code were exclusively addressing ritual purity (which is doubtful), this still would not validate the morality of homosexual activity. To illustrate, it is clear that Scripture prohibits child sacrifice because it was part of the ritual worship of the Canaanite God Molech (cf. Lev. 20:2-5; 2 Kings 16:1-4; 2 Chron. 28:1-4; Jer. 7:30-31; Ezek. 23:36-39). Yet child sacrifice is always wrong, whether it is connected to false worship or not, because it in essence constitutes a breach of the sixth commandment. Likewise, homosexuality is always wrong, for it is a violation of God's integral design of marriage and family. In short, then, *the context of Scripture's prohibition of a certain activity does not necessarily limit the immorality of that activity to that particular context.* This is especially true if the forbidden activity is prohibited throughout Scripture, as is homosexuality.

It seems clear, therefore, that the alternative interpretations of Leviticus 18:22 and 20:13 proposed by pro-homosexual exegetes come up short. Indeed, the sin prohibited in these two verses must be understood, as it traditionally has been, to be the general practice of homosexuality.[36]

HOMOSEXUALITY IN THE NEW TESTAMENT

Our major source concerning the New Testament's view of homosexuality is the apostle Paul, who refers to homosexuality in his letter to the Romans and in his first letters to the Corinthians and Timothy.[37] We will deal with these passages in turn, as in the Old Testament section above giving special attention to efforts at reinterpreting these passages over against the traditional understanding.[38]

The Letter to the Romans

The major passage on homosexuality in Paul's writings is found in the first chapter of his letter to the Romans, where his denunciation of homosexuality is part of his larger presentation of the universal sinfulness of humanity in its rejection of God the Creator (Rom. 1:18-23).[39] Because of this rejection, Paul contends, God gave depraved humanity over "in the lusts of their hearts to impurity, to the dishonoring of their bodies among themselves, because they exchanged the truth about God for a lie and worshiped and served the creature rather than the Creator" (1:24-25).

In what follows Paul elaborates in greater detail on precisely what he means by "the dishonoring of their bodies among themselves":

> For this reason God gave them up to dishonorable passions. For their *women exchanged natural relations for those that are contrary to nature*; and the *men likewise gave up natural relations with women and were consumed with passion for one another, men committing shameless acts with men* and receiving in themselves the due penalty for their error (Rom. 1:26-27).[40]

Paul proceeds to reiterate that these "shameless acts" are a result of people's rejection of God, who consequently "gave them up to a debased mind to do what ought not to be done" (Rom. 1:28). This is followed by a vice list, in which homosexuality is associated with a long litany of sinful human attitudes and behaviors (1:29-31; cf. 1 Cor. 6:9-10; 1 Tim. 1:9-10). Paul closes this section by issuing the indictment that though these people "know God's decree that those who practice such things deserve to die, they not only do them but give approval to those who practice them" (Rom. 1:32). Hence, God's judgment is pronounced not only on practicing homosexuals but also on those who condone such behavior (cf. 1 Cor. 5:1-13).

It is probably no coincidence that it is in Paul's letter to the Romans that this sweeping indictment of human depravity including a stern denunciation of homosexuality (as well as lesbianism, Rom. 1:26) is found. At the time of writing (c. A.D. 57), the Roman world was known

for its moral debauchery, sexual excess, and perversity.[41] The reign of
Claudius (A.D. 41–54) is notorious for such evils, as is that of his suc-
cessor, Nero (A.D. 54–68), during whose reign Paul penned his letter to
the Romans. A few decades later, the book of Revelation depicts the
Roman empire as the "whore Babylon," of whose "wine of the passion
of her sexual immorality" all nations have drunk (Rev. 18:3; cf. 18:9;
19:2). In the seer's vision, the woman is "arrayed in purple and scarlet,
and adorned with gold and jewels and pearls, holding in her hand a
golden cup full of abominations and the impurities of her sexual
immorality" (17:4) and identified by an inscription on her forehead,
"Babylon the great, mother of prostitutes and of earth's abominations"
(v. 5). This same woman is "drunk with the blood of the saints, the
blood of the martyrs of Jesus" (v. 6).

In light of the literary and cultural context of Paul's reference to
homosexuality in the first chapter of Romans, there seems little doubt
that he considered homosexuality at large, rather than merely more narrowly defined aberrant subsets of homosexual behavior, to be contrary
to God's created order and hence worthy of condemnation. What is
more, Paul condemns not only those who *engage* in homosexual behavior but also those who *condone* such behavior without themselves
engaging in it. However, recently attempts have been made to identify
the sin condemned in Romans and other New Testament writings as a
more narrow offense. Since these efforts often take their point of departure at the specific Greek word *arsenokoitēs*, which does not occur in
Romans but is found in Paul's two other references to the subject, we
will deal with these objections below.

First Corinthians

While Paul's denunciation of homosexuality in his letter to the Romans
involves his use of various circumlocutions for the practice ("dishonoring of their bodies among themselves," Rom. 1:24; "exchanged natural
relations for those that are contrary to nature," 1:26; "gave up natural
relations," "consumed with passion for one another," "men committing
shameless acts with men," 1:27), he employs the Greek term
arsenokoitēs, to refer to homosexuality in his other two major references

to the subject, 1 Corinthians 6:9 and 1 Timothy 1:10 (in 1 Cor. 6:9, the term *malakos* is used as well; see further below).[42]

Paul's reference to homosexuals in his first letter to the Corinthians is part of a section in which he deals with a variety of sexual issues confronting the Corinthian church.[43] It should be noted at the outset that first-century Corinth was notorious for its sexual immorality.[44] In 1 Corinthians 5, Paul addresses reports according to which the Corinthians tolerate a case where "a man has his father's wife," that is, he is having an ongoing sexual relationship with his stepmother (1 Cor. 5:1; cf. Lev. 18:8). Paul expresses his outrage at this false "tolerance" and urges the Corinthians to "deliver this man to Satan for the destruction of the flesh, so that his spirit may be saved in the day of the Lord" (1 Cor. 5:5). In a previous letter Paul had told the Corinthians not to associate with sexually immoral people (by which he meant not the sexually immoral of this world, but "anyone who bears *the name of brother*" [i.e., a fellow Christian] who is guilty of sexual immorality; 5:9-11). Such a person the Corinthians are to purge from their midst in the hope of repentance and restoration (5:13).

The Vice Lists Referring to Homosexuality in 1 Corinthians and 1 Timothy

1 CORINTHIANS 5:10; 6:9-10	1 TIMOTHY 1:9-10
. . . not at all meaning the sexually immoral of this world, or the greedy and swindlers, or idolaters . . .	. . . the law is not laid down for the just but for the lawless and disobedient, for the ungodly and sinners, for the unholy and profane,
Do not be deceived: neither the sexually immoral, nor idolaters, nor adulterers, nor **men who practice homosexuality,** nor thieves, nor the greedy, nor drunkards, nor revilers, nor swindlers will inherit the kingdom of God.	for those who strike their fathers and mothers, for murderers, the sexually immoral, **men who practice homosexuality,** enslavers, liars, perjurers, and whatever else is contrary to sound doctrine.

After chastising the Corinthians for engaging in public lawsuits against one another (1 Cor. 6:1-8), Paul asserts that "neither the sexually immoral, nor idolaters, nor adulterers, nor men who practice homosexuality [note: the original has two Greek words, possibly referring to both the passive and active partners in homosexual intercourse], nor thieves, nor the greedy, nor drunkards, nor revilers, nor swindlers will inherit the kingdom of God" (6:9-10; cf. 5:10).[45] Paul adds, "And such were some of you. But you were washed, you were sanctified, you were justified in the name of the Lord Jesus Christ and by the Spirit of our God" (6:11). In the following section Paul denounces Christians who have sex with prostitutes, contending that this is a gross misrepresentation of true Christian freedom and urging believers to flee from sexual immorality (6:12-20).

The vice list in 1 Corinthians 6:9-10, of which the two terms related to homosexuality are a part, expands the list in 5:10 by repeating all six items found in the antecedent passage.[46] In fact, the earlier list frames the subsequent one in that the first two and the last four items are repeated, with the four added characteristics being placed at the center. The terms "sexually immoral" and "idolaters" reflect the two major issues addressed in the context, sexual immorality (cf. 5:1-13; 6:12-20) and idolatry (cf. 8:1–11:1). Of the four new items, three (adulterers, *malakoi*, and *arsenokoitai*) are sexual; the fourth is thieves (though "robbers" may be more accurate). The vice list concludes with the four other items from 5:10-11.

Looking at the three items relevant for our present purposes, "adulterers" (*moichoi*) bears the straightforward meaning of married persons having sexual relations outside marriage (Ex. 20:14; Lev. 20:10; Deut. 5:18; cf. Luke 18:11). The next two terms, *malakoi* and *arsenokoitai,* require more extended comment. Both expressions have to do with homosexuality and are at times conflated into one English phrase in translation, such as the ESV's "men who practice homosexuality" (though keeping them as two separate terms seems preferable: cf. the NIV's "male prostitutes . . . homosexual offenders" and the TNIV's "male prostitutes . . . practicing homosexuals"). The first term, *malakos,* means literally "soft" (cf. Matt. 11:8 = Luke 7:25) and in Paul's day served as an epithet for the "soft" or effeminate (i.e., passive) partner in a homosexual (pederastic) relationship.[47] Importantly, *malakoi* (as well as *arsenokoitai*) refers to behavior and not mere orientation, as is implied by Paul's comment in 1 Corinthians 6:11, "And such were some of you."[48]

The meaning of the term *arsenokoitēs* (which is also found in 1 Tim. 1:9-10, on which see the discussion below) has been the subject of considerable debate in recent years.[49] Some pro-homosexual exegetes have sought to restrict the application of the term *arsenokoitēs* to a more narrow offense. John Boswell, for example, in an effort to demonstrate that the early church did not disapprove of homosexual acts as such, disavows any connection between the two terms *malakoi* and *arsenokoitai* in 1 Corinthians 6:9, translating the former as "masturbators" and the latter as *"male prostitutes."*[50] According to Boswell, if the term *arsenokoitai* were in fact referring to homosexuality in general, the term would not be absent "from so much literature about homosexuality."[51] Boswell also disavows any connection between the Levitical Holiness Code and the New Testament references to homosexuality, claiming that the New Testament writers would not have appealed to "the authority of the old to justify the morality of the new."[52]

Others, such as Robin Scroggs, contend that Paul's condemnation extends only to effeminate call boys in the context of an ancient homosexual practice called *pederasty,* sexual intercourse between an adult male and a young boy.[53] Unlike Boswell, Scroggs links the two nouns in 1 Corinthians 6:9 in his effort to demonstrate that only pederasty, but not homosexuality in general, was condemned by Paul.

Yet others have argued that Paul's reference to homosexuality is referring only to homosexual *acts,* not to *"celibate"* homosexual relationships (that is, relationships between persons with a homosexual orientation who do not have sexual relations).[54]

Another group alleges that the New Testament condemns merely the *negative dehumanizing pattern of homosexuality prevalent in first-century Hellenistic culture* and that it therefore cannot be applied directly to contemporary mutually consenting, non-exploitative homosexual relationships.[55] Dale Martin, for instance, while maintaining that no one actually knows what *arsenokoitai* meant, suggests some form of *exploitive sex* as the most likely alternative. According to Martin, *malakoi* simply refers to those who are effeminate (but not to the passive partner in homosexual intercourse), charging that the term serves as a malleable concept for condemning others of whose practice one does not approve.[56]

William Petersen, finally, while agreeing with David Wright's critique of John Boswell, objects to the translation "homosexuals" for *arsenokoitai* in 1 Corinthians 6:9 and 1 Timothy 1:10 on the grounds that, in his view, a major disjunction exists between the contemporary conception of homosexuality and that prevalent in the ancient world. While in Greco-Roman thought sexual acts, not sexual orientation, were what characterized a person's sexuality, Petersen maintains, modern usage defines "homosexual" primarily in terms of desire and orientation apart from actual behavior. Hence by using "homosexuals" for *arsenokoitai*, one improperly retrojects a modern concept into the ancient world "where no equivalent concept existed."[57]

To sum up the discussion thus far, it has been argued that the New Testament references ought to be restricted only to an aberrant subset of homosexual behavior, be it (1) homosexual prostitution, (2) pederasty, (3) homosexual acts but not "celibate" homosexual relationships, or (4) some negative, dehumanizing, and exploitive form of homosexual relationships but not homosexuality in general. Others object (5) that the concept of homosexuality has changed, so that using the term in modern translations of *arsenokoitai* is misleading. How are we to evaluate these arguments in light of the biblical evidence?

First, in light of the discussion of the teaching of the Old Testament and the book of Romans above it appears very unlikely that what is universally condemned in the Hebrew Scriptures might now, in New Testament times as well as in ours, be acceptable. As we concluded in our investigation of the Levitical Holiness Code above, the sin prohibited in these two verses [Lev. 18:22 and 20:13] must be understood, as it traditionally has been, to be the general practice of homosexuality, not a more narrow infraction such as homosexual acts performed by Canaanite temple prostitutes as part of the worship of false gods, as some pro-homosexual interpreters have argued.

Second, it appears likely that the term *arsenokoitēs*, which does not seem to occur in the extant literature prior to the present reference, was coined by Paul or someone else in Hellenistic Judaism from the Levitical prohibition against males "lying or sleeping with males" (Lev. 18:22, LXX: *arsenos . . . koitēn*; 20:13: *arsenos koitēn*).[58] This suggests that the term, as in the Levitical Holiness Code, is *broad and general* in nature and encompasses homosexuality *as a whole* rather than merely specific *aberrant subsets* of homosexual behavior.[59] As Gordon Wenham rightly notes, "lying with a male" relates to "every kind of male-male intercourse," including that between mutually consenting adults.[60] As to Boswell's argument that Christians would not have invoked the older order (i.e., the Levitical Holiness Code) to justify the new, in his first letter to the Corinthians Paul has already expressed his vehement opposition to the Corinthians' tolerance of incest, which is likewise proscribed in the Levitical Holiness Code (1 Corinthians 5; cf. Lev. 18:7-8; 20:11). As a Jew committed to the teaching and authority of the Hebrew Scriptures, Paul would have been equally persuaded of the unacceptability of homosexuality.[61] Boswell's objection that the term *arsenokoitai* is absent from much of ancient literature on homosexuality and hence should not be taken as a general reference is likewise not persuasive, since one should not expect to find the expression in writings predating Paul (who may have coined the term) and since the Greeks used a large variety of words and phrases to refer to homosexuality.[62] It should also be remembered that the prevailing form of male homosexuality in the Greco-Roman world was pederasty, so that one should expect the majority of references in Greco-Roman literature to be to this form of homosexual behavior.

Third, Scroggs's argument that Paul's references are merely to pederasty falls short on at least four counts.

(a) There was a clear and unambiguous Greek word for pederasty, the term *paiderastēs*. We have every reason to believe that if Paul had wished to condemn, not homosexuality at large, but only pederasty, he would have used the appropriate Greek term for this practice.

(b) The attempt to limit Paul's condemnation to pederasty (a practice in which the adult male desired homosexual intercourse with a passive sexual partner in the form of a young boy) is contradicted by Paul's reference to the male partners' *mutual desire for one another* in Romans 1:27 ("consumed with passion for one another").

(c) In the same passage, in Romans 1:26, Paul also condemns lesbian sex, which did not involve children, so that an appeal to pederasty does not adequately account for the prohibition of same-sex relations in this passage.

(d) Even if (for argument's sake only) Paul were to censure only pederasty in the passages under consideration, this would still not mean that,
as a Scripture-abiding Jew, he would have approved of homosexuality as
such. Quite to the contrary. In contrast to the surrounding Greco-Roman
world (which generally accepted homosexual acts), Hellenistic Jewish
texts universally condemn homosexuality and treat it (together with idolatry) as the most egregious example of Gentile moral depravity.[63]

Fourth, even if (for argument's sake) homosexual *acts* were the specific focus in the Pauline prohibitions (cf. Rom. 1:27, 32; though note the
references to the futility of people's thinking, their debased mind, and
their foolish and lustful hearts in 1:21, 24, 28), this does not mean that
he would have considered "celibate" homosexual relationships as being
within the scope of the divine creative will; for this would be to exchange
a man's "natural" function for what is "unnatural."[64] As Paul wrote in
his letter to the Romans, "their women exchanged *natural* relations for
those that are *contrary to nature;* and the men likewise gave up *natural*
relations with women and were consumed with passion for one another"
(Rom. 1:26-27). This makes clear that Paul considered homosexuality to
be "contrary to nature," that is, contrary to the created order.[65]

As noted above, this is borne out clearly by the Genesis narrative.
Not only does Genesis 1 repeatedly affirm that God made every creature "after its kind" (Gen. 1:21, 24), it also shows that God comple-
mented the man, not by creating another *man,* but by creating a *woman.*
God's creation of man as "male and female" is an integral part of the
created order, and it is *as male and female* that the man and the woman
reflect the divine image (1:27). This is not altered by a mere denial that
Paul in Romans speaks of homosexuality at large or by suggesting a distinction between homosexual acts and homosexual orientation; that
homosexuality is not in conflict with God's creation design can be maintained only by a decided *rejection of the biblical creation account itself.*
Demonstrably, and as mentioned, in the context of Genesis 1–2 there is
no place for homosexuality in that it is not even potentially procreative
and thus stands outside God's creative purposes of making humankind
in two sexes in order to "be fruitful and multiply."[66]

As Robert Gagnon contends, "The notion that first-century Jews,
such as Jesus and Paul, would have given general approval to a homo-

sexual lifestyle if they had only been shown adequate examples of mutually caring and non-exploitative same-sex relationships is fantastic. More or different information about same-sex intercourse would not have changed the verdict for any first-century Jew because the anatomical, sexual, and procreative complementarity of male and female unions, in contrast with those between female and female or male and male, would have remained indisputable."[67]

Fifth, not only is Paul's view of homosexuality as contrary to nature in keeping with the foundational creation narrative in Genesis 1 and 2, it is also illumined by prevailing views of homosexuality in contemporary Greco-Roman culture.[68] Stegemann, for example, has argued persuasively that the same-sex partner in homosexual intercourse inverts the natural mode of being in that one of the males must act like a woman or one of the women as the male.[69] Hence Philo (*Spec. Laws* 3.7 §§37-42) condemns pederasty in which "passive partners . . . habituate themselves to endure the disease of effemination, let both body and soul run to waste, and leave no ember of their male sex-nature to smolder," castigating them for violating nature by exchanging the male nature for the female and hence becoming guilty of unmanliness and effeminacy (*malakia*).

In the pagan world of Paul's day, on the other hand, pederasty was condoned because sexual acts were evaluated, not by God-given standards of morality, but by social values and norms.[70] Free males could choose women, boys, or slaves as sexual objects without causing offense as long as this did not interfere with their status as free males and as long as they did not "indulge in passive acts of love like a woman or a slave."[71] Remarkably, however, homosexual acts between free males were viewed with contempt because (as mentioned) one partner would need to adopt a passive (female) role. For this reason "[s]ociety would have considered same-sex sexual acts between two men of equal standing to be shameful. What some in modern society find acceptable—male same-sex eroticism between equals in a committed relationship—would have been condemned in ancient society"—and this in a culture that fell far short of biblical standards for morality on many counts, including its approval of pederastic same-sex intercourse.[72] This sheds a telling light on the contemporary debate concerning homosexuality, including that regarding same-sex marriages.[73] Yet while Paul, a Jew who sought to contextualize the gospel in the Greco-Roman world of his day, concurred with the reasoning that same-sex relations are contrary to nature, he "differed from his society's sexual mores in condemning *all* same-sex sexual acts."[74]

Sixth and last, Petersen's argument that the concept of homosexuality has changed, so that the translation "homosexuals" for *arsenokoitai* (*malakia*) is misleading, fails to convince since ancient sources do not support his thesis that homosexuality was defined exclusively in terms of homosexual acts but not orientation. The apostle Paul himself, in his letter to the Romans, refers both to homosexual acts (Rom. 1:27: "shameless acts"; 1:32: "those who practice") and underlying thoughts and passions (1:24: "lusts of their hearts"; 1:28: "debased mind"; cf. 1:21). Hence the dichotomy erected suggested by Petersen is false and is supported neither by Scripture nor by extrabiblical Greek literature.[75]

For these and many other reasons, attempts to limit the New Testament references to homosexuality to a more narrow subset of aberrant homosexual behavior must be judged unconvincing, and the traditional view must be upheld that the New Testament, as does the Old Testament, condemns homosexuality as sin and as incompatible with God's created order.

To this overall conclusion regarding homosexuality we may add several observations that flow from our study of 1 Corinthians 6:9-10 in particular:

(1) The church is told *not to tolerate sexual immorality in its midst* (1 Cor. 5:1-13). This includes those who practice homosexuality. It seems clear that the apostle Paul would not have tolerated openly practicing homosexuals as members (much less in leadership) of a Christian congregation.

(2) Homosexuality is *listed together with many other vices* as an attribute that will bar entrance into God's kingdom (1 Cor. 6:9-11; cf. 5:10). If homosexuality is not acceptable in heaven, the church must be clear that it is not acceptable in the church either.

(3) Paul makes clear that some of the members of the Corinthian church were *former homosexuals* (1 Cor. 6:11). This shows that true transformation of homosexuals is possible in Christ. As Paul notes, those individuals were cleansed from their sin ("washed," perhaps refer-

ring to spiritual regeneration, with possible secondary reference to baptism), set apart for God and his service ("sanctified"), and acquitted and made right with God ("justified") in Christ and by the Spirit (6:11; cf. 1:30). This is a hopeful note indeed for any homosexuals who are willing to repent of their sin and appropriate Christ's forgiveness and life-transforming power.[76]

We now turn to an investigation of the final New Testament passage that includes a reference to homosexuality, in Paul's first letter to Timothy. Since we have already adjudicated the debate concerning the meaning of *arsenokoitēs* in our discussion of 1 Corinthians 6:9-10, our comments here can be more brief.

First Timothy

The final significant reference to homosexuality in 1 Timothy, like that in 1 Corinthians, is included in a vice list. The reference is part of a digression (1 Tim. 1:8-11) that elaborates in further detail on the nature of the heretics' misuse of the law.[77] This is followed by a second digression (1:12-17) that presents Paul, in contrast to the false teachers, as the model of a sinner saved by grace. This makes clear that Paul is not exalting himself above his opponents because he is intrinsically superior to them. Rather, it is solely his acceptance of God's gracious offer of salvation and forgiveness in Christ that sets him apart from the heretics.

In this passage, Paul challenges the expertise claimed by these self-appointed "teachers of the law," who may have charged the apostle with antinomianism (an "anti-law" bias). Despite their confident demeanor, they understand neither the law's true purpose (1 Tim. 1:8) nor its intended recipients (vv. 9-10). According to Paul, the heretics' use of the law as a standard for Christian living was incompatible with "sound doctrine" (cf. 1 Tim. 6:3; 2 Tim. 1:13; 4:3; Titus 1:9; 2:1) that conformed to the "glorious gospel of the blessed God" which had been entrusted to Paul.

The law is not addressed to saved sinners nor does it need to be (cf. 1 Tim. 1:15-16); its primary purpose is to convict the unrighteous. To be sure, the law is good, if it is used properly. But if the law is given to restrain sin, and Christians have been set free from sin and are now leading quiet and godly lives, the law's purpose has, in the case of believers, already been fulfilled. This argument is consistent with Paul's earlier teaching on the purpose of the law in his letters to the Galatians and Romans (cf. Rom 7:7, 12-14, 16; 8:3-4; 13:8-10; Gal 5:14, 22-23).

The vices (or sinners), listed here in six groups of two (or three), plus a concluding catch-all phrase, are as follows:[78]

(1) lawbreakers and rebels;

(2) ungodly and sinful;

(3) unholy and irreligious (jointly echoing the first four commandments);

(4) those who kill their fathers or mothers, murderers (echoing the fifth and sixth commandments, "Honor your father and your mother" and "You shall not murder");

(5) adulterers and homosexuals (echoing the seventh commandment, "You shall not commit adultery");

(6) slave traders or kidnappers, liars, and perjurers (echoing the eighth and ninth commandments, "You shall not steal" and "You shall not give false testimony against your neighbor"); and whatever else is contrary to sound doctrine.

Within these pairs (or expressions of three), the offenses cited fall roughly within the same category. Thus, most relevant for our present purposes, both "adulterers" (*pornois*; cf. 1 Cor. 6:9: *pornoi, moichoi*) and "homosexuals" (*arsenokoitais*) refer to sexual sins that constitute a violation of the seventh commandment.[79] As indicated, it appears that Paul's list, after three general pairs (conveying the notion of godlessness, which may in some general sense be related to the first four commandments), follows the second portion of the Ten Commandments (Ex. 20:12-16; Deut. 5:16-20), specifically commandments five through nine.[80] Strong terms are chosen, perhaps to highlight the degree of evil in the pagan world and the need of law for those who have not heard the gospel (cf. Rom. 1:21-32).

The list of wrongdoers in 1 Timothy 1:9-10 leads Paul to discuss the "grace of our Lord" Christ Jesus coming into the world "to save sinners" (1:14-15). Paul himself was once in the category of those whose actions were condemned by the law; now he has been shown mercy. This holds out hope even for the false teachers and those guilty of violating any of the above-mentioned commandments—but only if they repent and desist from their improper use of the Mosaic law.

Once again, then, Paul includes homosexuality in a vice list (unlike in 1 Cor. 6:9-10, not distinguishing between the two partners in homosexual intercourse), in the present instance subsuming homosexuality together with adultery as a violation of the seventh commandment and hence indicating its unacceptability for Christians. We conclude with a brief summary of our findings and some practical implications.

CONCLUSION

The Biblical Verdict on Homosexuality

The biblical verdict on homosexuality is consistent. From the Pentateuch to the book of Revelation, from Jesus to Paul, from Romans to the Pastorals, Scripture with one voice affirms that homosexuality is sin and a moral offense to God. The contemporary church corporately, and biblical Christians individually, must bear witness to the unanimous testimony of Scripture unequivocally and fearlessly.[81]

In the contemporary climate of "political correctness," where those who denounce homosexuality as sin are accused of homophobia and where homosexuality is presented as an individual right similar to the rights of women or ethnic minorities, there is increasing pressure on the church to soften its stance toward homosexuality and to tolerate those who practice it, not only in the culture at large but even in its own ranks.[82] In recent years, some mainline denominations have even begun to appoint openly practicing homosexuals to leadership positions at both the local and the national level.

To be sure, the church's clear proclamation of the biblical teaching on homosexuality must be coupled with the proclamation of God's love for all people, including homosexuals. The beloved verse John 3:16, "For God so loved *the world,* that he gave his only Son, that whoever believes in him should not perish but have eternal life," includes homosexuals just as it does all sinners. Homosexuality is not the unpardonable sin, and forgiveness is always available (1 Cor. 6:11).

But forgiveness implies repentance, and repentance implies admission of wrong. The church would fail in its scriptural mandate if it were exercising tolerance *apart from* repentance and acceptance *apart from* admission of wrong (cf. 1 Corinthians 5). In fact, if the church were to soften its denunciation of homosexuality, or remove it altogether, it would effectively remove the incentive for homosexuals to repent. The message would be that homosexuality is acceptable, not only in the church, but also before God. In this case, at least, we must try, with God's help, to hate the sin but to love the sinner (which involves calling him or her to repentance).

Pro-Homosexual Interpretations of Biblical Passages on Homosexuality and Their Weaknesses

Texts Dealing with Homosexuality	PRO-HOMOSEXUAL INTERPRETATION	WEAKNESS
Gen. 18:17–19:29	Gang Rape	Offense not limited to gang rape
		Not just sexual immorality, but "unnatural desires" (Jude 6–7; cf. 2 Pet. 2:4-10)
		Gang rape never occurred, yet Sodom and Gomorrah still destroyed
	Inhospitality	*Yāda'* in Gen. 19:5 must mean "sexual relations" (not "get acquainted with") as it does in Gen. 19:8
		Though Lot supposedly broke the local hospitality code, it was the citizens who were killed
Lev. 18:22, Lev. 20:13	*Tō'ēbāh* ("abomination") refers to homosexual acts performed by Canaanite temple prostitutes as part of the worship of false gods	"Abomination" frequently does not have this connotation; it points to activities morally offensive to God
		Activities such as incest (Lev. 18:6-18), adultery (18:20), and bestiality (18:23) are also labeled as "abomination"
		Child sacrifice was also part of the ritual worship, yet it is always wrong

Texts Dealing with Homosexuality	PRO-HOMOSEXUAL INTERPRETATION	WEAKNESS
Rom. 1:18-32 1 Cor. 6:9-10 1 Tim. 1:9-10	*Arsenokoitēs* ("one who lies or sleeps with males") restricted to male prostitution, pederasty, homosexual acts, or the negative dehumanizing pattern of homosexuality prevalent in first-century Hellenistic culture; ancient and modern conceptions of homosexuality too different to use same term	Homosexuality in general universally condemned in OT; unlikely that it would be condoned in NT
		Term likely adapted from Leviticus, where it refers to every kind of male-male intercourse
		Reference to pederasty unlikely since there was a different Greek word for this; mutual desire not characteristic of pederasty; lesbian sex did not involve pederasty; Paul as Jew would not have approved of homosexuality
		"Celibate" homosexual relationships not acceptable because "contrary to nature"; Greco-Roman culture did not approve of homo-sexuality but held that it was "contrary to nature"
		Scripture sees no dichotomy between homosexual acts and orientation in Rom. 1:18-32

Practical Implications

But what are the practical implications of the Bible's unified witness against homosexuality? At the outset, we must be clear that the visible church ought to continue to oppose this distortion of the Creator's biblical/traditional model of marriage and family. Denominations that have departed from Christendom's historically orthodox position on homosexuality (either by openly endorsing homosexuality or by remaining silent on the issue) are certainly not in step with Judeo-Christian tradition nor, more importantly, with the Word of God.

Yet, for those who are within churches that oppose homosexuality or for Christians who are just personally convinced of the sinfulness of this practice, a more personal dilemma may surface. For example, what do you do if a friend or family member is involved in homosexuality, or if you are homosexual yourself? While this may seem like a daunting problem, especially for those involved, it must be remembered that, as for virtually every other transgression mentioned in the Bible, 1 John 1:9 applies: "If we confess our sins, he is faithful and just to forgive us our sins and to cleanse us from all unrighteousness."

Furthermore, as mentioned above, although Paul clearly condemned homosexuality in several of his letters, when writing to the Corinthians, he noted, "Do you not know that the unrighteous will not inherit the kingdom of God? Do not be deceived: neither the sexually immoral, nor idolaters, nor adulterers, nor men who practice homosexuality, nor thieves, nor the greedy, nor drunkards, nor revilers, nor swindlers will inherit the kingdom of God. *And such were some of you.* But you were washed, you were sanctified, you were justified in the name of the Lord Jesus Christ and by the Spirit of our God" (1 Cor. 6:9-11).

Clearly, then, homosexuality is a sin that can be overcome. Fortunately, a number of ministries and other resources are available for those who are trying to break away from homosexuality.[83]

11

SEPARATING WHAT GOD HAS JOINED TOGETHER: DIVORCE AND REMARRIAGE

WHILE THE BEAUTY OF God's plan for marriage is plainly laid out in Scripture and many long to experience the kind of intimacy and love found only in biblical marriage, the sad reality is that marriage relationships are often broken and fall short of the biblical ideal. This is recognized in the Mosaic stipulations regarding divorce in the Old Testament (Deut. 24:1-4) and is acknowledged also in the New Testament. While both Jesus and Paul strongly upheld the biblical ideal of a lifelong, monogamous marriage relationship, both also addressed the possibility of divorce and remarriage. As will be seen below, however, while there is consensus that lifelong monogamous marriage is the ideal, there is no universal agreement among Bible-believing Christians on whether or not Scripture permits divorce and remarriage in certain circumstances.[1]

THE OLD TESTAMENT BACKGROUND

Before investigating the New Testament teaching on divorce and remarriage, it will be helpful to look briefly at the Old Testament background. The most important text, which, as will be seen below, featured prominently in Jesus' debate with the Pharisees on the subject, is the Mosaic provision for divorce in Deuteronomy 24:1-4.[2] As Jesus made clear, the passage should not be construed as a divine endorsement of the practice but reflects an effort to regulate and mitigate existing practices (Matt.

19:8; Mark 10:5).[3] The critical phrase in the Deuteronomic stipulations that led to extensive rabbinic debate is the expression *'erwat dābār* (interpreted by the first-century rabbi Shammai as a synonym of *d'bar 'erwāh,* "a matter of nakedness," and by his contemporary Hillel separately as *'erwat,* "nakedness," and *dābār,* "something"; LXX: *aschēmon pragma,* "shameful thing"), commonly translated "some indecency" or "something indecent" (NIV, Deut. 24:1).

In Jesus' day rabbinic schools lined up behind two major interpretive traditions.[4] The school of Shammai interpreted the phrase as a reference to immodest behavior or sexual immorality (whether before or after marriage), while the school of Hillel (c. 60 B.C.–A.D. 20) focused on the earlier words in Deuteronomy 24:1, "finds no favor in his eyes," maintaining that divorce was allowed in any instance where a wife did something displeasing to her husband.[5] This more permissive interpretation seems to have held sway among most of Jesus' contemporaries (see Matt. 19:3), possibly including even some of Jesus' own disciples (cf. Matt. 19:10; see further below).

In its original context, the phrase was not needed to address the issue of divorce in the case of adultery, since according to Pentateuch adultery was punishable by death, not divorce (Lev. 20:10; Deut. 22:22).[6] At the same time, since marriage was held in high esteem in ancient Israel, the offense was surely not merely trivial but substantial. Possibly, what was in view is a variety of things a husband might have found objectionable, perhaps barrenness or some birth defect,[7] lewd, immoral behavior such as lesbianism or sexual misconduct short of intercourse,[8] or menstrual irregularity.[9] Again, Moses' stipulations must not be construed as condoning such divorces, but merely as regulating them. The thrust of Deuteronomy 24:1-4 is therefore *descriptive* rather than *prescriptive,* and this seems to be one thing Jesus' contemporaries had misconstrued.[10]

As the passage continues, if a man chooses to divorce his wife and she remarries, he may not take her back in the event of the woman's second divorce or her second husband's death (Deut. 24:2-4). This would be "an abomination before the LORD" (v. 4). The stipulation serves as a warning to the husband not to divorce too quickly. If he does, and the woman remains unmarried, he can still have her back (cf.

Hosea 3). Once the woman remarries, however, this option is no longer available. Beyond this, the stipulation may serve to protect the woman's husband from entering into his former wife's sinful pattern of immorality. Perhaps dowry-related issues were involved as well, but this is uncertain.[11]

JESUS' TEACHING ON DIVORCE

Restoring God's Original Design for Marriage

Despite the fact that the Mosaic Law included provisions regulating divorce, the Old Testament makes it clear that divorce falls short of God's ideal (Mal. 2:16).[12] Jesus took his listeners all the way back to the beginning, reminding them that God created humanity as male and female (Gen. 1:27) and stipulated that the man, upon marriage, was to leave his father and mother and be united to his wife (2:24) in a one-flesh union before God that people ought not to break: "So they are no longer *two* but *one* flesh. What therefore God has joined together, let not man separate" (Matt. 19:4-6; Mark 10:6-9).[13]

The response of Jesus' audience makes clear that they thought the Mosaic stipulations had in effect superseded God's original purposes at Creation. Why else would divorce have been regulated in the Deuteronomic law code (Deut. 24:1-4)? According to Jesus, however, the Mosaic statutes were interposed, not to replace the Creator's original intent, but merely in recognition of the reality of human hardness of heart (Matt. 19:7-8; Mark 10:5; cf. Matt. 5:31-32). In fact, marriage was *intended as a lifelong, faithful union of a man and a woman.*[14]

Hence it can be argued that while covenant language is clearly present in Genesis 2 (see, e.g., "leave" and "cleave" in Gen. 2:24), marriage is even *more* than a covenant, because it is rooted in creation and the will of the Creator himself. As Carson contends, "If marriage is grounded in creation, in the way God has made us, then it cannot be reduced to a merely covenantal relationship that breaks down when the covenantal promises are broken."[15] At the same time, God's pre-fall institution of marriage is clearly affected by the sin of the first man and woman in Genesis 3. The remainder of the Old Testament makes it clear that adultery strikes at the heart of the one-flesh union between a man and a woman ordained by God (e.g., Gen. 39:9).

The Disciples' Reaction

Recognizing the high standard set by Jesus, his original followers respond, finding his view unduly restrictive, "If such is the case . . . , it is better not to marry" (Matt. 19:10).[16] Jesus, brushing aside their objection,[17] replies that while a few may indeed have the gift of celibacy (19:11-12), God's original ideal for marriage (the single exception for *porneia* notwithstanding), still stands. Some argue that the disciples' response proves that Jesus' standard must have been extremely high— that is, no divorce or remarriage once the marriage has been consummated.[18] If Jesus aligned himself simply with the more conservative branch of Judaism of his day, why would his followers have been surprised? No, Jesus' standard must have been even stricter than "divorce on the grounds of adultery only"; the disciples' reaction proves that Jesus advocated a "no divorce once the marriage has been consummated" position.

Yet the above arguments remain inconclusive, especially since the disciples' reaction may not have been legitimate. Like many of their Jewish contemporaries,[19] Jesus' followers may have assumed a somewhat more lenient standard—perhaps they even assumed that Jesus' standard was more lenient based on his compassionate treatment of the adulterous woman mentioned in John 7:53–8:11 (assuming the historicity of the account)—and consequently were reacting against Jesus' severe-sounding pronouncement *even though* it included an exception for adultery.[20] Also, while contemporary Judaism *required* divorce in the case of sexual immorality (cf. *m. Soṭah* 5:1), Jesus merely *permitted* it (thus implying the need for forgiveness). The fact that Jesus' standard regarding divorce was higher even than that of the conservative school of Shammai would therefore adequately account for the disciples' horrified reaction to Jesus' teaching in Matthew 19.[21]

The "Exception Clause": "Except for Porneia"

Much discussion has centered on the one exception made by Jesus in which case divorce is permissible (though not mandated). This exception, mentioned in both Matthew 5:32 and 19:9 (though the Greek words are slightly different: *parektos logou porneias,* and *mē epi porneia*), stipulates that divorce is illegitimate "except for marital unfaithfulness" (NIV) or "sexual immorality" (ESV, ISV, NKJV, HCSB, TNIV; Greek: *porneia*).[22] The Synoptic parallels in Mark 10:11-12 and Luke 16:18 do not mention the exception, which has led some to argue that Jesus never actually made the exception but that Matthew (or someone else) added it at a later point.[23] Even if this were the case, however (which is unlikely), the "exception clause" would still be part of inerrant, inspired Scripture and thus authoritative for Christians today.[24]

Of those who maintain that Jesus did utter the exception, some endeavor to bring the Matthean exception clause into conformity with the absolute statements in Mark and Luke by contending that those Gospels, rather than Matthew, ought to be the ultimate point of reference.[25] Others are reluctant to subsume the Matthean exception clause too quickly under the absolute statement in Mark and Luke and argue that both sets of passages ought to be studied in their own right to appreciate Jesus' teaching on the issue at hand. The question turns to a significant extent on the meaning of *porneia* in light of its Old Testament and contemporary Jewish background and its relation to the terms *moicheia* and *moicheuō*.

The "Divorce and Remarriage for Adultery or Sexual Immorality" View

All four major evangelical views on divorce and remarriage acknowledge that Jesus allowed divorce under certain circumstances (if breaking of a betrothal is considered a "divorce" as well),[26] though there is no consensus on precisely what these circumstances are.[27] We will first consider the most widely held evangelical view, "divorce and remarriage for adultery or sexual immorality," and subsequently deal with more restrictive views, particularly the "no divorce once the marriage has been consummated" position that interprets the "exception clause" with reference to sexual unfaithfulness during the betrothal period.[28]

The incident recorded in Matthew 19:3-12 takes its point of departure from the Pharisees' question, "Is it lawful to divorce one's wife *for any cause?*" (NIV: "for any and every reason"; 19:3; cf. 5:31).[29] As at other occasions, Jesus' opponents seek to involve him in contradiction or otherwise present him with the apparent dilemma of choosing between opposing viewpoints.[30] The Pharisees' question brings into play the views held by the different rabbinic schools in Jesus' day. Though not compiled until around A.D. 200, the Mishnah provides pertinent information about the respective positions on divorce in first-century Judaism:

> The School of Shammai say: A man may not divorce his wife unless he has found unchastity in her, for it is written, "Because he has found in her indecency in anything" (Deut. 24:1). And the School of Hillel say: [He may divorce her] even if she spoiled a dish for him, for it is written, "Because he has found in her indecency in anything" (*m. Giṭṭin* 9:10).[31]

The above quote helps to put Jesus' pronouncement in perspective. While the spectrum ranged from conservative (Shammai, divorce only for "unchastity") to liberal (Hillel, divorce "for any cause"), virtually no first-century Jew would have questioned that *porneia* (whether defined more narrowly as "adultery" or more broadly as "sexual immorality") was a valid cause for divorce. What is more, proponents of this view note that in light of the Jewish divorce formula, divorce for *porneia* automatically entailed the right to remarry.[32] A marital breach as radical as adultery—a capital offense, whether or not this was enforced—was unquestioned as grounds for divorce by Jesus' contemporaries (e.g., *m. Soṭah* 1:1, 5).[33]

While it is sometimes alleged that *porneia* has a more narrow scope of reference, proponents of the "divorce for adultery or sexual immorality" view point out that the term in the New Testament generally refers broadly to sexual immorality, which may include, yet is not necessarily limited to, adultery, depending on the specific context.[34] Since in the present case the subject of debate seems to be marriage and its violation by one partner (not limited to breaking a betrothal), there seems to be no good reason to deny that adultery is included in the purview of the expression *porneia*.[35] In fact, "unchastity (i.e., *porneia*) has too broad a range of meaning to be interpreted so narrowly [e.g., as restricted to breaking a betrothal]. It may indeed *include* these narrow meanings, but it cannot be *restricted* to them."[36]

A brief look at what are perhaps the closest Old Testament parallels to the use of *porneia* and *moicheuō* in Matthew 19:9, that is, Jeremiah 3:8-10 and Hosea 2:2-5a (LXX: 2:4-7a), will prove to be instructive and help us arrive at a more definitive conclusion regarding the scope of reference of *porneia* in Matthew 19:9. In both of these passages Old Testament Israel is charged with spiritual "prostitution" (that is, the worship of gods other than the Creator and covenant God) as well as adultery (the breaking of her covenant with Yahweh). The passages read as follows:

> *Jeremiah 3:8-10:* "She [Judah] saw that for all the adulteries [*emoichato*] of that faithless one, Israel, I had sent her away with a decree of divorce [*biblion apostasiou*]. Yet her treacherous sister Judah did not fear, but she too went and played the whore [*eporneusen*]. Because she took her whoredom [*porneia*] lightly, she polluted the land, committing adultery [*emoicheusen*] with stone and tree. Yet for all this her treacherous sister Judah did not return to me with her whole heart, but in pretense, declares the LORD."

> *Hosea 2:2-5a (2:4-7a LXX):* "Plead with your mother, plead—for she is not my wife (*gynē*), and I am not her husband (*anēr*)—that she put away her whoring (*porneian*) from her face, and her adultery (*moicheian*) from between her breasts; lest I strip her naked and make her as in the day she was born. . . . Upon her children also I will have no mercy, because they are children of whoredom (*porneias*). For their mother has played the whore (*exeporneusen*); she who conceived them has acted shamefully."

In both of these passages, *porneia* and the related verb *porneuō* refer to the breaking of Israel's marriage covenant with Yahweh by way of spiritual "immorality," whereby the juxtaposed terms *porneia* and *moicheia* (or the corresponding verbs) are mutually referring. Not only is there *no sharp distinction* between these two expressions, there is in fact *essential continuity* between them.[37] In neither of these contexts is the scope of reference of *porneia* limited merely to breaking a betrothal. The reference is clearly to an *exclusive, lifelong marriage covenant*. Moreover, in Matthew 19:9, in addition to *porneia* and *moicheuō*, the term *gameō* (meaning "marry," or, in the present context, "remarry"), is used as well. For these reasons it seems very difficult to deny that *marriage and the violation of the marriage covenant*, not merely breaking a betrothal, is the topic of discussion in the present passage.[38]

Jesus vs. Hillel and Shammai

Assuming that Jesus himself uttered the "exception clause" (or at least that the Matthean insertion of it captures the sense of what Jesus actually said at this occasion),[39] how does Jesus align himself with or differ from the rabbinic schools of his day? Clearly, Jesus' view was infinitely stricter than that advocated by the school of Hillel, which held that divorce was permissible "for any cause" (cf. Matt. 19:3). On the surface at least, Jesus' view is much closer to that of the school of Shammai, which restricted legitimate divorce (with the possibility of remarriage) to marital unfaithfulness,[40] though, as mentioned, in contrast to Shammai, Jesus only *permitted* divorce in case of *porneia* while first-century Judaism *required* it.[41]

Yet, in a very important sense, Jesus' reply transcends the legalistic squabbles between those two rabbinic schools and goes to the very heart of the matter. Essentially, Jesus, in good rabbinic style, shifts the Old Testament warrant from one given passage (Deut. 24:1-4) to an earlier set of passages (Gen. 1:27; 2:24) and hence relativizes the (chronologically) later reference as merely an exception and concession which in no way mitigates the abiding principle established by the foundational texts.[42] Thus, by focusing on the original design of marriage in God's plan, Jesus teaches his followers the true meaning of marriage.[43] Not only does he stress the permanence of marriage as a divine rather than merely human institution, he contends that divorce is fundamentally at odds with God's purpose in creation.

What is more, Jesus' application of the same standard regarding divorce and remarriage to *both men and women* (see especially Mark 10:11) is nothing less than revolutionary. Despite regulations in the

Mosaic Law that stipulated equal treatment of men and women with regard to divorce (Lev. 20:10-12), in Old Testament times a double standard prevailed according to which women were required to be faithful to their husbands (or punishment ensued) while the standards for men were considerably more lenient. In Jesus' teaching, however, conjugal rights were set on an equal footing.[44] In fact, Jesus taught that lust for other women in a man's heart already constituted adultery (Matt. 5:28), which implies that extramarital affairs are equally wrong for men and women.[45]

Differences of Views Between the Schools of Shammai and Hillel and Jesus Concerning Divorce

Differences of Views	SHAMMAI	HILLEL	JESUS
OT background texts for marriage	Deut. 24:1-4	Deut. 24:1-4	Gen. 1:27; 2:24
Meaning of *porneia*	Immodest behavior or sexual immorality	Any instance where a wife did something displeasing to her husband	Immoral behavior on the part of the wife, including, but not restricted to, adultery (majority view)
Divorce for *porneia*	Required	Required	Permitted
The application of the standard for divorce and remarriage	Men only	Men only	Both men and women

WHY THE EXCEPTION?

Even so, however, Jesus *still* affirms *porneia* as an exception for divorce. If the original creation is the ideal, it may be asked, why did Jesus retain this exception at all (though there is disagreement as to the exact nature of this exception; see further below)? We cannot be certain. Most likely, the reason is that adultery violates the "one-flesh" principle underlying marriage,[46] which may be why at least in Old Testament times sexual marital unfaithfulness was punishable by death (Lev. 20:10; Deut. 22:22).[47] After all, it would be difficult to continue a marriage if the partner guilty of adultery had been put to death by stoning!

In many ways, therefore, the fundamental differences between the evangelical proponents of the "divorce and remarriage for adultery or sexual immorality" view and the adherents of the various "no divorce" positions turns on their *definition of marriage* itself, or more narrowly still, on their understanding of the sense in which marriage is viewed as a *covenant*. If one holds that the marriage covenant is *indissoluble under any circumstances* (as Roman Catholics and many adherents of the "no divorce once the marriage has been consummated" view do), because covenants *by their very nature* cannot be terminated, it is unlikely that any exegetical arguments from the study of Matthew 19 will prove persuasive that Jesus allowed divorce and/or remarriage in certain situations.[48] Those, on the other hand, who allow for the possibility that covenants can be broken will tend to be more open to the possibility that Jesus (or Paul) allowed for divorce and remarriage under exceptional circumstances.[49] This is not to say, of course, that some do not argue for or hold a "no divorce once the marriage has been consummated" position on exegetical grounds. In particular, the above observations do not apply to those who hold to a betrothal interpretation of the Matthean exception clauses but who accept the so-called "Pauline privilege" (see below).

ARGUMENTS ADVANCED AGAINST THE "DIVORCE AND REMARRIAGE FOR ADULTERY OR SEXUAL IMMORALITY" VIEW

The following arguments have been advanced against the "divorce for adultery or sexual immorality" position.[50]

(1) The question arises whether the present view places undue emphasis on what might be considered a more "difficult" passage on the issue, namely Matthew 19, rather than interpreting it in light of the more straightforward-seeming statements in the other Synoptic Gospels. Would Reformation-type exegesis not suggest that difficult passages be interpreted in light of clearer ones?

(2) The exception clause is limited to Matthew's Gospel. No exceptions in Jesus' teaching on divorce are mentioned by Mark, Luke, and Paul. This raises the possibility that these latter authors provide the general norm while Matthew deals with a special case of some kind.

(3) There appears to be a tension between Jesus' references to God's ideal for marriage at Creation in Matthew 19:4-6 and his allowing an exception for divorce in Matthew 19:9.

(4) If the exception for divorce made by Jesus in Matthew 19:9 is for sexual immorality/adultery, this would be different from the Mosaic grounds for divorce stipulated in Deuteronomy 24:1-4, which raises the question of continuity and makes Jesus appear to be in conflict with the Old Testament passage that forms the background for his discussion with the Pharisees in Matthew 19.

(5) According to this view, Jesus essentially answers the divorce question, put to him in Hillelite terms, in a Shammaite fashion. One would expect Jesus to posit a higher standard than either school rather than merely siding with the more conservative viewpoint of his day. A "no divorce once the marriage has been consummated" position would seem to be more consistent.

(6) There is some difficulty explaining the disciples' reaction. Their amazement would seem to presuppose a standard that seemed unattainable to them, higher than one that allowed for an exception in the case of adultery or sexual immorality.

(7) The "divorce for adultery or sexual immorality" view, by allowing for an exception, seems to take a lower view of the marriage covenant than seems warranted in light of the high view of the permanence of covenants in Scripture, especially the covenant between Christ and the church after which marriage is allegedly patterned.

RESPONSE

In response, proponents of this view would point out the following:

(1) Setting aside the Matthean passage as "difficult" and hence rendering it ineffectual in favor of the absolute statements in the other Synoptic Gospels is hermeneutically suspect, since the judgment of which passages are "difficult" and which are "clear" is itself unduly subjective. More appropriately, each passage ought to be properly interpreted and then harmonized with parallel passages, and all of these passages ought to be brought to bear on one's understanding of the biblical teaching on a given issue. Moreover, the "exception clause" is found not only in Matthew 19, but also in Matthew 5 (there in the context of

the "Sermon on the Mount"), so that according to Matthew the "exception clause" was a repeated aspect of Jesus' teaching on divorce and thus ought not to be dismissed lightly. On a related note, while speaking of Reformation principles, it should be noted that interpreting "except for *porneia*" as "except for sexual immorality" clearly seems to be the natural, most straightforward reading of the phrase in light of the word's semantic profile in the Greek.[51]

(2) The Markan, Lukan, and Pauline intentions were different from those of Matthew, which in their view accounts adequately for their omission of the exception clause (see further the survey of relevant passages for remarriage below); and even though the exception clause is found only in Matthew, it is still there and must be dealt with—we are not at liberty to set aside biblical teaching just because it is given *only once* (or twice; see the previous point).

(3) Jesus affirmed God's creation ideal as well as the Mosaic stipulations in Deuteronomy 24:1-4, rightly interpreted, thus upholding the validity of Scripture in both instances. If there is a tension, this is because of the presence of sin in this world, not undue compromise on Jesus' part. Allowing for an exception does not in any way put in question the ideal, norm, or general principle.

(4) While Jesus' pronouncement in Matthew 19:9 may appear to be in conflict with the Mosaic stipulations in Deuteronomy 24:1-4, there is essential continuity in principle: just as Moses allowed for exceptions because of people's hardness of heart (in his case, "some indecency"), so Jesus makes an exception (in his case, for *porneia,* that is, sexual immorality/adultery). Nevertheless, there is a deepening as well as a shift between the Mosaic code and Jesus' ruling.[52] While in the Old Testament adultery was punishable by death (so that the question of whether or not adultery constituted a legitimate grounds for divorce did not even arise), very few would dispute that according to New Testament teaching capital punishment for adultery no longer applies. For this reason the question naturally arises, what should be done in case of adultery? Jesus' answer appears to be that in this case divorce (no longer death) is permissible (though not required).

(5) As discussed above, Jesus' standard, while concurring with Shammai's interpretation of Deuteronomy 24:1-4, is in fact stricter by

merely permitting rather than requiring divorce in the case of *porneia* and by transcending the rabbinic debate and referring to God's creation ideal as the true norm (albeit not without exception).[53]

(6) The disciples' reaction may betray an unduly lenient view of divorce on their part (at least on the part of some). Also, Jesus' standard, even *with* the exception clause, is still higher than any of the various rabbinic schools in his day, including the more restrictive view of Shammai, in that he merely *permitted* rather than *required* divorce in the case of adultery.

(7) As developed in chapters 2 through 4, while biblical covenants are binding, and while marriage, properly understood, is indeed a covenant, there is reason to believe that some biblical covenants can be and in fact are terminated, so that equating the covenant nature of marriage with their absolute indissolubility may not be biblically warranted.[54]

More Restrictive Views: Divorce Only in Case of Breaking the Betrothal, Incest, Etc.

As mentioned, there is currently no evangelical consensus on the exact nature of the exception stipulated in Matthew 5:32 and 19:9. While a majority of evangelical scholars favors the position that *porneia* in these passages refers to sexual marital unfaithfulness, hence permitting divorce in cases of adultery or other sexual marital infidelity, some think a more narrow offense is in view, such as incest (i.e., marriage within forbidden degrees of kinship, Lev. 18:6-18; 20:17; Deut. 27:22) or the breaking of a betrothal (Deut. 22:20-21).[55]

The former view would allow divorce for those who had married unknowingly within forbidden degrees of kinship allowed by pagan law, which would have been important for Matthew's Jewish-Christian readers concerned about the large influx of Gentiles into the church. This view is rendered unlikely, however, by the fact that a marriage within the forbidden degrees of kinship would not have been recognized as a true marriage and thus would not have required a divorce.[56] Moreover, Deuteronomy 24 is a much more likely background for the present passage than Leviticus 18.[57]

The latter option, which interprets *porneia* as denoting sexual unfaithfulness during the betrothal period, is often viewed in its Matthean context as an attempt to show the legitimacy of Joseph's decision to divorce Mary upon hearing that she had become pregnant during the betrothal period.[58] By including Jesus' statement, with the exception clause, it is argued, Matthew shows Joseph's contemplated action to be that of a righteous man.[59] Those who hold this view point out that, in contrast to today, a betrothed couple was already considered "husband" and "wife" in Jewish society, so that a betrothal, like a marriage, could be severed only by issuing a formal certificate of divorce.[60] The proponents of this view maintain that it is only an as of yet unconsummated marriage (i.e., a betrothal) that can be severed by "divorce."[61] A marriage consummated by sexual union still exists in God's eyes even where divorce has occurred.[62]

Rather than viewing the absolute statements in Mark 10:11-12 and Luke 16:18 in light of Matthew 19, advocates of the "betrothal view" take the opposite approach. Mark and Luke, it is argued, represent Jesus' entire teaching on divorce of consummated marriages, and the Matthean passage, read correctly, likewise teaches a "no divorce once the marriage has been consummated" position, since breaking a betrothal does not constitute a true divorce (by modern standards) in the sense that a marriage is severed. Proponents of this view also observe that *porneia* is used alongside *moicheia*—and thus distinguished from it—in Matthew 15:19, and they contend that the two terms should also be distinguished in 19:9. Hence *porneia* cannot mean—or even include—adultery (i.e., marital sexual unfaithfulness) in Matthew 19:9, because if this had been his intention, Matthew would have used *moicheia,* not *porneia.*

As evidence for an instance where *porneia* refers to (alleged) sexual unfaithfulness during the betrothal period, representatives of the "betrothal view" typically cite John 8:41. If the expression refers to fornication in that instance, "fornication" could also be a legitimate meaning of the term in Matthew 19:9. Whether or not *porneia* refers to sexual unfaithfulness during the betrothal period, proponents of this view discern a link between the present passage and the account of Jesus' birth in Matthew 1:18-25. They conclude that Matthew included the exception clause in Matthew 19:9 to show that Joseph's decision to divorce Mary (on account of her supposed sexual infidelity during the betrothal period) was just and sanctioned by none other than Jesus himself.[63]

If the "betrothal view" is correct, therefore, Jesus' exception for divorce pertains only to sexual infidelity during the betrothal period, not to sexual marital unfaithfulness (the way "marriage" is understood today). This amounts to a "no divorce under any circumstances" view of Jesus' teaching on divorce, since no one today questions that an engaged person is free to break off the engagement if he or she discovers that his or her partner has been sexually unfaithful (or for any other reason, for that matter). As in the case of the "divorce for adultery or sexual immorality" view above, it will be helpful to discuss arguments that have been advanced against the "betrothal" position.

ARGUMENTS ADVANCED AGAINST THE "BETROTHAL" VIEW

The following arguments have been advanced against the "betrothal" view.[64]

(1) In the passage whose interpretation triggered the discussion in Matthew 19, that is, Deuteronomy 24:1-4, it is highly improbable that the discussion is *limited* to betrothal. Almost certainly, the passage *also* extends to marriage, divorce, and remarriage.

(2) There seems to be nothing in the *context of Matthew 19* that either explicitly or implicitly limits the expression *porneia* to betrothal. While breaking a betrothal may be *included* in the phrase, it is hardly *limited* to it.

(3) On a related point, the term *porneia*, unless narrowed by the context, is broader than sex during the betrothal period. It is not a technical term for fornication (as may be suggested by the KJV translation of Matt. 19:9), as would seem to be required by the betrothal view. The argument that if adultery were in view in Matthew 19:9, the term used would be *moicheia*, not *porneia*, with reference to Matthew 15:19, is not conclusive, because the broad expression *porneia* probably *includes moicheia* while not being limited to it (see the discussion of Jer. 3:8-10 and Hos. 2:2-5a above). The broad expression "some indecency" in

Deuteronomy 24:1 likely led to the use of a similarly broad term in Matthew 19:9.

(4) It may be observed that as to the tie posited between Matthew 1:18-25 and Matthew 19:3-12, the former passage (or issue) is not referred to in the latter, which is presented as a rabbinic dispute between Jesus and the Pharisees about a much broader issue, namely, under which circumstances (if any) divorce and remarriage are permissible, rather than exclusively the type of issue with which Joseph, Mary's betrothed, was faced. The alleged tie is further weakened by the fact that Matthew 19 is eighteen chapters removed from Matthew 1 and that *porneia* is not used in Matthew 1:18-25.

(5) In its argument that Mark and Luke provide us with Jesus' complete teaching on divorce while Matthew only deals with an exception related to betrothal, the proponents of the "betrothal view" inadequately recognize the common rabbinic practice of abbreviating an account for the sake of making it more memorable.[65] Rather than concluding that Jesus did not allow for any divorce in sexually consummated marriages, it is much more likely that he did not elaborate on points at which he agreed with the commonly held view in his day. As one authority on the subject notes,

> If Jesus said nothing about a universally accepted belief, then it is assumed by most scholars that this indicated his agreement with it. He is never recorded as saying anything about the immorality of sexual acts before marriage (to the dismay of many youth leaders), but not one assumes that he approved of them. Similarly, everyone assumes that he believed in monotheism, but it would be difficult to demonstrate this from the Gospel accounts. Also, Jesus nowhere explicitly allowed or forbade remarriage after the death of a spouse, but we assume that he did allow this because all Jews, including Paul, clearly allowed it.[66]

On all these matters we find it easy to assume that Jesus agreed with these commonly held positions because we, too, agree with them. In the present case, however, it seems that proponents of the "betrothal view" (illegitimately) construe Jesus' (alleged) silence on a subject as disagreement with the prevailing practice in Jesus' day.

(6) The fact that Mark, Luke, and Paul do not include the excep-

tion clause is not as disqualifying of the "divorce for adultery or sexual immorality" as the proponents of the "betrothal" view claim, since its omission by those writers can be accounted for by the purposes of these authors in their respective literary contexts. In fact, it may be argued that, rather than Mark and Luke, or Jesus himself, not mentioning an exception because there was none, they (or Jesus) may well not have elaborated on points at which Jesus' teaching was in line with the commonly held view in his day. As mentioned above, no first-century Jew questioned that divorce in the case of adultery was permissible. Construing Jesus' "silence" on exceptions for divorce in Mark and Luke as an indication that Jesus did not teach such an exception may therefore be less than decisive.

(7) If, as is likely, one of the reasons why the Pharisees raised this issue with Jesus is that John the Baptist had recently been killed because of his opposition to the marriage between Herod Antipas and Herodias (who had illegitimately divorced Herod's brother Philip; see esp. Mark's account), this would speak against the "betrothal (only) view" as well, since this was obviously not the issue in Herod and Herodias's case—illegitimate divorce of a marriage relationship and hence illegitimate remarriage was the issue.

RESPONSE

Proponents of the "betrothal view" offer the following response:

(1) A variety of responses are given. Some advocates of this position argue that Jesus' teachings transcend Deuteronomy 24:1-4. Others contend that the meaning of *porneia* in Matthew 19 is identical with that of *'erwat dābār* in Deuteronomy 24:1 and that the phrase denotes sexual indecency during the betrothal period in both instances.

(2) Again, responses vary. Most commonly, those who hold this view maintain that John 8:41 shows that *porneia* can refer to sexual unfaithfulness during the betrothal period, and that the link with Matthew 1:18-25 suggests that this is the term's likely meaning in Matthew 19. Others again stress the continuity between Deuteronomy 24 and Matthew 19.

(3) While it is true that *porneia* can have a broader scope of reference, proponents of the "betrothal view" respond that this is rendered

unlikely in Matthew 19 because of a variety of factors, be it the meaning of *'erwat dābār* in Deuteronomy 24:1, the link with Matthew 1:18-25, or other considerations.

(4) The tie between Matthew 1:18-25 and 19:3-12 may be remote literarily in Matthew's Gospel, but for Jesus, defending his earthly father was of very immediate concern; and while removed from Matthew 1, Jesus' validation of Joseph's contemplated action of divorcing Mary in his remarks in Matthew 19 still makes sense theologically in Matthew's Gospel.

(5) We have not found a response to this argument in the available literature on the subject. Proponents of the betrothal view might respond that it is one thing to shorten a statement for the purpose of memory, but it is quite another to shorten *and change* it. It is unlikely that Mark and Luke would record an absolute prohibition if Jesus gave an exception.

(6) The fact that the exception clause is found only in Matthew does appear to make it preferable to explain the Matthean exception in a way that it is congruent with the absolute statements in Mark, Luke, and Paul rather than *vice versa*. Matthew 19 is therefore a questionable starting point for one's study of the biblical teaching on divorce. Some advocates of the "betrothal view" also point out that, assuming that the "exception clause" in Matthew pertains only to the betrothal period, Mark and Luke, writing to predominantly Gentile readers, would have had no need to mention an exception that was irrelevant in a Greco-Roman context.

(7) Most proponents of the "betrothal view" would tend to minimize the role the political situation with Herod Antipas and Herodias played in the dispute at hand.

Summary

In double continuity with Moses, Jesus affirms both that God's ideal for marriage is a lifelong, "one flesh" union (cf. Gen. 2:24-25) and that, because of people's hardness of heart divorce is permissible (but not required) under certain circumstances. Within this context of essential continuity, Jesus is both "lighter" and "heavier" than Moses: on the one hand, the punishment for adultery is no longer death (an undeniable difference between the Old and the New Testament); on the other, adultery (now no longer punishable by death, which made further legislation unnecessary)—that is, any sexual sin by one of the marriage partners— and adultery (or sexual immorality) alone, is recognized as legitimate grounds for divorce.

Since adultery was clearly not the grounds for legitimate divorce in Deuteronomy 24, this means that Jesus, in a major break with Jewish law as well as with contemporary rabbinic schools, ruled out any Deuteronomy 24–type infractions as legitimate grounds for divorce (though, of course, the schools of Shammai and Hillel interpreted this passage differently), which explains the consternation his pronounce-ment caused among his hearers (including his own followers). Hence Jesus brilliantly upheld the true significance of the Mosaic law—God's ideal for marriage as well as an exception made on account of people's hardness of heart—while at the same time deepening people's under-standing of both the true intent of the law and the nature of the mar-riage union.

Since both Genesis passages quoted by Jesus in Matthew 19:4-6 (i.e., Gen. 1:27 and Gen. 2:24) refer to human sexuality, and since the indissolubility of the marriage Jesus defends is predicated upon the sex-ual ("one flesh") union referred to in Genesis 2:24, sexual promiscuity constitutes a *de facto* exception. While this violation of the marriage covenant may not necessitate divorce, "permission for divorce and remarriage under such circumstances, far from being inconsistent with Jesus' thought, is in perfect harmony with it."[67] And, as mentioned, "[w]ith the death penalty for marital *porneia* effectively abolished, 'the termination of the relationship might appropriately be effected by divorce.'"[68]

PAUL'S TEACHING ON DIVORCE

Paul addresses the same issue in a somewhat different context, that of a believer's desertion by an unbelieving spouse (1 Cor. 7:12-16).[69] Since Jesus had not dealt with this specific question, Paul must adjudicate the situation himself ("I, not the Lord," 7:12), which in no way diminishes the authoritative nature of Paul's apostolic pronouncement. According to Paul, a mixed marriage (i.e., one spouse is a believer, while the other is not) in such circumstances is preferable to divorce (cf. 1 Pet. 3:1-2), because it provides a Christian environment for the children of this marital union (1 Cor. 7:14).[70] Yet if the unbelieving spouse insists on leaving, the believer is not to hold him or her back, because God's desire is for peace, and there is no guarantee that the unbeliever will eventually be saved (7:15-16).[71]

Differences Between the "Divorce for Adultery or Sexual Immorality" View and the "No Divorce, No Remarriage" Position

	Potential weaknesses	Responses to weaknesses
DIVORCE FOR ADULTERY OR SEXUAL IMMORALITY (General interpretation; *porneia* referring to sexual marital unfaithfulness)	Why start with "more difficult passage"?	"More difficult" too subjective; "exception clause" also in Matt. 5:32; more natural reading
	The exception clause is limited to Matthew	Markan, Lukan, and Pauline intentions were different from those of Matthew
	There is a tension between Jesus' references to God's ideal for marriage at creation in Matt. 19:4-6 and his allowing an exception for divorce in Matt. 19:9	Jesus affirmed God's creation ideal as well as the Mosaic stipulations in Deut. 24:1-4; the tension is due to sin in the world
	How is there continuity between Moses in Deut. 24 and Jesus in Matt. 19?	Continuity in principle between God's ideal and exception because of people's hardness of heart
	Jesus essentially answers the divorce question, put to him in Hillelite terms, in a Shammaite fashion. One would expect Jesus to posit a higher standard than either school, namely "no divorce under any circumstance"	Jesus' standard in fact is stricter by permitting rather than requiring divorce and by referring to God's creation ideal as the true norm
	There is difficulty explaining the disciples' reaction	The disciples' reaction may betray an unduly lenient view of divorce on their part
	The view seems to take a lower view of the marriage covenant than seems warranted in light of the high view of the permanence of covenants in Scripture	There is reason to believe that covenants can be broken

	Potential weaknesses	Responses to weaknesses
NO DIVORCE/NO REMARRIAGE (Narrow interpretation; *porneia* referring to incest or sexual infidelity during the engagement period)	Deut. 24:1-4, which underlies the discussion in Matthew 19, is not limited to betrothal but extends also to marriage, divorce, and remarriage	Jesus' teaching transcends Deut. 24:1-4
	Nothing in the context of Matthew 19 inherently limits the expression *porneia* to bethrothal	As John 8:41 shows, *porneia* can indeed refer to premarital sexual unfaithfulness
	The term *porneia*, unless narrowed by the context, is broader than premarital sex	Though *porneia* can have a broader scope of reference, this is rendered unlikely in Matthew 19 because of larger theological considerations
	The alleged tie posited between Matt. 1:18-25 and Matt. 19:3-12 is unlikely	The tie between Matt. 1:18-25 and Matt. 19:3-12 makes perfect sense in the original Matthean context as a rehabilitation of Joseph through Jesus' teaching on divorce
	Rabbinic practice of abbreviating accounts inadequately recognized	It is one thing to shorten Jesus' statement but another to change its meaning
	The fact that Mark, Luke, and Paul do not include the exception clause can be explained by the respective purposes of these authors in their respective literary contexts	It is preferable to explain the Matthean exception in a way that is congruent with the absolute statements in Mark, Luke, and Paul rather than vice versa
	How is the issue of sexual immorality during betrothal period relevant to political issue of illegitimate divorce and remarriage of Herod Antipas and Herodias?	Advocates of this interpretation tend to minimize the relevance of the Herod/Herodias background

The Corinthian Context: Divorce for Desertion by Unbelieving Spouse

In order to appreciate Paul's ruling on divorce in the present passage, a proper understanding of the Corinthian context is indispensable.[72] Apparently some were teaching the superiority of singleness over marriage on the basis of a Greek dualism that disparaged sexual relations as inferior to the true spirituality of an ascetic lifestyle (1 Cor. 7:1, 5; cf. 1 Tim. 4:3). To counter this entirely non-Christian notion, Paul wrote that a wife must not divorce (*chōrizō*) her husband; but if she does (disobeying the apostle's ruling), she must either remain unmarried or be reconciled.[73] The same applies if circumstances are reversed (*aphiēmi*; 1 Cor 7:10-11). In the case of the *conversion* of one spouse, that believer must not initiate divorce. If the unbelieving spouse leaves, however, the remaining spouse is "not bound" (*dedoulōtai*): divorce is legitimate, and, many (though not all; see further below) infer, the believer is free to remarry.[74]

Needless to say, the dissimilarity between the Corinthian situation and the contemporary setting in this regard is readily apparent, since few today want to divorce their spouse in order to pursue a more perfect, sexless spirituality. In most cases, people have "fallen out of love" and simply want to get out of a present—now inconvenient—marriage to marry another, more desirable partner.[75] The injunction in verse 11, "(but if she does leave, let her remain unmarried, or else be reconciled to her husband)" (NASB), is at times taken as an absolute prohibition of remarriage under any circumstances. However, what is prohibited here is only remarriage after an illegitimate, not legitimate, divorce (assuming that there are some divorces that are legitimate; cf. v. 10: "the wife should not leave her husband" (NASB) with v. 11: "but if she does leave").

In the Corinthian context, then, a married person must not divorce his or her spouse (presumably, out of a desire to be more "spiritual"). Neither is it legitimate for a married person to observe continence, that is, to refrain permanently from sexual intercourse with his or her partner in marriage (1 Cor. 7:3-5). The only concession made by Paul is that believers who are deserted by their unbelieving spouse may divorce and (most, though not all, would agree; see further below) remarry. It would appear that the same principle applies today. If so, the divorce of those deserted by their unbelieving spouses ought to be considered legitimate, with the implication that remarriage would also be legitimate in those circumstances.

Jesus' and Paul's Teachings on Remarriage

There may therefore be two legitimate reasons for divorce stipulated by Jesus and Paul respectively: (1) adultery or marital unfaithfulness on account of sexual immorality (Matt. 5:32; 19:9; assuming that one adopts the majority view); and (2) desertion by an unbelieving spouse (1 Cor. 7:11-15). Beyond this, (3) death of a spouse also ends a marriage (and in this case at least, the remaining spouse is allowed to remarry, but "only in the Lord"; 1 Cor. 7:39; cf. Rom. 7:3).[76] But what does the New Testament teach regarding remarriage?

Survey of Relevant Passages

As we have already seen in the discussion above, Deuteronomy 24:1-4 serves as an important background passage, not only regarding divorce, but also on remarriage. Specifically, the Mosaic law code stipulates that once a man divorces his wife, and she marries another man who also divorces her, her first husband is not allowed to take her back. This passage looms behind the following New Testament texts, which likewise serve the purpose of warning men against arbitrarily divorcing their wives and against marrying illegitimately divorced women, and which also serve the purpose of protecting women.

In Matthew 5:31-32, as part of the Sermon on the Mount, Jesus contrasts the externalistic interpretation of rabbinic tradition with the true intent of the law. "It was also said, 'Whoever divorces his wife, let him give her a certificate of divorce.' But I say to you that everyone who divorces his wife, except on the ground of sexual immorality [or, discovery of indecency during the betrothal period, according to the "betrothal view"], makes her commit adultery. And whoever marries a divorced woman commits adultery." Why does illegitimate divorce cause both the wife and her second husband to commit adultery? The reason is that in God's eyes, the wife is still considered to be married to her first husband. The Mosaic stipulation in Deuteronomy 24:1 which is presupposed here sought to regulate divorce by requiring that a formal certificate of divorce be issued rather than that a wife merely be sent away. Jesus considerably ups the ante ("But I say to you") by limiting permissible (though not required) divorce to a single exception. The primary purpose of his pronouncement in the present passage seems to be that of protecting wives by limiting legitimate grounds for divorce to one sole exceptional instance.

Matthew 19:3-12 deals with the issue of divorce as part of a rabbinic dispute between Jesus and the Pharisees, which would be significant particularly for Matthew's Jewish audience.[77] In Matthew 19:9, Jesus says, "And I say to you: whoever divorces his wife, except for sexual immorality [or, indecency discovered during the betrothal period, according to the "betrothal view"], and marries another, commits adultery." Again, the reason is that God still considers that man to be married to his first wife. It seems to follow logically that if the divorce is for a wife's marital sexual unfaithfulness, and the husband marries another woman, he does *not* commit adultery (though this is disputed by some; others think the divorce referred to here is only for betrothed couples). The main purpose of Jesus' pronouncement here seems to be to issue a strong warning to husbands against divorcing wives illegitimately.

In the parallel account in Mark 10:11-12, Jesus is quoted as saying, "Whoever divorces his wife and marries another commits adultery *against her, and if she divorces her husband and marries another, she commits adultery.*" Over against Matthew, Mark includes the phrase "against her," emphasizing that the woman is the sinned-against party. He also adds that what is true for the husband is also true for the wife. In the context of Mark's Gospel, the function of Mark 10:11 seems to be to provide a commentary on John the Baptist's condemnation of the illicit marriage between Herod Antipas and Herodias, his brother Philip's former wife, which is mentioned in 6:17-19. Hence in this context it would not be meaningful to include the Matthean exception clause, because clearly this was not relevant to the case of Herod's marriage to Herodias.

The parallel passage in Luke's Gospel, Luke 16:18, combines the material in Mark 10:11 and Matthew 5:32b. It stands virtually alone without a context and reads as follows: "Anyone who divorces his wife and marries another woman commits adultery (= Mark 10:11), and the man who marries a divorced woman commits adultery" (= Matt. 5:32b) (NIV). Again, there is a warning to men not to divorce arbitrarily on the one hand and not to marry an illegitimately divorced woman on the other. The primary purpose, once again, is to protect women, which is a pronounced Lukan theme.

The final passage on the subject is found in 1 Corinthians 7:10-16. In verses 10-11, Paul draws on Jesus' teaching as follows: "To the married I give this charge (not I, but the Lord): the wife should not separate from her husband (but if she does, she should remain unmarried or else be reconciled to her husband), and the husband should not divorce his wife." As do Mark and Luke, Paul casts his statement in absolute terms, which makes Matthew the only New Testament document to include the exception clause regarding divorce for *porneia*. Husbands or wives should not divorce their spouses, yet if they do, they must not remarry. While 1 Corinthians 7:10-11 reads well under the assumption of a "no divorce, no remarriage" view, 7:15 seems to present a difficulty.

In this passage Paul proceeds to add the following apostolic pronouncement: "To the rest I say (I, not the Lord) that if any brother has a wife who is an unbeliever, and she consents to live with him, he should not divorce her," and *vice versa* (1 Cor. 7:12-13). After providing a rationale, the apostle concludes, "But if the unbelieving partner separates, let it be so. In such cases the brother or sister is not enslaved [NIV: "not bound"]. . . ." (7:15; the Greek word for "bound" is *douloō*). What is meant by "not bound" here? The parallel in 7:39 helps to shed some light on this question. There Paul writes, "A wife is *bound* [Greek *deō*] to her husband as long as he lives. But if her husband dies, she is *free to be married* to whom she wishes, only in the Lord." What seems only implied in 1 Corinthians 7:15 is spelled out more explicitly in 7:39, namely that "not bound" means "free to remarry." Unless further considerations emerge from the discussion under the next heading, it appears therefore that Paul would have allowed, not only divorce, but also remarriage, in the case of desertion by an unbelieving spouse.

The Current Discussion

The Mosaic stipulations in Deuteronomy 24:1-4 do allow remarriage in the case of divorce, albeit not to the same person. With regard to Matthew 5:32 and 19:9, some argue that divorce, but not remarriage, was permitted by Jesus in the case of sexual unfaithfulness during the betrothal period. These scholars contend that Matthew drops "and marries another woman" in Matthew 5:32 (cf. Mark 10:11 and Luke 16:18) and that the exception clause in Matthew 19:9 immediately follows the reference to divorce in the case of *porneia* but *precedes* the reference to remarriage, which they take to strongly imply that only divorce, but not remarriage, was allowed by Jesus in the case of *porneia* (and that only in the case of betrothal).[78] However, it seems that this view would require its proponents to argue that even Joseph would have been prohibited from "remarrying" (on the assumption that his betrothed was sexually unfaithful), which is hardly plausible. Also, even if *porneia* were to refer to *marital* sexual unfaithfulness, if Jesus were to allow for divorce on those grounds but then forbid remarriage, this would hardly constitute a divorce, but only a separation.[79]

With regard to 1 Corinthians 7:15, a majority of evangelical scholars interpret the passage in conjunction with 7:39 as teaching that the innocent party is free to remarry.[80] Paul's phrase "free to be married" in the latter passage resembles the Jewish divorce formula, "you are free to marry any man" (*m. Giṭṭin* 9:3). The Greek words *douloō* and *deō* are viewed as related and as used interchangeably.[81] The minority, however, counters that nothing is said explicitly about the possibility of remarriage and maintains that for the following reasons remarriage is not permitted even in the case of desertion by an unbeliever: (1) marriage is a creation ordinance, a covenant, which is permanently binding regardless of circumstances such as desertion by an unbelieving spouse; (2) Paul specifically prohibits remarriage in 1 Corinthians 7:10-11; (3) the words *douloō* and *deō* are not interchangeable; and (4) where Paul refers to the possibility of remarriage, this is always in the context of the death of one of the marriage partners (Rom. 7:2; 1 Cor. 7:39).

By way of response, the majority (note that not all proponents of the "betrothal view" agree at this point) observes that (1) the covenant nature of marriage raises the question of whether or not certain relevant covenants can be dissolved under any circumstances, which was dealt with in chapters 2 through 4; (2) Paul's argument in 1 Corinthians 7:15 proceeds beyond verses 10-11: verses 10-11 deal with the contemplated divorce of two believers, which is proscribed as illegitimate; in verse 12 the apostle speaks "to the rest"; and verse 15 deals with cases of abandonment where an unbeliever deserts his or her believing spouse; (3) while not identical, the terms *douloō* and *deō* do seem to inhabit the same semantic domain ("be under bondage," "be bound"), so that 1 Corinthians 7:39 seems to be admissible as a relevant parallel to 1 Corinthians 7:15; in addition, it should be noted that the verb tense of the phrase "not bound" (*ou dedoulōtai,* perfect tense) in 7:15 implies that the unbeliever abandoned the marriage in the past and that, as a result, the remaining believing spouse is *"no longer* bound" at the present time (with the effect of the abandonment continuing into the present); the burden of explaining how the Greek perfect tense here is compatible with a "no remarriage" position would seem to rest on those who advocate such a view; (4) Paul may be using an analogy, saying that when an unbelieving spouse deserts his or her partner, it is as if that person has died.[82]

On the basis of the discussion above, it is therefore on the whole more likely, and in keeping with first-century Jewish belief, that *in the cases of legitimate divorce, a legitimately divorced person is free to remarry.*[83] This is the view of a majority of evangelical interpreters today.[84] This conclusion is borne out also by the standard Jewish formula in the bill of divorce cited in the Mishnah, "See, you are free to marry any man" (*m. Giṭṭin* 9:3).[85] This also seems to be the assumption underlying Jesus' statement that "anyone who divorces his wife . . . causes her to become an adulteress [assuming remarriage as a matter of course], and anyone who marries the divorced woman commits adultery" (Matt. 5:32, NIV).[86]

The same would be true for those left widowed by the death of their spouse. Thus Paul encourages young widows to remarry (1 Tim. 5:14) and elsewhere rules more globally that a widow "is *free* . . . , and if she marries another man she is not an adulteress" (Rom. 7:3; cf. *m. Qid.* 1:1).[87] As mentioned, Paul writes in 1 Corinthians 7:39 that "a wife is *bound* to her husband as long as he lives. But if her husband dies, she is *free to be married* to whom she wishes, only in the Lord" (1 Cor. 7:39). Whether widowed (in which cases Paul explicitly encourages remarriage) or legitimately divorced, then, a person bereft of his or her spouse is free to remarry.

Whether or not remarriage is permitted for the victims of their spouse's sexual immorality (on the basis of the "divorce for adultery or sexual immorality" view) or unbelieving desertion, what about those who are the guilty party? What about the spouse who has committed adultery or left his or her partner because of that person's coming to faith? Regarding the former, it may be surmised that since adultery has already occurred, a new marriage on the part of the guilty party further compounds his or her guilt.[88] Regarding the latter, in practice the issue is inconsequential, since the unbeliever's major problem is that of unbelief, which is why that person will not be willing to subject himself or herself to the scriptural standard in any case.

The "Remarriage" and "No Remarriage" Positions
on 1 Corinthians 7

NO REMARRIAGE	REMARRIAGE
Marriage is a creation ordinance, a covenant, which is permanently binding regardless of circumstances	A covenant can be broken under certain circumstances
Paul specifically prohibits remarriage in 1 Cor. 7:10-11	1 Cor. 7:10-11 refers to believers, 1 Cor. 7:15 to believer abandoned by unbelieving spouse
The words *douloō* and *deō* are not interchangeable	While not identical, the terms *douloō* and *deō* do seem to inhabit the same semantic domain
Where Paul refers to the possibility of remarriage, this is always in the context of the death of one of the marriage partners (Rom. 7:2; 1 Cor. 7:39)	Paul may be using an analogy, saying that when an unbelieving spouse deserts his or her partner, it is as if that person has died

Summary

After discussing the various viewpoints on both Jesus' and Paul's teachings on divorce and remarriage, we conclude our discussion of the different views on these topics with a brief description and survey of the various positions held among evangelicals today. The first view espouses the biblical legitimacy of *divorce and remarriage for the innocent party of a spouse's adultery/sexual immorality and of an unbelieving spouse's desertion* ("divorce and remarriage"). This is sometimes labeled the "Erasmian view," since the well-known Reformer Erasmus of Rotterdam held this position, though other descriptions are used as well.[89] The position, which is found also in the Westminster Confession of Faith, represents the majority view among evangelicals today. Craig Blomberg, Don Carson, John Feinberg and Paul Feinberg, Gordon Hugenberger, David Clyde Jones, John MacArthur, John Murray,

Robert Stein, John Stott, and now also William Heth are among its most well-known proponents.[90]

The second view holds to *divorce for adultery and an unbelieving spouse's desertion but not remarriage* ("divorce, no remarriage"). This view was widespread among the church fathers. More recently, it has been embraced by Gordon Wenham and William Heth (but now Heth has changed his view; see above), Robert Gundry, Andrew Cornes, and the French scholar Jacques Dupont.[91]

The third view allows for *neither divorce nor remarriage in the case of adultery and for divorce but not remarriage in the case of desertion by an unbelieving spouse* ("no divorce, no remarriage"). This is the position of, among others, Abel Isaksson, James Montgomery Boice, Dwight Pentecost, and John Piper.[92] As is the case also with the other views, there are variations within the parameters of this position. In some cases the indissolubility of marriage (except in cases of the death of one spouse) is a strongly held belief by proponents of this view.

The fourth and final position[93] is that of *no divorce or remarriage for adultery but divorce and remarriage in the case of desertion by an unbeliever* ("no divorce, no remarriage/divorce, remarriage"). It should be noted that some proponents of the "betrothal view" discussed above hold to the third view (which does not accept the so-called "Pauline privilege"), while others subscribe to the fourth position (which does). In contrast to some proponents of the third view, those who advocate the fourth position do not subscribe to the notion of the absolute indissolubility of marriage. This view is held by Daniel Heimbach.[94]

CONCLUSION

We conclude with some pastoral implications and three parting principles.

Pastoral Implications

What are the pastoral implications of the above-presented positions on divorce and remarriage? First, the creation narrative upholds, and Jesus and Paul reaffirm, God's ordinance of marriage as a lifelong union between one man and one woman. God's ideal holds true even in a fallen world where sin is an ever-present reality and where divorce does occur.

Four Major Positions on Divorce and Remarriage

	DIVORCE AND REMARRIAGE FOR ADULTERY AND DESERTION	DIVORCE, NO REMARRIAGE FOR ADULTERY AND DESERTION	NO DIVORCE, NO REMARRIAGE FOR ADULTERY: DIVORCE BUT NO REMARRIAGE FOR DESERTION	NO DIVORCE, NO REMARRIAGE FOR ADULTERY; DIVORCE, REMARRIAGE FOR DESERTION
DEFINITION	Divorce and remarriage for the innocent party of a spouse's adultery/sexual immorality and of an unbelieving spouse's desertion	Divorce for adultery but not remarriage for both adultery and spousal desertion by an unbeliever	Neither divorce nor remarriage in the case of adultery, divorce but no remarriage in the case of desertion by an unbelieving spouse	No divorce or remarriage for adultery but divorce and remarriage in the case of desertion by an unbeliever

MAJOR REPRESENTATIVES	Erasmus
	Westminster Confession
	Craig Blomberg
	Don Carson
	John Feinberg and
	    Paul Feinberg
	Gordon Hugenberger
	David Clyde Jones
	John MacArthur
	John Murray
	Robert Stein
	John Stott
	William Heth
		Gordon Wenham
		William Heth
		  (prior to 2002)
		Robert Gundry
		Andrew Cornes
		Jacques Dupont
			Abel Isaksson
			James M. Boice
			Dwight Pentecost
			John Piper
				Daniel Heimbach

Second, some believe that according to Scripture, marriage is indissoluble, be it in a sacramental or a covenantal sense, except in the case of the death of one spouse. If so, divorce is never legitimate, and remarriage is always wrong as long as one's marriage partner is still living. This means that in the cases of adultery or desertion by an unbeliever the one whose partner committed sexual unfaithfulness or abandoned the marriage relationship is kept from remarrying under any circumstances. While this does safeguard a high standard of marriage, it carries the danger of placing too stringent a requirement on the one whose partner is guilty of sexual unfaithfulness or abandonment. If Paul, for example, strongly urged young widows to remarry, why ought victims of spousal sexual unfaithfulness whose partner has remarried be prohibited from entering into another marriage? Perhaps here there may be some legitimacy to the concern that a "no divorce, no remarriage" view may be unduly harsh toward the innocent party.

Third, there is, of course, the converse danger of being more lenient than Scripture allows. If the Bible were indeed to prohibit divorce and remarriage under any circumstances in order to uphold the indissolubility of marriage, anyone allowing for any exceptions (even adultery or abandonment) would be guilty of encouraging others to sin. It should be noted, however, that currently a majority of evangelical scholars favor allowing divorce and remarriage for adultery and desertion by an unbeliever. In most (if not all) cases, these scholars hold a high view of marriage (in many cases a covenant view) and cannot lightly be accused of allowing for exceptions simply because their view of marriage is inadequately low.

Unless one is very certain, therefore, that Scripture absolutely prohibits divorce and remarriage under any and all circumstances (only remarriage in the case of the death of one spouse excepted), it would seem wise to err on the side of mercy and to allow for divorce and remarriage in the cases of adultery and abandonment, lest people are held to a standard that may be higher even than the biblical one.

Fourth, divorce is never willed by God and is always the result of sin. Marital reconciliation and the restoration and preservation of marriages always ought to be the goal and prayer of the individuals concerned. Forgiveness is always required on the part of the victim of his partner's sexual unfaithfulness or desertion. Nevertheless, there is ultimately no control over the response of the sinning and/or unbelieving partner. Once remarriage on the part of that other partner has taken place, it would seem that there is now no possibility of restoration of the original union without breaking a second union that has now been established (cf. Deut. 24:1-4, esp. v. 4). Hence the pastoral strategy may at this point legitimately shift toward allowing the victimized partner the freedom to remarry.

Parting Principles

On the basis of these observations, then, we conclude with three parting principles. First, everything should be done to *uphold a high view of marriage* and to *preserve marriage* wherever possible (except in extreme cases, such as persistent spousal abuse, in which separation may be called for).

Second, on the assumption that divorce in cases of adultery or abandonment is permissible (though never mandated), and where there is no remaining possibility of restoring the original marriage, a *determination* should be made whether or not a given divorce is *biblically permissible* (though proponents of the indissolubility view will deny that such is ever the case). If so, a person may remarry, and a pastor may officiate at the wedding. Otherwise, he should decline to perform the ceremony.

Third, rather than adopting a "no fault" approach to divorce, a *clear distinction* should be drawn between the *guilty* and the *innocent party*.[95] The innocent party should be treated as if single or unmarried, the guilty party as divorced.[96]

Finally, one's views on divorce and remarriage have important ramifications not only in cases where regular church members are affected, but particularly when it comes to church leadership. Are there any circumstances under which a pastor or elder or deacon who has been divorced can legitimately and biblically be entrusted with this office? Or does Scripture bar such men from all church offices? While this issue is clearly related to the above discussion of the biblical teaching on divorce and remarriage in general, several other texts are brought into play here, so that we will defer discussion until the following chapter.

12

FAITHFUL HUSBANDS: QUALIFICATIONS FOR CHURCH LEADERSHIP

THE QUALIFICATIONS FOR church leadership stipulated in the Pastoral Epistles give prominent coverage to an applicant's marriage and family life.[1] In 1 Timothy 3:1-13, the primary passage on the subject, it is required that both overseers and deacons be "faithful husbands" (*mias gynaikas andra*, 3:2, 12; cf. Titus 1:6; see further below); that overseers keep their children under control with all dignity (1 Tim. 3:4; cf. Titus 1:6); and that they manage their own household well (1 Tim. 3:4). For, according to Pauline logic, "If anyone does not know how to manage his own family, how can he take care of God's church?" (3:5, NIV). Indeed, as the apostle makes clear later in the same chapter, the church is "God's household" (3:15, NIV).[2] There is thus a close relationship between church and family, and Christian maturity in the fulfillment of one's duties as husband and father becomes one of the most essential requirements for those aspiring to the office of pastor or elder.[3]

THE REQUIREMENT OF MARITAL FAITHFULNESS

The Meaning of the Phrase Mias Gynaikas Andra

English translations as well as commentators differ considerably regarding the meaning of the phrase *mias gynaikas andra* in 1 Timothy 3:2 and 12.[4] (1) Does Paul here require church leaders to be married (excluding unmarried officeholders)? (2) Is he seeking to prohibit applicants who are divorced? (3) Does the requirement bar widowers who remarried from holding ecclesiastical office (NRSV)? (4) Does the apostle speak out against polygamy (as is implied in the NIV)? (5) Or is he requiring that an officeholder be faithful in marriage if he is (and assuming that he usually is) in fact married, as opposed to being unfaithful to his wife while being married to her, as would be the case if he had one or several extramarital affairs? (This was often the case in the ancient world in the form of concubinage.) Virtually all of these positions are taken by at least certain translations and/or commentators.[5] How can this difficult issue be satisfactorily resolved, and which interpretation is most likely in light of the meaning of the phrase and the ancient cultural background?

First, it is unlikely that Paul, who himself was unmarried throughout most, if not all, his apostolic career (cf. 1 Cor. 7:8; see chapter 9) and who elsewhere extols the advantages of singleness for kingdom service (1 Cor. 7:32-35), would exclude single men from holding ecclesiastical office. Also, if the apostle's intention had been to limit the holding of church offices to those who were married, he could have said so much more unequivocally (e.g., by listing as a requirement that overseers be "married," *gamos*). It is therefore highly probable that the present requirement simply assumes that most potentially qualified candidates would likely be married and hence addresses a man's conduct toward his wife in marriage.

Second, if it had been Paul's intent to exclude divorcees, one can once again think of more direct ways in which he may have articulated this requirement (e.g., "not divorced"). At least on the face of it, this can at best be considered a possible inference (from the wording, "husband of *one* wife") rather than a direct statement. In fact, divorce is not mentioned anywhere in all of the Pastoral Epistles (neither is remarriage).

Third, it is also unlikely that Paul sought to prohibit widowers who remarried (who, by a literal reading, would in that case have been married, not once, but twice) from holding church office. Paul elsewhere encourages those who are widowed to remarry and adopts an entirely positive stance toward those who have lost their spouses.[6] It would be hard to understand why Paul would bar from church office widowers who follow his advice and remarry. This is true especially since many of these persons would be older, mature men who command respect and possess the life experience and spiritual seasoning to provide competent and distinguished leadership in the church (cf. Titus 2:2; 1 Pet. 5:5; see also 1 Thess. 5:12; Heb. 13:17). In the case of widowers who remarry, remarriage does not imply any character flaw or moral failure on their part. Nor does the presence of a new wife constitute an obstacle to such a man's eligibility, since he would be no different from other married men who seek and hold church office. There seems therefore to be no biblical, theological, or even commonsense reason why remarried widowers should be barred from church office.

Fourth, the theory that Paul sought to exclude polygamists from holding church office[7] runs into the difficulty that polygamy was not widely practiced in the Greco-Roman world at the time.[8] Considerably more likely is the possibility that the phrase *mias gynaikas andra* is geared toward barring men from holding church office who had one or several concubines, a widespread practice at that time.[9] Apparently, neither the Greeks nor the Romans regarded these practices as adulterous or polygamous. For Paul, however, concubinage was essentially equivalent to polygamy, since sexual union results in a "one flesh" relationship (cf. 1 Cor. 6:16).

For this reason, fifth, "faithful husband" is probably the best way to capture the essence of the expression *mias gynaikas andra*.[10] That the phrase constitutes a reference to marital faithfulness is suggested by the parallel in 1 Timothy 5:9, where a widow eligible for church support is required to have been "faithful to her husband" (NIV = TNIV) and where the equivalent phrase "wife of one husband" is used (cf. 1 Cor. 7:2-5). In the latter instance, the phrase cannot indicate a prohibition of polyandry (being married to more than one husband at a time, which in any case was virtually nonexistent in the ancient world) since it is made of a woman bereft of her husband. Moreover, it would hardly make sense for Paul first to encourage younger widows to get remarried and then disqualify them later on the grounds that they have (literally) been wives of more than one husband.[11] On a different note, the present requirement of marital faithfulness for church leaders (including deacons, 1 Tim. 3:12) is also consistent with the prohibition of adultery in the Decalogue (Ex. 20:14 = Deut. 5:18).[12]

If the above discussion is on target, therefore, it seems that the problem with the first four interpretations listed above is that they are based on a literalistic, if not rigid, reading of the phrase *mias gynaikas andros* as denoting *literally* marriage to only *one* woman *ever:* one as opposed to zero as in the case of single candidates for church office, or one as opposed to two or more wives, be it at the same time (polygamy) or consecutively (remarriage of widowers, divorcees). More likely, however, the phrase is to be understood *idiomatically* (designating "a one-wife-type-of-husband"), that is, as a term for marital faithfulness rather than as a literal enumeration of a certain number of marriages (one rather than zero or two or more) in which a candidate is required to be engaged.[13]

That this is in fact the case is further supported by inscriptional evidence regarding the Roman concept of a *univira,* that is, a "one husband"-type of wife.[14] This term denoting marital fidelity was initially applied to living women in relation to their husbands and later became an epithet given by husbands to their deceased wives. This is attested by numerous extant literary references and tombstone inscriptions. Hence the first-century B.C. poet Catullus wrote, "[T]o live content with one's husband alone is the greatest of compliments a wife can receive."[15] A Roman imperial inscription reads, "She lived fifty years and was satisfied with one husband."[16] The late-first-century B.C. *Laudatio Turiae* records a husband saying about his wife, "Rare are marriages, so long lasting, and ended by death, not interrupted by divorce . . ."[17]

For these reasons we conclude that the Pauline *mias gynaikas andra* requirement is best understood as stipulating that candidates for church office (both elder and deacon) be faithful husbands (assuming that they are currently married). If this is correct, what, then, are the implications of this requirement for the church today? In the following discussion we will briefly consider the implications of this requirement for single, divorced, and remarried candidates for church leadership.

Implications

The first implication of the "faithful husband" requirement is that younger candidates who have yet to prove their ability to manage their own households well should ordinarily not be put in ultimate leadership positions in the church. While they may possess proper formal training and may be both eager and otherwise qualified in terms of character and disposition, maturity and life experience are such an integral part of a church leader's necessary equipment for his role that any diminishing of this requirement may come dangerously close to appointing a recent convert, which is discouraged in Scripture in the strongest terms (1 Tim. 3:6; cf. 5:22).

Interpretations of the Phrase
Mias Gynaikas Andra in 1 Timothy 3:2, 12; Titus 1:6

	INTERPRETATIONS OF THE PHRASE *Mias Gynaikas Andra*	WEAKNESSES	UNDERSTANDING UPON WHICH THE INTERPRETATION OR MISINTERPRETATION IS BASED
UNLIKELY INTERPRETATIONS	The phrase excludes single men from holding ecclesiastical office	Paul was himself unmarried	**Literal:** *one* woman as opposed to *zero* (single) or *two* or *more* wives at the same time (polygamy) or consecutively (remarriage of divorcee or widower)
		Paul extols the advantages of singleness for kingdom service in 1 Cor. 7	
		Paul could have made this more plain	
	The phrase excludes divorcees	Paul could have made this more plain	
		Divorce is not mentioned anywhere in the Pastoral Epistles	
	The phrase prohibits widowers who remarried	Paul elsewhere encourages widowed to remarry	
		No good biblical, theological, or commonsense reason why remarried widowers should be barred from church leadership	
	Paul excludes polygamists	Polygamy was not widely practiced in the Greco-Roman world of that time	
MOST LIKELY INTERPRETATION	Geared toward excluding men who had one or several concubines or may otherwise have been unfaithful to their wives		**Idiomatic:** "a one-wife-type-of-husband" or "faithful husband"

Second, it is utter folly for someone to provide qualified, capable leadership for the church while neglecting his duties in his own family, be it because of busyness in ministry or because of improper priorities. Even while serving as pastor or elder, it is therefore imperative that men serving in this function regularly evaluate themselves to see whether or not they are able to oversee the church while continuing to be able to adequately fulfill their natural duties as husband and father. Otherwise, it may well be said with Paul that those men should beware, lest possibly, after having preached to others, they may themselves be disqualified (1 Cor. 9:27).

Third, theologically, by linking the family so closely to the church, the New Testament presents the latter as the eschatological extension of the former. That which reaches all the way back to the divine creation of the first man and woman is seen to be further extended and explicated in the "household of God," the church (cf. Eph. 5:31-32). Hence the requirements that an officeholder manage his own household well, and that he be faithful in marriage and keep his children under proper control, all form the indispensable prerequisite for his suitability for church office. Before he can lead the household of God, he must first show that he can properly discharge his leadership responsibilities in his own household.

CHURCH OFFICERS AND THE ISSUE OF DIVORCE

But what shall we say about divorced men serving as pastor/elder or deacon? In light of the fairly stringent statements made by both Jesus and Paul regarding divorce and remarriage (see the previous chapter), and in view of the fact that serving as pastor, elder, or deacon in the local church is a high calling of considerable responsibility, should men who have undergone a divorce be barred from serving in roles of church leadership, specifically those of pastor/elder or deacon? In light of the high moral qualifications required for those serving in those offices, this would seem to be almost a foregone conclusion. How else would those in charge of the church model Christlikeness to the rest of the congregation?

In fact, for those who hold a "no divorce, no remarriage" position, the question of whether a divorced man can serve in church leadership does not even arise—divorce is never legitimate for any Christian, including those aspiring to positions of leadership in the church. As such, a divorcee certainly could not be considered a "faithful husband" or "above reproach." For those open at least in principle to the possibility that divorce may be biblically legitimate in a limited number of circumstances (cf. Matt. 19:9; 1 Cor. 7:15), however, the issue is not quite as clear-cut. The major passages dealing with qualifications for leadership (1 Timothy 3; Titus 1) do not directly address this question, focusing instead on the requirement of a candidate's faithfulness in a present marriage. The issue therefore turns to a significant extent on the question of what is meant by the requirement of being a *mias gynaikas anēr*.[18]

If, as has been argued, the expression means "faithful husband," then it may be possible for men who experienced a divorce (especially if the divorce occurred prior to their conversion) to fulfill this requirement if they are faithful to their wife in their present marriage. Hence, divorced (and remarried) men would not necessarily be excluded from consideration as pastors/elders or deacons, especially if, in keeping with the general principles of the majority view outlined in the previous chapter, the divorce was legitimate. If the divorce was illegitimate (i.e., not covered by the Matthean "exception clause" or the Pauline privilege), service as pastor/elder or deacon would seem to be ruled out, because that person has an illegitimate divorce in his past, whether he repented of this sin or not.[19]

Overall, people should generally not be held to a stricter standard just to be "safe" and "conservative." If (and not all agree) both Jesus and Paul were willing to make an exception, we should be willing to follow their lead without fearing that a high view of marriage will thereby be compromised. Nevertheless, when coupled with the requirement that an overseer be "above reproach" (which includes community reputation), it may be best in many circumstances to weigh very carefully whether or not to appoint divorcees to the role of pastor/elder or deacon, especially when qualified candidates are available who did not undergo a divorce. This would seem to be the wisest course of action especially since there are many other avenues of service available to people in those kinds of circumstances apart from the highest ecclesiastical office.

Yet while the standard is one of *spiritual maturity* and *moral uprightness,* it is not that of *perfection.* In fact, the lists contain many attributes to which every Christian should aspire. To be sure, pastors ought to set an example of spiritual maturity, but their role is not to be conceived as representing Christ in such a way as to literally embody his own characteristics, be it in his unmarried state[20] or in his lack of divorce or remarriage. More appropriately, those officeholders who are married ought to model Christ's faithfulness to his spiritual bride, the church, by being faithful to their wife (cf. Eph. 5:25-30). This is fully compatible with the above-presented view that Paul requires marital faithfulness of officeholders while leaving open the question of whether or not those who have undergone a divorce that is biblically permissible (if this is considered possible) are at least in principle eligible to serve.

REQUIREMENTS PERTAINING TO CHURCH LEADERS' CHILDREN

Paul's letters to Timothy and Titus both include not only the "faithful husband" requirement but also a stipulation regarding the church leader's children. To Timothy, Paul writes that the candidate for office "must manage his own household well, with all dignity keeping his children submissive" (1 Tim. 3:4). In an argument from the lesser to the greater, Paul continues, "For if someone does not know how to manage his own household, how will he care for God's church?" (v. 5). The requirement mentioned in the letter to Titus seems to be even stricter, stipulating that a church leader's "children are *believers* and not open to the charge of debauchery or insubordination" (Titus 1:6; NIV: "whose children are *faithful* and not open to the charge of being wild and disobedient"; TNIV: "whose children *believe*"). Again, Paul follows up with a reason: "For an overseer, as God's steward, must be above reproach" (v. 7).

The Greek word underlying the rendering "believers" is *pistos*, which can mean either "believing" (ESV, TNIV) or "faithful" (NIV). While "believing" admittedly is the word's meaning in the majority of instances in the Pastorals, in the present case it is perhaps more likely that the expression means "faithful" in the sense of "obedient and submissive to their father's orders" (cf. 1 Tim. 3:11; 2 Tim. 2:2, 13).[21] The meaning "believing" is rendered less likely here in light of the context and the parallel in 1 Timothy 3:4, not to mention the theological difficulties of accommodating the doctrine of election within the scope of such a requirement.

The fact that the other two instances of "wild" (*asōtias*) relate to orgies of drunkenness (Eph. 5:18; 1 Pet. 4:4; cf. Prov. 28:7, LXX) and the other two instances of "disobedient" (lit., "unsubjected," *anypotakta;* cf. Heb. 2:8) to outright rebellion (1 Tim. 1:9; Titus 1:10) suggests that what is in view is not occasional disobedience but deep-seated rebellion against parental authority. Anyone who would be an elder in the church, which entails the exercise of authority over the congregation, must properly exercise authority at home, with his children responding in obedience and submission (whether or not they are spiritually regenerate). This is required if "God's manager" (*oikonomos theou;* cf. 1 Cor. 4:1, 2; 1 Pet. 4:10) is to be blameless (cf. 1 Tim. 3:5, 15).[22]

SINGLENESS AND CHURCH LEADERSHIP

We conclude our discussion of the relationship between marriage and family and church leadership with a few brief comments on singleness and church leadership. Similar to our discussion on divorced candidates above, we note that the phrase "faithful husband" does not directly apply to those who are unmarried and who aspire to a church office. Clearly, the requirement that church leaders be faithful husbands "does not mean that bishops had to be married; it just commends marriage as something that is not at all inconsistent with the episcopal office."[23] In light of Jesus' and Paul's positive treatment of celibacy elsewhere (see chapter 9 above), not to mention their own ministries which they carried out as unmarried men, it seems safe to conclude that a man's unmarried state does not disqualify him from serving as pastor or elder.[24]

There may, of course, be other issues that caution against appointing a relatively young single man to the pastoral office or to the office of elder—such as his inexperience, lack of proven track record, lack of spiritual maturity—but our point here is that singleness in and of itself is in no way disqualifying from positions of church leadership. In fact, as Paul notes in his major discussion of marriage and singleness in 1 Corinthians 7, singleness carries with itself several important advantages for kingdom service.[25] Single men who are fully devoted to the Lord and his work are free from the responsibilities of caring for a wife and children and can pursue Christian ministry to a larger extent than those who are married (1 Cor. 7:32-35). On the other hand, however, there may be limits to how effectively a single person can relate to the challenges faced by married couples and families in the church.

In the end, there is therefore no substitute for subjecting single candidates for church office to the same testing process and requirements as married men and to decide on their suitability to serve on an individual basis. To adapt Paul's words spoken with reference to deacons, "They must first be tested; and then if there is nothing against them, let them serve" (1 Tim. 3:10, NIV).

CONCLUSION

The present chapter applies much of what has been said earlier in this book regarding the biblical teaching on marriage and the family to the issue of qualifications for church leadership. In his letters to Timothy and Titus, the apostle Paul stipulates that candidates for both elder and deacon ought to be *mias gynaikas andra* (1 Tim. 3:2, 12; Titus 1:6). This phrase has been variously interpreted as requiring church leaders to be married (as opposed to unmarried); not divorced; not remarried (in the case of widowers); not polygamists (i.e., not married to more than one wife at the same time); or faithful in marriage (rather than unfaithful, as in the case of concubinage). After extended discussion, we concluded that the final option, requiring candidates for church office to be "faithful husbands," is the most likely understanding of this requirement.

After drawing several implications from this interpretation, we discussed the issue of divorce in relation to candidates for church office. We concluded that, technically, the "faithful husband" requirement does not directly address the issue of whether or not divorced candidates are eligible to be considered and to serve as elder and/or deacon. For this reason we counseled openness to this possibility in principle while registering several cautions.

Requirements pertaining to church leaders' children were discussed as well, again focusing on Paul's stipulations in the Pastoral Epistles (1 Tim. 3-5; Titus 1:6). In the former passage, Paul requires that an overseer "must manage his own household well, with all dignity keeping his children submissive." In the latter passage, Paul states that a church leader's children must be "faithful" or "believers" and "not open to the charge of being wild and disobedient" (NIV). After some discussion, we judged that the former rendering, "faithful," rather than "believers," seems to be more likely, both in light of the parallel in 1 Timothy 3:4 and on contextual and lexical grounds.

Our final topic of discussion was the issue of singleness and church leadership. We noted that single men should certainly be considered for church office, for at least the following reasons. First, the "faithful husband" requirement is not intended to stipulate that church leaders must be married, but simply that if they are married, they must be faithful to their spouse. Second, both Jesus and Paul commended the state of singleness by their own practice and instruction, pointing out advantages of singleness for ministry. At the same time, we noted that a specific single person may not qualify because of his youth, inexperience, or lack of spiritual maturity. We also noted that singles may face certain limitations in relating to challenges faced by the married members of their congregation. As any other candidates for church office, single persons should first be tested and then be appointed or not appointed depending on whether or not they meet the qualifications for leadership.

13

UNITING ALL THINGS IN HIM:
CONCLUDING SYNTHESIS

We have come to the end of our discussion, and it is now time to briefly summarize the findings of our study of the biblical teaching regarding marriage, the family, and related subjects. At the outset, we noted that for the first time in its history, Western civilization is confronted with the need to define the meaning of the terms "marriage" and "family." The cultural crisis that rages concerning the definitions of these terms was seen to be symptomatic of an underlying spiritual crisis that gnaws at the foundations of our once-shared societal values. In this spiritual cosmic conflict, Satan and his minions actively oppose the Creator's design for marriage and the family and seek to distort God's image as it is reflected in God-honoring Christian marriages and families. In light of the current confusion over marriage and the family and the lack of adequate Christian literature on the subject, there is a need for the kind of biblical and integrative treatment the present volume attempts to provide.

Human sexuality and relationships were seen to be rooted in the eternal will of the Creator as expressed in the way in which God made men and women. Man and woman are made in God's image (Gen. 1:27), and are called to representative rule (v. 28) involving procreation, whereby the man, as first-created, has ultimate responsibility before God, with the woman placed alongside him as his "suitable helper" (2:18, 20), within the context of monogamous marriage. The Fall led to serious consequences affecting both the man and the woman individually in their areas of involvement as well as the marital relationship. Men's work and the relational sphere of women have both been significantly affected and turned into a struggle for control. Nevertheless, the image of God in man is not eradicated, and marriage and the family continue as the primary divinely instituted order for the human race. Indeed, the Fall did not alter the Creator's design or standards for marriage and family, and he still expects these institutions to be marked by monogamy, fidelity, heterosexuality, fertility, complementarity, and durability.

In keeping with the roles established by the Creator in the beginning, the New Testament defines marital roles in terms of respect and love as well as submission and authority. While the husband and the wife are fellow heirs of God's grace (1 Pet. 3:7), and while "there is neither male nor female" as far as salvation in Christ is concerned (Gal. 3:28), there remains a pattern in which the wife is to emulate the church's submission to Christ and the husband is to imitate Christ's love for the church (Eph. 5:21-33). Thus a complementarian understanding of gender roles is borne out, not just by a few isolated problem passages but by biblical theology as a whole. Apart from their joint stewardship, the married couple has an important witnessing function in the surrounding culture and ought to understand itself within the larger framework of God's end-time purposes in Christ (cf. Eph. 1:10).

In a separate chapter, we investigated the three major models of marriage that describe marriage as a sacrament, as a contract, or as a covenant. We concluded that the biblical concept of marriage is best described as a covenant (or a creation ordinance with covenantal features) and defined marriage as *a sacred bond between a man and a woman, instituted by and publicly entered into before God (whether or not this is acknowledged by the married couple), normally consummated by sexual intercourse.* Rather than being merely a contract that is made for a limited period of time, conditional upon the continued performance of contractual obligations by the other partner, and entered into primarily or even exclusively for one's own benefit, marriage is a sacred bond that is characterized by permanence, sacredness, intimacy, mutuality, and exclusiveness.

As indicated in the just-cited definition of marriage, Scripture plainly reveals that the bearing and raising of children is an elemental part of

God's plan for marriage. In the Old Testament, children are presented as a blessing from the Lord, while barrenness is generally viewed as sign of divine disfavor (though there may be times where this is not actually the case), and the responsibilities of fathers, mothers, and children are spelled out in some detail. In the New Testament, parents are urged to bring up their children in the nurture and admonition of the Lord (Eph. 6:4), and women are to place special priority on their God-given calling as mothers and homemakers (1 Tim. 2:15; Titus 2:4-5). Likewise, in both Testaments fathers are reminded of their sacred duty to provide for their children, as well as to enforce discipline (Prov. 13:24; 2 Cor. 12:14; Heb. 12:6).

In the area of reproduction, several critical issues were addressed. First, Scripture is clear that life begins at conception and that abortion is morally unacceptable. Second, while contraception in general is a legitimate Christian option, this does not mean that every form of birth control is morally acceptable for believers. Only those devices that are contraceptive rather than abortive in nature are legitimate Christian options. Third, artificial reproductive technologies, likewise, raise a variety of complex ethical issues and call for judicious adjudication in order to determine which are and are not ethically permissible for believers today. Finally, the Bible presents adoption as an honored avenue for glorifying God and building a Christian family, especially for couples having difficulty conceiving children of their own.

In the area of Christian parenting, we weighed the pros and cons of particular methods of parenting, pointing out the dangers of approaches that focus on method to the detriment of cultivating a relationship with the child and of relying on the Spirit's guidance in parenting. In our treatment of single parenting, we adduced biblical teaching on God's concern for the fatherless and discussed some of the ways in which the church can assist single parents. The debate concerning physical punishment was surveyed as well, and while the biblical teaching prevents us from disallowing this form of discipline, important cautions were registered in this regard.

Fostering masculinity and femininity was identified as of utmost importance in our culture that is increasingly reaping the fruit of radical feminism's anti-male bias. We also identified several biblical principles of parental discipline that may be useful for holding children accountable for their actions. We also discussed the important topic of spiritual warfare pertaining to marriage and the family. Since marriage is such an important component of God's economy, the devil continually attacks this divinely instituted human relationship. Therefore, believers need to be ready to fight the good fight and defend their own marriages, as well the larger institution of matrimony.

We also discussed singleness, which may present itself at several life stages, for those who are either not yet married, are widowed, or are permanently unmarried (be it by choice or circumstance). While a couple is to refrain from sexual relations prior to entering into marriage, and while widowed individuals are permitted, in certain cases even encouraged, to remarry, permanent singleness (i.e., celibacy) is considered by both Jesus and Paul to be a special gift from God, though not a necessary requirement for church office (cf. 1 Tim. 3:2, 12; Titus 1:6). By promoting undistracted devotion to the Lord, singleness can actually be a unique opportunity for kingdom service (1 Cor. 7:32-35).

From creation it also becomes clear that heterosexuality, rather than homosexuality, is God's pattern for men and women. The sexes are created in distinctness, which must not be blurred or obliterated, and humanity exists as male and female for the purpose of complementarity and procreation, neither of which can be properly realized in same-sex sexual relationships. Moreover, the divine image was seen to be imprinted on man *as male and female,* so that homosexual unions fall short of reflecting God's own likeness as unity in diversity. Despite numerous attempts, even by some claiming to be followers of Christ, to reinterpret the biblical record, it is evident that Scripture universally views homosexuality in terms of rebellion against God and disregard for his creation order (Gen. 18:17–19:29; Lev. 18:22; 20:13; Rom. 1:24-27; 1 Cor. 6:9-10; 1 Tim. 1:9-10; 2 Pet. 2:4-10; Jude 6-7). Indeed, homosexuality offends the Creator's integrated design of marriage and family at almost every point, which may be why it is met with so strict a response in Scripture.

Because marriage is a divinely ordained covenant institution (Gen. 1:28; 2:24) rather than merely a human contractual agreement, according to the majority view divorce is permissible only in certain carefully delineated exceptional cases. According to this view, acceptable reasons for divorce include sexual marital unfaithfulness (adultery) as well as desertion by an unbeliever. Even in those cases, however, reconciliation is to be the aim, and divorce is only permitted, not commanded. Indeed, in all cases, divorce *remains the least preferable option,* for it falls short of God's design for marriage and the family. Where divorce is biblically "legitimate," however, most (including the authors of this volume) would agree, so is remarriage. The latter is *apropos* also in case of spousal death, "only in the Lord" (1 Cor. 7:39, NASB).

Faithfulness in marriage, obedient children, and proper household management are also considered of paramount importance among the requirements for church leaders in the Pastoral Epistles (see especially 1 Tim 3:2-5; Titus 1:6). There is a close link between the family and the church, which is God's "household" (1 Tim. 3:15), so that only those who are good husbands and fathers and who give adequate attention to managing their own homes are qualified to provide leadership also for the church. While this would not automatically preclude a divorced, single, or childless married man from the pastorate, it does highlight the need for one who holds the ultimate position of pastor in the visible Body of Christ to be truly a "one-wife-type-of husband" or a "one-woman-type-of man."

Both the Old and the New Testament present a coherent body of teachings pertaining to marriage and the family. From the Garden of Eden, to Israel, to Jesus, to the early church, to Paul, all uphold a very high standard in this crucial area of life. While countless times individuals fell and will fall short of God's ideal, Scripture makes clear that the Creator's standard for marriage and family remains intact—it was instituted at Creation, and is expected of humankind today. In this as well as in other areas, in the first century as today, Christianity towers above pagan cultures and displays the character of a holy God in the lives and relationships of his people.

CONCLUSION

We have come a long way in our understanding of the biblical teaching on marriage and the family. We can do no better than conclude this book by praying for our families Paul's prayer for the Ephesian believers who were also the recipients of the apostle's marvelous instructions regarding marriage, childrearing, and spiritual warfare:

> For this reason I bow my knees before the Father, *from whom every family in heaven and on earth is named,* that according to the riches of his glory he may grant you to be strengthened with power through his Spirit in your inner being, so that Christ may dwell in your hearts through faith—that you, being rooted and grounded in love, may have strength to comprehend with all the saints what is the breadth and length and height and depth, and to know the love of Christ that surpasses knowledge, that you may be filled with all the fullness of God.
>
> Now to him who is able to do far more abundantly than all that we ask or think, according to the power at work within us, *to him be glory* in the church and in Christ Jesus *throughout all generations,* forever and ever. Amen (Eph. 3:14-21).

Concerning the difficult and controversial issues that were dealt with in this book, Paul's words are apropos that, "For now we see in a mirror dimly, but then face to face. Now I know in part; then I shall know fully, even as I have been fully known. So now faith, hope, and love abide, these three; but the greatest of these is love" (1 Cor. 13:12-13). Indeed, "knowledge puffs up, but love builds up" (1 Cor. 8:1). May God use that which can contribute to his greater glory in this book and forgive whatever might fall short of his perfect wisdom. And may he receive ever greater glory through our marriages and families.

FOR FURTHER STUDY: HELPFUL RESOURCES

THE LITERATURE ON MARRIAGE and the family and related issues is vast and growing more expansive by the day. In the following pages we list what we consider to be the most helpful resources under the respective chapter headings. At times the material is broken up further under specialized subheadings. For the most part, the viewpoints represented by these publications are compatible with the positions taken in the present volume, though this is not invariably the case. Listing of a particular resource should in any case not be taken as an unqualified endorsement of all of its contents. We hope that the following bibliographies will prove useful to those who wish to study a given subject more fully on their own.

CHAPTER 1: THE CURRENT CULTURAL CRISIS: REBUILDING THE FOUNDATION

Clapp, Rodney. *A Peculiar People: The Church as Culture in a Post-Christian Society*. Downers Grove, Ill.: InterVarsity, 1996.

Colorado Statement on Biblical Sexual Morality, The. Commissioned by Focus on the Family. Appendix in Daniel Heimbach, *True Sexual Morality* (see listing below); also at https://www.family.org/cforum/foxi/abstinence.bv/a0028508.cfm.

Davies, Jon, and Gerard Loughlin, eds. *Sex These Days: Essays on Theology, Sexuality, and Society*. Sheffield, U.K.: Sheffield Academic Press, 1997.

Grudem, Wayne, ed. *Biblical Foundations for Manhood and Womanhood*. Wheaton, Ill.: Crossway, 2002.

Heimbach, Daniel R. *True Sexual Morality: Biblical Standards for a Culture in Crisis*. Wheaton, Ill.: Crossway, 2004.

Kassian, Mary A. *The Feminist Gospel: The Movement to Unite Feminism with the Church*. Wheaton, Ill.: Crossway, 1992.

———. *Women, Creation, and the Fall*. Wheaton, Ill.: Crossway, 1990.

Loughlin, Gerard. "The Want of Family in Postmodernity." In *The Family in Theological Perspective*. Edited by Stephen C. Barton. Edinburgh: T & T Clark, 1996, 307-327.

Moseley, N. Allan. *Thinking Against the Grain: Developing a Biblical Worldview in a Culture of Myths*. Grand Rapids, Mich.: Kregel, 2003.

Pyper, Hugh S., ed. *The Christian Family: A Concept in Crisis*. Norwich, U.K.: Canterbury, 1996.

Stanton, Glenn T. *Why Marriage Matters: Reasons to Believe in Marriage in Postmodern Society*. Colorado Springs: Piñon Press, 1997.

Thatcher, Adrian, and Elizabeth Stuart, eds. *Christian Perspectives on Sexuality and Gender*. Leominster, U.K.: Gracewing; Grand Rapids, Mich.: Eerdmans, 1996.

Wallerstein, Judith S., Julia M. Lewis, and Sandra Blakeslee. *The Unexpected Legacy of Divorce: A Twenty-five-year Landmark Study*. New York: Hyperion, 2000.

Wells, David F. *God in the Wasteland: The Reality of Truth in a World of Fading Dreams*. Grand Rapids, Mich.: Eerdmans, 1995.

CHAPTER 2: LEAVING AND CLEAVING: MARRIAGE IN THE OLD TESTAMENT

General Treatments of Marriage

Augustine. "On the Good of Marriage." [*De Bono Conjugali.*] In *The Nicene and Post-Nicene Fathers*. Edited by Philip Schaff. Grand Rapids, Mich.: Eerdmans, reprint 1980 [1887]. First Series, vol. 3, 397-413.

Barth, Karl. *Church Dogmatics*. Vol. 3, *The Doctrine of Creation*. Part 4. Translated by A. T. Mackay et al. Edinburgh: T & T Clark, 1961, 116-285.

Barton, Stephen C. *Life Together: Family, Sexuality, and Community in the New Testament and Today*. Edinburgh: T & T Clark, 2001.

Bromiley, Geoffrey W. *God and Marriage*. Grand Rapids, Mich.: Eerdmans, 1980.

Erickson, Millard J. *Christian Theology*. Second edition. Grand Rapids, Mich.: Baker, 1998, 517-536, 563-566.

Grudem, Wayne A. *Systematic Theology*. Grand Rapids, Mich.: Zondervan, 1994, 442-450, 454-470.

Luther, Martin. "The Estate of Marriage (1522)." In *Luther's Works*. Edited by Hilton C. Oswald. Translated by Edward Sittler. Saint Louis: Concordia, 1973. Vol. 28, 1-56.

————. "A Sermon on the Estate of Marriage (1519)." In *Martin Luther's Basic Theological Writings*. Edited by Timothy F. Lull. Minneapolis: Fortress, 1989, 630-637.

Wilson, Douglas. *Reforming Marriage*. Moscow, Idaho: Canon, 1995.

Biblical Background

Campbell, Ken M., ed. *Marriage and Family in the Biblical World*. Downers Grove, Ill.: InterVarsity, 2003.

Cohen, Shaye J. D., ed. *The Jewish Family in Antiquity*. Brown Judaic Studies 289. Atlanta: Scholars Press, 1993.

Hurley, James B. *Man and Woman in Biblical Perspective*. Grand Rapids, Mich.: Zondervan, 1981.

Osiek, Carolyn, and David L. Balch, eds. *Families in the New Testament World*. Louisville: Westminster/John Knox, 1997.

Perdue, Leo G., Joseph Blenkinsopp, John J. Collins, and Carol Meyers. *Families in Ancient Israel*. Louisville: Westminster/John Knox, 1997.

Towner, Philip H. "Household, Family." In *Dictionary of the Later New Testament and Its Developments*. Edited by Ralph P. Martin and Peter H. Davids. Leicester, U.K./Downers Grove, Ill.: InterVarsity, 1997, 511-520.

Tractate *Gittin* ("Bills of Divorce"). In *The Mishnah*. Translated by Herbert Danby. Oxford: Oxford University Press, 1933, 307-321.

Old Testament Teaching

Block, Daniel I. "Marriage and Family in Ancient Israel." In *Marriage and Family in the Biblical* World. Edited by Ken M. Campbell. Downers Grove, Ill.: InterVarsity, 2003, 33-102.

Hugenberger, Gordon P. *Marriage as a Covenant: A Study of Biblical Law and Ethics Governing Marriage Developed from the Perspective of Malachi*. Leiden, Netherlands: Brill, 1994. Reprint Grand Rapids, Mich.: Baker, 1998.

Ortlund, Raymond C., Jr. "Male-Female Equality and Male Headship." In *Recovering Biblical Manhood and Womanhood: A Response to Biblical Feminism*. Edited by John Piper and Wayne Grudem. Wheaton, Ill.: Crossway, 1991, 95-112.

Sex and Romance in Marriage

Akin, Daniel L. *God on Sex: The Creator's Ideas About Love, Intimacy, and Marriage*. Nashville: Broadman & Holman, 2003.

Bainton, Roland H. *What Christianity Says About Sex, Love, and Marriage*. New York: Association, 1957.

Dillow, Joseph C. *Solomon on Sex*. Nashville: Thomas Nelson, 1977.

Dobson, James. *What Wives Wish Their Husbands Knew About Women*. Wheaton, Ill.: Tyndale, 1975.

Elliot, Elisabeth. *Passion and Purity: Learning to Bring Your Love Life Under Christ's Control*. Grand Rapids, Mich.: Revell, 1984.

LaHaye, Tim, and Beverly LaHaye. *The Act of Marriage: The Beauty of Sexual Love*. Grand Rapids, Mich.: Zondervan, 1976.

Mahaney, C. J. "A Song of Joy: Sexual Intimacy in Marriage." In *Building Strong Families*. Edited by Dennis Rainey. Wheaton, Ill.: Crossway, 2002.

Rosenau, Douglas E. *A Celebration of Sex: A Guide to Enjoying God's Gift of Married Sexual Pleasure*. Nashville: Thomas Nelson, 1994.

Smedes, Lewis. *Sex for Christians*. Grand Rapids, Mich.: Eerdmans, 1976.

Wheat, Ed, and Gaye Wheat. *Intended for Pleasure: Sex Technique and Sexual Fulfillment in Christian Marriage*. Revised edition. Old Tappan, N.J.: Revell, 1981.

Chapter 3: No Longer Two, but One: Marriage in the New Testament

Ancient Household Codes

Balch, David L. "Household Codes." In *Graeco-Roman Literature and the New Testament: Selected Forms and Genres*. Edited by David E. Aune. Society of Biblical Literature Sources for Biblical Study 21. Atlanta: Scholars Press, 1988.

――――. *Let Wives Be Submissive: The Domestic Code in 1 Peter*. Society of Biblical Literature Monograph Series 26. Chico, Calif.: Scholars Press, 1981.

Dunn, James D. G. "The Household Rules in the New Testament." In *The Family in Theological Perspective*. Edited by Stephen C. Barton. Edinburgh: T & T Clark, 1996, 43-63.

Keener, Craig S. "Family and Household." In *Dictionary of New Testament Background*. Edited by Craig A. Evans and Stanley E. Porter. Leicester, U.K./Downers Grove, Ill.: InterVarsity, 2000, 353-368.

Towner, Philip H. "Households and Household Codes." In *Dictionary of Paul and His Letters*. Edited by Gerald F. Hawthorne et al. Leicester, U.K./Downers Grove, Ill.: InterVarsity, 1993, 417-419.

――――. "Household Codes." In *Dictionary of the Later New Testament and Its*

·*Developments.* Edited by Ralph P. Martin and Peter H. Davids. Leicester, U.K./Downers Grove, Ill.: InterVarsity, 1997, 513-520.

Marriage and Family

Adams, Jay. *Christian Living in the Home.* Phillipsburg, N.J.: Presbyterian & Reformed, 1989.

Barton, Stephen C. "Family." In *Dictionary of Jesus and the Gospels.* Edited by Joel B. Green et al. Leicester, U.K./Downers Grove, Ill.: InterVarsity, 1992, 226-229.

———. *Discipleship and Family Ties in Mark and Matthew.* Cambridge: Cambridge University Press, 1994.

———. "Hospitality." In *Dictionary of the Later New Testament and Its Developments.* Edited by Ralph P. Martin and Peter H. Davids. Leicester, U.K./Downers Grove, Ill.: InterVarsity, 1997, 501-507.

Barton, Stephen C., ed. *The Family in Theological Perspective.* Edinburgh: T & T Clark, 1996.

Beam, Joe. *Becoming One: Emotionally, Spiritually, and Sexually.* West Monroe, La.: Howard, 1999.

Dominian, Jack. *Marriage, Faith, and Love.* New York: Crossroad, 1982.

Elliot, Elisabeth. *The Shaping of a Christian Family.* Grand Rapids, Mich.: Revell, 2000.

Garland, Diana S. Richmond, and Diane L. Pancoast, eds. *The Church's Ministry With Families: A Practical Guide.* Dallas: Word, 1990.

Gilder, George. *Men and Marriage.* Gretna, La.: Pelican, 1986.

Gross, Edward. *Will My Children Go to Heaven? Hope and Help for Believing Parents.* Phillipsburg, N.J.: Presbyterian & Reformed, 1995.

Gushee, David P. *Getting Marriage Right: Realistic Counsel for Saving and Strengthening Relationships.* Grand Rapids, Mich.: Baker, 2004.

Hess, Richard S., and M. Daniel Carroll R., eds. *Family in the Bible: Exploring Customs, Culture, and Context.* Grand Rapids, Mich.: Baker, 2003.

Hughes, Kent, and Barbara Hughes. *Disciplines of a Godly Family.* Wheaton, Ill.: Crossway, 2004.

Jenkins, Jerry B. *Hedges: Loving Your Marriage Enough to Protect It.* Dallas: Word, 1990.

Keener, Craig S. "Marriage." In *Dictionary of New Testament Background.* Edited by Craig A. Evans and Stanley E. Porter. Leicester, U.K./Downers Grove, Ill.: InterVarsity, 2000, 680-693.

———. "Family and Household." In *Dictionary of New Testament Background.*

Edited by Craig A. Evans and Stanley E. Porter. Leicester, U.K./Downers Grove, Ill.: InterVarsity, 2000, 353-368.

Köstenberger, Andreas J. "Marriage and Family in the New Testament." In *Marriage and Family in the Biblical World*. Edited by Ken M. Campbell. Downers Grove, Ill.: InterVarsity, 2003, 240-284.

Lewis, Robert. *Raising a Modern-Day Knight: A Father's Role in Guiding His Son to Authentic Manhood*. Wheaton, Ill.: Tyndale, 1999.

MacArthur, John. *Different By Design. Discovering God's Will for Today's Man and Woman*. Wheaton, Ill.: Victor, 1994.

O'Brien, Peter T. *The Letter to the Ephesians*. Pillar New Testament Commentary. Grand Rapids, Mich.: Eerdmans, 1999, 405-438.

O'Donovan, Oliver. *Marriage and the Church's Task*. London: Church Information Office, 1978.

Packer, J. I. "Marriage and Family in Puritan Thought." In *A Quest for Godliness: The Puritan Vision of the Christian Life*. Wheaton, Ill.: Crossway, 1990, 259-273.

Patterson, Dorothy Kelley. *The Family*. Nashville: Broadman & Holman, 2001.

Sproul, R. C., ed. *Family Practice: God's Prescription for a Healthy Home*. Phillipsburg, N.J.: Presbyterian & Reformed, 2001.

Strobel, Lee, and Leslie Strobel. *Surviving a Spiritual Mismatch in Marriage*. Grand Rapids, Mich.: Zondervan, 2002.

Thomas, Gary. *Sacred Marriage*. Grand Rapids, Mich.: Zondervan, 2000.

Twelker, Paul A. "The Biblical Design for Marriage: The Creation, Distortion, and Redemption of Equality, Differentiation, Unity, and Complementarity." Posted at http://www.tiu.edu/psychology/design.htm.

Various authors. *Studies in Christian Ethics: Christianity and the Family* 9, no. 1 (1996).

See also the bibliography listed at http://www.familymin.org/private/bib_full.html and http://www.familymin.org/private/bib_full2.html; and the section entitled "Suggested Reading" in Gushee, *Getting Marriage Right*, 239-257.

Men, Masculinity, and Fatherhood

Beck, Stephen. *A Father's Stew: Biblical Integration of Family, Work, and Ministry*. Bryan, Tex.: Ranger Press, 2002.

Blankenhorn, David. *Fatherless America: Confronting Our Most Urgent Social Problem*. New York: HarperCollins, 1995.

Doriani, Daniel. *The Life of a God-Made Man: Becoming a Man After God's Own Heart*. Wheaton, Ill.: Crossway, 2001.

Eberly, Don E., ed. *The Faith Factor in Fatherhood: Renewing the Sacred Vocation of Fathering.* Lanham, Md.: Rowman & Littlefield, 1999.

Elliot, Elisabeth. *The Mark of a Man.* Grand Rapids, Mich.: Revell, 1981.

Farrar, Steve. *Anchor Man.* Nashville: Thomas Nelson, 2000.

———. *Point Man.* Revised edition. Sisters, Ore.: Multnomah, 2003.

Farris, Michael. *What a Daughter Needs from Her Dad: How A Man Prepares His Daughter for Life.* Minneapolis: Bethany, 2004.

———. *The Home Schooling Father.* Nashville: Broadman & Holman, 2001.

Hughes, R. Kent. *Disciplines of a Godly Man.* Wheaton, Ill.: Crossway, 1991.

Lancaster, Philip. *Family Man, Family Leader.* San Antonio: Vision Forum, 2004).

Minirth, Frank, Brian Newman, and Paul Warren. *The Father Book: An Instruction Manual.* Minirth-Meier Clinic Series; Nashville: Thomas Nelson, 1992.

Palkovitz, Rob. *Involved Fathering and Men's Adult Development: Provisional Balances.* Mahwah, N.J.: Lawrence Erlbaum Associates, 2002.

Ryle, J. C. *Thoughts for Young Men.* Amityville, N.Y.: Calvary Press, 1999.

Scott, Stuart. *The Exemplary Husband: A Biblical Perspective.* Bemidji, Minn.: Focus, 2002.

Vitz, Paul C. *Faith of the Fatherless: The Psychology of Atheism.* Dallas: Spence, 1999.

Weber, Stu. *Four Pillars of a Man's Heart.* Sisters, Ore.: Multnomah, 1997.

Wilson, Douglas. *Federal Husband.* Moscow, Idaho: Canon, 1999.

Roles of Men and Women

Bordwine, James E. *The Pauline Doctrine of Male Headship.* Vancouver, Wash.: Westminster Institute; and Greenville, S.C.: Greenville Seminary Press, 1996.

Clark, Stephen B. *Man and Woman in Christ: An Examination of the Roles of Men and Women in Light of Scripture and the Social Sciences.* Ann Arbor, Mich.: Servant, 1980.

DeMoss, Nancy Leigh. *Biblical Womanhood in the Home.* Wheaton, Ill.: Crossway, 2002.

Doriani, Daniel. *Women and Ministry: What the Bible Teaches.* Wheaton, Ill.: Crossway, 2003.

Grenz, Stanley J., with Denise Muir Kjesbo. *Women in the Church: A Biblical Theology of Women in Ministry.* Leicester, U.K./Downers Grove, Ill.: InterVarsity, 1995.

Grudem, Wayne. *Evangelical Feminism and Biblical Truth: An Analysis of 118 Disputed Questions.* Sisters, Ore.: Multnomah, 2004.

House, H. Wayne. *The Role of Women in Ministry Today.* Grand Rapids, Mich.: Baker, 1995.

Hove, Richard. *Equality in Christ? Galatians 3:28 and the Gender Dispute.* Wheaton, Ill.: Crossway, 1999.

Hunt, Susan. *By Design: God's Distinctive Calling for Women.* Wheaton, Ill.: Crossway, 1998.

Impson, Beth. *Called to Womanhood: The Biblical View for Today's Woman.* Wheaton, Ill.: Crossway, 2001.

Jones, Rebecca. "Does Christianity Squash Women?" Posted at http://www.cbmw.org.

Knight, George. *The Role Relationship of Men and Women.* Phillipsburg, N.J.: Presbyterian & Reformed, 1989.

Köstenberger, Andreas J. *Studies in John and Gender: A Decade of Scholarship.* New York: Peter Lang, 2001, 173-352. (See also the bibliography on pages 364-376.)

Köstenberger, Andreas J., Thomas R. Schreiner, and H. Scott Baldwin, eds. *Women in the Church: A Fresh Analysis of 1 Timothy 2:9-15.* Grand Rapids, Mich.: Baker, 1995. (See also the extensive bibliography on pages 307-321.) Note: a second edition is scheduled to appear in 2005.

Neuer, Werner. *Man and Woman in Christian Perspective.* Translated by Gordon J. Wenham. Wheaton, Ill.: Crossway, 1991 [1981].

Piper, John, and Wayne Grudem, eds. *Recovering Biblical Manhood and Womanhood: A Response to Evangelical Feminism.* Wheaton, Ill.: Crossway, 1991.

Saucy, Robert, and Judith TenElshof, eds. *Women and Men in Ministry: A Complementarian Perspective.* Chicago: Moody, 2001.

Strauch, Alexander. *Men and Women: Equal Yet Different.* Littleton, Colo.: Lewis & Roth, 1999.

Sexual Ethics

Grenz, Stanley J. *Sexual Ethics: A Biblical Perspective.* Dallas: Word, 1990. Reprint *Sexual Ethics: An Evangelical Perspective.* Louisville: Westminster/John Knox, 1997.

Moseley, N. Allan. "Sex and 'The Wicked Bible.'" Chapter 8 in *Thinking Against the Grain: Developing a Biblical Worldview in a Culture of Myths.* Grand Rapids, Mich.: Kregel, 2003.

Thielicke, Helmut. *The Ethics of Sex*. Translated by John W. Doberstein. New York/Evanston/London: Harper & Row, 1964. Reprint Grand Rapids, Mich.: Eerdmans, 1978.

Watson, Francis. *Agape, Eros, Gender: Towards a Pauline Sexual Ethics*. Cambridge: Cambridge University Press, 2000.

Women and Femininity

Clarkson, Sally. *Seasons of a Mother's Heart*. Walnut Springs, Tex.: Whole Heart Ministries, 2001.

———. *The Ministry of Motherhood*. Colorado Springs: WaterBrook, 2002.

———. *The Mission of Motherhood*. Colorado Springs: WaterBrook, 2002.

DeMoss, Nancy Leigh. *Lies Women Believe: And the Truth that Sets Them Free*. Chicago: Moody, 2002.

Elliot, Elisabeth. *Let Me Be a Woman*. Wheaton, Ill.: Tyndale, 1976.

George, Elizabeth. *A Woman After God's Own Heart*. Eugene, Ore.: Harvest, 2001.

Hughes, Barbara. *Disciplines of a Godly Woman*. Wheaton, Ill.: Crossway, 2001.

Patterson, Dorothy Kelley. *BeAttitudes for Women: Wisdom from Heaven for Life on Earth*. Nashville: Broadman & Holman, 2000.

Peace, Martha. *Becoming a Titus 2 Woman*. Bemidji, Minn.: Focus, 1997.

———. *The Excellent Wife: A Biblical Perspective*. Revised edition. Bemidji, Minn.: Focus, 1997.

Schaeffer, Edith. *The Hidden Art of Homemaking*. Wheaton, Ill.: Tyndale, 1985.

Wilson, Nancy. *Praise Her in the Gates: The Calling of Christian Motherhood*. Moscow, Idaho: Canon, 2000.

———. *The Fruit of Her Hands: Respect and the Christian Woman*. Moscow, Idaho: Canon, 1997.

CHAPTER 4: THE NATURE OF MARRIAGE: SACRAMENT, CONTRACT, OR COVENANT?

Atkinson, David. *To Have and to Hold: The Marriage Covenant and the Discipline of Divorce*. Grand Rapids, Mich.: Eerdmans, 1979.

Augustine. "On the Good of Marriage." [*De Bono Conjugali.*] In *The Nicene and Post-Nicene Fathers*. Edited by Philip Schaff. Grand Rapids, Mich.: Eerdmans, reprint 1980 [1887]. First Series, vol. 3, 397-413.

Chapman, Gary D. *Covenant Marriage: Building Communication and Intimacy*. Nashville: Broadman & Holman, 2003.

Dunstan, Gordon R. "Marriage Covenant." *Theology* 78 (May 1975): 244-252.

Grisez, Germain. "The Christian Family as Fulfillment of Sacramental Marriage." *Studies in Christian Ethics* 9, no. 1 (1996): 23-33.

Hugenberger, Gordon P. *Marriage as a Covenant: Biblical Law and Ethics as Developed from Malachi.* Grand Rapids, Mich.: Baker, 1998 [1994].

Köstenberger, Andreas J. "The Mystery of Christ and the Church: Head and Body, 'One Flesh.'" *Trinity Journal* 12 n.s. (1991): 79-94.

Levitt, Laura S. "Covenant or Contract? Marriage as Theology." *Cross Currents* 48, no. 2 (Summer 1998): 169-184.

Lowery, Fred. *Covenant Marriage: Staying Together for Life.* West Monroe, La.: Howard, 2002.

Palmer, Paul F. "Christian Marriage: Contract or Covenant?" *Theological Studies* 33 (1972): 617-665.

Tarwater, John K. "The Covenantal Nature of Marriage in the Order of Creation in Genesis 1 and 2." Ph.D. diss., Southeastern Baptist Theological Seminary, 2002.

von Soden, Hans. "ΜΥΣΤΗΡΙΟΝ und sacramentum in den ersten zwei Jahrhunderten der Kirche." *Zeitschrift für die neutestamentliche Wissenschaft* 12 (1911): 188-227.

Waugh, Philip, ed. *Covenant Marriage: The Experience of a Lifetime.* Nashville: Broadman & Holman, forthcoming.

Witte, John. *From Sacrament to Contract: Marriage, Religion, and Law in the Western Tradition.* Louisville: Westminster/John Knox, 1997.

CHAPTER 5: THE TIES THAT BIND:
FAMILY IN THE OLD TESTAMENT

Children and Parenting (General)

Bunge, Marcia J., ed. *The Child in Christian Thought and Practice.* Grand Rapids, Mich.: Eerdmans, 2001.

Carroll, John T. "Children in the Bible." *Interpretation* 55 (2001): 121-134. *Note:* The entire issue is devoted to the topic "The Child."

Clarkson, Clay. *Heartfelt Discipline.* Colorado Springs: WaterBrook, 2002.

Dobson, James. *Bringing Up Boys.* Carol Stream, Ill.: Tyndale, 2001.

———. *Preparing for Adolescence.* Updated edition. Ventura, Calif.: Regal, 1997.

Farris, Michael. *What a Daughter Needs from Her Dad: How A Man Prepares His Daughter for Life.* Minneapolis: Bethany, 2004.

Keathley, J. Hampton III. "Biblical Foundations for Child Training." Dallas: Biblical Studies Press, 1997. Posted at http://www.bible.org.

Lewis, Robert. *Real Family Values: Leading Your Family into the Twenty-first Century with Clarity and Conviction*. Sisters, Ore.: Multnomah, 2000.

MacArthur, John. *Safe in the Arms of God: Truth from Heaven About the Death of a Child*. Nashville: Thomas Nelson, 2003.

————. *What the Bible Says About Parenting*. Waco, Tex.: W Publishing Group, 2000.

Miller, Donna. *Growing Little Women: Capturing Teachable Moments with Your Daughter*. Chicago: Moody, 1997.

Plowman, Ginger. *Don't Make Me Count to Three: A Mom's Look at Heart-Oriented Discipline*. Wapallopen, Pa.: Shepherd, 2004.

Priolo, Louis Paul. *Teach Them Diligently: How to Use the Scriptures in Child Training*. Woodruff, S.C.: Timeless Texts, 2000.

Rainey, Dennis, and Barbara Rainey. *Parenting Today's Adolescent*. Nashville: Thomas Nelson, 2002.

Sproul, R. C., Jr. *Bound for Glory: God's Promise for Your Family*. Wheaton, Ill.: Crossway, 2003.

Strange, William A. *Children in the Early Church: Children in the Ancient World, the New Testament, and the Early Church*. Carlisle: Paternoster, 1996.

Tripp, Paul. *Age of Opportunity: A Biblical Guide to Parenting Teens*. Phillipsburg, N.J.: Presbyterian & Reformed, 2001.

Tripp, Tedd. *Shepherding a Child's Heart*. Wapallopen, Pa.: Shepherd, 1998.

Wilson, Douglas. *Future Men*. Moscow, Idaho: Canon, 2001.

Wood, Diana, ed. *The Church and Childhood*. Studies in Church History 31. Rochester, N.Y.: Boydell & Brewer, 1997. First published Oxford: Blackwell, 1994, for The Ecclesiastical Historical Society.

CHAPTER 6: THE CHRISTIAN FAMILY:
FAMILY IN THE NEW TESTAMENT

Children and Parenting in the New Testament

Balla, Peter. *The Child-Parent Relationship in the New Testament and Its Environment*. Wissenschaftliche Untersuchungen zum Neuen Testament 155. Tübingen: Mohr-Siebeck, 2003.

Barton, Stephen C. "Child, Children." In *Dictionary of Jesus and the Gospels*. Edited by Joel B. Green et al. Leicester, U.K./Downers Grove, Ill.: InterVarsity, 1992, 100-104.

Derrett, J. D. M. "Why Jesus Blessed the Children (Mk 10.13-16 Par.)." *Novum Testamentum* 25 (1983): 1-18.

Francis, James. "Children and Childhood in the New Testament." In *The Family in Theological Perspective*. Edited by Stephen C. Barton. Edinburgh: T & T Clark, 1996, 65-85.

O'Brien, Peter T. *The Letter to the Ephesians*. Pillar New Testament Commentary. Grand Rapids, Mich.: Eerdmans, 1999, 439-447.

The Church as Family

Aasgaard, Reider. *"My Beloved Brothers and Sisters": Christian Siblingship in the Apostle Paul*. Studies of the New Testament and Its World. Edinburgh: T & T Clark, 2003.

Hellerman, Joseph H. *The Ancient Church as Family*. Minneapolis: Fortress, 2001.

CHAPTER 7: TO HAVE OR NOT TO HAVE CHILDREN: SPECIAL ISSUES RELATED TO THE FAMILY (PART 1)

Abortion

Gorman, Michael J. *Abortion and the Early Church: Christian, Jewish and Pagan Attitudes in the Greco-Roman World*. New York: Paulist, 1982.

Grisanti, Michael A. "The Abortion Dilemma." *The Master's Seminary Journal* 11, no. 2 (Fall 2000): 169-190.

Hoffmeier, James K., ed. *Abortion: A Christian Understanding and Response*. Grand Rapids, Mich.: Baker, 1987.

Lindemann, Andreas. "'Do Not Let a Woman Destroy the Unborn Babe in Her Belly': Abortion in Ancient Judaism and Christianity." *Studia theologica* 49 (1995): 253-271.

Olasky, Marvin, and Susan Olasky. *More than Kindness: A Compassionate Approach to Crisis Childbearing*. Wheaton, Ill.: Crossway, 1990.

Schlossberg, Terry, and Elizabeth Achtemeier. *Not My Own: Abortion and the Marks of the Church*. Grand Rapids, Mich.: Eerdmans, 1995.

Waltke, Bruce K. "Reflections from the Old Testament on Abortion." *Journal of the Evangelical Theological Society* 19 (1976): 3-13.

Contraception

Alcorn, Randy. *Does the Birth Control Pill Cause Abortions?* Gresham, Ore.: Eternal Perspective Ministries, 2000.

Bevington, Linda K., and Russell DiSilvestro, eds. *The Pill: Addressing the Scientific and Ethical Question of the Abortifacient Issue*. Bannockburn, Ill.: The Center for Bioethics and Human Dignity, 2003.

Cutrer, William. *Family Building: Fact, Fallacy, and Faith: A Christian Doctor Looks at Contraception.* N.p.: Aspire, 2002.

McLaren, Angus S. *A History of Contraception.* Oxford: Blackwell, 1992.

Noonan, John T., Jr. *Contraception: A History of its Treatment by the Catholic Theologians and Canonists.* Cambridge, Mass.: Harvard University Press, 1965.

O'Donovan, Oliver. *Begotten or Made?* Oxford: Clarendon/Oxford University Press, 2002 [1984].

Thielicke, Helmut. *The Ethics of Sex.* Translated by John W. Doberstein. New York: Harper & Row, 1964, 200-225.

Waters, Brent. *Reproductive Technology: Towards a Theology of Procreative Stewardship.* Cleveland: Pilgrim, 2001.

Infertility and Artificial Reproductive Technologies

Anderson, Ray. "God Bless the Children—and the Childless." *Christianity Today,* August 7, 1987, 28.

Baskin, Judith. "Rabbinic Reflections on the Barren Wife." *Harvard Theological Review* 82 (1989): 101-114.

Callaway, Mary. *Sing, O Barren One: A Study in Comparative Midrash.* Society of Biblical Literature Dissertation Series 91. Atlanta: Scholars Press, 1986.

Colson, Charles W., and Nigel M. de S. Cameron, eds. *Human Dignity in the Biotech Century: A Christian Vision for Public Policy.* Downers Grove, Ill.: InterVarsity, 2004.

Daube, David. *The Duty of Procreation.* Edinburgh: Edinburgh University Press, 1977.

Glahn, Sandra L., and William R. Cutrer. *The Infertility Companion: Hope and Help for Couples Facing Infertility.* Grand Rapids, Mich.: Zondervan, 2004.

Halverson, Kaye. *The Wedded Unmother.* Minneapolis: Augsburg, 1980.

Kilner, John F., Paige C. Cunningham, and W. David Hager, eds. *The Reproduction Revolution: A Christian Appraisal of Sexuality, Reproductive Technologies, and the Family.* Grand Rapids, Mich.: Eerdmans, 2000.

Smietana, Bob. "When Does Personhood Begin? And What Difference Does It Make?" *Christianity Today,* July 2004, 24-28.

Stout, Martha. *Without Child: A Compassionate Look at Infertility.* Grand Rapids, Mich.: Zondervan, 1985.

Van Regenmorter, John. "Frozen Out: What to Do with Those Extra Embryos." *Christianity Today,* July 2004, 32-33.

Van Regenmorter, John, and Sylvia Van Regenmorter. *When the Cradle Is*

Empty: Answering Tough Questions About Infertility. Wheaton, Ill.: Tyndale/Focus on the Family, 2004.

Van Seters, John. "The Problem of Childlessness in Near Eastern Law and the Patriarchs of Israel." *Journal of Biblical Literature* 87 (1968): 401-408.

Adoption

Andersen, David V. "When God Adopts." *Christianity Today,* July 19, 1993, 36-39.

Gilman, Lois. *The Adoption Resource Book*. San Francisco: HarperCollins, 1998.

Kincaid, Jorie. *Adopting for Good: A Guide for People Considering Adoption*. Downers Grove, Ill.: InterVarsity, 1997.

Packer, J. I. "Amazing Adoption." *Christianity Today,* July 19, 1993, 38.

Ring, June M. "Partakers of the Grace: Biblical Foundations for Adoption." Posted at http://www.ppl.org/adopt.html.

Schooler, Jayne. *The Whole Life Adoption Book*. Colorado Springs: NavPress, 1993.

CHAPTER 8: REQUIRING THE WISDOM OF SOLOMON:
SPECIAL ISSUES RELATED TO THE FAMILY (PART 2)

Physical and Other Forms of Discipline

Aries, Philippe. *Centuries of Childhood: A Social History of Family Life*. New York: Vintage, 1962.

Florea, Jesse. "Does Spanking Work for all Kids?" *Focus on Your Child*. Posted at http://www.focusonyourchild.com/develop/art1/A0000507.html.

"Focus on the Family Defends Parents' Right to Discipline," at http://www.charitywire.com/charity63/03826.html.

Gangel, Kenneth O., and Mark F. Rooker. "Response to Oosterhuis: Discipline Versus Punishment." *Journal of Psychology and Theology* 21, no. 2 (Summer 1993): 134-137.

Gillogly, Robert R. "Spanking Hurts Everybody." *Theology Today* 37, no. 4 (January 1981): 415-424.

Greenleaf, B. K. *Children Through the Ages: A History of Childhood*. New York: Barnes & Noble, 1978.

Haeuser, Adrienne A. "Swedish Parents Don't Spank." *The No Spanking Page*. Posted at http://www.neverhitachild.org.

Larimore, Walter L. "Is Spanking Actually Harmful to Children?" Posted at http://www.health.family.org/children/articles/a0000513.html.

Larzelere, Robert E. "Response to Oosterhuis: Empirically Justified Uses of Spanking: Toward a Discriminating View of Corporal Punishment." *Journal of Psychology and Theology* 21, no. 2 (1993): 142-147.

Miller, Alice. "Against Spanking." *Tikkun* 15, no. 2 (March/April 2000): 17-19.

Mohler, R. Albert, Jr. "Should Spanking Be Banned? Parental Authority Under Assault." 6/22/2004, at http://www.crosswalk.com/news/weblogs/mohler/1269621.html.

Mollenkott, Virginia Ramey. "Gender, Ethics, and Parenting." Review of *The Case Against Spanking: How to Discipline Your Child Without Hitting*, by Irwin A. Hyman. *The Witness* (April 2000): 28-29.

Oosterhuis, Alyce. "Abolishing the Rod." *Journal of Psychology and Theology* 21, no. 2 (Summer 1993): 127-133.

Pike, Patricia. "Response to Oosterhuis: To Abolish or Fulfill?" *Journal of Psychology and Theology* 21, no. 2 (1993): 138-141.

Rainey, Dennis, and Barbara Rainey. "Deciding When to Spank," at http://www.familylife.com/articles/article_detail.asp?id=322.

————. "What to Do About Children Expressing Anger Through Hitting." Posted at http://www.familylife.com/articles/article_detail.asp?id=321.

Child Protection Reform. "Spanking as Disicipline, Not Abuse," at http://www.childprotectionreform.org/policy/spanking_home.htm.

Straus, Murray A., and Denise A. Donnelly. *Beating the Devil Out of Them: Corporal Punishment in American Families and Its Effect on Children.* Second edition. New Brunswick, N.J.: Transaction, 2001.

Straus, Murray A., and Anita K. Mathur. "Social Change and Trends in Approval of Corporal Punishment by Parents from 1968 to 1994." Durham, N.H.: Family Research Laboratory, University of New Hampshire, 1996. Posted at http://www.unh.edu/frl/cp27.htm.

Whelchel, Lisa. *Creative Correction: Extraordinary Ideas for Everyday Discipline.* Minneapolis: Bethany, 2000.

Family Worship

Alexander, James W. *Thoughts on Family Worship.* Morgan, Pa.: Soli Deo Gloria, 1998 [1847].

Clarkson, Clay. *Our Twenty-four Family Ways: Family Devotional Guide.* Colorado Springs: Whole Heart Press, 2004.

Cromarty, Jim. *A Book for Family Worship.* Harrisburg, Pa.: Evangelical Press, 1997.

Gaither, Gloria, and Shirley Dobson. *Creating Family Traditions: Making Memories in Festive Seasons.* Sisters, Ore.: Multnomah, 2004.

Hughes, Kent, and Barbara Hughes. *Disciplines of a Godly Family.* Wheaton, Ill.: Crossway, 2004.

Johnson, Terry L. *The Family Worship Book: A Resource Book for Family Devotions.* Fearn: Christian Focus Publications, 2000.

Prince, David E. "Family Worship: Calling the Next Generation to Hope in God." Posted at http://www.cbmw.org.

Piper, Noël. *Treasuring God in Our Traditions.* Wheaton, Ill.: Crossway, 2003.

Ptacek, Kerry. *Family Worship: The Biblical Basis, Historical Reality, and Current Need.* Greenville, S.C.: Greenville Seminary Press, 2000.

Spiritual Warfare

Arnold, Clinton E. *Three Crucial Questions About Spiritual Warfare.* Grand Rapids, Mich.: Baker, 1997.

——— *Powers of Darkness: Principalities and Powers in Paul's Letters.* Leicester, U.K./Downers Grove, Ill.: InterVarsity, 1992.

O'Brien, Peter T. *Gospel and Mission in the Writings of Paul: An Exegetical and Theological Analysis.* Grand Rapids, Mich.: Baker, 1995, 109-131.

Page, Sydney H. T. *Powers of Evil: A Biblical Study of Satan and Demons.* Grand Rapids, Mich.: Baker, 1995.

Powlison, David. *Power Encounters: Reclaiming Spiritual Warfare.* Grand Rapids, Mich.: Baker, 1995.

Various authors. "Elements/Elemental Spirits of the World," "Power," and "Principalities and Powers." In *Dictionary of Paul and His Letters.* Edited by Gerald F. Hawthorne et al. Leicester, U.K./Downers Grove, Ill.: InterVarsity, 1993, 229-233, 723-725, and 746-752.

CHAPTER 9: UNDIVIDED DEVOTION TO THE LORD: THE DIVINE GIFT OF SINGLENESS

Singleness

Arterburn, Stephen, and Fred Stoeker. *Every Man's Battle: Winning the War on Sexual Temptation One Victory at a Time.* Colorado Springs: WaterBrook, 2000.

Arterburn, Stephen, Fred Stoeker, and Mike Yorkey. *Every Man's Battle Guide: Weapons for the War Against Sexual Temptation.* Colorado Springs: WaterBrook, 2003.

Birkett, Kirsten, and Lois Hagger. "Gift of Singleness? You're not Serious? A Look at Paul's Call to Singleness in 1 Corinthians 7." *Journal of Biblical Manhood and Womanhood* 5, no. 2 (Fall 2000): 8-9.

Chapman, John. "The Holy Vocation of Singleness: The Single Person in the Family of God." *Journal of Biblical Manhood and Womanhood* 5, no. 2 (Fall 2000): 4-5.

Clarkson, Margaret. *So You're Single.* Wheaton, Ill.: Harold Shaw, 1978.

Deming, Will. *Paul on Marriage and Celibacy: The Hellenistic Background of 1 Corinthians 7.* Grand Rapids, Mich.: Eerdmans, 2004.

Elliot, Elisabeth. *Passion and Purity: Learning to Bring Your Love Life Under Christ's Control.* Grand Rapids, Mich.: Revell, 2002.

Farmer, Andrew. *The Rich Single Life.* Gaithersburg, Md.: PDI Communications, 1998.

Foster, Richard J. *The Challenge of the Disciplined Life.* San Francisco: HarperCollins, 1985, 114-133 = "Sexuality and Singleness." In *Readings in Christian Ethics.* Vol. 2, *Issues and Applications.* Edited by David K. Clark and Robert V. Rakestraw. Grand Rapids, Mich.: Baker, 1996, 155-165.

Harris, Joshua, *Not Even a Hint.* Sisters, Ore.: Multnomah, 2003.

———. *Boy Meets Girl: Say Hello to Courtship.* Sisters, Ore.: Multnomah, 2000.

———. *I Kissed Dating Goodbye.* Sisters, Ore.: Multnomah, 1997.

Harris, Monford. "Pre-marital Sexual Experience: A Covenantal Critique." *Judaism* 19 (1970): 134-144.

Hsu, Albert Y. *Singles at the Crossroads. A Fresh Perspective on Christian Singleness.* Downers Grove, Ill.: InterVarsity, 1997.

Köstenberger, Andreas J. "Review Article: The Apostolic Origins of Priestly Celibacy." *European Journal of Theology* 1 (1992): 173-179.

Lum, Ada. *Single and Human.* Downers Grove, Ill.: InterVarsity Press, 1976.

Piper, John. "Foreword: For Single Men and Women (and the Rest of Us)." In *Recovering Biblical Manhood and Womanhood.* Edited by John Piper and Wayne Grudem. Wheaton, Ill.: Crossway, 1991, xvii-xxviii.

Ramsey, Paul. *One Flesh: A Christian View of Sex Within, Outside, and Before Marriage.* Grove Booklets on Ethics 8. Bramcote, U.K.: Grove, 1975.

Swindoll, Luci. *Wide My World, Narrow My Bed.* Portland, Ore.: Multnomah, 1982.

Taylor, Rhena. *Single and Whole.* Downers Grove, Ill.: InterVarsity Press. 1984.

Treas, Judith, and Deirdre Giesen. "Sexual Infidelity Among Married and

Cohabiting Americans." *Journal of Marriage and the Family* 62 (2000): 48-60.

Weising, Edward F., and Gwen Weising. *Singleness: An Opportunity for Growth and Fulfillment.* Springfield, Mo.: Gospel Publishing, 1982.

Wenham, David. "Marriage and Singleness in Paul and Today." *Themelios* 13, no. 2 (1988): 39-41.

Wilson, Douglas. *Her Hand in Marriage: Biblical Courtship in the Modern World.* Moscow, Idaho: Canon, 1997.

Yoder, John Howard. *Singleness in Ethical and Pastoral Perspective.* Elkhart, Indiana: Associated Mennonite Biblical Seminaries, 1974.

Single Parenting

Barnes, Robert G. *Single Parenting.* Wheaton, Ill.: Tyndale, 1992.

Blackwelder, David. "Single Parents: In Need of Pastoral Support." In *Clinical Handbook of Pastoral Counseling,* Edited by Robert J. Wicks and Richard D. Parsons. Mahwah, N.J.: Paulist, 1993. Vol. 2, 329-359.

Brandt, Patricia, with Dave Jackson. *Just Me and the Kids: A Course for Single Parents.* Elgin, Ill.: David C. Cook, 1985.

Cynaumon, Greg. *Helping Single Parents with Troubled Kids: A Ministry Resource for Pastors and Youth Workers.* Colorado Springs: NavPress, 1992.

Garfinkel, Irwin, and Sara McLanahan. *Single Mothers and Their Children: A New American Dilemma.* Washington, D.C.: The Urban Institute Press, 1986.

Hannah, Jane, and Dick Stafford. *Single Parenting with Dick and Jane: A Biblical, Back-to-Basics Approach to the Challenges Facing Today's Single Parent.* Nashville: Family Touch, 1993.

Kerr, Gerri. "Making It Alone: The Single-Parent Family." In *Family Ministry,* edited by Gloria Durka and Joanmarie Smith. Minneapolis: Winston, 1980, 142-167.

Olsen, Richard P., and Joe H. Leonard, Jr. *Ministry with Families in Flux: The Church and Changing Patterns of Life.* Louisville: Westminster/John Knox, 1990.

Richmond, Gary. *Successful Single Parenting.* Eugene, Ore.: Harvest, 1990.

Sandefur, Gary. *Growing Up with a Single Parent: What Hurts, What Helps.* Cambridge, Mass.: Harvard University Press, 1994.

Warren, Ramona. *Parenting Alone.* Family Growth Electives. Elgin, Ill.: David C. Cook, 1993.

Modesty

DeMoss, Nancy Leigh, *The Look: Does God Really Care What I Wear?* (Buchanan, Mich.: Revive Our Hearts, n.d.).

Gresh, Dannah. *The Secret Keeper: The Delicate Power of Modesty*. Chicago: Moody, 2002.

Mohler, Mary K. "Modeling Modesty." Louisville: The Southern Baptist Theological Seminary, n.d. Posted at www.albertmohler.com/Modeling Modesty.pdf.

Pollard, Jeff. *Christian Modesty and the Public Undressing of America*. San Antonio: Vision Forum, 2003.

Shalit, Wendy. *A Return to Modesty: Discovering the Lost Virtue*. New York: Free Press, 1999.

CHAPTER 10: ABANDONING NATURAL RELATIONS: THE BIBLICAL VERDICT ON HOMOSEXUALITY

Balch, David L., ed. *Homosexuality, Science, and the "Plain Sense" of Scripture*. Cambridge/Grand Rapids, Mich.: Eerdmans, 2000.

Burtoff, Larry. "Setting the Record Straight." Focus on the Family. Posted at http://www.family.org.

Cole, Sherwood O. "Biology, Homosexuality, and the Biblical Doctrine of Sin." *Bibliotheca Sacra* 157 (July–September 2000): 348-361.

Dallas, Joe, *Desires in Conflict: Hope for Men Who Struggle with Sexual Identity*. Eugene, Ore.: Harvest, 2003.

————. *A Strong Delusion*. Eugene, Ore.: Harvest, 1996.

Davies, Bob, and Lori Rentzel. *Coming Out of Homosexuality: New Freedom for Men and Women*. Downers Grove, Ill.: InterVarsity, 1994.

De Young, James B. *Homosexuality: Contemporary Claims Examined in Light of the Bible and Other Ancient Literature and Law*. Grand Rapids, Mich.: Kregel, 2000.

————. "The Source and NT Meaning of *Arsenokoitai*, with Implications for Christian Ethics and Ministry." *The Master's Seminary Journal* 3 (1992): 191-215.

Dobson, James. *Marriage Under Fire: Why We Must Win This Battle*. Sisters, Ore.: Multnomah, 2004.

Gagnon, Robert A. J. *The Bible and Homosexual Practice: Texts and Hermeneutics*. Nashville: Abingdon, 2001.

Gagnon, Robert A. J., and Dan O. Via. *Homosexuality and the Bible: Two Views*. Minneapolis: Fortress, 2003.

Garland, David E. *1 Corinthians*. Baker Exegetical Commentary on the New Testament. Grand Rapids, Mich.: Baker, 2003, 212-218.

Haley, Mike. *101 Frequently Asked Questions About Homosexuality*. Eugene, Ore.: Harvest, 2004.

Halperin, D. M. "Homosexuality." *Oxford Classical Dictionary*. Third edition. Edited by Simon Hornblower and Antony Spawforth. Oxford/New York: Oxford University Press, 1996, 720-723.

Hays, Richard B. "Relations Natural and Unnatural: A Response to John Boswell's Exegesis of Romans 1." *Journal of Religious Ethics* 14 (1986): 184-215.

Lutzer, Erwin W. *The Truth About Same-Sex Marriage: Six Things You Need to Know About What's Really at Stake*. Chicago: Moody, 2004.

Mohler, R. Albert, Jr. "The Compassion of Truth: Homosexuality in Biblical Perspective." Posted at http://www.henryinstitute.org.

Montoya, Alex D. "Homosexuality and the Church." *The Master's Seminary Journal* 11, no. 2 (Fall 2000): 155-168.

Moseley, N. Allan. "Homosexuality and the Christian Worldview." Chapter 9 in *Thinking Against the Grain: Developing a Biblical Worldview in a Culture of Myths*. Grand Rapids, Mich.: Kregel, 2003.

Paul, Anne. *Restoring Sexual Identity: Hope for Women Who Struggle with Same-Sex Attraction*. Eugene, Ore.: Harvest, 2003.

Pope, M. H. "Homosexuality." *The Interpreter's Dictionary of the Bible: Supplementary Volume*. Nashville: Abingdon, 1976, 415-417.

Satinover, Jeffrey. *Homosexuality and the Politics of Truth*. Grand Rapids, Mich.: Baker, 1996.

———. "The Gay Gene?" Posted at http://www.cbmw.org.

Schmidt, Thomas E. *Straight or Narrow? Compassion and Clarity in the Homosexuality Debate*. Leicester, U.K./Downers Grove, Ill.: InterVarsity, 1995.

Sears, Alan, and Craig Osten. *The Homosexual Agenda: Exposing the Principal Threat to Religious Freedom Today*. Nashville: Broadman & Holman, 2003.

Stanton, Glenn T., and Bill Maier. *Marriage on Trial: The Case Against Same-Sex Marriage and Parenting*. Downers Grove, Ill.: InterVarsity, 2004.

Staver, Mathew D., *Same-Sex Marriage: Putting Every Household at Risk* (Nashville: Broadman & Holman, 2004).

Stegemann, Wolfgang. "Paul and the Sexual Mentality of His World." *Biblical Theology Bulletin* 23 (1993): 161-168.

Jones, Stanton L., and Mark A. Yarhouse. *Homosexuality: The Use of Scientific*

Research in the Church's Moral Debate. Downers Grove, Ill.: InterVarsity, 2000.

Stott, John R. W. "Homosexual Partnerships?" In *Involvement: Social and Sexual Relationships in the Modern World,* vol. 2. Old Tappan, N.J.: Revell, 1984.

Taylor, J. Glen. "The Bible and Homosexuality." *Themelios* 21, no. 1 (1995): 4-9.

Turner, P. D. M. "Biblical Texts Relevant to Homosexual Orientation and Practice: Notes on Philology and Interpretation." *Christian Scholar's Review* 26 (1997): 435-445.

Wenham, Gordon J. "The Old Testament Attitude to Homosexuality." *Expository Times* 102 (1991): 359-363.

White, James, and Jeffrey D. Niell. *The Same Sex Controversy: Defending and Clarifying the Bible's Message About Homosexuality.* Minneapolis: Bethany, 2002.

Worthen, Anita, and Bob Davies. *Someone I Love is Gay: How Family and Friends Can Respond.* Downers Grove, Ill.: InterVarsity, 1996.

Wright, David F. "Homosexuality." In *Dictionary of Paul and His Letters.* Edited by Gerald F. Hawthorne et al. Leicester, U.K./Downers Grove, Ill.: InterVarsity, 1993, 413-415.

———. "Homosexuality: The Relevance of the Bible." *Evangelical Quarterly* 61 (1989): 291-300.

CHAPTER 11: SEPARATING WHAT GOD HAS JOINED TOGETHER: DIVORCE AND REMARRIAGE

Adams, Jay, *Marriage, Divorce, and Remarriage in the Bible.* Grand Rapids, Mich.: Zondervan, 1986.

Atkinson, David. *To Have and to Hold: The Marriage Covenant and the Discipline of Divorce.* London: William Collins Sons, 1979.

Blomberg, Craig L. "Marriage, Divorce, Remarriage, and Celibacy." *Trinity Journal* 11 (1990): 161-196.

Carson, D. A. *Matthew.* Expositor's Bible Commentary 8. Grand Rapids, Mich.: Zondervan, 1984, 412-419.

Collins, Raymond F. *Divorce in the New Testament.* Collegeville, Minn.: Liturgical Press, 1992.

Cornes, Andrew. *Divorce and Remarriage: Biblical Principles and Pastoral Care.* Grand Rapids, Mich.: Eerdmans, 1993.

Ellisen, Stanley A. *Divorce and Remarriage in the Church.* Grand Rapids, Mich.: Zondervan, 1980.

Fee, Gordon D. *The First Epistle to the Corinthians.* New International

Commentary on the New Testament. Cambridge/Grand Rapids, Mich.: Eerdmans, 1987, 290-306.

Fitzmyer, Joseph A. "The Matthean Divorce Texts and Some New Palestinian Evidence." *Theological Studies* 37 (1976): 197-226.

Harrell, P. E. *Divorce and Remarriage in the Early Church: A History of Divorce and Remarriage in the Ante-Nicene Church.* Austin, Tex.: Sweet, 1967.

Hawthorne, Gerald F. "Marriage and Divorce, Adultery and Incest." In *Dictionary of Paul and His Letters.* Edited by Gerald F. Hawthorne et al. Leicester, U.K./Downers Grove, Ill.: InterVarsity, 1993, 594-601.

Heth, William A. "Jesus on Divorce: How My Mind Has Changed." *Southern Baptist Journal of Theology* 6, no. 1 (2002): 4-29.

Heth, William A., and Gordon J. Wenham. *Jesus and Divorce: The Problem with the Evangelical Consensus.* Nashville: Thomas Nelson, 1985. Updated edition. Carlisle, U.K.: Paternoster, 1997.

House, H. Wayne, ed. *Divorce and Remarriage: Four Christian Views.* Leicester, U.K./Downers Grove, Ill.: InterVarsity, 1990.

Instone-Brewer, David. *Divorce and Remarriage in the Bible: The Social and Literary Context.* Grand Rapids, Mich.: Eerdmans, 2002.

Jensen, Joseph. "Does *Porneia* Mean Fornication? A Critique of Bruce Malina." *Novum Testamentum* 20 (1978): 161-184.

Jones, David Clyde. *Biblical Christian Ethics.* Grand Rapids, Mich.: Baker, 1994, 177-204.

Keener, Craig S. *. . . And Marries Another: Divorce and Remarriage in the Teaching of the New Testament.* Peabody, Mass.: Hendrickson, 1991.

———. "Adultery, Divorce." In *Dictionary of New Testament Background.* Edited by Craig A. Evans and Stanley E. Porter. Leicester, U.K./Downers Grove, Ill.: InterVarsity, 2000, 6-16.

———. "Marriage, Divorce and Adultery." In *Dictionary of the Later New Testament and Its Developments.* Edited by Ralph P. Martin and Peter H. Davids. Leicester, U.K./Downers Grove, Ill.: InterVarsity, 1997, 712-717.

Murray, John. *Divorce.* Phillipsburg, N.J.: Presbyterian & Reformed, 1989.

Norman, R. Stanton. "Biblical, Theological, and Pastoral Reflections on Divorce, Remarriage, and the Seminary Professor: A Modest Proposal." *Journal for Baptist Theology and Ministry* 1, no. 1 (Spring 2003): 78-100.

Piper, John. "Divorce and Remarriage: A Position Paper"; and "On Divorce and Remarriage in the Event of Adultery." Posted at www.desiringgod.org.

Smith, David L. "Divorce and Remarriage: From the Early Church to John Wesley." *Trinity Journal* 11 (1990): 131-142.

Stein, Robert H. "Divorce." *Dictionary of Jesus and the Gospels.* Edited by Joel B. Green et al. Leicester, U.K./Downers Grove, Ill.: InterVarsity, 1992, 192-199.

Stott, John R. W. "Marriage and Divorce." In *Involvement: Social and Sexual Relationships in the Modern World,* vol. 2. Old Tappan, N.J.: Revell, 1984.

Wenham, Gordon J. "The Biblical View of Marriage and Divorce." *Third Way* 1, Nos. 20-22 (October and November 1997).

———. "The Syntax of Matthew 19.9." *Journal for the Study of the New Testament* 28 (1986): 17-23.

———. "The Restoration of Marriage Reconsidered." *Journal of Jewish Studies* 30 (1979): 36-40.

CHAPTER 12: FAITHFUL HUSBANDS:
QUALIFICATIONS FOR CHURCH LEADERSHIP

Baugh, Steven M. "1–2 Timothy, Titus." In *Zondervan Illustrated Bible Backgrounds Commentary.* Edited by Clinton E. Arnold. Grand Rapids, Mich.: Zondervan, 2002. Vol. 3, 444-511.

Knight, George W. *The Pastoral Epistles.* New International Greek Testament Commentary. Grand Rapids, Mich.: Eerdmans; Carlisle: Paternoster, 1992.

Köstenberger, Andreas J. "Hermeneutical and Exegetical Challenges in Interpreting the Pastoral Epistles." *Southern Baptist Journal of Theology* 7, no. 3 (Fall 2003): 4-13.

———. *The Pastoral Epistles.* New Expositor's Bible Commentary, vol. 12. Grand Rapids, Mich.: Zondervan, forthcoming.

Lightman, Majorie, and William Zeisel. "Univira: An Example of Continuity and Change in Roman Society." *Church History* 46 (1977): 19-32.

Merkle, Benjamin L. "Hierarchy in the Church? Instruction from the Pastoral Epistles Concerning Elders and Overseers." *Southern Baptist Journal of Theology* 7, no. 3 (Fall 2003): 32-43.

Mounce, William D. *The Pastoral Epistles.* Word Biblical Commentary. Nashville: Thomas Nelson, 2000.

Page, Sidney. "Marital Expectations of Church Leaders in the Pastoral Epistles." *Journal for the Study of the New Testament* 50 (1993): 105-120.

CHAPTER 13: UNITING ALL THINGS IN HIM:
CONCLUDING SYNTHESIS

Note: What follows is a selection of resources listed above for chapters 1–11 that the authors find particularly helpful for strengthening and protecting one's marriage and family.

Akin, Daniel L. *God on Sex: The Creator's Ideas About Love, Intimacy, and Marriage*. Nashville: Broadman & Holman, 2003.

Alexander, James W. *Thoughts on Family Worship*. Morgan, Pa.: Soli Deo Gloria, 1998.

Arterburn, Stephen, and Fred Stoeker. *Every Man's Battle: Winning the War on Sexual Temptation One Victory at a Time*. Colorado Springs: WaterBrook, 2000.

Arterburn, Stephen, Fred Stoeker, and Mike Yorkey. *Every Man's Battle Guide: Weapons for the War Against Sexual Temptation*. Colorado Springs: WaterBrook, 2003.

Cromarty, Jim. *A Book for Family Worship*. Harrisburg, Pa.: Evangelical Press, 1997.

Dobson, James. *Bringing Up Boys*. Carol Stream, Ill.: Tyndale, 2001.

———. *Preparing for Adolescence*. Updated edition. Ventura, Calif.: Regal, 1997.

Farris, Michael. *What a Daughter Needs from Her Dad: How A Man Prepares His Daughter for Life*. Minneapolis: Bethany, 2004.

Hughes, Kent, and Barbara Hughes. *Disciplines of a Godly Family*. Wheaton, Ill.: Crossway, 2004.

Jenkins, Jerry B. *Hedges: Loving Your Marriage Enough to Protect It*. Dallas: Word, 1990.

Johnson, Terry L. *The Family Worship Book: A Resource Book for Family Devotions*. Fearn: Christian Focus Publications, 2000.

Lewis, Robert. *Raising a Modern-Day Knight: A Father's Role in Guiding His Son to Authentic Manhood*. Wheaton, Ill.: Tyndale, 1999.

———. *Real Family Values: Leading Your Family into the Twenty-first Century with Clarity and Conviction*. Sisters, Ore.: Multnomah, 2000.

MacArthur, John. *Different By Design. Discovering God's Will for Today's Man and Woman*. Wheaton, Ill.: Victor, 1994.

Miller, Donna. *Growing Little Women: Capturing Teachable Moments with Your Daughter*. Chicago: Moody, 1997.

Ptacek, Kerry. *Family Worship: The Biblical Basis, Historical Reality, and Current Need*. Greenville, S.C.: Greenville Seminary Press, 2000.

Rainey, Dennis, and Barbara Rainey. *Parenting Today's Adolescent*. Nashville: Thomas Nelson, 2002.

Tripp, Paul. *Age of Opportunity: A Biblical Guide to Parenting Teens*. Phillipsburg, N.J.: Presbyterian & Reformed, 2001.

Tripp, Tedd. *Shepherding a Child's Heart*. Wapallopen, Pa.: Shepherd, 1998.

Douglas Wilson. *Future Men*. Moscow, Idaho: Canon, 2001.

PERSONAL AND GROUP STUDY GUIDE

WE TRUST THAT THE study of issues related to marriage and family from an integrative and biblical point of view will prove beneficial for different types of readers: from seminary students to pastors, Bible study groups, and individuals. The following study guide is designed to help you assimilate the information presented in this book.

Before beginning your personal or group study of *God, Marriage, and Family*, you may want to keep in mind the following practical suggestions:

- As you go through this study guide, you may want to focus on one chapter of the book per week. While some of the information may be familiar to you, the assimilation will still take time and concentration. Going through the book too quickly may result in missing some of the benefits of reading it. Alternatively, you may want to read through the book once and then work through it more slowly a second time using the Study Guide.
- Set aside a regular time for reading the chapter and answering the questions. This is important in view of the many distractions and daily obligations that make it difficult for all of us to complete projects we started. If you are leading a group study, allocate also a regular time when all the participants can meet together to discuss the assigned chapter.
- Make sure that you write down your observations and notes as you read the chapter, as well as the answers to the questions posed in the study guide. This will help you to better retain the information. We suggest that you have a special notebook where you record all your notes and answers.

- In a group study setting, each member should have his or her own copy of the book, in order to be able to study the material at a convenient time. This is helpful, given our particular habits when reading a book. Some of us like to underline paragraphs; others write notes in the margins; yet others prefer to leave the book "untouched."

Each section of the Study Guide includes the following features:

- *Chapter Theme:* A brief statement summarizing the chapter.
- *Discussion Starters:* A set of questions designed to start off the discussion of the respective chapter topic and to draw in those participating in the study by engaging their personal experience and convictions.
- *Discussion Questions:* A list of questions intended to help identify the main points of each chapter, to structure the information for better retention, and to stimulate individual discovery or group participation. The answers are provided in a separate section at the end of this volume.
- *Personal Application Questions:* A list of questions intended to help each participant apply the knowledge gained through his or her study of a given chapter.
- *Issues for Prayer:* Suggestions on how one may pray based on the truths learned during the session.
- *Assignment:* Activities to be completed prior to the next session which are designed to deepen the integration of biblical truths learned into one's own experience.

CHAPTER 1: THE CURRENT CULTURAL CRISIS: REBUILDING THE FOUNDATION

Chapter Theme

The current cultural crisis concerning marriage and the family is symptomatic of a deeper spiritual crisis. The present volume provides an integrated, biblical study on marriage and the family to help alleviate the current confusion and the lack of adequate Christian literature on marriage and the family.

Discussion Starters

1. Without giving names, do you know of a family (even confessing Christians) that has gone through divorce? Can you list some of the causes for that divorce and the results it has had on each member of the family? Do you think the church could have done more to prevent the divorce and even heal such a marriage? List several ways the church could have gotten involved more effectively in that marriage.
2. Have you previously participated in a conference or group study on marriage and family? What issues received central attention? Do you think the Bible was given proper emphasis?

Discussion Questions

1. What are the two reasons why a biblically integrated treatment of the subject of marriage and family is needed?
2. Describe the paradigm shift we are seeing today with regard to marriage and family.
3. What are the negative effects of the paradigm shift?

Personal Application Questions

When faced with the shift from a biblical view of marriage and family toward a more libertarian understanding, do you tend to conform to the cultural mores and adopt the views of culture? Or do you go to the Bible as the final authority on any issue? Do you consider the Bible sufficient to deal with this issue?

Issues for Prayer

Ask God to make you sensitive to the teaching of his Word on the issues of marriage and family, to open your mind to the information presented in this book, and to help you identify specific ways in which you can integrate the information in your thinking, in your daily family living, and in your interaction with other people (and families). Ask him to give you the discernment of the Holy Spirit to see clearly the biblical principles on these issues and to identify ways to apply them.

Assignment

Make a list of the various ways in which society distorts the biblical model for marriage and family. Pay close attention to advertisements, the media, and personal interaction with other families. These are a good source for detecting the generally accepted views on marriage and family promoted by society but contrary to Scripture.

CHAPTER 2: LEAVING AND CLEAVING: MARRIAGE IN THE OLD TESTAMENT

Chapter Theme

The Old Testament teaches that marriage is a sacred bond between a man and a woman instituted by and entered into before God. Humanity was created in God's image to rule the earth for him, whereby the man was given ultimate responsibility and the woman placed alongside him as his "suitable helper." The Fall led to several negative consequences for the marital union, yet God's ideal for marriage is upheld in biblical wisdom literature such as Proverbs 31 or the Song of Solomon.

Discussion Starters

1. Do you think that modern society has departed from the biblical understanding of marriage as described in Genesis 2:24? If yes, name some ways in which that change is seen today.
2. Do you think that the government should promote laws that encourage a biblical understanding of marriage and family? Should the state have legislative power to impose upon families God's intention for marriage and family as seen in creation? How much involvement do you think the state should have in such matters?

Discussion Questions

1. What are three principles pertaining to marriage and family established in the beginning?
2. There are three major views on the image of God in man. What are they, and which understanding is most likely?
3. What is the difference between essential or ontological subordination and functional subordination?
4. In which expression applied to the woman in Genesis 2 can we see both equality and distinctiveness, complementarity and submission/authority?
5. What are the marital roles stipulated in the Old Testament for husbands toward their wives and vice versa?
6. In what ways does the history of Israel show that God's ideal of marriage established at Creation was compromised?

Personal Application Questions

Do you contribute in your home to the building of a marriage and family that is informed by the Bible, or do your marriage and family mirror the surrounding culture? If you are a wife, do you display the characteristics of the "excellent wife" in Proverbs 31? What are some of the areas in your life that could use improvement? If you are a husband, do you offer your wife an environment that encourages godly character? In reading the Song of Solomon, in what ways do you think you could prove your love to your wife?

Issues for Prayer

Whether you are a wife or a husband, ask God to give you the grace to do away with those aspects of your life that hinder the building up of a marriage as intended by God. Many families are easily influenced by the standards imposed by culture. Ask God to help you think biblically about marriage and family and give you the strength to choose always to follow his principles rather than those of society.

Assignment

After reading Proverbs 31 and Song of Solomon, make a list of the characteristics that you think you lack or in which you need to grow in order to be the wife or the husband God wants you to be. Make also a list of the characteristics that you think are praiseworthy in your spouse.

CHAPTER 3: NO LONGER TWO, BUT ONE: MARRIAGE IN THE NEW TESTAMENT

Chapter Theme

The New Testament reaffirms the Old Testament ideal of marriage as a sacred bond between a man and a woman before God. Jesus teaches that what God has joined together, humans should not sever. Paul presents marriage in analogy to the relationship between Christ and the church, with the husband as the head of his wife, which entails both the exercise of authority and sacrificial love, and the wife submitting to her husband as the church does to Christ.

Discussion Starters

1. How would you characterize the ideal marriage? What should the husband and the wife do to encourage such a marriage? In order for such an ideal marriage to be achievable, what must characterize both spouses?
2. Sin has brought a reversal of male-female roles. If you are a woman, relate a time when you usurped the authority of your husband. If you are a man, relate a time when you were abusive rather than loving in the exercise of your leadership. What were the consequences of such a reversal?

Discussion Questions

1. What was Jesus' view of the nature of marriage?
2. List the important passages where Paul addresses the topic of marriage and briefly summarize their content.
3. Give some important principles for marriage from the book of Ephesians.
4. What are three applications from Ephesians 5 on marital relationships?

Personal Application Questions

What do you think you should do in order to make your marriage more reflective of the biblical ideal? If you are a wife, are you being submissive to the leadership of your husband? If you are a husband, are you leading by love, or by force?

Issues for Prayer

Ask God for the power to fulfill your biblical role in your family as he requires. If you are a wife, pray that God would help you accept the leadership of your husband, understanding the seriousness of his role. If you are a husband, pray that God would make you more sensitive to the needs of your wife, understanding that she is a "weaker vessel," and to create a loving environment in which her submission may be out of joy rather than being coerced.

Assignment

Meditate together, as a couple, on Ephesians 5:21-33. Determine one area in which you are each lacking. For an entire week, pray every day for one another that each may be strengthened to live the quality of life that glorifies Christ.

CHAPTER 4: THE NATURE OF MARRIAGE: SACRAMENT, CONTRACT, OR COVENANT?

Chapter Theme

The present chapter provides a discussion and critique of the three major approaches to the nature of marriage: the sacramental, contractual, and covenantal models.

Discussion Starters

1. Is defining the nature of marriage important to the discussion of marriage and the family? Why or why not?
2. Have you personally thought about the nature of marriage and family? In your religious upbringing, was there one particular model of marriage that was emphasized? If so, how has it impacted you and your marriage?

Discussion Questions

1. What are the three major models for the nature of marriage? Define and give the roots of each model.
2. Give three weaknesses of the sacramental model for marriage.
3. Give three weaknesses of the contractual model.
4. What biblical support can be offered for the covenantal view of marriage?
5. What are the five important aspects of the marriage covenant?
6. What concerns have been raised regarding the covenantal model?

Personal Application Questions

God has designed marriage to be 1) permanent, 2) a sacred bond between a man and a woman, 3) the most intimate of human relationships, 4) mutual, and 5) exclusive. How are you, both husband and wife, doing in each of these five areas? Spend time pondering this before the Lord, pouring out your heart to him regarding any struggles you might experience in relation to your spouse. Then find appropriate ways to share these with your spouse.

Issues for Prayer

Pray that God would help you to a faithful husband or wife, understanding that your marriage is a sacred bond before God. Pray that the Lord would increase the intimacy of your marriage, not merely in the sexual area but also in the sharing of your lives and in mutual understanding, support, and love.

Assignment

Set aside some uninterrupted time with your spouse and discuss the five important aspects of the marriage covenant. For each aspect, discuss ways you can strengthen your marriage by committing or recommitting yourselves to God's plan for marriage in this area. Write down specific measures you can take to make every one of these five aspects a more permanent part of your marriage relationship.

CHAPTER 5: THE TIES THAT BIND:
FAMILY IN THE OLD TESTAMENT

Chapter Theme

God's command for the man and the woman to be fruitful and multiply indicates that procreation is an integral part of his plan for marriage. The Old Testament stipulates a series of roles and responsibilities for fathers, mothers, and children. It also provides both good and bad examples of parenting and underscores the importance of teaching children about God.

Discussion Starters

1. Do you think that refraining from discipline is part of the solution? Explain. How have you dealt with a rebellious child in the past?
2. If you are a father, how do you exercise your responsibility as the head of the home? If you are a mother, how do you apply the Bible's teaching on the responsibilities of mothers? Give an example of how you exercise your responsibility.

Discussion Questions

1. List at least three responsibilities for fathers according to the Old Testament.
2. List at least three responsibilities for mothers according to the Old Testament.
3. List at least three responsibilities for children according to the Old Testament.

Personal Application Questions

Do you think that you fulfill your responsibilities as a father or mother according to Old Testament teaching? Comparing your parenting with some of the examples in the Scriptures, which one does your parenting resemble the most?

Issues for Prayer

Ask God to help you be the kind of father or mother you should be for your child. Ask the Lord to give you wisdom to know how to instill the positive attributes found in Scripture (especially the book of Proverbs) in your child or children.

Assignments

Discuss with your spouse what you consider to be your roles as father or mother. Make a list, compare it to the biblical characteristics described in this chapter, and pray over it for the next week, asking God to help you carry out the biblical mandate for parenting.

CHAPTER 6: THE CHRISTIAN FAMILY: FAMILY IN THE NEW TESTAMENT

Chapter Theme

During his earthly ministry Jesus repeatedly showed his love for children and used them as examples for discipleship. Paul provided instructions on how fathers, mothers, and children ought to conduct themselves in the family of God.

Discussion Starters

1. List several ways by which a parent's behavior can unintentionally provoke the child to anger, which later may lead to rebellion. How can you avoid such a crisis?
2. Describe a situation in which you wronged your child, realized it, and asked the child's forgiveness. How did this change your relationship with your child?

Discussion Questions

1. What are two ways in which children figured prominently in Jesus' ministry and teaching?
2. What are several ways in which children came to typify desirable attitudes in believers in the early church?
3. What are the assumptions underlying the New Testament authors' use of the "household codes"?
4. What are the responsibilities and roles of each individual in a household? Give at least one Scripture reference for each.
5. What are the four characteristics older women are to exemplify, according to Titus 2?
6. What are Paul's instructions for young women?
7. Give eight observations that can be drawn from Paul's teaching on the woman's relationship to her husband and children.

Personal Application Questions

Have you been too lenient or too harsh in disciplining your child? Do you train up your children in the ways of the Lord? Do you pray for them?

Issues for Prayer

Ask the Lord to help you view your child the way Jesus approached children during his earthly ministry. Pray for the Lord to show you how he would have you develop your child's potential for serving him once he or she is grown, and to help you be the example that may inspire your child or children to follow after him.

Assignments

Over the next week, when a situation of tension appears between you and your child, take note of the cause of the tension, of how you sought to resolve it, and of the aftermath. Write down what you think you could have done to deal more effectively with the situation and note the improvements you see from previous dealings with tension.

CHAPTER 7: TO HAVE OR NOT TO HAVE CHILDREN:
SPECIAL ISSUES RELATED TO THE FAMILY (PART 1)

Chapter Theme

Among the items related to marriage and the family addressed in this chapter are childlessness and related medical issues, abortion, contraception, artificial reproductive technologies, and adoption.

Discussion Starters

1. Do you know someone who has had an abortion? What are some of the consequences that they have suffered as a result? Do you think the church has done enough to help that individual?
2. Have you or someone you know had difficulty having children? How have you or the person you know dealt with this issue?

Discussion Questions

1. What is the biblical teaching regarding children, the killing of children, and God's involvement in procreation? What were ancient Greco-Roman, Jewish, and the early Christians' views toward abortion?
2. What are potentially acceptable forms of contraception?
3. What are morally unacceptable forms of contraception?
4. What are some principles for evaluating modern artificial reproductive technologies?
5. What are some instances of adoption in Scripture?

Personal Application Questions

Do you place the same value on life as God does? How does your commitment show itself in the way you help those who struggle with related issues such as abortion or childlessness?

Issues for Prayer

Pray for those whom you know to be struggling with not being able to have children. Ask the Lord to give you wisdom in counseling those who are either considering or have already undergone an abortion. Consider prayerfully whether the Lord may want you to get actively involved in a pregnancy support ministry or an adoption agency.

Assignment

During the next week get information from a Christian pregnancy center or adoption agency. Discuss with your spouse some of the ways in which you may be used by the Lord in the lives of those who struggle with abortion or childlessness.

CHAPTER 8: REQUIRING THE WISDOM OF SOLOMON: SPECIAL ISSUES RELATED TO THE FAMILY (PART 2)

Chapter Theme

The present chapter takes up special issues related to Christian parenting in today's world, including the selection of a given method of parenting, single parenting, physical punishment and other forms of discipline, cultivating masculinity and femininity in boys and girls, and principles of discipline. The important issue of spiritual warfare pertaining to marriage and the family is addressed as well.

Discussion Starters

1. Which parenting method do you use? Are there any books or materials that have had a significant influence on you in this regard? Are there any people in your life who have served as major examples or role models in parenting?
2. Which approach to physical discipline do you take? What is the stance toward physical discipline in the general culture? What do you consider to be the biblical teaching in this regard?

Discussion Questions

1. Give advantages and weaknesses of a "method" approach to parenting.
2. Give the three typical critiques of physical punishment in child-rearing.
3. Cite seven biblical principles of disciplining children.
4. What three instruments in the "devil's toolbox" does he use to destroy marriages and subvert family life? Give at least one biblical reference for each.
5. What are three important lessons to be learned as one fights the spiritual warfare in a family?

Personal Application Questions

Have you been aware of the spiritual warfare surrounding your marriage and family? If so, how have you engaged the enemy within (your sinful nature) and without (the devil and the world)? By and large, have you been successful? How are you going to apply the biblical principles for spiritual warfare covered in this chapter?

Issues for Prayer

Pray that the Holy Spirit might make you more sensitive to issues related to spiritual warfare, particularly as related to marriage and the family. Ask the Lord to show you how you can avoid giving the devil an opportunity to disrupt your marriage or your family life. Pray also that God may help you find ways to strengthen your marriage and to be the father or mother he wants you to be. Make it a habit to commit your spouse and your children daily to the Lord for his protection and encouragement.

Assignment

Make a chart with one column each for your spouse and each of your children. Then, pray for each of them on a daily basis for one week specifically in the area of spiritual warfare. Identify specific issues in your loved ones' lives in which the power of the devil and/or sin needs to be broken, and pray for God's victory in this regard. Ask your spouse to do the same for you.

CHAPTER 9: UNDIVIDED DEVOTION TO THE LORD: THE DIVINE GIFT OF SINGLENESS

Chapter Theme

Singleness was rare in Old Testament times and for the most part limited to the categories of widows; eunuchs; those who could not marry because of disease, economic distress, or a divine call; the divorced; and unmarried young men and women. In the New Testament, both Jesus and Paul point out the advantages of singleness for Christian ministry. The Scriptures provide helpful counsel for singles—be it young unmarried men or women, widows or widowers, single parents, or divorcees—and the variety of issues with which they are confronted.

Discussion Starters

1. Describe the attitude of your church toward singles, particularly those who have never been married. Does the church seek to integrate them into the social life and ministry of the church or are they marginalized? Is the issue of singleness addressed from the pulpit? List several ways in which your church (and even your family) could be a blessing to singles. If you have children who are grown but not yet married, how do you deal with the fact that they are still single while most of their peers already have families?

2. Describe the way in which your church deals with those who are single as a result of divorce or the death of a spouse. What are some ways in which your church could reach out to them to help them (socially, spiritually, financially, etc.)?

Discussion Questions

1. What are the six categories of singleness in the Old Testament?
2. What is the New Testament view of celibacy?
3. How can young, unmarried men stay pure in the vulnerable area of sexuality?
4. What are the biblical qualifications for a "true" widow?
5. Give three observations concerning singleness and marriage.

Personal Application Questions

How do you relate to singles in your church? Do you view singleness as an abnormal state, an undesirable and unnatural condition? Do you try to diagnose the problem of those who remain single well into their twenties and thirties? Or do you view singleness as a gift from God that presents certain advantages for the ministry?

Issues for Prayer

Ask God to help you find ways in which you can be a blessing and an encouragement to singles in your church. Ask God to help you view singleness as the Bible views it. If you have a grown child who is still single, pray for him or her to be receptive to God's will for his or her life and not to be affected by the unbiblical views of society.

Assignment

Over the next week, invite a single person over to your house and plan some activities with him or her. Try to find out what single persons think the church is doing right concerning singles and what they see as needing improvement so that they may feel better integrated into the life of the church.

CHAPTER 10: ABANDONING NATURAL RELATIONS: THE BIBLICAL VERDICT ON HOMOSEXUALITY

Chapter Theme

Homosexuality is universally condemned as sin throughout Scripture, most importantly in the Sodom and Gomorrah narrative in Genesis, the Levitical Holiness Code, and Paul's letter to the Romans and his first letters to the Corinthians and Timothy. The chapter shows how pro-homosexual interpreters have sought to relativize the biblical teaching on homosexuality in a number of ways and concludes that Scripture condemns homosexuality in general rather than merely certain forms of homosexual behavior.

Discussion Starters

1. Describe a situation (if you have experienced one) in which you had some interaction with a practicing homosexual. Do you think you related to this person in a normal way or did you feel awkward? Were you condemning in your heart or did you look at this man or woman as a person in need of salvation? Imagine a situation in which a homosexual person comes for a visit to your home. Describe how you, as a Christian, would behave.

2. List several biblical truths (and verses) you think a gospel presentation should contain when talking to a homosexual. Do you think that it should be different from a presentation of the gospel to a heterosexual? Explain. What are some key truths that the gospel should contain in such an encounter?

Discussion Questions

1. Give several components of the biblical/traditional model of marriage and family that homosexuality violates.

2. Give the two major pro-homosexual interpretations of the biblical account of Sodom and Gomorrah (Gen. 18:17–19:29). How would you respond to those interpretations?

3. Explain the pro-homosexual interpretation of Leviticus 18:22 and 20:13. How would you respond to this view?

4. What are the various pro-homosexual interpretations of *arsenokoitēs* ("one who lies or sleeps with males") in 1 Cor. 6:9-10 and 1 Timothy 1:9-10? How would you respond to these views?

Practical Application Questions

Do you have an attitude of condemnation and judgment toward those who practice homosexuality? Do you think that there is still grace for them? Do you think that God can change their sinful behavior, or are they without hope? If you know someone who practices such sinful behavior, can you love that person as the Bible requires? Would you feel comfortable sharing the gospel with such a person if the opportunity were to present itself?

Issues for Prayer

Ask God to give you compassion and love for those who have abandoned God's intended design for sexual expression. Ask God to give you the strength and the courage to witness to such people, without backing away from presenting the whole truth of the gospel, which includes leaving behind sinful behavior.

Assignment

Over the next week, based on media, personal contacts, and advertisements, take note of how the world views homosexual behavior. In a parallel column, write down how the teaching of the Bible contrasts with the world's view.

CHAPTER 11: SEPARATING WHAT GOD HAS JOINED TOGETHER: DIVORCE AND REMARRIAGE

Chapter Theme

While evangelicals concur that Scripture teaches a high view of marriage and views the breaking of the marriage bond in a negative light, there are differences of opinion as to whether the New Testament allows for exceptional cases in which divorce is legitimate. The chapter surveys Jesus' and Paul's teaching on the subject and discusses strengths and weaknesses of the major evangelical positions on divorce and remarriage.

Discussion Starters

1. Imagine that a couple comes to you for marital counseling. How would you advise such a couple to deal with their problems (pick one particular problem)? What would a process of healing entail, in your opinion? Would you ever think that divorce could be an option? Give reasons for your answer.

2. Without giving names, think of a couple who have gone through divorce and explain the consequences of this divorce for their children, for themselves individually, for their faith, etc.

Discussion Questions

1. What is the most important text on divorce and remarriage in the Old Testament? Explain the critical phrase in the text, according to the schools of Hillel and Shammai. Give the most likely interpretation.

2. In what ways does Jesus' reply to a question about the issue of divorce (Matt. 19:3-12 and parallels) differ from the two rabbinic schools?

3. What is the fundamental difference between the evangelical proponents of the "divorce and remarriage for adultery or sexual immorality" view and the adherents of the "no divorce, no remarriage" position? Explain. Moreover, how do they differ concerning the reference to *porneia* in the exception clause?

4. List arguments advanced against the "divorce for adultery or sexual immorality" view and responses given.

5. List arguments advanced against the "betrothal" view and responses given.

6. According to the majority view, what are the two legitimate reasons for divorce stipulated by Jesus and Paul respectively? What other possible reasons exist for divorce and/or remarriage?
7. What arguments are put forth against and for remarriage from 1 Corinthians 7:15, 39?
8. What are the pastoral implications of the positions on divorce and remarriage?
9. What major implications should be drawn from the discussion on divorce and remarriage?

Practical Application Questions

Do you think that divorce is an option in your marriage? Are you doing everything within your power to build up your marriage, rather than tear it down? Are you aware of the devil's temptations in regard to the opposite sex, and do you stay away from any contact with the opposite sex that may gradually lead to unfaithfulness to your spouse? Are you easily angered by the mistakes of your spouse or do you have patience and a forgiving spirit? Do you focus on what you appreciate about your mate, or do you tend to find fault with him or her? Are you selfish in your relationship with your spouse or do you enjoy him or her? Do you ask forgiveness when you have done something wrong?

Issues for Prayer

Ask God to help you be the kind of marriage partner that he would want you to be, and to make you loving, patient, edifying, and forgiving. Ask God to help you fulfill the role he has designed for you in marriage. Ask God to bless your marriage in such a way that you may be a positive example to other couples. Pray for wisdom concerning how to counsel a couple with marital problems.

Assignment

Make a list of your strengths and weaknesses in the way you relate to your spouse. Make a separate list of what you consider to be the strengths and weaknesses of your spouse. Exchange the two lists with your spouse, discuss the opinions, and specific ways in which each of you can help the other improve the quality of the relationship, and pray for each other for the rest of the week with a specific focus on the elements listed.

CHAPTER 12: FAITHFUL HUSBANDS: QUALIFICATIONS FOR CHURCH LEADERSHIP

Chapter Theme

The chapter discusses biblical requirements for church leaders related to their conduct as husbands and fathers. Special attention is given to Paul's stipulation that an elder or overseer be a "one-wife-type-of husband" or a "one-woman-type-of man."

Discussion Starters

1. What is your opinion about singles serving in the leadership of you church, either as deacon, elder, or pastor? What age is too young for leadership positions in the church, in your opinion? What about men who have been divorced? Would you be comfortable with them fulfilling leadership roles in the church? What about women serving in leadership positions in the church? How would you react if you went to a church where a woman was teaching a Sunday school class or even preaching from the pulpit?

2. How do you relate to the leadership in your church? Have you had any disagreement with anyone in leadership in your church? If so, how has the situation influenced your way of thinking about church?

Discussion Questions

1. What are four unlikely understandings of the phrase *mias gynaikas andra* in 1 Timothy 3:2, 12, and Titus 1:6, and what are their weaknesses? What is the most likely interpretation and translation that best captures the essence of the expression?

2. What is the difference in understanding between the first four interpretations and the one we have settled on in this book?

3. What are three implications of the "faithful husband" requirement?

Practical Application Questions

If you are in a leadership position in your church and have a family, are you a positive example for other families in the church? Are you offering godly leadership in your family? What are you teaching those who observe your family life? What are your motives for desiring a leadership position? Is it honor, money, or power? Or is it the desire to serve? Compare your motives to those found in 1 Peter 5:2-4.

Issues for Prayer

Ask God to bless those in leadership positions in your church with wisdom, vision, integrity, and the empowerment of the Holy Spirit. Also ask God to help you obey and submit to those "who watch over you" (Heb. 13:17). If you desire to serve in such a position, ask God to give you a clear understanding of where he wants you to serve and of the spiritual qualifications that you need to work on with the help of the Holy Spirit.

Assignment

Maybe you feel the call of God upon you to serve him in some capacity in your church, or perhaps as a minister in another church. Evaluate your life in light of the qualifications found in the New Testament. On a scale of 1 to 10, how would you rate yourself regarding spiritual readiness to serve in a leadership position? Talk also with those in leadership in your church about your desire. They may either confirm your calling or raise doubts about your readiness for such a role.

CHAPTER 13: UNITING ALL THINGS IN HIM:
CONCLUDING SYNTHESIS

Chapter Theme

This concluding chapter summarizes the major contents of each of the
preceding chapters of the book.

Discussion Starters

1. Give an example of a situation in which this study has helped
   you in your parenting or marital relationship.
2. How has this study impacted your thinking on the nature of
   marriage and the family and your role as father or mother? Give
   three specific examples.

Discussion Questions

1. Discuss the contemporary cultural crisis surrounding marriage
   and the family and sketch out the spiritual solution required to
   address it.
2. What are the three major principles regarding the husband-wife
   relationship that can be gleaned from Genesis 1–3, and what are
   the six ways in which God's ideal for marriage was compromised in the history of Israel? Cite specific Scripture passages
   that support the principles.
3. What are the roles of the husband and the wife according to Paul's
   teaching in Ephesians 5:21-33? Discuss the implications of the
   analogy between Christ and the church and husband and wife.
4. Discuss several of the major Old Testament passages that speak
   of parents' responsibility to teach children about God and provide an overview of the major responsibilities of fathers, mothers, and children according to Old Testament teaching.
5. Discuss the roles and responsibilities of fathers, mothers, and
   children according to Paul's teaching in the New Testament.
   Give scriptural support for your answers.

6. Choose one of the three major issues related to childbearing, abortion, infertility, or adoption. For your chosen topic, provide a survey of the biblical teaching. Then discuss the major contemporary ethical issues involved and lay out what you would consider a proper Christian approach to these issues.

7. Give an account of the contemporary debate surrounding physical punishment of children. What are the major objections raised against physical discipline? How would you respond to these concerns in light of Scripture?

8. What are the different forms of singleness in the Old and the New Testament? Do you discern any development in the biblical teaching on singleness? Wherever possible, give scriptural support for you answer.

9. Discuss and critique one pro-homosexual interpretation of an Old Testament passage regarding homosexuality (either Sodom and Gomorrah or the Levitical Holiness Code) and discuss and critique at least three ways in which advocates of homosexuality have sought to limit the scope of biblical references to homosexuality. In your treatment of the New Testament material, be sure to include a discussion of the meaning of *arsenokoitai* in 1 Corinthians 6 and 1 Timothy 1, and the phrase "contrary to nature" in Romans 1.

10. Provide a thorough, verse-by-verse commentary on Jesus' discussion of divorce in Matthew 19:3-12, with special emphasis on the meaning of the phrase "except for *porneia*." Discuss the viewpoints of the two major interpretive schools on this passage, then list at least three major arguments advanced against each position plus responses given. Conclude your essay with an articulation of your own beliefs on this issue, including a brief rationale for it.

11. What are the five interpretations of the phrase *mias gynaikas anēr* in 1 Timothy 3:2, 12 and Titus 1:6? Evaluate the strengths and weaknesses of each approach and indicate your own preference, including a rationale for your position.

Personal Application Questions

Has this study helped you to gain a better and more biblical understanding of the issues related to marriage and family? Are you motivated to implement the principles learned in improving your family and marriage responsibilities?

Issues for Prayer

Ask God to bless your marriage and family and to make it a blessing to others. Ask him to give you the strength and wisdom to apply what your have learned so that your marriage and family may bring glory to God.

ANSWERS TO DISCUSSION QUESTIONS

THE PRECEDING *Personal and Group Study Guide* featured a list of discussion questions for each chapter to help identify the main points of each chapter, to structure the information for better retention, and to stimulate individual discovery or group participation. It is highly recommended that the reader attempt to answer the questions on his or her own before checking the answers below.

CHAPTER 1: THE CURRENT CULTURAL CRISIS:
REBUILDING THE FOUNDATION

1. What are the two reasons why a biblically integrated treatment of the subject of marriage and family is needed?

   • the cultural confusion regarding marriage and family
   • the lack of adequate Christian literature on marriage and family

2. Describe the paradigm shift we are seeing today with regard to marriage and family.

   • shift from the biblical/traditional model of marriage and family to libertarian ideology elevating human freedom of self-determination

3. What are the negative effects of the paradigm shift?

   • high divorce rates

GOD, MARRIAGE, AND FAMILY

- sex outside marriage
- homosexuality
- gender role confusion

CHAPTER 2: LEAVING AND CLEAVING:
MARRIAGE IN THE OLD TESTAMENT

1. What are three principles pertaining to marriage and family established in the beginning?

   - the man and the woman were created in God's image to rule the earth for God
   - the man's being created first establishes his ultimate responsibility for the marital union before God; the woman's role in relation to man is that of a "suitable helper"
   - the Fall has abiding consequences

2. There are three major views on the image of God in man. What are they, and which understanding is most likely?

   - substantive = reflection of God's essence
   - relational = reflection of God's relational nature
   - functional = representative rule (most likely, possibly in combination with substantive)

3. What is the difference between essential or ontological subordination and functional subordination?

   - ontological subordination = distinction in nature
   - functional subordination = distinction in roles

4. In which expression applied to the woman in Genesis 2 can we see both equality and distinctiveness, complementarity and submission/authority?

   - "suitable helper"

5. What are the marital roles stipulated in the Old Testament for husbands toward their wives and vice versa?

Husbands:
- no explicit "job description"
- primary responsibility for marriage, ultimate authority over family (Genesis 2)
- provision of food, clothing, and marital rights (Ex. 21:10)

Wives:
- presenting her husband with children (Gen. 1:28; 30:1, 23)
- managing the household (Gen. 1:28; cf. 2:5)
- providing her husband with companionship (Gen. 2:18, 20; cf. Mal. 2:11)

6. In what ways does the history of Israel show that God's ideal of marriage established at Creation was compromised?

- polygamy (rather than monogamy)
- divorce (rather than durability)
- adultery (rather than fidelity)
- homosexuality (rather than heterosexuality)
- sterility (rather than fertility)
- dilution of gender distinctions (rather than complementarity)

CHAPTER 3: NO LONGER TWO, BUT ONE:
MARRIAGE IN THE NEW TESTAMENT

1. What was Jesus' view of the nature of marriage?

- marriage is a sacred bond between a man and a woman, established by and entered into before God (Matt. 19:6; cf. Gen. 1:27; 2:24)
- marriage is to be permanent (Matt. 19:6)
- marriage is limited to this life; no marriage in heaven (Matt. 22:30 par.)

2. List the important passages where Paul addresses the topic of marriage, and briefly summarize their content.

- 1 Corinthians 7:2-5 (fulfill marital obligations toward spouse)

- 1 Timothy 2:15 (women "preserved by" childbearing); 4:1-4 (do not forbid marriage)
- Ephesians 5:21-33 (wives, submit to your husbands; husbands, love your wives; analogy between Christ-church and husband-wife relationship)

3. Give some important principles for marriage from the book of Ephesians.

- the marriage relationship must be seen within the compass of God's larger salvation-historical, end-time purposes (Eph. 1:10)
- Paul's commands are directed to Spirit-filled believers (Eph. 5:18)
- Paul does not call for "mutual submission" in terms of identical roles but for submission "one to another," i.e., wives to husbands (Eph. 5:21)
- "headship" entails not merely nurture and protection but also a position of and the exercise of authority (Eph. 5:22-24)
- female submission is not merely a result of the Fall (Gen. 2:18, 20)
- the restored pattern for marriage in Christ does not transcend that of submission/authority (Eph. 5:22; Col. 3:18)

4. What are three applications from Ephesians 5 for marital relationships?

- wives are called to follow their husband's loving leadership in their marriage and family
- there is a difference between traditional and biblical marriage
- improper caricatures of the biblical teaching of wifely submission and the husband's loving leadership (e.g., subservience and hierarchical views) must be rejected

CHAPTER 4: THE NATURE OF MARRIAGE:
SACRAMENT, CONTRACT, OR COVENANT?

1. What are the three major models for the nature of marriage? Define and give the roots of each model.

- sacramental: marriage as a means of obtaining grace; marriage is rooted in church law
- contractual: marriage as a bilateral contract that is voluntarily formed, maintained, and dissolved by two individuals; marriage rooted in civil law
- covenantal: marriage as a sacred bond between a man and a woman instituted by and entered into before God; marriage rooted in the standards of divine law

2. Give three weaknesses of the sacramental model of marriage.

- there is nothing in the institution of marriage itself that "mystically" dispenses divine grace
- it does not cohere with the thrust of biblical teaching on marriage as a whole; the Creator designed marriage to be a wellspring of new physical life (through procreation), not a mechanism for attaining spiritual life
- it subordinates the husband-wife relationship to the control of the church

3. Give three weaknesses of the contractual model.

- reductionistic; not found in Scripture to describe nature of marriage as a whole
- it provides an extremely weak basis for the permanence of marriage—people's ability not to sin
- it opens the door to a variety of marital arrangements prohibited by Scripture

4. What biblical support can be offered for the covenantal view of marriage?

- covenantal language in Genesis 2
- references to marriage as a "covenant" (Prov. 2:16-17; Mal. 2:14)
- biblical analogies and passages in which marriage is viewed in covenantal terms

5. What are the five important aspects of the marriage covenant?

- the permanence of marriage (Matt. 19:6 par. Mark 10:9)
- the sacredness of marriage (Gen. 2:22)
- the intimacy of marriage (Gen. 2:23-25)
- the mutuality of marriage (Eph. 5:25-30)
- the exclusiveness of marriage (Gen. 2:22-25; 1 Cor. 7:2-5)

6. What concerns have been raised regarding the covenantal model?

- marriage is not explicitly referred to as a covenant in the New Testament
- marriage transcends the notion of a covenant; it is part of God's created order
- there is no clear demonstrable distinction between marriage as a contract and marriage as a covenant in the Old Testament terminology for marriage

CHAPTER 5: THE TIES THAT BIND:
FAMILY IN THE OLD TESTAMENT

1. List at least three responsibilities of fathers according to the Old Testament.

- personally modeling strict personal fidelity to Yahweh
- instructing the family in the traditions of the exodus and the Scriptures
- providing for the family's basic needs for food, shelter, clothing, and rest

2. List at least three responsibilities of mothers according to the Old Testament.

- instructing her children
- managing the affairs of her household and caring for her husband and children
- providing wise counsel to her husband

3. List at least three responsibilities of children according to the Old Testament.

- respecting their parents
- helping in and around the home
- providing for their parents in their old age

CHAPTER 6: THE CHRISTIAN FAMILY:
FAMILY IN THE NEW TESTAMENT

1. What are two ways in which children figured prominently in Jesus' ministry and teaching?

   - Jesus frequently restored children to their parents by miraculous healing
   - Jesus used children to teach on the nature of discipleship

2. What are several ways in which children came to typify desirable attitudes in believers in the early church?

   - as an image representing the needy, the "little ones" who are members of the church (Mark 9:42; Matt. 18:6-14; cf. Acts 20:35)
   - as a metaphor for learning in expressing the relationship of pupil to teacher as child to parent (Mark 10:24b; 2 Cor. 12:14; 1 Tim. 1:2; 1 John 2:1)
   - as a symbol of hope and new beginning (Isa. 9:6; cf. Luke 2:12-14) in association with imagery of birthing a new creation, be it in elaboration of the pupil-teacher relationship (Gal. 4:4) or with reference to the birth pangs of the messianic age (John 16:21; Rom. 8:22; 1 Thess. 5:3; Rev. 12:2; cf. Isa. 26:16-19; 66:7-14)

3. What are the assumptions underlying the New Testament authors' use of the "household codes"?

   - the order in the household will promote order on a larger societal scale
   - believer's conformity to the ethical standards of such a code would bring Christianity respect in the surrounding culture (1 Tim. 3:7, 6:1; Titus 2:5, 8, 10, 3:8; 1 Pet. 2:12)
   - aid in the church's evangelistic mission (1 Thess. 4:12)

4. What are the responsibilities and roles of each individual in a household? Give at least one Scripture reference for each.

Fathers:
- provide for children (2 Cor. 12:14)
- ensure proper nurture and discipline (Prov. 13:24; Heb. 12:6)

Mothers:
- raising of children, motherhood (1 Tim. 2:15)
- managing the home (1 Tim. 5:14)

Children:
- obedience to parents (Eph. 6:1-3)
- care for them in old age (1 Tim. 5:8)

5. What are the four characteristics older women are to exemplify, according to Titus 2?

- they are to be reverent in the way they live
- they are not to be slanderers
- they are not to be addicted to much wine
- they are to be "teachers of the good"

6. What are Paul's instructions for young women?

- they are to be certain kinds of wives and mothers
- they are to be cultivating Christian character
- they are to be engaged in activities with the right kind of attitude
- they are to be subject to their own husbands

7. Give eight observations that can be drawn from Paul's teaching of the woman's relationship to her husband and children.

- while marriages are to be strong, young women need other significant relationships
- love of husbands comes before love of children
- wives are called both to love and to submit to their husbands
- women need self-control in dealing with their husbands and children

- women's hearts are to be pure and their attitude toward others in the home to be kind rather than antagonistic or hostile
- women are to be devoted first and foremost to the home
- God has in store blessings for women who defy secular stereotypes and focus on their God-given calling related to family and the home
- the desired result of proper wifely submission and diligent homemaking will be that no one will revile the word of God

CHAPTER 7: TO HAVE OR NOT TO HAVE CHILDREN:
SPECIAL ISSUES RELATED TO THE FAMILY (PART 1)

1. What is the biblical teaching regarding children, the killing of children, and God's involvement in procreation? What were ancient Greco-Roman, Jewish, and early Christians' views toward abortion?

- the Bible teaches that children are a blessing from God and regards the killing of children with particular horror; God is shown to be active in the creation of human beings from the time of conception
- the exposure of a newborn child was a frequent practice in the ancient world; Jewish law prohibited abortion and the exposure of children on the basis of Exodus 21:22-25; the early Christians likewise condemned both practices

2. What are potentially acceptable forms of contraception?

- *general principle*: those that are contraceptive in nature, i.e., exclusively prohibit conception
- abstinence
- "rhythm method"
- "barrier methods" (diaphragm, cervical cap, condoms, and spermicides)

3. What are morally unacceptable forms of contraception?

- *general principle:* all forms of induced abortion
- IUD (intrauterine device)
- RU-486 ("morning after pill")

4. What are forms of contraception that require special consideration and extra care?
   - sterilization (vasectomy, tubal occlusion)
   - "the pill" and its many applications (combined and progestin-only contraceptives)

5. What are some principles for evaluating modern artificial reproductive technologies?

   - respect for the sanctity of human life
   - respect for all human beings as image bearers
   - respect for the fidelity of the marriage bond
   - the heart of the one wanting to use those methods

6. What are some instances of adoption in Scripture?

   - Jacob adopting Naphtali, Ephraim, and Manasseh (Gen. 30:3-8; 48:5)
   - Moses being adopted by Pharaoh's daughter (Ex. 2:10)
   - Esther's adoption by Mordecai (Est. 2:7)
   - Jesus' adoption by Joseph (Matt. 1:25; 2:13-15; Luke 2:22-24)
   - the metaphorical use of adoption for New Testament believers (Rom. 8:15, 23; 9:4; Gal. 4:5; Eph. 1:5)

CHAPTER 8: REQUIRING THE WISDOM OF SOLOMON:
SPECIAL ISSUES RELATED TO THE FAMILY (PART 2)

1. Give advantages and weaknesses of a "method" approach to parenting.

   Advantages:
   - it increases the confidence of parents that they have a plan and purpose in their parenting
   - it provides for predictability and consistency
   - it brings parents together with other parents who use the same method

   Weaknesses:
   - parental confidence may in fact give them a false sense of security that all is well when at least in the long run it may not be

• it places the emphasis on an abstract set of principles rather than on people
• it tends to give inadequate respect to the individuality and uniqueness of each child
• it tends to lose sight of the various stages of development in a child and young person's life, which requires flexibility and constant adjustment

2. Give the three typical critiques of physical punishment in child-rearing.

• spanking a child is tantamount to physical abuse
• spanking is archaic and psychologically damaging
• a discontinuity exists between the Old and New Testament views on children and discipline

3. Cite seven biblical principles of disciplining children.

• discipline must be consistent
• discipline ought to be age-appropriate
• it must adhere to the universal biblical principles of fairness and justice (the punishment should fit the offense)
• discipline should be child-specific
• it should be administered in love and not anger
• it should be future-oriented and forward-looking
• it must be part of a relationship between parent and child that is larger and more permanent than any temporary form of discipline

4. What three instruments in the "devil's toolbox" does he use to destroy marriages and subvert family life? Give at least one biblical reference for each.

• sexual temptation (1 Cor. 7:5)
• unresolved anger (Eph. 4:26-27; 6:4)
• the husband's insensitivity toward his wife (1 Pet. 3:7; Col. 3:19)

5. What are three important lessons to be learned as one fights the spiritual warfare in a family?

- awareness of the fact that there is a battle
- knowledge of one's spiritual enemy
- use of proper spiritual weapons

CHAPTER 9: UNDIVIDED DEVOTION TO THE LORD: THE DIVINE GIFT OF SINGLENESS

1. What are the six categories of singleness in the Old Testament?

- widows
- eunuchs
- those who could not marry for reasons of disease or economic difficulties
- divine call
- divorced
- unmarried young men and women

2. What is the New Testament view of celibacy?

- it is a gift of God (1 Cor. 7:7)
- it is a voluntary state (Matt. 19:11-12)

3. How can young, unmarried men stay pure in the vulnerable area of sexuality?

- they must pray and trust God to deliver them from temptation
- they must grow strong in the Lord and the knowledge of his Word
- they must make every effort to cultivate the virtues of self-control and purity of heart
- they must seek the company and accountability of other, like-minded male believers
- they must understand that the temptation is not the sin
- they must realize that when we sin, God stands ready to forgive

- they are not to shun younger women but to love them as their sisters in the Lord
- they should not overestimate their ability to resist temptation nor underestimate the power of the temptation and the tempter himself

4. What are the biblical qualifications for a "true" widow?

- she has no relatives to care for her
- she puts her hope in God and does not indulge in a pleasure-seeking lifestyle
- she must be at least sixty years old
- she must have been faithful to her deceased husband
- she must be well-known for her good deeds:

  - bringing up children
  - showing hospitality
  - "washing the feet of the saints"
  - helping those in trouble
  - devoting herself to all kinds of good deeds

5. Give three observations concerning singleness and marriage.

- the married state is not the final destiny of anyone (Matt. 2:30; cf. Rom. 7:3; 1 Cor. 7:39)
- singles ought to learn to be content (1 Tim. 6:6; cf. Phil. 4:13)
- all who forsake marriage and family in the present world for the sake of God are rewarded with a new family in the body of Christ, as well as with an eternal family in the kingdom of heaven (Luke 18:28-29)

CHAPTER 10: ABANDONING NATURAL RELATIONS: THE BIBLICAL VERDICT ON HOMOSEXUALITY

1. Give several components of the biblical/traditional model of marriage and family that homosexuality violates.

- heterosexuality
- complementarity

- fertility
- monogamy, fidelity, durability

2. Give the two major pro-homosexual interpretations of the biblical account of Sodom and Gomorrah (Gen. 18:17–19:29). How would you respond to those interpretations?

Gang rape not homosexuality:
- offense not limited to gang rape
- not just sexual immorality but "unnatural desire": see Jude 6-7; cf. 2 Peter 2:4-10
- intended rape never occurred, yet Sodom and Gomorrah still destroyed

Inhospitality not homosexuality:
- the word *yāda'* ("know") must mean "sexual relations" (not "get acquainted with") in Genesis 19:5 in light of the parallel in Genesis 19:8
- it was the citizens, not Lot, who were killed, though supposedly it was Lot who broke the local hospitality code

3. Explain the pro-homosexual interpretation of Leviticus 18:22 and 20:13. How would you respond to this view?

The word translated "abomination" refers possibly to homosexual acts performed by Canaanite temple prostitutes as part of the worship of false gods:

- "abomination" frequently does not have this connotation but that of activities morally offensive to God
- activities like incest in Leviticus 18:6-18, adultery in Leviticus 18:20, bestiality in Leviticus 18:23 are also labeled "abomination"
- child sacrifice was also part of the ritual worship, yet it was always wrong

4. What are the various pro-homosexual interpretations of *arsenokoitēs* ("one who lies or sleeps with males") in 1 Corinthians 6:9-10 and 1 Timothy 1:9-10? How would you respond to these views?

The meaning is restricted to (1) male prostitution, (2) pederasty, (3) homosexual acts, (4) the negative dehumanizing pattern of homosexuality prevalent in first-century Hellenistic culture, or (5) the ancient and the modern conception of homosexuality are too different to use the same term for both:

- homosexuality in general is universally condemned in the Old Testament; it is unlikely that the New Testament would condone this practice
- the term was very likely adapted from the Levitical Holiness Code, where it includes every kind of male-male intercourse
- reference to pederasty is unlikely, since there was a different Greek word for pederasty. Romans 1:27 speaks of mutual desire, which does not fit the pattern of pederasty. No pederasty was involved in lesbian sex, which is mentioned in Romans 1:26, and even if pederasty were in view in the Romans passage, Paul as a Scripture-abiding Jew would still not have approved of homosexuality as such
- Paul would not have allowed for "celibate" homosexual relationships, because according to Romans 1:26-27 he considered homosexuality as "contrary to nature"
- Paul's view of homosexuality as "contrary to nature" also coheres with the prevailing view in Greco-Roman culture, which held that one of the same-sex partners had to compromise their natural gender identity
- Paul's comments in Romans 1:18-32 do not support the dichotomy suggested between homosexual acts and homosexual orientation; in this passage Paul makes mention of both homosexual acts and the thoughts and passions underlying homosexual activity

CHAPTER 11: SEPARATING WHAT GOD HAS JOINED TOGETHER: DIVORCE AND REMARRIAGE

1. What is the most important text on divorce and remarriage in the Old Testament? Explain the critical phrase in the text, according to the schools of Hillel and Shammai. Give the most likely interpretation.

   - Deuteronomy 24:1-4
   - *'erwat dābār* ("shameful thing," "some indecency")
   - the conservative school of Shammai states that the phrase is a reference to immodest behavior or sexual immorality
   - the liberal school of Hillel claimed that the phrase was a reference to any instance where a wife did something displeasing to her husband
   - the most likely interpretation is that the phrase refers to various forms of immoral behavior on the part of the wife

2. In what ways does Jesus' reply to a question about the issue of divorce (Matt. 19:3-12 and parallels) differ from the two rabbinic schools?

   - Jesus only *permitted* divorce in case of *porneia* while even the conservative school of Shammai *required* it
   - Jesus' reply transcends the legalistic squabbles between those two rabbinic schools and goes to the heart of the matter; he focuses on the original design of marriage as a divine rather than merely human institution (Gen. 1:27; 2:24); divorce, in this case, is at odds with God's purpose in creation
   - Jesus applies the standard regarding divorce and remarriage to both men and women

3. What is the fundamental difference between the evangelical proponents of the "divorce and remarriage for adultery or sexual immorality" view and the adherents of the "no divorce, no remarriage" position? Explain. Moreover, how do they differ concerning the reference to *porneia* in the exception clause?

- the difference turns on their definition of marriage itself, or more narrowly still, on their understanding of the senses in which marriage is viewed as a covenant; it all depends on whether the covenant can be broken or not
- for the first view, *porneia* is general, referring to sexual marital unfaithfulness, while for the second view *porneia* is more narrowly defined as incest or sexual infidelity during the engagement period

4. List arguments advanced against the "divorce for adultery or sexual immorality" view and responses given.

Arguments against:
- why start with the "more difficult" passage?
- the exception clause is limited to Matthew's Gospel
- there is a tension between Jesus' references to God's ideal for marriage at Creation in Matthew 19:4-6 and his allowing an exception for divorce in Matthew 19:9
- how is there continuity between Moses in Deuteronomy 24 and Jesus in Matthew 19?
- Jesus essentially answers the divorce question, put to him in Hillelite terms, in a Shammaite fashion; one would expect Jesus to posit a higher standard than either school, namely "no divorce under any circumstances"
- there is difficulty explaining the disciples' reaction
- the view seems to take a lower view of marriage covenant than seems warranted in light of the high view of the permanence of covenants in Scripture

Responses:
- "more difficult" is too subjective; also mentioned in Matthew 5:32; view is most straightforward, natural reading of text
- Markan, Lukan, and Pauline intentions were different from those of Matthew
- Jesus affirmed God's creation ideal as well as the Mosaic stipulations in Deuteronomy 24:1-4; the tension is due to sin in the world

- continuity in principle: God's ideal upheld; exception because of people's hardness of heart; but shift in punishment for adultery from death to permissible divorce
- Jesus' standard is in fact stricter by permitting rather than requiring divorce and by referring to God's creation ideal as the true norm
- the disciples' reaction may betray an unduly lenient view of divorce on their part
- some covenants can be broken

5. List arguments advanced against the "betrothal" view and responses given.

Arguments against:
- Deuteronomy 24:1-4, which underlies the discussion in Matthew 19, is not limited to betrothal but extends also to marriage, divorce, and remarriage
- nothing in the context of Matthew 19 limits the expression *porneia* to betrothal
- the term *porneia*, unless narrowed by the context, is broader than premarital sex
- the alleged tie posited between Matthew 1:18-25 and Matthew 19:3-12 is unlikely
- the "betrothal" view does not adequately consider the first-century rabbinic practice of abbreviating an account
- the fact that Mark, Luke, and Paul do not include the exception clause can be explained by the respective purposes of these authors in their respective literary contexts
- the issue of sexual immorality during the betrothal period would have been irrelevant for the political issue of the illicit marriage between Herod Antipas and Herodias

Responses:
- Jesus' teaching transcends Deuteronomy 24:1-4
- as John 8:41 shows, *porneia* can indeed refer to premarital sexual unfaithfulness
- though *porneia* can have a broader scope of reference, this is rendered unlikely in Matthew 19 because of larger theological consideration

- the tie between Matthew 1:18-25 and Matthew 19:3-12 makes perfect sense in the original Matthean context as a rehabilitation of Joseph through Jesus' teaching on divorce
- abbreviate perhaps—but change?
- it is preferable to explain the Matthean exception in a way that is congruent with the absolute statements in Mark, Luke, and Paul rather than vice versa
- Herod Antipas/Herodias minimized as relevant background for Matthew 19 and parallels

6. According to the majority view, what are the two legitimate reasons for divorce stipulated by Jesus and Paul respectively? What other possible reasons exist for divorce and/or remarriage?

- sexual immorality or adultery
- desertion by an unbelieving spouse
- death of a spouse
- other extreme circumstances when confronted through the process laid out in Matthew 18:15-17

7. What arguments are put forth against and for remarriage from 1 Corinthians 7:15, 39?

Against remarriage:
- marriage is a creation ordinance, a covenant, which is permanently binding regardless of circumstances
- Paul specifically prohibits remarriage in 1 Corinthians 7:10-11
- the words *douloō* and *deō* are not interchangeable
- where Paul refers to the possibility of remarriage, this is always in the context of the death of one of the marriage partners

For remarriage:
- a covenant can be broken under certain circumstances
- 1 Corinthians 7:10-11 refers to believers, 1 Corinthians 7:15 addresses a believer being abandoned by an unbelieving spouse

- while not identical, the terms *douloō* and *deō* do seem to inhabit the same semantic domain
- Paul may be using an analogy, saying that when an unbelieving spouse deserts his or her partner, it is as if that person has died

8. What are the pastoral implications of the positions on divorce and remarriage?

- the creation narrative upholds, and Jesus and Paul reaffirm, God's ordinance of marriage as a lifelong union between one man and one woman
- there is the danger of placing too stringent a requirement on the one whose partner is guilty of sexual unfaithfulness or abandonment
- there is the converse danger of being more lenient than Scripture allows
- divorce is never willed by God and is always the result of sin

9. What major implications should be drawn from the discussion on divorce and remarriage?

- everything should be done to preserve marriages
- one must determine if a given divorce is or has been legitimate
- a clear distinction should be drawn between the guilty and the innocent party

CHAPTER 12: FAITHFUL HUSBANDS:
QUALIFICATIONS FOR CHURCH LEADERSHIP

1. What are four unlikely understandings of the phrase *mias gynaikas andra* in 1 Timothy 3:2, 12, and Titus 1:6, and what are their weaknesses? What is the most likely interpretation and translation that best captures the essence of the expression?

The phrase excludes single men from holding ecclesiastical office:

- Paul was himself unmarried

- Paul extols advantages of singleness for ministry in 1 Corinthians
- Paul would have said so much more unequivocally

The phrase excludes divorcees:

- Paul could have said this more directly
- divorce is not mentioned anywhere in all of the Pastoral letters

The phrase prohibits widowers who remarried

- Paul elsewhere encourages those who are widowed to remarry
- no good biblical, theological, or commonsense reason to bar widowers from church leadership

Paul excludes polygamists

- polygamy was not widely practiced in the Greco-Roman world of that time
- geared toward men who had one or several concubines or may otherwise have been unfaithful to their wives
- translation: "faithful husband"

2. What is the difference in understanding between the first four interpretations and the one we have settled on in this book?

- literal interpretation: *one* woman as opposed to *zero* (single) or *two* or *more* wives at the same time (polygamy) or consecutively (remarriage)
- idiomatical interpretation: "a one-wife-type-of-husband"

3. What are three implications of the "faithful husband" requirement?

- younger candidates who have yet to prove their ability to manage their own households well should ordinarily not be put in ultimate positions in the church

- it is utter folly for someone to provide qualified, capable leadership for the church while neglecting his duties in his own family
- by linking the family so closely to the church, the New Testament presents the latter as the eschatological extension of the former

CHAPTER 13: UNITING ALL THINGS IN HIM: CONCLUDING SYNTHESIS

For answers to the questions for chapter 13, review the answers to the discussion questions in the previous twelve chapters.

NOTES

CHAPTER 2:
LEAVING AND CLEAVING: MARRIAGE IN THE OLD TESTAMENT

1. As is the case with many other topics addressed in Scripture, Christians who have dealt with this issue are not all agreed. Evangelicals who have written on issues related to marriage and the family generally fall into two broad groups, complementarians (who affirm that Scripture stipulates distinct roles for men and women) and egalitarians (who believe that there are no differences in role between men and women according to Scripture). Along complementarian lines see John Piper and Wayne Grudem, eds., *Recovering Biblical Manhood and Womanhood: A Response to Evangelical Feminism* (Wheaton, Ill.: Crossway, 1991); Andreas J. Köstenberger, Thomas R. Schreiner, and Henry S. Baldwin, eds., *Women in the Church: A Fresh Analysis of 1 Timothy 2:9-15* (Grand Rapids, Mich.: Baker, 1995); Andreas J. Köstenberger, "Women in the Pauline Mission," in Peter Bolt and Mark Thompson, eds., *The Gospel to the Nations: Perspectives on Paul's Mission* (Downers Grove, Ill.: InterVarsity Press, 2000), 236-237 (reprinted in Andreas J. Köstenberger, *Studies on John and Gender: A Decade of Scholarship* [New York: Peter Lang, 2001], 348-350); Robert L. Saucy and Judith K. TenElshof, eds., *Women and Men in Ministry: A Complementary Perspective* (Chicago: Moody, 2001); and Wayne Grudem, *Evangelical Feminism and Biblical Truth: An Analysis of 118 Disputed Questions* (Sisters, Ore.: Multnomah, 2004). Along egalitarian lines see Stanley J. Grenz with Denise Muir Kjesbo, *Women in the Church: A Biblical Theology of Women in Ministry* (Downers Grove, Ill.: InterVarsity Press, 1995); Alvera Mickelsen, ed., *Women, Authority, and the Bible* (Downers Grove, Ill.: InterVarsity Press, 1986); and Ruth A. Tucker and Walter Liefeld, *Daughters of the Church: Women and Ministry from New Testament Times to the Present* (Grand Rapids, Mich.: Zondervan, 1987). For a comparison of views see James R. Beck and Craig L. Blomberg, eds., *Two Views on Women in Ministry* (Grand Rapids, Mich.: Zondervan, 2001). For contours of a biblical theology of human sexuality, including marriage and the family, see Charles H. H. Scobie, *The Ways of Our God: An Approach to Biblical Theology* (Grand Rapids, Mich./Cambridge: Eerdmans, 2003), 802-811, 827, 835-842, 859, 864-869.

2. Contra William J. Webb, *Slaves, Women, and Homosexuals: Exploring the Hermeneutics of Cultural Analysis* (Downers Grove, Ill.: InterVarsity Press, 2001), 142-143, who claims that the "whispers of patriarchy in the garden may have been placed there in order to anticipate the curse" and that what Genesis 2–3 represents is "a way of describing the past through present categories. The creation story may be using the social categories that Moses' audience would have been familiar with." But see the competent refutation of Webb's view of Genesis 2–3 in specific and of his "redemptive-movement hermeneutic" in general by Wayne Grudem in the *Journal of the Evangelical Theological Society* 47, no. 2 (June 2004): 299-347.

3. Cf. Matthew 19:5-6; Mark 10:9; 1 Corinthians 6:16; Ephesians 5:31; cf. Malachi 2:10-16, especially v. 10.

4. See Raymond C. Ortlund, Jr., "Male-Female Equality and Male Headship," in *Recovering Biblical Manhood and Womanhood,* 95-112.

5. Beyond this, many have detected covenantal language in Genesis 1 and 2. Because the term "covenant" is not used in these chapters, and because a full-fledged discussion of the so-called "covenantal model" of marriage involves several other Old Testament and New Testament texts, we will defer treatment of this issue and deal with it in a separate chapter (chapter 4) below.

6. The (roughly synonymous) Hebrew terms used in Genesis 1:26-27 are *tselem* for "image" (in the sense of "replica," cf. Num. 33:42; 1 Sam. 6:5, 11; 2 Kings 11:18; Ezek. 7:27; 16:17; 23:14) and *demût* for "likeness" (in the sense of "resemblance," cf. 2 Kings 16:10; 2 Chron. 4:3-4; Ps. 58:4; Ezek. 23:15).

7. Cf. Millard J. Erickson, *Christian Theology,* 2d ed. (Grand Rapids, Mich.: Baker, 1998), 532-534; see also his survey on pages 520-529 of the three major views on the image of God in man: (1) substantive (Luther, Calvin, and more recently Wayne Grudem, *Systematic Theology* [Grand Rapids, Mich.: Zondervan, 1994], 445-449); (2) relational (Barth, Brunner); and (3) functional (several Reformed scholars; Anthony Hoekema, *Created in God's Image* [Grand Rapids, Mich.: Eerdmans, 1986], especially 72-73, favors a combination of (2) and (3), with (3) being primary). For the ancient background see especially Hans Walter Wolff, *Anthropology of the Old Testament* (Philadelphia: Fortress, 1973), 160, followed by William Dyrness, *Themes in Old Testament Theology* (Downers Grove, Ill.: InterVarsity Press, 1979), 83, and others. See also G. C. Berkouwer, *Man: The Image of God* (Grand Rapids, Mich.: Eerdmans, 1962), 70.

8. Note the notion of "likeness" (cf. Gen. 5:3). See also the reiteration in Genesis 9:6 and the statement in James 3:9.

9. Wolff, *Anthropology of the Old Testament,* 160.

10. All scriptural quotations in this book are from the English Standard Version unless indicated otherwise.

11. See especially Hoekema, *Created in God's Image,* 73: "To see man as the image of God is to see both the task and the gifts. But the task is primary; the gifts are secondary. The gifts are the means for fulfilling the task."

12. See James B. Hurley, *Man and Woman in Biblical Perspective* (Grand Rapids, Mich.: Zondervan, 1981), 210-212. Since naming typically conveys the notion of authority, it is perhaps significant to note that Adam named his wife twice, once before the Fall ("woman," Gen. 2:23) and once after the Fall ("Eve," Gen. 3:20). Hence the husband's authority is not merely the result of the Fall.

13. Cf. Larry J. Kreitzer, "Adam and Christ," in Gerald F. Hawthorne, Ralph P. Martin, and Daniel G. Reid, eds., *Dictionary of Paul and His Letters* (Leicester, U.K./Downers Grove, Ill.: InterVarsity Press, 1993), 10: "The historicity of Adam as the first created person appears to have been taken for granted by the apostle Paul."

14. See chapter 9 for a discussion of singleness.

15. See R. David Freedman, "Woman, a Power Equal to Man," *Biblical Archaeological Review* 9, no. 1 (1983): 56-58; Joy L. E. Fleming, *A Rhetorical Analysis of Genesis 2–3 with Implications for a Theology of Man and Woman* (Ph.D. diss.; University of Strasburg, 1987); and many egalitarian writers.

16. On the distinction between "being" and "function," see Helmut Thielicke, *Theological Ethics. Volume 3: Sex,* trans. John W. Doberstein (Grand Rapids, Mich.: Eerdmans, 1979 [1964]), 20-26.

17. Cf. Stephen D. Kovach and Peter R. Schemm, Jr., "A Defense of the Doctrine of the

Eternal Subordination of the Son," *Journal of the Evangelical Theological Society* 42 (1999): 461-476.

18. See especially 1 Corinthians 11:9. Cf. the insightful observations on 1 Corinthians 11:7 in Thielicke, *Theological Ethics,* 281.

19. Cf. Andreas J. Köstenberger, "Ascertaining Women's God-Ordained Roles: An Interpretation of 1 Timothy 2:15," *Bulletin of Biblical Research* 7 (1997): 107-144.

20. Thomas R. Schreiner argued this position in the first edition of *Women in the Church,* but he has now changed his view (see the forthcoming second edition of this work).

21. In God's curse of Adam and Eve, he allowed them to reap the fruit of the seeds that they had sown. In other words, the Lord had a design for marriage and the family that included perfect harmony and order with male headship and female submission. Adam and Eve, however, chose to abandon their God-ordained gender roles, which resulted in their fall. In God's curse upon the first couple, he sentenced them (by way of their new sin nature) to fulfill the roles that they had chosen when they opted to abandon God's creation design. Viewed in this light, the judgment inherent in God's curse upon Adam and Eve essentially consisted in God's allowing them to experience the results of their own sinful choices. Another example of God's judicial act of allowing people to experience the results of their own sinful actions is the thrice-mentioned "God handed them over" (*paredōken*) in Romans 1:24, 26, and 28. God's followers are similarly judged today (cf. Gal. 6:7-9).

22. See Susan T. Foh, "What Is the Woman's Desire (Gen 3:16, 4:7)," *Westminster Theological Journal* 37 (1975): 376-383.

23. Regarding later rabbinic discussions of how long a man could abstain from sexual relations with his wife, see David Instone-Brewer, *Divorce and Remarriage in the Bible: The Social and Literary Context* (Grand Rapids, Mich.: Eerdmans, 2002), 106 (citing *m. Ketub.* 5:6-7).

24. Cf. Daniel I. Block, "Marriage and Family in Ancient Israel," in Ken M. Campbell, ed., *Marriage and Family in the Biblical World* (Downers Grove, Ill.: InterVarsity Press, 2003), 40-48, and the discussion in chapter 5 below.

25. Cf. Instone-Brewer, *Divorce and Remarriage in the Bible,* 99-110, who also documents the influence of this passage on Jewish divorce laws, which stipulated the permissibility of divorce for both material ("food and clothing," 103-105) and emotional neglect ("conjugal rights," 106-110). Instone-Brewer proceeds to argue that Jesus' silence on divorce on the basis of Exodus 21:10-11 should be construed as his agreement with the Jewish consensus view at this point (166, 181-182, 185) and that Paul's allusion to this passage in 1 Corinthians 7 should be taken to imply that Paul, too, allowed for divorce because of marital neglect (193-194, 212). We find Instone-Brewer's arguments from silence precarious, however. In Jesus' case, one would have expected him to add marital neglect to *porneia* as a second exception for divorce if he had approved of neglect as a legitimate ground for divorce. In Paul's case, it is one thing to say that he alluded to Exodus 21:10-11 but quite another to say that this implies that he approved of divorce for marital neglect. Especially in light of the major ramifications of such a view (namely, that this would render divorce for marital neglect biblically legitimate today), it seems reasonable to require more explicit biblical warrant than the double argument from silence provided by Instone-Brewer.

26. Or, possibly, her *ointment/oil.* See Block, "Marriage and Family in Ancient Israel," 48, who points out that while the immediate point of reference (at least in his view) is not to a man's wife but his concubine who would bear children for him, according to the rabbinic principle of *qal-wa-homer* (what applies in a minor case will apply all the more in a major one) it seems reasonable to assume that this basic care applied to a man's concubines was true all the more regarding a husband's treatment of his

wife. As Block (ibid., 48, n. 67) notes, the Old Testament has no specific designation for "wife" other than *iššâ*, "woman."

27. The Tanakh interprets the final term (which occurs only here in the Old Testament) as referring to a wife's "conjugal rights." Instone-Brewer, *Divorce and Remarriage in the Bible*, 100, states that there was virtual unanimity regarding the rendering "conjugal rights" among early and later Jewish interpreters. But see the argument for "ointment/oil" in Shalom M. Paul, "Exod. 21:10: A Threefold Maintenance Clause," *Journal of Near Eastern Studies* 28 (1969): 48-51; idem, *Studies in the Book of the Covenant in the Light of Cuneiform and Biblical Law*, Vetus Testamentum Supplement 18 (Leiden, Netherlands: Brill, 1970), 56-61 (cited by Block, "Marriage and Family in Ancient Israel," 48, n. 69). Instone-Brewer, *Divorce and Remarriage in the Bible*, 9, 45, n. 37, 100, concludes that it began as a reference to "oil" and changed to conjugal rights (he glosses the phrase as "love").

28. Another common task fulfilled by husbands toward their wives was that they provided them with a proper burial when they died (e.g., Gen. 23:16; 35:19-20).

29. Cf., e.g., Genesis 16:1, 16; 17:17, 19, 21; 21:2, 3, 5, 7, 9; 22:20, 23; 24:15, 24, 47; 25:2, 12.

30. See the additional examples cited in Block, "Marriage and Family in Ancient Israel," 72-73, n. 185.

31. The rabbinic passage is cited by Instone-Brewer, *Divorce and Remarriage in the Bible*, 103, who dates it prior to A.D. 70. The same author also adduces Exodus 21:10-11, which was taken to imply that men must provide food and material (or the money to purchase them), while women must prepare the meals and make the items of clothing.

32. See the survey in ibid., 59-61.

33. But cf. ibid., 21, who claims that "it is unlikely that [Gen. 2:24] was interpreted in this way [i.e., as indicating that monogamy was the ideal for marriage in the Pentateuch] until almost the time of the New Testament." In any case, there is certainly little doubt that Jesus himself interpreted Genesis 2:24 in this way (Matt. 19:4-6 par. Mark 10:6-9), as Instone-Brewer himself acknowledges (ibid., 136-141).

34. For a brief survey see Scobie, *Ways of Our God*, 807, who states that the ideal of monogamy is established in Genesis 2:24, assumed in the law (Deut. 28:54, 56) and in the Prophets (Jer. 5:8; 6:11; Mal. 2:14), and upheld in the wisdom literature (Prov. 5:18; 31:10-31; Eccles. 9:9).

35. Though note Instone-Brewer, *Divorce and Remarriage in the Bible*, 59-60, who points out that there is no evidence that polygamy was widespread in Israel, except possibly after wars had decimated the male population (cf. Isa. 3:25; 4:1); that polygamy was frequently (Instone-Brewer says "almost always") related to childlessness (e.g., Gen. 16:1-4; 1 Samuel 1); and that its presence among leaders and kings like Gideon, Samson, David, and Solomon was probably due to their imitation of the leaders of other nations (cf. 1 Sam. 8:5, 19-20, criticized in Deut. 17:17).

36. Cf. David W. Chapman, "Marriage and Family in Second Temple Judaism," in *Marriage and Family in the Biblical World*, 217. "Polygyny" is the move appropriate term, since, technically, "polygamy" refers to multiple spouses of either sex.

37. See Gordon P. Hugenberger, *Marriage as a Covenant: Biblical Law and Ethics as Developed from Malachi* (Grand Rapids, Mich.: Baker, 1998), 112, 115-118.

38. Cf. Instone-Brewer, *Divorce and Remarriage in the Bible*, 59, with reference to Louis M. Epstein, *Marriage Laws in the Bible and Talmud*, Harvard Semitic Series 12 (Cambridge, Mass.: Harvard University Press, 1942), 4.

39. See especially Jesus' citation and interpretation of Genesis 2:24 in Matthew 19:4-6 par. Mark 10:6-9.

40. On the various approaches to translating Malachi 2:16 see chapter 11 below.

41. Contra Instone-Brewer, *Divorce and Remarriage in the Bible,* 98 (citing Louis M. Epstein, *The Jewish Marriage Contract: A Study in the Status of the Woman in Jewish Law* [New York: Johnson Reprint Corp., 1968 (1942)]), who claims that "the law allowing polygamy made it technically impossible for a man to be sexually unfaithful to his wife."

42. Interestingly, while the penalty for adultery was death, there are no accounts in the Old Testament of this penalty being enforced. The closest examples are God's threatened execution of Abimelech if he caused Sarah to become an adulteress (Gen. 20:7), Abimelech's threatened execution of anyone who caused Rebekah to become an adulteress (Gen. 26:11), and Judah's planned, but averted, burning of Tamar (Gen. 38:24). Note that all of these events occurred in the book of Genesis, *before* the giving of the law. Also, it is interesting to note that the Old Testament does not specify the method of execution for those guilty of adultery. While Judah planned to burn Tamar, rabbinic tradition specified strangulation as the method of death, and in New Testament times the method of execution was apparently stoning (cf. John 8:5).

43. For a survey of the biblical condemnation of sexual relations outside marriage see Scobie, *Ways of Our God,* 804-806, who covers adultery (Ex. 20:14; Deut. 5:18; cf. Lev. 18:20; 20:10), prostitution (Lev. 19:29; Deut. 23:17; cf. Prov. 2:18-19), bestiality (Ex. 22:19; Lev. 18:23; Deut. 27:21), and homosexuality (Lev. 18:22; 20:13 et al., though there are some problems with Scobie's coverage here).

44. Instone-Brewer, *Divorce and Remarriage in the Bible,* 92, notes that later Jewish rabbis taught that if couples had been married for ten years with no children, they were expected to divorce and remarry so as to have children (though there was no consensus on this).

45. Related issues, such as dealing with infertility or implications for birth control, will be treated in chapter 7 below.

46. See the above discussion of Genesis 1–3.

47. Contrary to some, the Old Testament practice of paying a dowry for a wife (cf. Gen. 29:18; 34:12; Ex. 22:16-17; 1 Sam. 18:25) should not be viewed as violating the principle of complementarity on the grounds that it reflects a view of females as the property of their fathers and hence of less value than men. According to the best available evidence, the dowry primarily fulfilled an economic function which served the purpose of strengthening the woman's standing rather than suggesting that she was of inferior status. Cf. the discussions on dowry in *Marriage and Family in the Biblical World,* 13-14, 54, and 193-198. See also Instone-Brewer, *Divorce and Remarriage in the Bible,* 5, who views the function of the dowry in the ancient Near East as providing a measure of personal security to the bride and as constituting the legal seal on the marriage covenant.

48. In Leviticus 12 the Mosaic civil legislation prescribed a period of uncleanness for a new mother of seven days for the birth of a male child (12:2) and fourteen days for the birth of a female child (12:5). Some have suggested that this shows an inherent male bias or unequal worth between the sexes that is built into the Mosaic law; yet, this civil prescription ought not to be viewed as an indicator of the lower worth of women, but rather as a stigma on women for Eve's part in the fall of mankind (cf. 1 Tim. 2:14, 15).

49. The apostle Peter sums up the Old Testament pattern as follows: "For this is how the holy women who hoped in God used to adorn themselves, by submitting to their husbands, as Sarah obeyed Abraham, calling him lord" (1 Pet. 3:5-6).

50. Cf. John MacArthur, Jr., *Different By Design: Discovering God's Will for Today's Man and Woman* (Wheaton, Ill.: Victor, 1994), 77. See the helpful discussion of the Proverbs 31 woman on pages 75-82 under the following six headings: Her Character

as a Wife; Her Devotion as a Homemaker; Her Generosity as a Neighbor; Her Influence as a Teacher; Her Effectiveness as a Mother; and Her Excellence as a Person.

51. See also the section on mothers and motherhood in the writings of the apostle Paul, in chapter 6 below.

52. For a helpful biblical and practical treatment, see Daniel Akin, *God on Sex: The Creator's Ideas About Love, Intimacy, and Marriage* (Nashville: Broadman & Holman, 2003). See also Duane A. Garrett, *Proverbs, Ecclesiastes, Song of Songs,* New American Commentary (Nashville: Broadman & Holman, 1993); Othmar Keel, *The Song of Songs: A Continental Commentary,* trans. Frederick J. Gaiser (Minneapolis: Fortress, 1994); and the survey by Scobie, *Ways of Our God,* 803-804. For a brief discussion of "A Christian View of Sex," see Allan N. Moseley, *Thinking Against the Grain* (Grand Rapids, Mich.: Kregel, 2003), 170-183, who presents the following seven points: (1) God created sex (Gen. 1:27-28; 2:24-25); (2) God's original purposes for sex were unitive (i.e., designed to produce union) and procreative (Gen. 2:24); (3) God intends sex to be pleasurable for husbands and wives (Song of Solomon; Prov. 5:18-20; 1 Cor. 7:3-5); (4) sexual intimacy between unmarried partners is wrong (1 Thess. 4:3-5; Heb. 13:4); (5) illicit sex is harmful (Prov. 5:10-11; 6:28-29, 32-33); (6) Christians can and should resist sexual temptation (Rom. 16:19); and (7) there is more to life and love than sex (Col. 3:4; 1 Cor. 13:1-13).

53. See, e.g., Jerry B. Jenkins, *Hedges: Loving Your Marriage Enough to Protect It* (Dallas: Word, 1990).

54. See especially Foh, "What Is the Woman's Desire?"

55. In support of the eschatological reading advocated here, cf., e.g., Francis Landy, in Robert Alter and Frank Kermode, eds., *The Literary Guide to the Bible* (Cambridge, Mass.: Belknap Press of Harvard University Press, 1987), 318: "Through it [the Song of Solomon] we glimpse, belatedly, by the grace of poetry, the possibility of paradise"; and Raymond B. Dillard and Tremper Longman III, *An Introduction to the Old Testament* (Grand Rapids, Mich.: Zondervan, 1994), 265: "The book pictures the restoration of human love to its pre-Fall bliss."

56. Keel, *Song of Songs,* 252. We owe this reference to our colleague Bob Cole.

57. In an unpublished paper "Song of Songs/Canticles," Bob Cole develops the inter-canonical links between the Song of Solomon and a variety of other passages, including (but not limited to) Genesis 2–3; 49:9; Exodus 30:23, 25; Numbers 24:7-9; Psalm 45; Proverbs 5:15-20; Isaiah 5:1; 35:1-2; and Hosea 14:6-7. These links make clear that the Song of Solomon is not an isolated collection of love poetry but an integral part of the salvation-historical thread of Scripture.

58. In the subsequent Genesis narrative, the emphasis is repeatedly on wives' bearing children for their husbands (Gen. 4:1-2, 17, 25; 5:3; etc.).

59. Incredibly, Abraham's son Isaac later repeats his father's sin when he identifies his beautiful wife as his sister and is confronted by Abimelech (the son or grandson of the ruler in Abraham's day) for his deceit (Gen. 26:7-11).

60. For helpful background information on Abraham, Sarah, and Hagar, as well as Jacob, Rachel, and Leah (on whom see below) see Joe M. Sprinkle, "Law and Narrative in Exodus 19–24," *Journal of the Evangelical Theological Society* 47 (2004): 248-249.

61. The tensions experienced between Leah and Rachel, Jacob's two wives, are indirect evidence that monogamy rather than polygamy is God's plan.

62. Subsequently, we read, however, that David had also married *Ahinoam* of Jezreel, and that Saul had given Michal to another man, Paltiel son of Laish (1 Sam. 25:43-44), which may indicate neglect on David's part (cf. Ex. 21:10-11) or, perhaps more likely, suggest a measure of revenge sought by Saul. Later, David demands that his wife Michal be returned to him, to the great distress of Michal's second husband

(2 Sam. 3:13-14; cf. 1 Sam. 25:43-44). However, when David leapt and danced for joy upon the ark's return to Israel, Michal looked out of the window and despised David in her heart (2 Sam. 6:16; 1 Chron. 15:29), and when David returned to bless his household, she reproached him for uncovering and abasing himself before his servants' female servants (2 Sam. 6:20). Michal bore no further children after this. This may constitute a lesson for wives not to chastise their husbands for zeal in the Lord's service that they may find excessive.

63. Later, Abigail and one of David's other wives, Ahinoam, were captured by the Amalekites, and David bravely rescued them (1 Sam. 30:5, 18). In this David provides a positive example of courage and initiative in marriage.

64. While Scripture prohibits interfaith marriage (e.g., Deut. 7:1-5), it nowhere pronounces a negative verdict on inter-racial marriage. For materials on this topic, see J. Daniel Hays, *From Every People and Nation: A Biblical Theology of Race* (Downers Grove, Ill.: InterVarsity Press, 2003); and George A. Yancey and Sherelyn Whittum Yancey, *Just Don't Marry One: Interracial Dating, Marriage, and Parenting* (Valley Forge, Pa.: Judson Press, 2002).

CHAPTER 3:
NO LONGER TWO, BUT ONE: MARRIAGE IN THE NEW TESTAMENT

1. For a brief survey see Charles H. H. Scobie, *The Ways of Our God: An Approach to Biblical Theology* (Grand Rapids, Mich./Cambridge: Eerdmans, 2003), 835-840. The editors and several of the contributors to the project *Does Christianity Teach Male Headship? The Equal-Regard Marriage and Its Critics* (Grand Rapids, Mich.: Eerdmans, 2004), contend that the New Testament teaching on marriage and the family is essentially Aristotelian and "worked its way into the texts of early Christianity" such as Ephesians 5:21-33, Colossians 3:18-25, and 1 Peter 3:1-7 (4; see also 94-95, 133). They argue that Christian marriages and families ought to replace a headship and submission model with an "equal-regard," neighbor love approach in which "the wife can be Christ to the husband just as the husband can mediate the love of Christ to the wife" (138). While a full critique of this position is beyond the scope of this volume, it is hard to see how this position awards final authority to the New Testament's teaching on male headship and wifely submission and thus is based on a high view of Scripture.

2. See the following chapter.

3. See the previous chapter.

4. Diana S. Richmond Garland and Diane L. Pancoast, eds., *The Church's Ministry with Families: A Practical Guide* (Dallas: Word, 1990), in a volume that grew out of a 1987 conference on marriage and the family, advocate a broader, "ecological" definition of family, transcending that of marriage as "parents and their children" or "persons related by blood or marriage," according to which the nuclear family—a married couple and children—is assumed to be the norm. Following A. Hartman and J. Laird, *Family-Centered Social Work Practice* (New York: Free Press, 1983), they define marriage as "the relationships through which persons meet their needs for intimacy, sharing of resources, tangible and intangible help, commitment, responsibility, and meaningfulness over time and contexts" (11), including friendships, roommates, workplace "families," and communal groups. David Garland's essay in *Church's Ministry with Families* concludes that "[t]he definitive characteristics of the family can no longer be considered to be legal marriage and biological parenting; instead, they are summed up in *mutual* commitment" (33). On these premises, then, family ministry consists in "strengthening the relationships among ecological family members" (14). There are several problems with this approach, however.

First, this definition of family is too broad to be meaningful. Second, the definition is inadequately rooted in biblical morality, which denounces homosexual unions, which would seem to be included (doubtless unintentionally) in this broad definition. Third, the definition is primarily sociological rather than theological and biblical in nature, in that it fails to acknowledge Scripture as the final authority in the realm of social relationships. Fourth, it inadequately recognizes that Jesus, while placing a high premium on discipleship that transcends flesh and blood ties, also held a very high view of marriage, reaffirming God's original purposes for marriage (Matt. 19:4-6; cf. Gen. 2:24), so that one (discipleship) should not be pitted over against the other (marriage). The shift from a more traditional definition of marriage and the family via Jesus' teaching on discipleship to a broad, sociological definition accentuating family networks formed by shared commitments and marked by cohesion is therefore illegitimate.

5.   Note that the word "two" is found in the Greek Septuagint but not the Hebrew Masoretic text. Matthew 19 will be discussed more fully in the chapter on divorce below (chapter 10).

6.   John R. W. Stott, "Marriage and Divorce," in *Involvement: Social and Sexual Relationships in the Modern World*, vol. 2. (Old Tappan, N.J.: Revell, 1984), 167. See the discussion on the nature of marriage at the end of this chapter. On ancient Jewish marriage and weddings, see Craig S. Keener, "Marriage," in Craig A. Evans and Stanley E. Porter, eds., *Dictionary of New Testament Background* (Downers Grove, Ill.: InterVarsity Press, 2000), 684-686.

7.   Though Cynthia Long Westfall, "Family in the Gospels and Acts," in Richard S. Hess and M. Daniel Carroll R., eds., *Family in the Bible* (Grand Rapids, Mich.: Baker, 2003), 146, may erect perhaps a bit too sharp a dichotomy when she writes, "However, Jesus did not intend the family to be the most important institution on earth or the central unit of a Christian's identity and purpose."

8.   For a brief survey of the New Testament's teaching on sexual relations outside marriage which reveals the coherence between Jesus, Paul, and other New Testament authors, see Scobie, *Ways of Our God*, 837-838, who covers adultery (Matt. 5:27-28; 19:18 pars.; Rom. 13:9; James 2:11), fornication (Matt. 15:19 par. Mark 7:21; Acts 15:20, 29; 1 Cor. 6:9, 13, 18), prostitution (Luke 7:48; 1 Cor. 6:15-16; Heb. 13:4), and homosexuality (Rom. 1:18-32 et al.).

9.   This in no way amounts to a license for husbands to abuse their wives physically or in any other way, nor does it preclude the necessity for wives to separate from their abusive husbands in order to avoid serious harm. The delicate pastoral implications of such situations call for considerable wisdom in each individual case. For an enlightening account of a marriage between a believing wife and an unbelieving husband including helpful advice on how to deal with this issue see Lee and Leslie Strobel, *Surviving a Spiritual Mismatch in Marriage* (Grand Rapids, Mich.: Zondervan, 2002).

10. Peter even says that "Sarah . . . obeyed Abraham and called him her master" (1 Pet. 3:6, NIV; cf. Gen. 18:12).

11. But see the caution registered in note 9, above.

12. Wayne Grudem, *1 Peter,* Tyndale New Testament Commentaries (Grand Rapids, Mich.: Eerdmans, 1988), 144, notes that "any kind of weakness" on the part of the woman may be in view, including physical weakness, weakness in terms of lacking authority, and greater emotional sensitivity. Thomas R. Schreiner, *1, 2 Peter, Jude,* New American Commentary (Nashville: Broadman & Holman, 2003), 160 (citing Kelly, Cranfield, Michaels, Davids, Hillyer, and others), rejects the views that women are weaker intellectually, emotionally, morally, or spiritually and believes "sheer [physical] strength" is in view.

13. See especially Ephesians 5:21-33 par. Colossians 3:18-19. For a discussion of 1 Thess. 4:3-8 and 1 Corinthians 7 including bibliographic references to the New Testament

teaching on marriage up to 1985, see O. Larry Yarbrough, *Not Like the Gentiles: Marriage Rules in the Letters of Paul,* SBL Dissertation Series 80 (Atlanta: Scholars Press, 1985), especially 65-125.

14. Cf. David Instone-Brewer, *Divorce and Remarriage in the Bible: The Social and Literary Context* (Grand Rapids, Mich.: Eerdmans, 2002), 193-194 (with further bibliographical references on 194, n. 7), who argues persuasively that Paul here alludes to Exodus 21:10-11. See further chapter 2 above and chapter 10 below.

15. See also the interesting recent discussion of Ephesians 5 by Francis Watson, *Agape, Eros, Gender: Towards a Pauline Sexual Ethic* (Cambridge: Cambridge University Press, 2000), 183-259. Watson keenly observes that both viewing Ephesians 5 as "a legitimation of patriarchal marriage" and claiming that it "transforms patriarchal marriage by subjecting it to the criterion of love" simplify the passage by ignoring its complexities (229, n. 6), referring to Ben Witherington, *Women and the Genesis of Christianity* (Cambridge: Cambridge University Press, 1990), 156; and Sarah J. Tanzer, "Ephesians," in Elisabeth Schüssler Fiorenza, ed., *Searching the Scriptures*, vol. 2, *A Feminist Commentary* (New York: Crossroad, 1994), 325-348, especially 341.

16. For Christ is not the *source* of demons, but their *head*. Contra Catherine Clark Kroeger, "Head," in Gerald F. Hawthorne, Ralph P. Martin, and Daniel G. Reid, eds., *Dictionary of Paul and His Letters* (Leicester, U.K./Downers Grove, Ill.: InterVarsity Press, 1993), 375-377, see the critique by Wayne Grudem, "The Meaning of κεφαλή ('Head'): An Evaluation of New Evidence, Real and Alleged," *Journal of the Evangelical Theological Society* 44 (2001): 25-65, reprinted in Wayne Grudem, ed., *Biblical Foundations for Manhood and Womanhood* (Wheaton, Ill.: Crossway, 2002).

17. On Genesis 3:16, see especially Susan T. Foh, "What Is the Woman's Desire (Gen 3:16, 4:7)," *Westminster Theological Journal* 37 (1975): 376-383, who rightly interprets Genesis 3:16 in light of Genesis 4:7 where "desire" conveys a sense of attempted mastery or control. See also the scenario at the Fall (Genesis 3), which is cited by Paul in 1 Timothy 2:14-15 as one of two reasons for his prohibition of women teaching or exercising authority over a man in the church (cf. 1 Tim. 2:12).

18. Note that Gentiles comprise the majority of Paul's readership in Ephesians.

19. See further at Ephesians 5:32 below. The usual English translation of this expression by "mystery" is somewhat misleading in that "mystery" is at best a partial cognate of the Greek term *mystērion*. In fact, in a very important sense *mystērion* conveys the very opposite sense of "mystery," for while the English term means "something secret or unrevealed" or even "something intrinsically unknowable," the Greek expression refers to a truth that was previously undisclosed but has now been made known (see Andreas J. Köstenberger, "The Mystery of Christ and the Church: Head and Body, 'One Flesh,'" *Trinity Journal* 12 n.s. [1991]: 80-83). Other *mystērions* in Scripture include Christ himself (Col. 2:2; 4:3), the sanctification of believers (1 Tim. 3:16), the transformation (rapture?) of believers (1 Cor. 15:51), the current blindness of Israel (Rom. 11:25), and general lawlessness (2 Thess. 2:7).

20. See Andreas J. Köstenberger, "What Does It Mean to Be Filled with the Spirit? A Biblical Investigation," *Journal for the Evangelical Theological Society* 40 (1997): 229-240 for a detailed discussion of Ephesians 5:18 and related passages.

21. Cf. Timothy G. Gombis, "Being the Fullness of God in Christ by the Spirit: Ephesians 5:18 in Its Epistolary Setting," *Tyndale Bulletin* 53, no. 2 (2002): 262-264; citing Thomas R. Schreiner, *Paul, Apostle of God's Glory in Christ: A Pauline Theology* (Downers Grove, Ill.: InterVarsity Press, 2001), 338; Köstenberger, "What Does It Mean to Be Filled with the Spirit?" 233; and Gordon D. Fee, *Paul, the Spirit, and the People of God* (Peabody, Mass.: Hendrickson, 1996), 63-73.

22. See, e.g., chapter 8 in Instone-Brewer, *Divorce and Remarriage in the Bible,* especially

236-237, who maintains "that there is no longer any need to teach submission. . . . In NT days it would cause a scandal if the submission of wives were omitted from moral instruction, but now it is likely to cause an equal scandal if it is included. The threefold teaching of submission did not have a Christian origin, and the number of caveats and explanations added to this teaching by NT authors suggests that they were somewhat uncomfortable with it. They attempted to Christianize it by adding that the head of the household should show respect for those submitting to him, and perhaps submit to them in return." For this reason, Instone-Brewer says that no bride should be "forced" to vow submission to her husband, but if she opts to make such a vow, her husband should likewise vow to submit to his wife. For our part, we fail to see clear textual evidence for the New Testament authors' "discomfort" with teaching wifely submission. We certainly do not advocate "forcing" wives to vow to submit to their husbands. It is clearly fallacious to say, however, that, because the Christian teaching of submission to authorities had non-Christian origins (assuming this to be the case for the sake of argument), it follows that this scriptural teaching is non-authoritative. Nor does it appear to be possible to extricate biblical sexual morality from the submission principle. The analogy between the headship of Christ over the church and the husband's headship over the wife in Ephesians 5:23-25, too, militates against setting aside the husband's headship and wifely submission as irrelevant and inapplicable for today. For these and other reasons, Instone-Brewer's reasoning and conclusions must be judged not to cohere with Scripture's own message on the subject.

23. See Wayne Grudem, "The Myth of Mutual Submission as an Interpretation of Ephesians 5:21," in Wayne Grudem, ed., *Biblical Foundations for Manhood and Womanhood* (Wheaton, Ill.: Crossway, 2002), 221-231, who suggests that the force of the Greek term *allēlois* is "some to others" (contra Roger R. Nicole, "The Wisdom of Marriage," in J. I. Packer and Sven K. Soderlund, eds., *The Way of Wisdom: Essays in Honor of Bruce K. Waltke* [Grand Rapids, Mich.: Zondervan, 2000], 290; Scobie, *Ways of Our God*, 839 et al.). Rather than speaking of "mutual submission," it may be more appropriate to speak of "mutual humility" (note the shift from submission to humility in 1 Pet. 5:5-6). See also Daniel Doriani, "The Historical Novelty of Egalitarian Interpretations of Ephesians 5:21-22," in *Biblical Foundations for Manhood and Womanhood*, 203-219; and Wayne Walden, "Ephesians 5:21: A Translation Note," *Restoration Quarterly* 45, no. 4 (2003): 254, who points out that the pronoun *allēlōn* is not so much reciprocal or mutual as showing "random or distributive activity within the group" (Walden provides the examples of people trampling one another [Luke 12:1]; envying one another [Gal. 5:26]; and killing one another [Rev. 6:4], which hardly should be understood in a mutual sense). Hence Ephesians 5:21 does not call for "mutual submission" of husband and wife, but calls on wives to submit to their husbands and for husbands to love their wives.

24. Andrew T. Lincoln, *Ephesians*, Word Biblical Commentary (Dallas: Word, 1990), 366, quoted in Gerald F. Hawthorne, "Marriage and Divorce," in *Dictionary of Paul and His Letters*, 596. See also the discussion in Watson, *Agape, Eros, Gender*, 219-259.

25. In that context, a husband's love is further defined as not being harsh with one's wife (cf. 1 Pet. 3:7).

26. Cf. Hawthorne, "Marriage and Divorce," 596.

27. See, for example, Stanley J. Grenz, *Sexual Ethics: A Biblical Perspective* (Dallas: Word, 1990), 28. Also, "Men, Women, and Biblical Equality," the statement of evangelical egalitarian beliefs by Christians for Biblical Equality, states, "The Bible teaches that woman and man were created for full and equal partnership. . . . The rulership of Adam over Eve resulted from the Fall and was therefore not a part of the original created order" (paragraphs 2 and 5).

28. See especially Raymond C. Ortlund, Jr., "Male-Female Equality and Male Headship," in John Piper and Wayne Grudem, eds., *Recovering Biblical Manhood and Womanhood: A Response to Evangelical Feminism* (Wheaton, Ill.: Crossway, 1991), 95-112, especially 106-111.

29. Cf. Peter T. O'Brien, *The Letter to the Ephesians,* Pillar New Testament Commentary (Grand Rapids, Mich.: Eerdmans, 1999), 429-435.

30. See Köstenberger, "Mystery of Christ and the Church," 79-94.

31. On spiritual warfare in relation to marriage and the family, see further the discussion in chapter 7 below.

32. For a thorough monograph-length treatment of the spiritual warfare theme within the context of Ephesians as a whole, see Timothy Gombis, "The Triumph of God in Christ: Divine Warfare in the Argument of Ephesians" (Ph.D. diss., University of St. Andrews, forthcoming 2005). See also the same author's forthcoming essay, "A Radically New Humanity: The Function of the *Haustafel* in Ephesians," in the *Journal of the Evangelical Theological Society.* For an interesting treatment of Ephesians 6:10-18 within the context of the entire Ephesian letter, see Donna R. Hawk-Reinhard, "Ephesians 6:10-18: A Call to Personal Piety or Another Way of Describing Union with Christ?" (paper presented at the 2004 Midwest Regional Meeting of the Evangelical Theological Society).

33. When we talk about the God-ordained "primary sphere" and "center" of men's and women's activity, we do not advocate or condone a husband's neglect of his wife and family or seek to confine a woman to the home as may be the case in traditional arrangements. Nor do we seek to take away from the man's and woman's joint responsibility to rule the earth for God. We are merely reflecting the biblical teaching in passages such as Genesis 3:16-19 that seem to draw a distinction regarding the man's and the woman's primary spheres of activity, indicating distinct yet complementary roles. Rather than pitting the husband's work outside the home against his devotion to marriage and family, it should be viewed within the larger context of his fulfilling his responsibility to provide for his family. As to the woman, her role in childbearing already indicates that, biologically, her role centers on children and family in a way that is distinctive and unique.

34. Some may object to the notion of gender roles ostensibly being suspended "for a limited time" as in the scenario described here. It should be pointed out, however, that such an arrangement does not necessarily constitute a suspension of proper biblical gender roles. Rather, in the above example (and other examples that could be adduced) the husband's pursuit of an education may in fact be a manifestation of his headship in and provision for his family. The temporary adjustment in roles may merely constitute a means to that end. The husband's leadership of the family will entail finding prayerful solutions to a specific family's individual circumstances or crises. As we have described in this chapter, headship and submission are unfailing biblical principles, the normative pattern with which we are continually called to align ourselves. At the same time, the specific application of these fixed principles ought to remain flexible and may be modified temporarily as circumstances warrant without affecting the validity of the biblical principles themselves.

35. See our comments with regard to Abraham and Sarah in the equivalent section at the end of chapter 2 above.

36. For further information on Priscilla and Aquila in the context of the Pauline mission, see Andreas J. Köstenberger, "Women in the Pauline Mission," in Peter Bolt and Mark Thompson, eds., *The Gospel to the Nations: Perspectives on Paul's Mission* (Downers Grove, Ill.: InterVarsity Press, 2000), 227-228.

37. C. E. B. Cranfield, *The Epistle to the Romans,* International Critical Commentary (Edinburgh: T. & T. Clark, 1979), 2.784.

38. James D. G. Dunn, *Romans 9–16*, Word Biblical Commentary (Dallas: Word, 1988), 892.

CHAPTER 4:
THE NATURE OF MARRIAGE: SACRAMENT, CONTRACT, OR COVENANT?

1. While in this chapter we only discuss the three models of marriage that are most prevalent today, we realize that a host of other models have been suggested and held by Christians. For example, author John Witte interacts with the "social model" and the "commonwealth model" of marriage in his text *From Sacrament to Contract: Marriage, Religion, and Law in the Western Tradition* (Louisville: Westminster/John Knox, 1997). Also, John K. Tarwater mentions a "non-covenantal evangelical model," which is often referred to as the "divine institution model," in his work "The Covenantal Nature of Marriage in the Order of Creation in Genesis 1 and 2" (Ph.D. diss., Southeastern Baptist Theological Seminary, 2002), 13-15.

2. See Andreas J. Köstenberger, "The Mystery of Christ and the Church: Head and Body, 'One Flesh,'" *Trinity Journal* 12 n.s. [1991]: 79-94, especially 86-87, with reference to Hans von Soden, "ΜΥΣΤΗΡΙΟΝ und sacramentum in den ersten zwei Jahrhunderten der Kirche," *Zeitschrift für die neutestamentliche Wissenschaft* 12 (1911): 188-227.

3. Augustine, "On the Good of Marriage" [*De bono conjugali*], in Philip Schaff, ed., *The Nicene and Post-Nicene Fathers* (Grand Rapids, Mich.: Eerdmans, reprint 1980 [1887]), First Series, vol. 3, pages 397-413. See also Augustine, "On Marriage and Concupiscence" [*De nuptiis et concupiscentia*], book 1, chapter 11, *Nicene and Post-Nicene Fathers*, First Series, Vol. 5, 268; idem, "On the Grace of Christ, and on Original Sin" [*De gratia Christi, et de peccato originali*], book 2, chapter 39, *Nicene and Post-Nicene Fathers*, First Series, Vol. 5, 251. Attitudes to sexuality, marriage, and family in the patristic period are chronicled by Peter Brown, *The Body and Society: Men, Women, and Sexual Renunciation in Early Christianity* (London: Faber & Faber, 1990).

4. See the "Doctrine on the Sacrament of Matrimony" from the twenty-fourth session of the Council of Trent in James Waterworth, ed. and trans., *The Canons and Decrees of the Sacred and Oecumenical Council of Trent* (London: Dolman, 1848), 192-232. For a basic presentation of Roman Catholic sacramental theology see Alan Schreck, *Basics of the Faith: A Catholic Catechism* (Ann Arbor, Mich.: Servant, 1987), 147-182.

5. Schreck, *Basics of the Faith*, 152, emphasis added.

6. It should be noted that, in addition to conceiving of marriage as a sacrament, the Roman Catholic Church also teaches that marriage is a covenant. Cf. Schreck, *Basics of the Faith*, 177, who writes that "[t]he relationship of a married couple is a *covenant*, a solemn promise involving the man, the woman, and God himself at the center. This covenant is modeled upon the New Covenant between Jesus Christ and the church, sealed by the blood of Christ. . . . The man and the woman who make this covenant receive special graces [the "sacramental" dimension of marriage] to remain faithful to the covenant and to carry out the duties of this state of life with the Spirit of Christ. . . . As part of their marriage covenant, Catholic couples vow to receive children lovingly from God."

7. Cf. Germain Grisez, "The Christian Family as Fulfillment of Sacramental Marriage," *Studies in Christian Ethics* 9, no. 1 (1996): 23-33.

8. Cf. Köstenberger, "Mystery of Christ and the Church," 87.

9. See further the third criticism lodged below.

10. For other criticisms, see Köstenberger, "Mystery of Christ and the Church," 86, summarizing Markus Barth, *Ephesians 4–6*, Anchor Bible (New York: Doubleday, 1974), 748-749.

11. See Witte, *From Sacrament to Contract,* who argues that Western Christianity has moved steadily from a sacramental to a contractual view of marriage; Paul F. Palmer, "Christian Marriage: Contract or Covenant?" *Theological Studies* 33, no. 4 (December 1972): 617-665; Laura S. Levitt, "Covenant or Contract? Marriage as Theology," *Cross Currents* 48, no. 2 (Summer 1998): 169-184.

12. See David Instone-Brewer, *Divorce and Remarriage in the Bible: The Social and Literary Context* (Grand Rapids, Mich.: Eerdmans, 2002), 1-19.

13. Cf. Gary D. Chapman, *Covenant Marriage: Building Communication and Intimacy* (Nashville: Broadman & Holman, 2003), 8-10, who contrasts contracts with covenants, which (1) are initiated for the benefit of the other person; (2) are unconditional; (3) are based on steadfast love; (4) view commitments as permanent; (5) require confrontation and forgiveness (13-24). See also the more popular treatment in Fred Lowery, *Covenant Marriage: Staying Together for Life* (West Monroe, La.: Howard, 2002), 81-95.

14. Gordon R. Dunstan, "Marriage Covenant," *Theology* 78 (May 1975): 244.

15. Though see the discussion of the Old Testament notion of marriage as a contract in Instone-Brewer, *Divorce and Remarriage in the Bible,* 1-19. It is important not to confuse a contract to marry (cf. Luke 1:17; 2:5) with marriage being a contract in the secular sense of the term.

16. Palmer, "Christian Marriage: Contract or Covenant?" 618-619.

17. In defining the nature of marriage as a covenant it is important that one not limit marriage to the theological boundaries that have been set for understanding traditional salvific covenants. This is especially true since the New Testament writers do not explicitly label marriage as a covenant (although they do describe it as being *similar* to a covenant—cf. Eph. 5:22-33). As David Instone-Brewer notes, "Although the distinction between 'covenant' and 'contract' is a useful one in theological language, we must take care not to read later theological development back into the Old Testament. The theological distinction between covenant and contract helps to distinguish between a relationship based on legalism and one based on grace and trust. The term 'covenant' is useful for emphasizing the gracious aspect of God's covenant with Israel and with the church. However, the theological development of this term should not determine the way in which Old Testament language is understood" (Instone-Brewer, *Divorce and Remarriage in the Bible,* 16-17). See further the cautions registered below.

18. Cf. Gordon P. Hugenberger, *Marriage as a Covenant: Biblical Law and Ethics as Developed from Malachi* (Grand Rapids, Mich.: Baker, 1998 [1994]). See also David Atkinson, *To Have and to Hold: The Marriage Covenant and the Discipline of Divorce* (Grand Rapids, Mich.: Eerdmans, 1979); and John MacArthur, *Matthew 16–23,* The MacArthur New Testament Commentary (Chicago: Moody, 1988), 166, who defines marriage as "a mutual covenant, a God-ordained obligation between a man and a woman to lifelong companionship." Tarwater, "Covenantal Nature of Marriage," 13-14, equating "covenant" with "absolute indissolubility," improperly labels MacArthur's view "non-covenantal" because MacArthur allows for the possibility of divorce in certain exceptional circumstances (see chapter 11 below).

19. For general information about biblical covenants, see Meredith G. Kline, *Treaty of the Great King: The Covenant Structure of Deuteronomy* (Grand Rapids, Mich.: Eerdmans, 1963); Klaus Baltzer, *The Covenant Formulary in Old Testament, Jewish, and Early Christian Writings* (Philadelphia: Fortress, 1971); Delbert R. Hillers, *Covenant: The History of a Biblical Idea* (Baltimore: Johns Hopkins University Press, 1969); Ernest W. Nicholson, *God and His People: Covenant Theology in the Old Testament* (Oxford: Clarendon, 1986); Dennis J. McCarthy, *Old Testament Covenant: A Survey of Current Opinions* (Richmond, Va.: John Knox, 1973); Paul Kalluveettil, *Declaration and Covenant: A Comprehensive Review of Covenant*

Formulae from the Old Testament and the Ancient Near East (Rome: Biblical Institute Press, 1982); and O. Palmer Robertson, *The Christ of the Covenants* (Phillipsburg, N.J.: Presbyterian & Reformed, 1980).

20. For a list of covenantal traits of marriage see David P. Gushee, *Getting Marriage Right: Realistic Counsel for Saving and Strengthening Relationships* (Grand Rapids, Mich.: Baker, 2004), 136-138, who says marriage is a covenant because (1) it is a freely entered agreement between two people; (2) it publicly ratifies a relationship between a man and a woman and subjects it to objective standards and social responsibilities; (3) it spells out the mutual responsibilities and moral commitments that both parties are taking on in this new form of community; (4) it is sealed by various oath signs that publicly symbolize and even "perform" the solemn commitments being made; (5) it is a lifetime commitment; (6) God is the witness and guarantor of its promises; (7) there are dire consequences for breaking its terms and great rewards for keeping them.

21. John R. W. Stott, "Marriage and Divorce," in *Involvement: Social and Sexual Relationships in the Modern World,* vol. 2 (Old Tappan, N.J.: Revell, 1984), 163. Cf. Hugenberger, *Marriage as a Covenant,* 171, who defines covenant as "an elected, as opposed to natural, relationship of obligation established under divine sanction."

22. Paul R. Williamson, "Covenant," in T. Desmond Alexander and Brian S. Rosner, eds., *New Dictionary of Biblical Theology* (Leicester, U.K./Downers Grove, Ill.: InterVarsity Press, 2000), 420. See also Leslie W. Pope, "Marriage: A Study of the Covenant Relationship as Found in the Old Testament" (M.A. thesis, Providence Theological Seminary, 1995), especially 74-78; and Instone-Brewer, *Divorce and Remarriage in the Bible,* 15, who contends that, in contemporary English, the best translation for the ancient Near Eastern concept of "covenant" is that of "contract," so that a "biblical 'marriage covenant' should therefore be understood as a 'marriage contract.'"

23. See further below.

24. The implications of a covenant view of marriage for the notion of the indissolubility of marriage will be explored in chapter 11 below.

25. Instone-Brewer, *Divorce and Remarriage in the Bible,* 17.

26. E.g., Jeremiah 31:32; Ezekiel 16:8, 59-62; Hosea 2:18-22; Ephesians 5:22-33; cf. 1 Samuel 18-20. See especially Hugenberger, *Marriage as a Covenant,* 294-312; and Tarwater, "Covenantal Nature of Marriage," 65-98. On Ezekiel 16, see Marvin H. Pope, "Mixed Marriage Metaphor in Ezekiel 16," in Astrid Beck, ed., *Fortunate the Eyes That See: Essays in Honor of David Noel Freedman in Celebration of His Seventieth Birthday* (Grand Rapids, Mich.: Eerdmans, 1995), 384-399.

27. Cf. Hugenberger, *Marriage as a Covenant,* 216-279.

28. Cf. Michael V. Fox, *Proverbs 1–9,* Anchor Bible (New York: Doubleday, 2000), 120-121; and the very thorough discussion in Hugenberger, *Marriage as a Covenant,* 296-302.

29. Fox, *Proverbs 1–9,* 121. Hence, in its biblical context, the notion of covenant includes that of a contractual arrangement. See also Pieter A. Verhoef, *The Books of Haggai and Malachi,* New International Commentary on the Old Testament (Grand Rapids, Mich.: Eerdmans, 1987), 274, who notes that marriage qualifies as "a covenant of God" in that it is contracted in submission to the revealed will of God (Ex. 20:14) and with the expectation of his blessing (Gen. 1:28); the monograph-length treatment by Hugenberger, *Marriage as a Covenant,* especially 27-47; and Daniel I. Block, "Marriage and Family in Ancient Israel," in Ken M. Campbell, ed., *Marriage and Family in the Biblical World* (Downers Grove, Ill.: InterVarsity Press, 2003), 44, who states unequivocally that "[a]ncient Israelites viewed marriage as a covenant relationship," citing Proverbs 2:17 and Malachi 2:14 (cf. John Calvin,

Commentaries on the Twelve Minor Prophets: Zechariah and Malachi, trans. John Owen [Grand Rapids, Mich.: Eerdmans, 1950], 5.552-553, cited in Tarwater, "Covenantal Nature of Marriage," 5).

30. See further the discussion in chapter 11 below.

31. Cf. Gushee, *Getting Marriage Right,* who argues that the nature of marriage as a "covenant" ought to be emphasized to strengthen marriages today (though he allows divorce in cases of sexual infidelity, desertion, and violence).

32. See chapter 11 below.

CHAPTER 5:
THE TIES THAT BIND: FAMILY IN THE OLD TESTAMENT

1. For a historical survey of the child in Christian thought (especially the essay "The Least and the Greatest: Children in the New Testament" by Judith M. Gundry-Volf on pages 29-60), see Marcia J. Bunge, ed., *The Child in Christian Thought* (Grand Rapids, Mich.: Eerdmans, 2001). For a survey of biblical teaching on parents and children see Charles H. H. Scobie, *The Ways of Our God: An Approach to Biblical Theology* (Grand Rapids, Mich./Cambridge: Eerdmans, 2003), 808-809, 841-842. While in the preceding chapters we have embraced a covenant view of marriage, there are no necessary connections between viewing marriage as a covenant and speaking of "covenant families." The latter concept is based on covenant theology, which emphasizes continuities between the biblical covenants (cf. R. C. Sproul, Jr., *Bound for Glory: God's Promise for Your Family* [Wheaton, Ill.: Crossway, 2003]; Gregg Strawbridge, ed., *The Case for Covenantal Infant Baptism* [Phillipsburg, N.J.: Presbyterian & Reformed, 2003]).

2. This would rule out cohabiting couples as well as same-sex marriages or domestic partnerships. Cf. George Rekers, chairman, *The Christian World View of the Family* (Sunnyvale, Calif.: The Coalition on Revival, 1989), 6: "We affirm that the Biblical definition of family is the nuclear family of a heterosexual married couple with its natural and adopted children, together with family branches consisting of all nuclear families descended from common ancestors" (posted at http://www.reformation.net/COR/cordocs/family.pdf). Contra Diana S. Richmond Garland and Diane L. Pancoast, eds., *The Church's Ministry with Families: A Practical Guide* (Dallas: Word, 1990), 9-12, 235-239, who contend that definitions such as "parents and their children" or "persons related by blood or marriage" are inadequate and instead propose what they call an "ecological model" (following Hartman and Laird) which centers on the meeting of biological, social, and psychological needs of the individuals involved in a mutually agreed upon environment which is characterized by shared values and cohesion or closeness. We have lodged a critique of this model in chapter 3.

3. Of course, spiritually speaking, all believers have been adopted into God's family and are brothers and sisters in Christ.

4. Cf. Daniel I. Block, "Marriage and Family in Ancient Israel," in Ken M. Campbell, ed., *Marriage and Family in the Biblical World* (Downers Grove, Ill.: InterVarsity Press, 2003), 35, to whom the following discussion is indebted. See also idem, "The Foundations of National Identity: A Study in Near Eastern Perceptions" (Ph.D. diss., University of Liverpool, 1983).

5. Cf. Block, "Marriage and Family in Ancient Israel," 35-40. For illustrations of this family structure see Joshua 7:16-26 and Judges 6-8.

6. Ibid., 40. The following discussion proceeds along the lines sketched out by Block in his essay.

7. Ibid., 41.

8. See the chart in ibid., 42.

9. See further the discussion and additional examples in ibid., 43, n. 41.

10. Ibid., 47.

11. Cf. the examples of Noah (Gen. 6:9), Abraham (Gen. 17:1-7; 26:5), Joshua (Josh. 24:15), and Hezekiah (2 Kings 18:3). See also Deuteronomy 6:4-9, on which see further the discussion below, and Boaz's example even before he is married (Ruth 2:12).

12. This included the Passover (Ex. 12:1-20), the Festival of Weeks (Deut. 16:9-12), and the Festival of Booths (Deut. 16:13-17).

13. Cf. Deuteronomy 6:4-9, 20-25; 11:18-25.

14. See chapter 2 above.

15. Block, "Marriage and Family in Ancient Israel," 54.

16. Ibid., 53-54.

17. E.g., Genesis 16:15; 17:19; Exodus 2:22; 2 Samuel 12:24; Hosea 1:4.

18. Cf. Exodus 13:2, 12-15; 22:29; 34:1-20; Numbers 3:11-13; 8:16-18; 18:15.

19. E.g., Psalm 103:13; Proverbs 3:12; 13:24; Hosea 11:1-4.

20. Cf. Exodus 12:24; 13:8; Deuteronomy 6:7-9, 20-25. Regarding the catechetical and didactic responsibilities of fathers see Christopher J. H. Wright, *God's People in God's Land: Family, Land, and Property in the Old Testament* (Grand Rapids, Mich.: Eerdmans, 1990), 81-84.

21. Cf. Deuteronomy 8:5; 2 Samuel 7:14; Proverbs 13:24; 19:18; 22:15; 23:13-14. See further the discussion below and the special section on parental discipline in chapter 8.

22. Block, "Marriage and Family in Ancient Israel," 54-55.

23. See ibid., 56-58.

24. See the discussion in ibid., 55, n. 102.

25. As Daniel Block writes in private correspondence dated May 26, 2004, we may extrapolate that since the reading of the Torah was to take place in the company of all—men, women, and children (Deut. 31:9-31; Neh. 8:3), we may assume that all were to be made aware of God's revelation in accordance with the covenant. Also, *banim* (often rendered gender-specifically as "sons") may be used inclusively with reference to children in general in Deuteronomy 6:7. In a general sense, sons are called in Proverbs 1:8 to listen to their father's and mother's instruction; it seems reasonable to infer that daughters were the recipients of their parents' teaching as well. Finally, Proverbs 31:10-31 may derive from some sort of acrostic domestic catechism that mothers might have taught their daughters, though this would have been primarily practical and domestic rather than theological and scriptural in nature.

26. See Block, "Marriage and Family in Ancient Israel," 65; see also ibid., 66, for a list of "clear signals of functional ordering" in the male-female relationship as presented in Genesis 1 and 2.

27. Ibid., 66-68.

28. Genesis 29:31; 30:6; 35:18; 38:28; Judges 13:24; 1 Samuel 1:20; 4:20; Isaiah 7:14. Block (ibid., 67, n. 153) notes that of the forty-six recorded instances of naming children in the Old Testament, in twenty-eight the name was given by the mother.

29. Exodus 20:12; Deuteronomy 5:16; the order is reversed in Leviticus 19:3.

30. Mothers (as well as grandmothers) also had an important role in teaching Scripture to their children, especially if the father was not a believer. The best-known New Testament example is probably Timothy, who was reared in the faith by his mother Eunice and his grandmother Lois (2 Tim. 1:5; cf. 2 Tim. 3:14-15; Acts 16:1).

31. For examples, see Block, "Marriage and Family in Ancient Israel," 67, n. 157.

32. See the extensive discussion in ibid., 68, notes 159, 160, and 161.

33. See ibid., 69-70 for polygamy; ibid., 49-50 for divorce; and ibid., 71-72 for widowhood.

34. Ibid., 64-65 (with footnotes refuting the feminist Phyllis Trible's attempt to "redeem Gen. 1–3 of its patriarchal and sexist stance" and demonstrating servant leadership in the case of kings, judges, priests, and prophets in Old Testament times). See the discussion in ibid., 61-64.

35. See ibid., 73-77 and further below.

36. See ibid., 77-78.

37. For a discussion of rabbinic attitudes toward procreation including references, see Craig S. Keener, "Marriage," in Craig A. Evans and Stanley E. Porter, eds., *Dictionary of New Testament Background* (Downers Grove, Ill.: InterVarsity Press, 2000), 681, who notes that rabbis required husbands to divorce their wives who after a trial period proved unable to bear children (*m. Yebam.* 6:6). For a brief survey of the Old Testament-Jewish context, see Gundry-Volf, "Least and the Greatest," 34-36.

38. What is more, in the ancient world, prior to social security and health care systems, sons were also an economic necessity for women. On infertility and the Bible, see Judith Baskin, "Rabbinic Reflections on the Barren Wife," *Harvard Theological Review* 82 (1989): 101-114; Mary Callaway, *Sing, O Barren One: A Study in Comparative Midrash,* SBL Dissertation Series 91 (Atlanta: Scholars Press, 1986); David Daube, *The Duty of Procreation* (Edinburgh: Edinburgh University Press, 1977); and John Van Seters, "The Problem of Childlessness in Near Eastern Law and the Patriarchs of Israel," *Journal of Biblical Literature* 87 (1968): 401-408. Regarding contemporary implications, see the discussion below.

39. Contra Gerald Loughlin, "The Want of Family in Postmodernity," in Stephen C. Barton, ed., *The Family in Theological Perspective* (Edinburgh: T & T Clark, 1996), 323, who contends that "procreation, though natural, is an inessential part of marriage" (quoting Karl Barth, *Church Dogmatics* [Edinburgh: T & T Clark, 1961], vol. 3, part 4, 266). Opposing the comment that married couples need a good reason for not having children, Loughlin writes that, "[t]o the contrary, Christian couples need a good reason *for* having children, since faith in the resurrected Christ frees them from the necessity to reproduce . . ." (323, n. 48). However, there is no scriptural evidence that Christ "frees" believers from "the necessity to reproduce" (a potentially misleading phrase). No dichotomy must be erected between God's created order and life in Christ. Paul's teaching on marriage and parenting in Ephesians 5 and his qualifications for church leaders in 1 Timothy 3 and Titus 1, for instance, clearly (re)affirm marriage and children as the general norm for believers (see also 1 Tim. 2:15; 4:3; etc.).

40. See Block, "Marriage and Family in Ancient Israel," 89-90.

41. For a detailed discussion and listing of terms see ibid., 79-80.

42. See ibid., 80-82.

43. For biblical references see ibid., 80, notes 212 and 213.

44. See the extensive discussion in ibid., 82-85.

45. See ibid., 92-94.

46. For biblical references see ibid., 92, notes 278 and 279.

47. Note that Leviticus 19:3 even mentions mothers before fathers, a fact that did not escape later Jewish rabbis (see references in Craig S. Keener, "Family and Household," in *Dictionary of New Testament Background,* 355). The New Testament makes clear that this command includes widows as well (1 Tim. 5:4, 8).

48. Block, "Marriage and Family in Ancient Israel," 93.

49. We will not include an extended discussion of grandparents and their role and responsibilities in the present chapter (or volume), since Scripture, for a variety of

reasons, provides little material in this regard. One major difference between the ancient and the contemporary context is that, unlike in much of Western society today, in biblical times grandparents lived together with their children and grandchildren in an extended household and hence were an integral part of day-to-day living (e.g., Gen. 31:55; 45:10; 46:7; Ex. 10:2; cf. Judg. 12:14; 1 Chron. 8:40), while in our day they typically constitute a separate household, often at a considerable distance from the nuclear family. Nevertheless, grandparents are part of "family," and these ties should be nurtured wherever possible. In one of the few New Testament references to grandparents, the apostle Paul urges children and grandchildren to take care of their widowed mothers or grandmothers (1 Tim. 5:4). He also notes the positive influence of Timothy's grandmother Lois, who together with his mother Eunice imparted her sincere faith to Timothy (2 Tim. 1:5).

50. On the Shema, see especially Daniel I. Block, "How Many Is God? An Investigation into the Meaning of Deuteronomy 6:4-5," *Journal of the Evangelical Theological Society* 47 (2004): 193-212, whose translation forms the basis for the rendering chosen here.

51. An interesting New Testament example is Timothy, who was taught the Scriptures by his Jewish mother and grandmother, since apparently his Gentile father was not a Christian (2 Tim. 1:5; 3:15; cf. Acts 16:1). Peter Balla, *The Child-Parent Relationship in the New Testament and Its Environment*, Wissenschaftliche Untersuchungen zum Neuen Testament 155 (Tübingen: Mohr Siebeck, 2003), 83-84, also cites examples from Jewish literature such as 4 Maccabees 18:10 (where the mother of the seven martyrs says to her sons, "While he [their father] was still with you, he taught you the law and the prophets") and Josephus, *Against Apion* 2.204 (children "should be taught to read, and shall learn both the laws and the deeds of their forefathers, in order that they may imitate the latter").

52. Hence Christian parenting is inadequate that conceives of the parental task as merely exposing a child to all the various religious options available, such as Christianity, Judaism, Islam, Hinduism, Buddhism, and so on, without seeking to inculcate in his or her heart and mind the truth of Scripture, in the misguided belief that it is illegitimate to influence a child's free determination of their own spiritual direction.

53. Cf. C. Hassell Bullock, *An Introduction to the Old Testament Poetic Books*, rev. and exp. ed. (Chicago: Moody, 1988), 162. One important implication of the fact that Proverbs 22:6 does not constitute a divine promise is that if a child does not choose to follow Christ once he or she is grown this cannot be construed as God breaking his promise. Neither is there a direct cause-and-effect relationship between parenting and how children turn out. Not every wrong decision made by children can or should be traced to parental failure. As Derek Kidner, *Proverbs*, Tyndale Old Testament Commentary (Leicester, U.K./Downers Grove, Ill.: InterVarsity Press, 1964), 51-52, points out, "even the best training cannot instill wisdom, but only encourage the choice to seek it (e.g. 2:1ff). . . . While there are parents who have only themselves to thank for their shame (29:15), it is ultimately the man himself who must bear his own blame, for it is *his* attitude to wisdom (29:3a; 2:2ff.) . . . which sets his course." Similarly, the church father Jerome: "Parents should not be faulted if, having taught their children well, these turn out badly later" (*Commentary on Titus,* per J.-P. Migne, ed., *Patrologia Graeca* [Paris: Migne, 1857-1886], 26:599BC, cited in Peter Gorday, ed., *Ancient Christian Commentary on Scripture: New Testament*, vol. 9, *Colossians, 1–2 Thessalonians, 1–2 Timothy, Titus, Philemon* [Downers Grove, Ill.: InterVarsity Press, 2000], 287).

54. As Kidner, *Proverbs,* 147, notes, the training prescribed is, literally, "according to his [the child's] way, which may imply respect for his individuality and vocation (though not his or her self-will; cf. Prov. 22:5; 14:12)." For an extensive treatise on childrearing, including a discussion of and practical principles for discipline, see

J. Hampton Keathley, "Biblical Foundations for Child Training" (Dallas: Biblical Studies Press, 1997), posted at http://www.bible.org.

55. For a lucid discussion of the teaching of the book of Proverbs with a view of training young men in wisdom see Block, "Marriage and Family in Ancient Israel," 89-92.

56. The Scripture references in parentheses are illustrative rather than exhaustive. The attributes are listed in order of first occurrence in the book of Proverbs.

57. E.g., John T. Carroll, "Children in the Bible," *Interpretation* 55 (2001): 125-126, with references to the works of others on 125, n. 14.

58. See especially the helpful study "Parents and Children" in Kidner, *Proverbs,* 50-52, who notes that "the rod is no panacea" and that the "parents' chief resource is constructive, namely their 'law,' taught with loving persistence" (50). For a discussion of the controversy surrounding physical forms of punishment in our culture today, as well as principles for parental discipline, see chapter 8 below.

CHAPTER 6:
THE CHRISTIAN FAMILY: FAMILY IN THE NEW TESTAMENT

1. On gender roles in Palestinian and geographically related Jewish traditions, see Craig S. Keener, "Marriage," in Craig A. Evans and Stanley E. Porter, eds., *Dictionary of New Testament Background* (Downers Grove, Ill.: InterVarsity Press, 2000), 690, who notes that wives' standard duties in first-century Palestine were largely domestic: grinding wheat, washing, nursing, and sewing (*m. Ketub.* 5:5). See also David Instone-Brewer, *Divorce and Remarriage in the Bible: The Social and Literary Context* (Grand Rapids, Mich.: Eerdmans, 2002), 103; and Daniel I. Block, "Marriage and Family in Ancient Israel," in Ken M. Campbell, ed., *Marriage and Family in the Biblical World* (Downers Grove, Ill.: InterVarsity Press, 2003), 73-74, who mentions tending the garden, harvesting grain, cooking food, and clothing the family.

2. Curiously, only the female equivalent, "Like mother, like daughter," is found explicitly in Scripture (Ezek. 16:44), though the maxim is clearly presupposed in biblical passages such as John 5:17-23 or 8:34-59. Daniel I. Block, *The Book of Ezekiel Chapters 1–24,* New International Commentary on the Old Testament (Grand Rapids, Mich.: Eerdmans, 1997), 506, n. 252, cites the phrase "Like the father, so the son" in Ezekiel 18:4, though there the context is somewhat different.

3. The best historical evidence indicates that Jesus' trade was not limited to working with wood (which may be suggested by the term "carpenter"), hence we have chosen the expression "craftsman" to convey the larger scope of Jesus' occupation. See the forthcoming essay by Ken M. Campbell, "What Was Jesus' Occupation?" in the *Journal of the Evangelical Theological Society.*

4. Cf. James Francis, "Children and Childhood in the New Testament," in Stephen C. Barton, ed., *The Family in Theological Perspective* (Edinburgh: T & T Clark, 1996), 67, with reference to Hans R. Weber, *Jesus and the Children* (Geneva: World Council of Churches, 1979), 52-53. See Johannes P. Louw and Eugene A. Nida, *Greek-English Lexicon of the New Testament Based on Semantic Domains,* 2d ed. (New York: United Bible Societies, 1989), 1:109-111, semantic domain "Children."

5. Note that Hugenberger sees this as evidence that marriage is a covenant. See Gordon P. Hugenberger, *Marriage as a Covenant: Biblical Law and Ethics as Developed from Malachi* (Grand Rapids, Mich.: Baker, 1998), 176-181. For some interesting background material see Joseph H. Hellerman, *The Ancient Church as Family* (Minneapolis: Fortress, 2001).

6. Note the conclusion by Stephen C. Barton, *Discipleship and Family Ties in Mark and Matthew* (Cambridge: Cambridge University Press, 1994), 56, that there is "strong precedent for the apparent 'hostility' to family in the context of discipleship of Jesus found in the gospels," pointing to Judaism from the story of Abraham onwards, the

renunciation of family life at Qumran (as idealized by Philo and Josephus), and the communities of "Therapeutae" (Philo). But see the perceptive review and critique by John Barclay in *Studies in Christian Ethics* 9, no. 1 (1996): 47-50.

7. Luke 14:26; cf. Matthew 10:37: "*loves* father or mother/son or daughter *more* than me."

8. Cf. the creative and suggestive treatment by Cynthia Long Westfall, "Family in the Gospels and Acts," in Richard S. Hess and M. Daniel Carroll R., *Family in the Bible* (Grand Rapids, Mich.: Baker, 2003), 125-147, who discusses Jesus' family ties under the rubrics "Mary the Unwed Mother," "Joseph the Stepfather," "Jesus the Illegitimate Son," and "The Displacement of Jesus' Family" and whose entire essay focuses almost exclusively on Jesus' own identity and experience in his earthly family.

9. Francis's calling (in an otherwise excellent article) Acts 1:14 "a reaffirmation of family ties" strikes us as rather curious (James Francis, "Children and Childhood in the New Testament," 81).

10. Cf. Rodney Clapp, *Families at the Crossroads: Beyond Traditional and Modern Options* (Leicester, U.K./Downers Grove, Ill.: InterVarsity Press, 1993); and the critique in Stephen C. Barton, "Biblical Hermeneutics and the Family," in *Family in Theological Perspective*, 10-16; as well as Nicholas Peter Harvey, "Christianity Against and for the Family," *Studies in Christian Ethics* 9, no. 1 (1996): 34-39; and the response by Linda Woodhead in ibid., 40-46.

11. Cf. Barton, *Discipleship and Family Ties*.

12. Cf. Stephen C. Barton, "Family," in Joel B. Green, Scot McKnight and I. Howard Marshall, eds., *Dictionary of Jesus and the Gospels* (Downers Grove, Ill.: InterVarsity Press, 1992), 226-229.

13. Though Westfall, "Family in the Gospels and Acts," 146, may erect perhaps a bit too sharp a dichotomy when she writes, "However, Jesus did not intend the family to be the most important institution on earth or the central unit of a Christian's identity and purpose."

14. See chapter 4, "The Gospel Tradition," in Peter Balla, *The Child-Parent Relationship in the New Testament and Its Environment*, Wissenschaftliche Untersuchungen zum Neuen Testament 155 (Tübingen: Mohr Siebeck, 2003), 114-156; John T. Carroll, "Children in the Bible," *Interpretation* 55 (2001): 121-134; William A. Strange, *Children in the Early Church: Children in the Ancient World, the New Testament, and the Early Church* (Carlisle, U.K.: Paternoster, 1996), especially chapter 2, 38-65; and Judith M. Gundry-Volf, "The Least and the Greatest," in Marcia J. Bunge, ed., *The Child in Christian Thought* (Grand Rapids, Mich.: Eerdmans, 2001), 29-60 (with further bibliography on 29-30, n. 2), who discusses children in the Gospels under the following five headings: (1) and (2) children as recipients of, and models of entering, the reign of God (Mark 10:13-16 pars.); (3) humble like a child (Matt. 18:1-5); (4) and (5) serving children and being great; and welcoming children and welcoming Jesus (Mark 9:33-37 pars.). Note that apart from the following examples, Jesus also referred to children playing in Matthew 11:16-19.

15. Examples include Jairus's daughter in Mark 5:21-24, 35-43; the daughter of a Syrophoenician woman in Mark 7:24-30; and a demon-possessed boy in Mark 9:14-29. See especially Stephen C. Barton, "Child, Children," *Dictionary of Jesus and the Gospels*, 100-104; and Francis, "Children and Childhood in the New Testament," 65-85 (note further bibliographic references to childhood in the ancient world on 66, n. 2 and to childhood and the teaching of Jesus on 72, n. 12).

16. See James D. M. Derrett, "Why Jesus Blessed the Children (Mk 10.13-16 Par.)," *Novum Testamentum* 25 (1983): 1-18; James I. H. McDonald, "Receiving and Entering the Kingdom: A Study of Mk 10.15," *Studia Evangelica* 6 (1973): 328-332.

17. Cf. Francis, "Children and Childhood in the New Testament," 75, who correlates this to the recollection of Israel's own experience with God in passages such as Deuteronomy 7:7-8; Hosea 11:1-4; Ezekiel 16:3-8; and Ps. 74:21.

18. For bibliography on children in Luke's Gospel, see ibid., 78, nn. 26 and 27.

19. Ibid., 79. Francis also notes negative connotations conveyed by children in the New Testament—but remarkably not in Jesus' teaching—such as lack of maturity (80).

20. Cf. David L. Balch, "Household Codes," in David E. Aune, ed., *Graeco-Roman Literature and the New Testament: Selected Forms and Genres,* Society of Biblical Literature Sources for Biblical Study 21 (Atlanta: Scholars Press, 1988); idem, *Let Wives Be Submissive: The Domestic Code in 1 Peter,* Society of Biblical Literature Monograph Series 26 (Chico, Calif.: Scholars Press, 1981); Craig S. Keener, "Family and Household," *Dictionary of New Testament Background,* 353-368; idem, "Marriage," *Dictionary of New Testament Background,* 687; and Philip H. Towner, "Households and Household Codes," in Gerald F. Hawthorne, Ralph P. Martin, and Daniel G. Reid, eds., *Dictionary of Paul and His Letters* (Leicester, U.K./Downers Grove, Ill.: InterVarsity Press, 1993), 417-419, who also notes the related passages 1 Timothy 2:1-15; 5:1-2; 6:1-2, 17-19; Titus 2:1–3:8; and 1 Peter 2:13–3:7; "Household Codes," in Ralph P. Martin and Peter H. Davids, eds., *Dictionary of the Later New Testament and Its Developments* (Downers Grove, Ill.: InterVarsity Press, 1997), 513-520; and James D. G. Dunn, "The Household Rules in the New Testament," in *Family in Theological Perspective,* 43-63 (including the list on 44-46, plus the bibliography listed on 49, nn. 7 and 8).

21. This does not mean, of course, that rendering Christianity respectable in the surrounding culture is the *supreme* or *only* principle at stake in living out one's marriage relationship according to biblical truth and revelation. Even if certain aspects of the Christian message or Christian living are countercultural, this may challenge the surrounding culture to ponder the distinctness and difference of the gospel. The church is certainly not authorized to alter biblical principles in order to accommodate itself to the surrounding culture, be it in the form of egalitarianism or otherwise diluting the principles set forth in chapters 2 and 3 above as well as the present chapter.

22. For a treatment of the responsibilities of children and parents in Paul's teaching with special emphasis on the Christian adaptation of the household code format, see Gundry-Volf, "Least and the Greatest," 53-58.

23. On ancient conditions with regard to children, including infant mortality rates and exposure of children, see Keener, "Family and Household," 359-360. On a figurative level, children are often presented in the New Testament as metaphorical for those who are deficient in understanding (1 Cor. 3:1-4; Heb. 5:13). In 1 Corinthians 13:11-12, Paul contrasts adulthood with childhood as the stage of entering into maturity. Believers must "no longer be infants, tossed back and forth by the waves, and blown here and there by every wind of teaching" (Eph. 4:14); together, they must grow up in Christ (Eph. 4:15).

24. See Peter T. O'Brien, *The Letter to the Ephesians,* Pillar New Testament Commentary (Grand Rapids, Mich.: Eerdmans, 1999), 442, n. 13.

25. For a full-monograph treatment of children in the New Testament and its environment see Balla, *Child-Parent Relationship.*

26. Ibid.

27. The phrase "for this is right" probably indicates not a separate reason for children to obey their parents but introduces the following quotation from the Decalogue. To reflect this understanding, we changed the period to a colon in the ESV translation. See O'Brien, *Letter to the Ephesians,* 442, with reference to Thorsten Moritz, *A*

Profound Mystery: The Use of the Old Testament in Ephesians, Novum Testamentum Supplement 85 (Leiden, Netherlands: Brill, 1996), 171-174, especially 171.

28. Cf. O'Brien, *Letter to the Ephesians,* 439, who notes that this is the fifth result participle in this passage; and the discussion of Ephesians 5:18 in the context of the letter as a whole, in chapter 3 above. On the notion of "being filled with the Spirit," see Andreas J. Köstenberger, "What Does It Mean to Be Filled with the Spirit? A Biblical Investigation," *Journal for the Evangelical Theological Society* 40 (1997): 229-240, who notes that there is no biblical reference to believers asking to be filled with the Spirit but that in Scripture God is shown to fill believers at his own time and discretion to empower them for ministry or bold witness (cf. Acts 2:4; 4:8, 31; 9:17; 13:9, 52). Christians already have the indwelling Holy Spirit in them at all times (e.g., Rom. 8:9-11) and should focus on living in obedience with God's revealed will in Scripture and on not quenching or grieving the Holy Spirit (1 Thess. 5:19; Eph. 4:30).

29. Note also Jesus' reference to the fifth commandment in Matthew 15:4 par. Mark 7:10 (as well as to negative consequences for disobedience in Ex. 21:17 par. Lev. 20:9).

30. See O'Brien, *Letter to the Ephesians,* 441.

31. Ibid., 440-441.

32. This teaching echoes a concern found both in the Old Testament (especially Proverbs) and Judaism (such as Philo, Josephus, 4 Maccabees, and some of the rabbis); see Moritz, *Profound Mystery,* 159-163.

33. In Ephesians 6:4, the Greek word translated "provoke" is *parorgizō* (elsewhere in the New Testament only with the same meaning in Rom. 10:19; variant in Colossians 3:21; see also Dan. 11:36, LXX; Sir. 4:3, LXX; T. Job 43:9; T. Levi 3:10?; 3 Bar. 16:2). In Colossians 3:21, the Greek word translated "provoke" is *erethizō* (elsewhere in the New Testament only in 2 Cor. 9:2, where the expression has a positive sense; cf. 1 Macc. 15:40 and further extrabiblical Greek examples in W. Bauer, F. W. Danker, W. F. Arndt, and F. W. Gingrich, *A Greek-English Lexicon of the New Testament and Other Early Christian Literature,* 3d ed. (BDAG) (Chicago: University of Chicago Press, 2000), 391, which include the ideas of "irritate" or "embitter"; indeed, many fathers "irritate" their children, which is an abuse of their authority).

34. O'Brien, *Letter to the Ephesians,* 445, notes that while *hoi pateres* in certain contexts can mean "parents" in general (Heb. 11:23), in Ephesians 6:4 there is a change of wording from *goneis,* "parents," in Ephesians 6:1 to *pateres* in Ephesians 6:4, which makes it likely that the present reference is specifically to fathers. This is supported also by the fact that fathers were responsible for educating and disciplining their children in both the Jewish and the Greco-Roman world.

35. Ibid., 440.

36. Andrew T. Lincoln, *Ephesians,* Word Biblical Commentary (Dallas: Word, 1990), 406.

37. See Balla, *Child-Parent Relationship,* 83-84. It is an indication of the powerful dynamics of natural father-child relations that this kind of language was applied also to older and younger men who were not biologically related. Thus younger men could call older men "fathers" and older men could address younger men as "sons." Teachers likewise might refer to their disciples as children (John 13:33; 21:5; 3 John 4), while disciples might call their teachers "fathers" (2 Kings 2:12; Matt. 23:9).

38. Cf. Philo, *Special Laws* 2.232, who writes of the parents' authority to "impose harsh punishments" on children (cited in Carroll, "Children in the Bible," 123).

39. See parallels in Keener, "Family and Household," 357.

40. Indeed, how many children have a distorted view of our heavenly Father because of a poor or even abusive earthly father? In such cases, the requirement is to forgive and to focus on God the Father who alone is perfect and able to meet all our needs. See, e.g., Mary A. Kassian, *In My Father's House: Women Relating to God as Father*

(Nashville: LifeWay, 1999).

41. This pronouncement is almost unbearable for some contemporary scholars, such as Carolyn Osiek and David L. Balch, *Families in the New Testament World: Households and House Churches* (Louisville: Westminster/John Knox, 1997), 122, who write, "It is theologically and morally outrageous when this 'Pauline' author argues that a woman 'will be saved through childbearing' (1 Tim. 2:15)." For a detailed treatment of the interpretation of 1 Timothy 2:15, see Andreas J. Köstenberger, "Ascertaining Women's God-Ordained Roles: An Interpretation of 1 Timothy 2:15," *Bulletin of Biblical Research* 7 (1997): 107-144. On hospitality, see Stephen C. Barton, "Hospitality," in *Dictionary of the Later New Testament and Its Developments,* 501-507.

42. See Köstenberger, "Ascertaining Women's God-Ordained Roles," 142-144, especially 143.

43. On this issue see especially Larry Burkett, *Women Leaving the Work Place* (Chicago: Moody, 1999); Cheryl Gochnauer, *So You Want to Be a Stay-at-Home Mom* (Downers Grove, Ill.: InterVarsity Press, 1999); and Donna Otto, *The Stay-at-Home Mom: For Women at Home and Those Who Want to Be* (Eugene, Ore.: Harvest, 1997).

44. Köstenberger, "Ascertaining Women's God-Ordained Roles," 143.

45. The Greek word is *diabolos;* cf. 1 Timothy 3:11; 2 Timothy 3:3.

46. Cf. 2 Peter 2:19; Romans 6:18, 22; 1 Corinthians 7:15; Galatians 4:3. This attribute is also required of elders and deacons (1 Tim. 3:3, 8).

47. Cf. 1 Timothy 5:2. "And so" at the beginning of Titus 2:4 renders a purpose clause (*hina*) in the original. Contrary to the implication of certain works on spiritual disciplines, growth in godly character ought not to be seen in isolation from service to others in the context of healthy relationships in the church. Otherwise, such "spirituality" can easily foster spiritual pride and a judgmental attitude toward others who are perceived as less "spiritual." On a different note, interestingly, Titus is not told to teach young women directly.

48. See already the portrait of the excellent wife (and mother) in Proverbs 31, which is discussed in chapter 2 above.

49. See chapter 3 for a discussion of wifely submission in Ephesians 5:21-33. The dichotomy erected by John R. W. Stott, *Guard the Truth: The Message of 1 Timothy and Titus* (Downers Grove, Ill.: InterVarsity Press, 1996), 189, that "masculine 'headship' [is one] not of authority . . . but of responsibility and loving care" is false.

50. Stanley N. Helton, "Titus 2:5—Must Women Stay at Home?" in Carroll D. Osburn, ed., *Essays on Women in Earliest Christianity* (Joplin, Mo.: College Press, 1995), 376.

51. See also the discussion of contemporary issues in parenting, including single parenting, physical discipline, and principles of disciplining one's children, in chapter 7 below.

52. Gifted children, for example, may be easily bored and come across as disrespectful or rebellious. Merely exhorting them to be respectful without dealing with the issue of the child's need for additional challenges will prove inadequate. Some children thrive on formal structure, others need a larger scope of freedom. Some children tend to be more compliant, others frequently push the limits. A one-size-fits-all approach to discipline is therefore inadequate.

53. On family worship, see especially James W. Alexander, *Thoughts on Family Worship* (Morgan, Pa.: Soli Deo Gloria, 1998); Kerry Ptacek, *Family Worship: The Biblical Basis, Historical Reality, and Current Need* (Greenville, S.C.: Greenville Seminary Press, 2000). See further the section on "Family Ways" in chapter 8 below.

54. Dietrich Bonhoeffer, *Ethics,* trans. Neville Horton Smith (London: SCM, 1955), 183.

CHAPTER 7:
TO HAVE OR NOT TO HAVE CHILDREN:
SPECIAL ISSUES RELATED TO THE FAMILY (PART 1)

1. For contemporary implications with regard to marriage and the family, see especially part 2 in Stephen C. Barton, ed., *The Family in Theological Perspective* (Edinburgh: T & T Clark, 1996), a volume reflecting the editor's concerns as first articulated in his "Marriage and Family Life as Christian Concerns," *Expository Times* 106, no. 3 (1994): 69-74.

2. On ancient Jewish attitudes toward abortion, see Craig S. Keener, "Marriage," in Craig A. Evans and Stanley E. Porter, eds., *Dictionary of New Testament Background* (Downers Grove, Ill.: InterVarsity Press, 2000), 681. On contraception, see John T. Noonan, Jr., *Contraception: A History of Its Treatment by the Catholic Theologians and Canonists* (Cambridge, Mass.: Harvard University Press, 1965); Angus S. McLaren, *A History of Contraception* (Oxford: Blackwell, 1992). See also William A. Strange, *Children in the Early Church: Children in the Ancient World, the New Testament, and the Early Church* (Carlisle, U.K.: Paternoster, 1996), 4-5, who cites the common ancient practice of exposure of unwelcome children, in particular girls (*Oxyrhynchus Papyrus* 744) and those with birth defects. The Jews, by contrast, took the Law of Moses to condemn abortion (Ex. 21:22-25). On birth control, see Helmut Thielicke, *The Ethics of Sex*, trans. John W. Doberstein (New York: Harper & Row, 1964), 200-225, whose discussion is considerably more nuanced than that of Mary Pride, *The Way Home: Beyond Feminism, Back to Reality* (Westchester, Ill.: Crossway, 1985), who advocates letting God give a couple as many children as he desires by practicing no birth control. On infertility, see Martha Stout, *Without Child: A Compassionate Look at Infertility* (Grand Rapids, Mich.: Zondervan, 1985); Kaye Halverson, *The Wedded Unmother* (Minneapolis: Augsburg, 1980); and John and Sylvia Van Regenmorter, *When the Cradle Is Empty: Answering Tough Questions About Infertility* (Wheaton, Ill.: Tyndale/Focus on the Family, 2004).

3. For a survey of the biblical teaching on abortion see Charles H. H. Scobie, *The Ways of Our God: An Approach to Biblical Theology* (Grand Rapids, Mich./Cambridge: Eerdmans, 2003), 801, 834, 862, who notes that "the OT has nothing directly to say about abortion, the killing of the unborn, probably because such a practice would have been unthinkable for God's people" (801). See also Michael A. Grisanti, "The Abortion Dilemma," *The Master's Seminary Journal* 11, no. 2 (Fall 2000): 169-190.

4. James K. Hoffmeier, ed., *Abortion: A Christian Understanding and Response* (Grand Rapids, Mich.: Baker, 1987), 55, cited in Scobie, *Ways of Our God*, 801. Scobie, in ibid., 834, also points out that the same word (*brephos*) used for Elizabeth's unborn child in Luke 1:41, 44 is used for a newborn child (Jesus) in Luke 2:12 (and, for that matter, for the children brought to Jesus in Luke 18:15). Grisanti, "Abortion Dilemma," 178, also cites Genesis 4:1 and Job 3:3 in support of the notion that "[t]he Bible recognizes no essential difference between the being in the womb and the being after birth."

5. Scobie, *Ways of Our God*, 801, who also notes that the LXX has a significant variant that distinguishes between fetuses that are and those that are not "fully formed" (ibid., citing Michael J. Gorman, *Abortion and the Early Church* [New York: Paulist, 1982], 35). See also Bruce K. Waltke, "Reflections from the Old Testament on Abortion," *Journal of the Evangelical Theological Society* 19 (1976): 13: "the fetus is human and therefore to be accorded the same protection to life granted every other human being."

6. C. Hassell Bullock, "Abortion and Old Testament Prophetic and Poetic Literature," in *Abortion: A Christian Understanding*, 68.

7. Some pro-abortion exegetes cite Exodus 21:22-25 to support their position. However, this view is based on the questionable translation of the Hebrew *yeled* as

"miscarriage" (RSV, NASB). For a thorough treatment of the passage and refutation of the "miscarriage" view, see John S. Feinberg and Paul D. Feinberg, *Ethics for a Brave New World* (Wheaton, Ill.: Crossway, 1993), 63-65, who demonstrate that (1) even if miscarriage were in view, in contrast to abortion (which is an intentional intervention with the express purpose of terminating an unborn life) the death that ensues in verse 22 is *accidental;* and (2) the Hebrew terms used in verse 22 refer to *premature live childbirth* (rather than miscarriage) elsewhere in the Old Testament (cf. the NIV rendering of Exodus 21:22 as "she gives birth prematurely"). See also the very thorough treatment in Grisanti, "Abortion Dilemma," 180-187, who notes that the Hebrew term for "child" in Ex. 21:22 is *yeled,* which "never refers elsewhere [in the Old Testament] to a child unrecognizable as human or incapable of existence outside the womb" (it refers to newborns in Ex. 1:17-18; 3:6-9; weaned children in Gen. 21:8; and to teenagers, youths, or young men in Gen. 21:14-16; 2 Kings 2:24; Dan. 1:4, 10, 15, 17) and registers important key observations on 186-187; and the brief comments by Scobie, *Ways of Our God,* 801, who also cites Walter C. Kaiser, *Toward Old Testament Ethics* (Grand Rapids, Mich.: Zondervan, 1983), 102-104, 170-172; Hoffmeier, *Abortion: A Christian Understanding,* 57-61; and John Jefferson Davis, *Evangelical Ethics: Issues Facing the Church Today,* 2d ed. (Phillipsburg, N.J.: Presbyterian & Reformed, 1993), 136-137.

8. See Everett Ferguson, *Backgrounds of Early Christianity,* 2d ed. (Grand Rapids, Mich.: Eerdmans, 1993), 73-74, who cites other sources on 73, n. 27. See also M. J. Gorman, *Abortion and the Early Church,* 24-32 and idem, "Abortion and the New Testament," in *Abortion: A Christian Understanding,* 74-75.

9. Cited in Ferguson, *Backgrounds of Early Christianity,* 74; see also Strange, *Children in the Early Church,* 4-5. The word *ektithēmi* occurs in Acts 7:19, 21 with reference to the exposure of baby Moses in Egypt, though the circumstances were, of course, very different. See also Keener, "Marriage," 681, who cites Quintilian, *Institutio Oratoria* 8.1.14 (written prior to A.D. 96) and Juvenal, *Satires* 6.602-609 (second century A.D.).

10. See the discussion in David W. Chapman, "Marriage and Family in Second Temple Judaism," in Ken M. Campbell, ed., *Marriage and Family in the Biblical World* (Downers Grove, Ill.: InterVarsity Press, 2003), 224-227, especially 226-227. See also Keener, "Marriage," 681, who notes that many philosophers, physicians, and others disliked abortion and ancients debated whether or not the embryo was a person and hence abortion should be legal. For abortion and birth control in the ancient Near East, see Victor H. Matthews, "Marriage and Family in the Ancient Near East," in *Marriage and Family in the Biblical World,* 21-22; and Andrew E. Hill, "Abortion in the Ancient Near East," in *Abortion: A Christian Understanding,* 31-36.

11. Cf. Andreas Lindemann, "'Do Not Let a Woman Destroy the Unborn Babe in Her Belly': Abortion in Ancient Judaism and Christianity," *Studia theologica* 49 (1995): 253-271.

12. For a helpful survey of the legal background of abortion in the United States, see Grisanti, "Abortion Dilemma," 171-173, who on 176-178 also provides a spectrum of views on abortion, ranging from (1) "always" ("abortion on demand") to (2) "sometimes" (under certain circumstances, such as rape, incest, and threats to the mother's health, see also 187-190) to (3) "rarely" (ectopic or tubal pregnancy; his view) to (4) "never." For the ethical issues involved in abortion see chapter 6, "Abortion" in Davis, *Evangelical Ethics.*

13. The only possible exception may be cases where the principle of the sanctity of the life of the unborn conflicts with that of the preservation of the mother's life, primarily in the case of ectopic or tubal pregnancies (cf. Grisanti, "The Abortion Dilemma," 177-178 and the previous footnote). See also the discussions under the headings "Abortion" and "Prochoice or Prolife" in Scobie, *Ways of Our God,* 862 and 864.

Scobie rightly points to alternatives to abortion and urges the church to assist those wrestling with this issue. Help in this area is offered by the following organizations: National Right to Life (http://www.nrlc.org), Prolife America (http://www.pro-lifeinfo.org), Life Issues Institute (http://www.lifeissues.org), America's Pregnancy Helpline (http://www.thehelpline.org), CareNet (http://www.care-net.org), and Hope After Abortion (http://www.hopeafterabortion.com). See also John Piper, *A Hunger for God: Desiring God Through Fasting and Prayer* (Wheaton, Ill.: Crossway, 1997), 155-172; Stanley J. Grenz, *Sexual Ethics: A Biblical Perspective* (Dallas: Word, 1990), 135-138; and Richard B. Hays, *The Moral Vision of the New Testament: A Contemporary Introduction to New Testament Ethics* (San Francisco: Harper, 1996), 456-460. Contra Beverly W. Harrison, *Our Right to Choose: Toward a New Ethic of Abortion* (Boston: Beacon, 1983), 70, who claims that "the ancient moral ethos reflected in Scripture . . . has been superseded by a more adequate morality . . ."

14. Mohler, "Can Christians Use Birth Control? (parts 1 and 2)," 3/29/2004 and 3/30/2004, at http://www.albertmohler.com/radio_archive.html.

15. Pope Paul VI, *Humanae Vitae* 14-17.

16. See Deuteronomy 22 for related "crimes" and punishments.

17. Albert Mohler, "Can Christians Use Birth Control?" Further resources on the issue of contraception in general, identified on the websites of Ethics and Medicine (Ben Mitchell; posted at http://www.ethicsandmedicine.com) and the Center for Bioethics and Human Dignity (President John Kilner; http://cbhd.org), are Oliver O'Donovan, *Begotten or Made?* (Oxford: Clarendon/Oxford University Press; reprint 2002 [1984]); and Brent Waters, *Reproductive Technology: Towards a Theology of Procreative Stewardship* (Cleveland: Pilgrim Press, 2001; originally published London: Darton, Longman & Todd, 2001; chapter 3 deals more specifically with the issue of childlessness and ethics).

18. In order to understand how the biblical principle of respect for human life applies to this question, it is important to make a distinction regarding terms that are often erroneously used interchangeably. The term "contraception" comes from the root words *contra*, meaning "against," and *ception*, referring to "conception." Thus, the term literally means to prohibit fertilization and thus avoid conception that would result in a pregnancy once the zygote implants in the uterine wall. In contrast, the term "birth control" is much broader in its scope. Controlling birth *may include* contraceptive measures *but is not limited to the prevention of conception* as a means of controlling the birth of a child. It may also include practices that are abortive in nature, that is, that which kills a growing child after the conception has taken place (either before or after the conceived child implants in the uterine wall of the mother). Based on the earlier discussion regarding abortion, any form of "birth control" that endangers the life of a child or seeks to terminate the life of a child either before or after implantation in the uterine wall as a means to controlling birth and family planning is morally reprehensible and must be rejected.

19. The most popular form of the rhythm method (calendar method) is called the Billings Method, which is explained in Evelyn Billings and Ann Westmore, *The Billings Method,* updated edition (Melbourne: Penguin, 2003 [1980]).

20. Matthew 5:29-30 is not relevant here, since Jesus' reference to gouging out an eye or cutting off a hand is hyperbolic in nature and relates not to parts of the body that are functioning normally but are inconvenient, but to those that are "causing" a person to sin.

21. John Jefferson Davis, "Theologically Sound," in David B. Biebel, ed., *The Sterilization Option: A Guide for Christians* (Grand Rapids, Mich.: Baker, 1995), 72.

22. Virtually all discussions on the morality of sterilization are by Roman Catholic moral theologians, owing in large part to their opposition to contraceptive measures in

general. Pope Paul VI laid out the official catholic teaching on this issue in paragraph 14 of the papal encyclical *Humanae Vitae*. Among the Catholic moral theologians who have expressly disagreed with the pope are James Burtchaell ("'Human Life' and Human Love," *Commonweal* [November 13, 1968]: 248-250); and Richard A. McCormick, S.J. ("Sterilization and Theological Method," *Theological Studies* 37, no. 3 [September 1976]: 471-477). *First Things* published a very interesting and informative discussion on the topic of contraception entitled "Contraception: A Symposium" that included responses by Protestant, Catholic, and Jewish thinkers (*First Things* 88 [December 1988]: 17-29). Unfortunately, the topic of sterilization received very little direct attention. Clearly, this is an area in which further discussion among evangelicals is needed.

23. For instance, one might argue that God himself built in menopause, at which time the woman's reproductive ability comes to an end. It may therefore not be inappropriate to conclude a couple's childbearing activity by way of sterilization at an earlier time.

24. *Physician's Desk Reference,* 50th ed. (Montvale, N.J.: Medical Economics, 1996): Norplant, 3281; Depro-Prevara, 2435.

25. Statistically speaking, when taken as designed, these various types of hormone-based birth control methods are effective 99.5 percent of the time, meaning that even when taken as directed, one out of every 200 acts of sexual intercourse (on average) will result in a pregnancy. From this fact one can know for certain that while "the pill" is effective in preventing ovulation and preventing fertilization, it does not prevent all fertilization. While there is no statistical data to indicate how many births are terminated by the third mechanism, one can be assured that it does occur.

26. Posted at http://www.pdrhealth.com/content/women_health/chapters/fgwh21.shtml (emphasis added).

27. The following is a list of combination oral contraceptives that function in the manner described above, organized alphabetically by brand name. The page number from the 54th edition of the *Physician's Desk Reference* is also included for the reader's convenience. This is an updated and expanded list from that originally compiled by Debra Evans, *The Christian Woman's Guide to Sexuality* (Wheaton, Ill.: Crossway, 1996), 290. The list (with *PDR* page numbers) is as follows: ALESSE - 21 (Wyeth-Ayerst), 3203; ALESSE - 21 (Wyeth-Ayerst), 3209; BREVICON-21 (Searle), 2891; BREVICON-28 (Searle), 2891; DEMULEN 1/35 (Searle), 2911; DEMULEN 1/50 (Searle), 2911; DESOGEN (Organon), 2085; LO/OVRAL (Wyeth-Ayerst), 3267; ESTROSTEP 21 (Parke-Davis), 2246; ESTROSTEP Fe (Parke-Davis), 2246; LEVLEN 21 (Berlex), 749; LEVLEN 28 (Berlex), 749; LEVLITE 21 (Berlex), 749; LEVLITE 21 (Berlex), 749; LEVORA (Watson), 3174; LOESTRIN 21 (Parke-Davis), 2257; LOESTRIN 28 (Parke-Davis), 2257; LO/OVRAL 28 (Wyeth-Ayerst), 3272; MICRONOR (Ortho-McNeil), 2165; MIRCETTE (Organon), 2097; MODICON - 21 (Ortho), 2184; MODICON -28 (Ortho), 2184; NECON 0.5/35 Watson), 3180; NECON 1/35 Watson), 3180; NECON 1/50 Watson), 3180; NECON 1/50 Watson), 3180; NECON 10/11 Watson), 3180; NORDETTE 21 (Wyeth-Ayerst), 3275; NORDETTE 28 (Wyeth-Ayerst), 3277; NORINYL 1+35-21 (Searle), 2891; NORINYL 1+35-28 (Searle), 2891; NORINYL 1+50-21 (Searle), 2891; NORINYL 1+50-21 (Searle), 2891; NOR-QD (Watson), 3184; ORTHO-CEPT (Ortho-McNeil), 2168; ORTHO-CYCLEN (Ortho-McNeil), 2198; ORTHO-NOVUM 1/35 (Ortho-McNeil), 2184; ORTHO-NOVUM 1/50 (Ortho-McNeil), 2178; ORTHO-NOVUM 7/7/7 (Ortho-McNeil), 2184; ORTHO-NOVUM 10/11 (Ortho-McNeil), 2184; ORTHO TRI-CYCLEN (Ortho-McNeil), 2191; OVCON (Bristol-Meyers Squibb), 838; OVRAL (Wyeth-Ayerst), 3289; OVRETTE (Wyeth-Ayerst), 3289; PLAN B (Women's Capitol), 3201; PREVEN EMERGENCY (Gynetics), 1335; TRI-LEVLEN (Berlex), 749; TRI-NORINYL (Searle), 2929; TRIPHASIL-21 (Wyeth-Ayerst), 3328;

TRIPHASIL-28 (Wyeth-Ayerst), 3333; TIVORA (Watson), 3187; ZOVIA 1/35E (Watson), 3190; ZOVIA 1/50E (Watson), 3190.

28. The reader might find it interesting to note the position statement of the Christian Medical and Dental Association (CMDA) regarding this issue. It reads in part as follows: "CMDA recognizes that there are differing viewpoints among Christians regarding the broad issue of birth control and the use of contraceptives. The issue at hand, however, is whether or not hormonal birth control methods have post-conceptional effects (i.e., cause abortion). CMDA has consulted many experts in the field of reproduction who have reviewed the scientific literature. While there are data that cause concern, our current scientific knowledge does not establish a definitive causal link between the routine use of hormonal birth control and abortion. However, neither are there data to deny a post-conceptional effect." For further reading one can access the rest of the position statement at http://www.epm.org/articles/CMDAstate.html. Also, Randy Alcorn's website for his *Eternal Perspectives Ministries* is very helpful and attempts to treat both sides of the issue fairly while taking a conservative approach to this issue. See http://www.epm.org/prolife.html or http://www.epm.org/articles/26doctor.html for two of several interesting discussions related to this topic. See also Tom Strode, "To Be or Not to Be: The Pill May Be Controlling Births in Ways You've Never Considered," *Light* (November/December 2002): 8-9; and Walter L. Larimore and Randy Alcorn, "Using the Birth Control Pill Is Ethically Unacceptable," in John F. Kilner, Paige C. Cunningham, and W. David Hager, eds., *The Reproduction Revolution: A Christian Appraisal of Sexuality, Reproductive Technologies and the Family* (Grand Rapids, Mich.: Eerdmans, 2000), 179-191.

29. Evans, *Christian Woman's Guide to Sexuality,* 196.

30. For additional information on this topic see Randy Alcorn, *Does the Birth Control Pill Cause Abortions?* (Gresham, Ore.: Eternal Perspective Ministries, 2000); Linda K. Bevington and Russell DiSilvestro, eds., *The Pill: Addressing the Scientific and Ethical Question of the Abortifacient Issue* (Bannockburn, Ill.: The Center for Bioethics and Human Dignity, 2003).

31. This is hardly satisfactory, however, since, to be consistent, the proponents of this kind of argument would also have to conclude that the use of any medical intervention for a medical problem is likewise inappropriate.

32. While different in nature from the direct and gracious intervention of God on behalf of Sarah, Hannah, and Elizabeth, these new medical procedures are nonetheless wondrous in their own right.

33. See further the description below. While the topic of cloning is beyond the scope of this chapter, see the following resources for some helpful discussion of the topic: Scott B. Rae's *Moral Choices: An Introduction to Ethics,* 2d ed. (Grand Rapids, Mich.: Zondervan, 2000), 169-180; and Glen H. Stassen and David P. Gushee's short but helpful discussion in *Kingdom Ethics: Following Jesus in Contemporary Context* (Downers Grove, Ill.: InterVarsity Press, 2003), 262-264.

34. Karen Dawson, *Reproductive Technology: The Science, the Ethics, the Law, and the Social Issues* (Melbourne: VCTA Publishing, Macmillan Education Australia, 1995), 49.

35. Rae, *Moral Choices,* 149. For additional information on artificial insemination, in vitro fertilization, and related issues, see Gary P. Stewart, John F. Kilner, and William R. Cutrer, eds., *Basic Questions on Sexuality and Reproductive Technology: When Is It Right to Intervene?* (Grand Rapids, Mich.: Kregel, 1998); Kilner, Cunningham, and Hager, eds., *Reproduction Revolution;* and John F. Kilner, C. Ben Mitchell, Daniel Taylor, eds., *Does God Need Our Help? Cloning, Assisted Suicide, and Other Challenges in Bioethics* (Wheaton, Ill.: Tyndale, 2003).

36. John Van Regenmorter, "Frozen Out: What to Do with Those Extra Embryos," *Christianity Today,* July 2004, 33.

37. A possible analogy is provided by the Old Testament practice of men seeking offspring from women other than their wives in the case of their wives' infertility— often with their wives' consent (e.g., Abraham and Hagar, at Sarah's prompting; Gen. 16:1-4). To be sure, the analogy breaks down in that, in the case of modern reproductive technology, sexual intercourse with a person of the opposite sex other than one's spouse is not required. Nevertheless, in both cases an effort is made to have children through the involvement of someone outside the marriage bond. In Scripture, at least in Abraham's case, this is viewed as resulting from a lack of faith. Trusting God to remove barrenness, if possible, or choosing to adopt, may therefore be preferable alternatives.

38. Rae, *Moral Choices,* 154. Some have suggested that the Old Testament practice of levirate marriage (Deut. 25:5-10) legitimates the use of donor sperm from a family member other than one's spouse. It would seem wise, however, not to draw too close a parallel, for there are notable and important differences between the two practices. To begin with, the close relative of the deceased husband actually married the woman, which is very different from accepting donor sperm from someone other than one's husband. Also, in the case of levirate marriage, no provisions were made to assist a *living* spouse in having children. The purpose was rather to provide an inheritance and material security when a woman's husband had passed away.

39. For a helpful, compassionate treatment of the subject see June M. Ring, "Partakers of the Grace: Biblical Foundations for Adoption," posted at http://www.ppl.org/ adopt.html. June Ring serves as the adoption resources coordinator for Presbyterians Pro-Life. See also Roland de Vaux, *Ancient Israel: Its Life and Institutions,* trans. John McHugh (New York: McGraw-Hill, 1961), 51-52.

40. Other possible examples include Abram adopting Eliezer of Damascus (Genesis 15) and Eli and Samuel (1 Samuel 1).

41. Cf. Daniel I. Block, "Marriage and Family in Ancient Israel," in *Marriage and Family in the Biblical World,* 87-88.

42. For a practical discussion of the contemporary practice of adoption in light of its biblical foundation see the above-mentioned article by June Ring, "Partakers of the Grace." See also Lois Gilman, *The Adoption Resource Book* (San Francisco: HarperCollins, 1998); Jorie Kincaid, *Adopting for Good: A Guide for People Considering Adoption* (Downers Grove, Ill.: InterVarsity Press, 1997); and Jayne Schooler. *The Whole Life Adoption Book* (Colorado Springs: NavPress, 1993).

43. See especially James M. Scott, *Adoption as Sons of God: An Exegetical Investigation into the Background of ΥΙΟΘΗΣΙΑ in the Corpus Paulinum,* Wissenschaftliche Untersuchungen zum Neuen Testament 2/48 (Tübingen: Mohr Siebeck, 1992). On Paul's spiritual use of family language see Reider Aasgaard, *'My Beloved Brothers and Sisters': Christian Siblingship in the Apostle Paul,* Studies of the New Testament and Its World (Edinburgh: T & T Clark, 2003).

44. For a concise summary, see James M. Scott, "Adoption," in Gerald F. Hawthorne, Ralph P. Martin, and Daniel G. Reid, eds., *Dictionary of Paul and His Letters* (Leicester, U.K./Downers Grove, Ill.: InterVarsity Press, 1993), 15-18. See also John T. Carroll, "Children in the Bible," *Interpretation* 55 (2001): 123.

45. Cf. John 1:12-13; Romans 8:14-17, 29; Galatians 3:23-36; 4:1-7; Ephesians 1:5; 1 John 3:1-2, 10; 5:19. See especially Edmund P. Clowney, "Interpreting the Biblical Models of the Church: A Hermeneutical Deepening of Ecclesiology," in D. A. Carson, ed., *Biblical Interpretation and the Church: Text and Context* (Exeter, U.K.: Paternoster, 1984), 75-76, who also refers to Ephesians 3:14; 2 Corinthians 6:18; Matthew 12:49-50; 23:28; and 1 John 4:21.

46. 1 Corinthians 12-14; Romans 12; Ephesians 4. On the preceding two paragraphs, see Ray Anderson, "God Bless the Children—and the Childless," *Christianity Today,* August 7, 1987, 28.

CHAPTER 8:
REQUIRING THE WISDOM OF SOLOMON:
SPECIAL ISSUES RELATED TO THE FAMILY (PART 2)

1. See, e.g., Gary Ezzo and Anne M. Ezzo, *Growing Kids God's Way: Biblical Ethics for Parenting,* 4th ed. (Chatsworth, Calif.: Growing Families International, 1997); but note the controversy surrounding this ministry: see http://www.ezzo.info and the two-part critique in the *Christian Research Journal,* at http://www.equip.org/free/DG233.htm and http://www.equip.org/free/DG234.pdf. Less regimented and more aimed at capturing the essence of the parenting task is Tedd Tripp, *Shepherding a Child's Heart* (Wapallopen, Pa.: Shepherd, 1998). See also the various parenting resources published by William Sears and Martha Sears. On a note of interest, the first work offering advice on childrearing in the patristic period was written by John Chrysostom (c. A.D. 347–407), *On the Vainglory of the World and on the Education of Children.*

2. E.g., homeschooling, private Christian schools, charter schools, and so on. On some ancient background for homeschooling and private Christian schools see William A. Strange, *Children in the Early Church: Children in the Ancient World, the New Testament, and the Early Church* (Carlisle, U.K.: Paternoster, 1996), 80-81, who notes that "[w]e hear of no Christian schooling outside the home in the early centuries. . . . Christian parents were still content for their children to share a common education with their pagan neighbours, and the church was slow to copy the [*sic*] synagogue in providing an alternative pattern of schooling. Even when John Chrysostom . . . wrote the first Christian treatise on the education of children . . . , he addressed himself to parents, and said nothing about sending children to specifically Christian schools. The first Christian schools seem to have been those founded by the monasteries from the fourth century onwards." Strange notes that, at least in those days, "[t]o set up their own separate educational provision would have been to withdraw from the common life they shared with their pagan neighbours."

3. Cf. Alice B. Tolbert, "The Crisis of Single-Parent Families," *Urban Mission* 7 (1989): 9-15, especially 11-12.

4. The absence of the father in a family where the mother serves as the single parent is hard to compensate. Works describing the father's importance in the development of children include Don E. Eberly, "The Collapse and Recovery of Fatherhood," in Don E. Eberly, ed., *The Faith Factor in Fatherhood: Renewing the Sacred Vocation of Fathering* (Lanham, Md.: Rowman & Littlefield, 1999), 4-20; Rob Palkovitz, *Involved Fathering and Men's Adult Development: Provisional Balances* (Mahwah, N.J.: Lawrence Erlbaum Associates, 2002); Paul C. Vitz, *Faith of the Fatherless: The Psychology of Atheism* (Dallas: Spence, 1999); David Blankenhorn, *Fatherless America: Confronting Our Most Urgent Social Problem* (New York: HarperCollins, 1995); and Frank Minirth, Brian Newman, and Paul Warren, *The Father Book: An Instruction Manual,* Minirth-Meier Clinic Series (Nashville: Thomas Nelson, 1992).

5. Cf. F. Charles Fensham, "Widow, Orphan, and the Poor in Ancient Near Eastern Legal and Wisdom Literature," *Journal of Near Eastern Studies* 21 (1962): 129-139; Mark Sneed, "Israelite Concern for the Alien, Orphan, and Widow: Altruism or Ideology?" *Zeitschrift für die alttestamentliche Wissenschaft* 111 (1999): 498-507; Harold V. Bennett, *Injustice Made Legal: Deuteronomic Law and the Plight of Widows, Strangers, and Orphans in Ancient Israel* (Grand Rapids, Mich.: Eerdmans, 2002).

6. Deuteronomy 24:17; 27:19; Psalm 23:10; Isaiah 1:17; Jeremiah 7:6; 22:3; Zechariah

7:10. See also Deuteronomy 26:12, which instructs that a portion of the tithes were to be distributed to "the alien, the fatherless, and the widow."

7. Isaiah 1:23; 10:2; Jeremiah 5:28; 7:6; Ezekiel 22:7; Zechariah 7:10-14; Malachi 3:5.

8. For materials related to parenting and ministry to single parents see, e.g., Blake J. Neff, "The Diverse-Traditional Family," in Blake J. Neff and Donald Ratcliff, eds., *Handbook of Family Religious Education* (Birmingham: Religious Education Press, 1995), 121-124; Jane Hannah and Dick Stafford, *Single Parenting with Dick and Jane: A Biblical, Back-to-Basics Approach to the Challenges Facing Today's Single Parent* (Nashville: Family Touch, 1993); Ramona Warren, *Parenting Alone*, Family Growth Electives (Elgin, Ill.: David C. Cook, 1993); Robert G. Barnes, *Single Parenting* (Wheaton, Ill.: Tyndale, 1992); Greg Cynaumon, *Helping Single Parents with Troubled Kids: A Ministry Resource for Pastors and Youth Workers* (Colorado Springs: NavPress, 1992); Gary Richmond, *Successful Single Parenting* (Eugene, Ore.: Harvest, 1990); Richard P. Olsen and Joe H. Leonard, Jr., *Ministry with Families in Flux: The Church and Changing Patterns of Life* (Louisville: Westminster/John Knox, 1990); Patricia Brandt with Dave Jackson, *Just Me and the Kids: A Course for Single Parents* (Elgin, Ill.: David C. Cook, 1985); Gerri Kerr, "Making It Alone: The Single-Parent Family," in Gloria Durka and Joanmarie Smith, eds., *Family Ministry* (Minneapolis: Winston, 1980), 142-167. See also Andrew J. Weaver, Linda A. Revilla and Harold G. Koenig, *Counseling Families Across the Stages of Life: A Handbook for Pastors and Other Helping Professionals* (Nashville: Abingdon, 2002), 101-118; and David Blackwelder, "Single Parents: In Need of Pastoral Support," in Robert J. Wicks and Richard D. Parsons, eds., *Clinical Handbook of Pastoral Counseling*, vol. 2 (Mahwah, N.J.: Paulist, 1993), 329-359.

9. See Susan Graham Mathis, "Good Samaritans for Single Parents," *Focus on the Family* (April 2004), 20-21. *Focus on the Family* magazine has a special edition just for single parents, which can be ordered at http://www.family.org.

10. We gratefully acknowledge the assistance of Alan Bandy in the research for this and the previous section.

11. We are indebted for the preceding information to R. Albert Mohler, Jr., "Should Spanking Be Banned? Parental Authority Under Assault," 6/22/2004, at http://www.crosswalk.com/news/weblogs/mohler/1269621.html. Mohler answers the question, "Does the Bible instruct parents to spank their children?" with an emphatic yes, contending that "[t]oday's outbreak of out-of-control children can be directly traced to the failure of parents to discipline their children." He notes that spanking should be "not the result of a parental loss of temper, nor of a parent's whim, but of moral necessity."

12. Alyce Oosterhuis, "Abolishing the Rod," *Journal of Psychology and Theology* 21, no. 2 (Summer 1993): 132.

13. Ibid.

14. Cf. Robert R. Gillogly, "Spanking Hurts Everybody," *Theology Today* 37, no. 4 (January 1981): 415. But see Robert E. Larzelere, "Child Abuse in Sweden," http://people.biola.edu/faculty/paulp/sweden2.html, who notes a possible increase in child abuse as one of the undesirable consequences of outlawing spanking.

15. Alice Miller, "Against Spanking," *Tikkun* 15, no. 2 (March/April 2000): 19.

16. Ibid., 17.

17. Mary S. Van Leeuwen, *Gender and Grace* (Downers Grove, Ill.: InterVarsity Press, 1990), 170; quoted in Oosterhuis, "Abolishing the Rod," 131.

18. Virginia Ramey Mollenkott, "Gender, Ethics, and Parenting," review of *The Case Against Spanking: How to Discipline Your Child Without Hitting*, by Irwin A. Hyman, *The Witness* (April 2000): 28. She notes that "Irwin Hyman, who teaches school psychology at Temple University, is nationally known for his campaign

against spanking on such television shows as *Oprah, Today,* and *Good Morning America.* In 1996 when California legislators voted on reintroducing physical punishment in their school systems, the motion was defeated in part by Hyman's photographs of bruised and welted children who had been legally paddled in one of the 23 states that still permit such abuses. Any adult who assaulted another adult and left welts and bruises would be prosecuted; why would it be legal to do to helpless children what adults are not permitted to do to one another?"

19. Oosterhuis, "Abolishing the Rod," 128.

20. See also Gillogly, "Spanking Hurts Everybody," 40.

21. Miller, "Against Spanking," 17. She states further that, "Severe traumas inflicted on infants lead to an increase in the release of stress hormones that destroy the existing, newly formed neurons and their interconnections." Once again, she is using strong rhetoric that assumes spanking is abusive and traumatizing. Also, "severe traumas" experienced by infants suggests something far more sinister and damaging than spanking.

22. Ibid., 18.

23. Ibid. She equates spanking with physical abuse.

24. Kenneth O. Gangel and Mark F. Rooker, "Response to Oosterhuis: Discipline Versus Punishment," *Journal of Psychology and Theology* 21, no. 2 (Summer 1993): 135. They write, "While it is true that certain Old Testament practices (e.g., sacrifices) were not to be continued in the New Testament age, there is more continuity between the Testaments than the author assumes. In her zeal to point out the antiquated nature of the use of the rod in the Old Testament, Oosterhuis overemphasizes the difference or discontinuity between the teaching of the Old and New Testament."

25. Gillogly, "Spanking Hurts Everybody," 41; Oosterhuis, "Abolishing the Rod," 129.

26. Oosterhuis, "Abolishing the Rod," 129.

27. Patricia Pike, "Response to Oosterhuis: To Abolish or Fulfill?" *Journal of Psychology and Theology* 21, no. 2 (1993): 138-141.

28. Ibid., 132. She states, "To deny historical development as central to God's management results in a stultifying adherence to the past at the cost of having God's word speak to the present." It should be noted at this point that Hebrews 12:5-11 does in fact suggest a continuity between the Old and the New Testament concepts of discipline. Although Hebrews 12 does not specifically mention using the "rod," its direct reference to Proverbs 3:12 warrants this conclusion.

29. For the legal aspect concerning parents' rights to spank see, *Child Protection Reform,* "Spanking as Discipline, not Abuse," at http://www.childprotectionreform.org/policy/spanking_home.htm.

30. Robert E. Larzelere, "Response to Oosterhuis: Empirically Justified Uses of Spanking: Toward a Discriminating View of Corporal Punishment," *Journal of Psychology and Theology* 21, no. 2 (1993): 142-147.

31. For information about the benefits of spanking from a Christian perspective see Walter L. Larimore, "Is Spanking Actually Harmful to Children?" *Focus On Your Family's Health,* at http://www.health.family.org/children/articles/a0000513.html.

32. E.g., some children may aptly respond to a stern verbal rebuke, while some may clearly get the message only when they receive a spanking. See Jesse Florea, "Does Spanking Work for All Kids?" *Focus on Your Child,* at http://www.focusonyourchild.com/develop/art1/A0000507.html.

33. See Lisa Whelchel, *Creative Correction: Extraordinary Ideas for Everyday Discipline* (Minneapolis: Bethany, 2000).

34. See James Dobson, *Bringing Up Boys* (Carol Stream, Ill.: Tyndale, 2001).

35. Robert Lewis, *Raising a Modern-Day Knight: A Father's Role in Guiding His Son to*

Authentic Manhood (Wheaton, Ill.: Tyndale, 1997). Lewis lists the following principles of manhood: (1) rejecting passivity; (2) accepting responsibility; (3) leading courageously; and (4) expecting a greater reward (60); and lists ten biblical ideals a wise father can impart to his son: loyalty, servant-leadership, kindness, humility, purity, honesty, self-discipline, excellence, integrity, and perseverance.

36. On same-sex marriage, see James Dobson, *Marriage Under Fire: Why We Must Win This Battle* (Sisters, Ore.: Multnomah, 2004); Erwin Lutzer, *The Truth About Same-Sex Marriage* (Chicago: Moody, 2004); Glenn T. Stanton and Bill Maier, *Marriage on Trial: The Case Against Same-Sex Marriage and Parenting* (Downers Grove, Ill.: InterVarsity Press, 2004); Mathew D. Staver, *Same-Sex Marriage: Putting Every Household at Risk* (Nashville: Broadman & Holman, 2004); and James R. White and Jeffrey D. Niell, *The Same Sex Controversy: Defending and Clarifying the Bible's Message About Homosexuality* (Minneapolis: Bethany, 2002).

37. See especially Clinton E. Arnold, *Three Crucial Questions About Spiritual Warfare* (Grand Rapids, Mich.: Baker, 1997) and *Powers of Darkness: Principalities and Powers in Paul's Letters* (Leicester, U.K./Downers Grove, Ill.: InterVarsity Press, 1992); Sydney H. T. Page, *Powers of Evil: A Biblical Study of Satan and Demons* (Grand Rapids, Mich.: Baker, 1995); and the articles on "Elements/Elemental Spirits of the World," "Power," and "Principalities and Powers," in Gerald F. Hawthorne, Ralph P. Martin, and Daniel G. Reid, eds., *Dictionary of Paul and His Letters* (Leicester, U.K./Downers Grove, Ill.: InterVarsity Press, 1993), 229-233, 723-725, and 746-752. See also the helpful survey entry by David Beck, "Spiritual Warfare," in Michael J. Anthony, ed., *Evangelical Dictionary of Christian Education* (Grand Rapids, Mich.: Baker, 2001), 660-662.

38. The only partial exception is Evelyn Christenson, *What Happens When We Pray for Our Families* (Colorado Springs: Chariot, 1992). There is no discussion of spiritual warfare in such popular books on marriage as Gary Chapman's *The Five Love Languages* (Chicago: Moody, 1995); Larry Crabb's *The Marriage Builder* (Grand Rapids, Mich.: Zondervan, 1992); Kay Arthur's *A Marriage Without Regrets* (Eugene, Ore.: Harvest, 2000); Willard Hartley's *His Needs, Her Needs* (Grand Rapids, Mich.: Revell, 1990); *The Language of Love*, by Gary Smalley and John Trent (Pomona, Calif.: Focus on the Family, 1988); or Laura Walker's *Dated Jekyll, Married Hyde* (Minneapolis: Bethany, 1997). There is nothing in best-selling books on parenting such as *Relational Parenting*, by Ross Campbell (Chicago: Moody, 2000); *Raising Heaven-bound Kids in a Hell-bent World*, by Eastman Curtis (Nashville: Thomas Nelson, 2000); *Children at Risk*, by James Dobson and Gary Bauer (Dallas: Word, 1990); or *The Gift of Honor*, by Gary Smalley and John Trent (Nashville: Thomas Nelson, 1987).

39. For an example from the life of David, see Köstenberger, "Marriage and Family in the New Testament," in Ken M. Campbell, ed., *Marriage and Family in the Biblical World* (Downers Grove, Ill.: InterVarsity Press, 2003), 279.

40. Peter T. O'Brien, *The Letter to the Ephesians*, Pillar New Testament Commentary (Grand Rapids, Mich.: Eerdmans, 1999), 457.

41. See Andreas J. Köstenberger, "What Does It Mean to Be Filled with the Spirit? A Biblical Investigation," *Journal for the Evangelical Theological Society* 40 (1997): 229-240.

42. On Ephesians 6:10-20 in the context of the letter of Ephesians as a whole, see especially the writings of Peter T. O'Brien: *Gospel and Mission in the Writings of Paul: An Exegetical and Theological Analysis* (Grand Rapids, Mich.: Baker, 1995), 109-131; *Letter to the Ephesians*, 456-490, especially 457-460; and Andreas J. Köstenberger and Peter T. O'Brien, *Salvation to the Ends of the Earth: A Biblical Theology of Mission*, New Studies in Biblical Theology (Leicester, U.K./Downers Grove, Ill.: InterVarsity Press, 2001), 196-198.

43. See, similarly, Beck, "Spiritual Warfare," 661, who identifies four critical issues: (1) underestimating the enemy; (2) identifying the enemy; (3) the nature of the weapons; and (4) the objective of the warfare.

44. For a discussion of biblical principles for dealing with sexual temptation see the heading "Young Men" in chapter 9 below.

45. On the background to 1 Corinthians 7 and for an exposition of verse 5, see especially Gordon D. Fee, *The First Epistle to the Corinthians*, New International Commentary on the New Testament (Grand Rapids, Mich.: Eerdmans, 1987), 266-283.

46. The question of whether it is only the husband's prayers (probably the immediate focus) or the couples' prayers (the necessary implication) that are hindered need not concern us here (see the relevant commentary literature; e.g., P. H. Davids, *The First Epistle of Peter*, New International Commentary on the New Testament [Grand Rapids, Mich.: Eerdmans, 1990], 123, n. 20). In the end, it is clearly the prayers of both members of the couple that are negatively affected by the husband's insensitivity toward his wife.

47. There are many excellent ministries aimed at strengthening Christian marriages and families. Among the best are Focus on the Family (http://www.family.org), FamilyLife (http://www.familylife.com), Family Dynamics (http://www.familydynamics.net) and the "Kingdom Family Initiative," which is part of the "Empowering Kingdom Growth" movement in the Southern Baptist Convention (http://www.sbc.net/ekg/default.asp; see especially the seven pillars of a kingdom family at http://www.sbc.net/ekg/EKG-7pillars.asp). Another organization that includes promoting biblical principles for marriage and family is the Council on Biblical Manhood and Womanhood (http://www.cbmw.org).

48. See, e.g., James W. Alexander, *Thoughts on Family Worship* (Morgan, Pa.: Soli Deo Gloria, 1998 [1847]); Clay Clarkson, *Our Twenty-four Family Ways: Family Devotional Guide* (Colorado Springs: Whole Heart Press, 2004); Jim Cromarty, *A Book for Family Worship* (Harrisburg, Pa.: Evangelical Press, 1997); Terry L. Johnson, *The Family Worship Book: A Resource Book for Family Devotions* (Fearn: Christian Focus Publications, 2000); David E. Prince, "Family Worship: Calling the Next Generation to Hope in God," posted at http://www.cbmw.org; Kerry Ptacek, *Family Worship: The Biblical Basis, Historical Reality, and Current Need* (Greenville, S.C.: Greenville Seminary Press, 2000).

49. See, e.g., Gloria Gaither and Shirley Dobson, *Creating Family Traditions: Making Memories in Festive Seasons* (Sisters, Ore.: Multnomah, 2004); Nöel Piper, *Treasuring God in Our Traditions* (Wheaton, Ill.: Crossway, 2003); Kent and Barbara Hughes, *Disciplines of a Godly Family* (Wheaton, Ill.: Crossway, 2004), 43-56.

CHAPTER 9:
UNDIVIDED DEVOTION TO THE LORD: THE DIVINE GIFT OF SINGLENESS

1. One indicator of the marginalization of singles in the contemporary church is the lack of Christian literature available on the topic. For example, while there are literally hundreds of Christian titles currently in print on issues related to marriage, a perusal of mainline Christian publishers reveals that there are at the most a few dozen titles currently in print that are solely devoted to singleness and related issues.

2. Rose M. Kreider and Tavia Simmons, *Marital Status: 2000* (Washington, D.C.: U.S. Census Bureau, 1993), 3. Note that this percentage includes the widowed, divorced, separated, and never married.

3. A 1989 survey of more than 20,000 missionaries from nineteen of the major mission sending agencies found that 16.3 percent of their missionaries were single. Nearly 85 percent of the single missionaries surveyed were female. Howard Erickson, "Single Missionary Survey," *Fundamentalist Journal* 8, no. 1 (January 1989): 27.

4. Daniel I. Block, "Marriage and Family in Ancient Israel," in Ken M. Campbell, ed., *Marriage and Family in the Biblical World* (Downers Grove, Ill.: InterVarsity Press, 2003), 57, n. 113. An older source is chapter 9 in Alfred Edersheim, *Sketches of Jewish Social Life in the Days of Christ* (London: Hodder & Stoughton, 1876).

5. Some argue that even today, adolescence is but a myth: see David Alan Black, *The Myth of Adolescence: Raising Responsible Children in an Irresponsible Society* (Danbury, Conn.: Davidson, 1999).

6. On widows, see the following essays in *Marriage and Family in the Biblical World*: Victor H. Matthews, "Marriage and Family in the Ancient Near East," 22-24; Block, "Marriage and Family in Ancient Israel," 71-72; Steven M. Baugh, "Marriage and Family in Ancient Greek Society," 111-112; and David W. Chapman, "Marriage and Family in Second Temple Judaism," 215-217. Note that for at least two reasons there were very few single widowers in Old Testament times. First, as today, in ancient times females enjoyed a longer lifespan than males. Thus, if a marriage partner passed away, it was usually the husband. Second, if a man was left single due to the death of his wife, it was comparably easy for him to remarry, especially if he was financially established (e.g., Abraham in Gen. 25:1). The most notable example of a widower in the Old Testament is Ezekiel, whose wife, "the delight of [his] eyes," was taken by Yahweh as a sign of Jerusalem's coming grief (Ezek. 24:15-27). The term for widower, *ʾalmān*, is found in the Old Testament only in a metaphorical sense in Jeremiah 51:5.

7. Block, "Marriage and Family in Ancient Israel," 71, notes that almost one third of the occurrences of the word for "widow," *ʾalmānâ*, are found in Mosaic legislation providing for the well-being of other vulnerable groups, such as orphans, aliens, and Levites.

8. However, high priests were explicitly forbidden to marry widows (Lev. 21:14). Interestingly, regular priests were allowed to marry widows (Lev. 21:7), yet both regular priests and high priests were forbidden to marry divorcees, prostitutes, or defiled women.

9. See Block, "Marriage and Family in Ancient Israel," 93-94; Chapman, "Marriage and Family in Second Temple Judaism," 216-217.

10. Cf. Exodus 22:22; Deuteronomy 14:29; 16:11, 14; 24:19-21; 27:19; Isaiah 1:17; Jeremiah 22:3; Zechariah 7:10.

11. Cf. Exodus 22:23; Psalm 68:5; 146:9; Proverbs 15:25; Malachi 3:5.

12. S. Safrai, "Home and Family," in S. Safrai and M. Stern, eds., *The Jewish People of the First Century* (Philadelphia: Fortress Press, 1987), 748. Cf. *m. Ketubbot* 13:5; *b. Ketubbot* 82b.

13. Safrai claims that "none of the ascetic trends within Pharisaic Judaism advocated celibacy, neither did most other movements" ("Home and Family," 748). However, both Philo and Pliny note that the Essenes rejected marriage (Philo, *Hypothetica* 2.14-17; Pliny, *Natural History* 5.73), yet Josephus was aware of a branch of the Essenes that did allow marriage (*Jewish War* 12.160-161). For more on celibacy in ancient Judaism, including the Qumran community, see Craig S. Keener, "Marriage," in Craig A. Evans and Stanley E. Porter, eds., *Dictionary of New Testament Background* (Downers Grove, Ill.: InterVarsity Press, 2000), 682-683; see also Chapman, "Marriage and Family in Second Temple Judaism," 211-215.

14. Perhaps another extrabiblical example of a divine call to celibacy is recorded in *b. Yebamot* 63b, where mention is made of a first-century Jew named Simeon ben Azzai who did not marry because "my soul lusts for the Torah." Note also the requirement for Levitical priests to abstain from sexual relations for the sake of ceremonial purity which, though different from compulsory celibacy, may present certain parallels with Jesus' category of "eunuchs for the kingdom" (see below).

15. See Block, "Marriage and Family in Ancient Israel," 49-52.

16. For a father's concern that his daughter might not find a husband see Sirach 42:9a: "A daughter keeps her father secretly wakeful, and worry over her robs him of sleep; when she is young, lest she do not marry . . ." Yet a father's worries concerning his daughter extend even further. The passage continues, ". . . or if married, lest she be hated; while a virgin, lest she be defiled or become pregnant in her father's house; or having a husband, lest she prove unfaithful, or, though married, lest she be barren" (Sir. 42:9b-10).

17. Thus, Paul can stipulate that church leaders are to be "faithful husbands" (1 Tim 3:2, 12). See chapter 11.

18. Clearly, their reasons differed. The Baptist's calling and lifestyle would have made marriage exceedingly difficult. In Jesus' case, it would have been unthinkable for the Christ and the Son of God to enter into marriage with a human female during his brief earthly sojourn, a fact that is supported biblically, historically, and theologically. Contra the unconvincing pop-theology presented in such works as Dan Brown, *The Da Vinci Code* (New York: Doubleday, 2003); William E. Phipps, *Was Jesus Married? The Distortion of Sexuality in the Christian Tradition* (New York: Harper & Row, 1970); Margaret Starbird, *The Woman with the Alabaster Jar: Mary Magdalene and the Holy Grail* (Santa Fe, N.M.: Bear, 1993); and the teaching of the Mormon church that Jesus had multiple wives. Cf., e.g., Darrick T. Evenson, *The Gainsayers* (Bountiful, Utah: Horizon, 1988). Contra also Darrell L. Bock, *Breaking the Da Vinci Code* (Nashville: Thomas Nelson, 2004), 33-34, who, though opposing the view that Jesus was married, writes that "if He [Jesus] had been married and fathered children, His marital relationship and His parenthood would not theoretically undercut His divinity but would have been reflections of His complete humanity. . . . Had Jesus been married, theoretically He still could have been and done all He did." However, it is hard to see how Jesus' deity (note the miraculous virgin birth) would have permitted him to engage in sexual union with a human female. Bock's discussion of the argument that Jesus, as a good Jew, and as a Jewish rabbi, would have been married, is also not entirely unproblematic. His point that "Jesus had no recognized official role within Judaism" and thus "was not technically a rabbi" (37) does not adequately acknowledge the fact that Jesus, in keeping with first-century Jewish custom, *took on the role* of a Jewish rabbi and was addressed as such by his followers and others (see Andreas J. Köstenberger, "Jesus as Rabbi in the Fourth Gospel," *Bulletin of Biblical Research* 8 [1998]: 97-128; his distinction between "rabbi" and "teacher" from Luke's Gospel is improperly founded as well; see John 1:38: "Rabbi" [which means Teacher]; similarly, John 20:16). Moreover, in his discussion, "Would being single make Jesus un-Jewish?" on pages 47-59, Bock seems to overstate how common and culturally acceptable it would have been for Jewish males in the first century to remain unmarried (cf. the above discussion of the fourth category of singleness in Old Testament times which was related to some type of divine call). On Paul, see further the discussion below.

19. Contra Albert Y. Hsu, who has argued that singleness *ought not* to be understood as a gift in the same sense as other spiritual gifts disclosed in Scripture. Cf. chapter 3, "The Myth of the Gift" in Albert Y. Hsu, *Singles at the Crossroads: A Fresh Perspective on Christian Singleness* (Downers Grove, Ill.: InterVarsity Press, 1997).

20. Of course, Paul also taught that even married people are to devote as much attention as possible to the advancement of the Kingdom of God. In the words of the apostle, "This is what I mean, brothers: the appointed time has grown very short. From now on, *let those who have wives live as though they had none,* and those who mourn as though they were not mourning, and those who rejoice as though they were not rejoicing, and those who buy as though they had no goods, and those who deal with the world as though they had no dealings with it. For the present form of this world

is passing away" (1 Cor. 7:29-31). Jesus, too, noted that family may be a hindrance in service of God (cf. Matt. 24:19; Luke 14:26).

21. One way to know, then, whether or not a person may be called to singleness is to see whether or not they can exercise self-control and remain sexually pure (1 Cor. 7:9). Beyond this, there is no substitute for following God's personal step-by-step leading through the Holy Spirit; and one's understanding of one's own calling will of necessity be provisional, since it is impossible to know what God might have in store for someone in the future.

22. There is some debate as to Paul's marital status (see especially F. F. Bruce, *Paul: Apostle of the Heart Set Free* [Grand Rapids, Mich.: Eerdmans, 1990; orig. Exeter, U.K.: Paternoster, 1977], 269-270; and David E. Garland, *1 Corinthians,* Baker Exegetical Commentary on the New Testament [Grand Rapids, Mich.: Baker, 2003], 276-277). The reference in 1 Corinthians 7:8 ("unmarried, as I am") would seem to suggest that Paul was single at least at the time of writing 1 Corinthians if not for most or all of his apostolic career. Yet on the basis of the fact that Paul was a rabbi and (possibly) a member of the Sanhedrin (cf. Acts 26:10; Phil. 3:5-6), which some claim would have required marriage, as well as other reasons (see further below), others have argued that Paul was either widowed or divorced. Apart from the fact that it is far from certain whether or not Paul was in fact a member of the Sanhedrin in the first place (Garland, *1 Corinthians,* 277), however, the best evidence does not support the argument that Sanhedrin membership required marriage. The Jewish Mishnah considers "rabbinical learning as the sole test of a candidate's eligibility" (cf. *m. Sanh.* 4:4; it may be taken for granted that the Sanhedrin was composed exclusively of Jews; cf. Emil Schürer, *The History of the Jewish People in the Age of Jesus Christ* [175 B.C.–A.D. 135], rev. and ed. Geza Vermes, Fergus Millar and Matthew Black [Edinburgh: T & T Clark, 1979], 2.211; it is doubtful that *b. Sanh.* 36b, "We do not appoint as members of the Sanhedrin an aged man, a eunuch or one who is childless," applied in the first century A.D. [Garland, *1 Corinthians,* 277]; another later rabbinic passage that is sometimes cited is *m. Yebamot* 6:6; see further below). While doubtless many (if not most) Sanhedrin members were married, this is different from saying that because Paul was a member of Sanhedrin at one time, he *must* therefore have been married.

23. But see the highly speculative view that Paul was married throughout his apostolic ministry based on the phrase *gnēsie syzyge* ("true yokefellow") in Philippians 4:3, which some have taken as a reference to Paul's wife (C. Wilfred Griggs, "I Have a Question," *Ensign* 6 [February 1976]: 36, adducing Clement of Alexandria, *Stromata* 3.53.1; Origen, *Commentary on the Epistle to the Romans* 1:1; cf. Sabine Baring-Gould, *A Study of St. Paul, His Character and Opinions* [London: Isbister, 1897], 213-214 [noting Eusebius's reference to Clement of Alexandria, see *Ecclesiastical History* 3.20], who entertains the possibility, only to reject the idea, that the "true yokefellow" in Philippians 4:3 may have been Lydia [so already the nineteenth-century French scholar Ernest Renan], whom Paul had married; see also the helpful entry in BDAG 954). According to Griggs, Paul in Philippians 4:3 asks "his wife to assist some of the women who had done so much on his behalf." However, this argument, which is highly conjectural and dubious on lexical grounds, has proved persuasive to few and in no way overturns Paul's explicit statement to the contrary in 1 Corinthians 7:8 (note that the view is not even mentioned in the recent magisterial commentary by Garland, *1 Corinthians,* 276-277; and Peter T. O'Brien, *Commentary on Philippians,* New International Greek Testament Commentary [Grand Rapids, Mich.: Eerdmans, 1991], 480, n. 22, includes it under "fanciful guesses"). See also Veselin Kesich, "Paul: Ambassador for Christ or Founder of Christianity?" *St. Vladimir's Theological Quarterly* 43, no. 3-4 (1999): 375-401, who asserts that "Paul was probably married" (392).

24. See the interchange between Joachim Jeremias, "War Paulus Witwer?" *Zeitschrift für die neutestamentliche Wissenschaft* 25 (1926): 310-312, who argues that Paul, as Sanhedrin member, must have been married (adducing *m. Yebamot* 6:6) and that he was probably widowed already at the time of his conversion; Erich Fascher, "Zur Witwerschaft des Paulus und der Auslegung von I Cor 7," *Zeitschrift für die neutestamentliche Wissenschaft* 28 (1929): 62-69; and Joachim Jeremias, "Nochmals: War Paulus Witwer?" *Zeitschrift für die neutestamentliche Wissenschaft* 28 (1929): 321-323; see also C. K. Barrett, *The First Epistle to the Corinthians,* Harper's New Testament Commentaries (New York: Harper & Row, 1968), 161; Edmund Arens, "Was Paul Married?" *Bible Today* 66 (1973): 1191; Jeremy Moiser, "A Reassessment of Paul's View of Marriage with Reference to 1 Cor. 7," *Journal for the Study of the New Testament* 18 (1983): 108; Gordon D. Fee, *The First Epistle to the Corinthians,* New International Commentary on the New Testament (Grand Rapids, Mich.: Eerdmans, 1987), 288, n. 7; and Jerome D. Murphy-O'Connor, *Paul: A Critical Life* (Oxford: Clarendon, 1996), 62-65. See also John McArthur, Jr., *1 Corinthians,* The MacArthur New Testament Commentary (Chicago: Moody, 1984), 163, who says that Paul "[l]ikely was a widower" primarily on the grounds of the other instances of "unmarried" (*agamos*) in 1 Corinthians 7 (i.e., 1 Cor. 7:11: divorced; 1 Cor. 7:34: divorced or widowed). However, it seems best to view *agamos* as the general term for being unmarried (BDAG 5), which would leave open, at least on the basis of 1 Corinthians 7:8, Paul's previous marital status.

25. Considered plausible and a real possibility by Bruce, *Paul: Apostle of the Heart Set Free,* 270. See also W. E. Phipps, "Is Paul's Attitude Toward Sexual Relations Contained in 1 Cor. 7.1?" *New Testament Studies* 28 (1982): 128; Simon J. Kistemaker, *1 Corinthians,* New Testament Commentary (Grand Rapids, Mich.: Baker, 1993), 215.

26. Garland, *1 Corinthians,* 277, who does acknowledge that "many argue that he [Paul] was not" married.

27. For an attempted reconstruction of the Corinthian background of 1 Corinthians 7 see chapter 10 below.

28. See further the discussion below.

29. From Eusebius, *Ecclesiastical History* 6.8.1: "At this time while Origen was conducting catechetical instruction at Alexandria, a deed was done by him which evidenced an immature and youthful mind, but at the same time gave the highest proof of faith and continence. For he took the words, 'There are eunuchs who have made themselves eunuchs for the kingdom of heaven's sake,' in too literal and extreme a sense. And in order to fulfill the Savior's word, and at the same time to take away from the unbelievers all opportunity for scandal, for, although young, he met for the study of divine things with women as well as men, he carried out in action the word of the Savior."

30. When priests could marry and have children (in accord with earlier medieval tradition), their children often became priests as well. The effect was that there were more and more priests, which resulted in a diluting of ecclesiastical power. Promoting celibacy was one way to ensure that only a select few were chosen as priests by the church hierarchy, which enabled it to recentralize its control over the church.

31. Augustine, *City of God* 14.26.

32. Aquinas, *Summa Theologica* 2.2.151-152.

33. Though note that Jesus uses "eunuchs" in a figurative rather than literal sense in Matthew 19:12.

34. See the discussion above. Despite efforts to demonstrate the contrary, the Roman Catholic understanding owes significantly more to later ecclesiastical tradition than to

New Testament teaching. See Andreas J. Köstenberger, "Review Article: The Apostolic Origins of Priestly Celibacy," *European Journal of Theology* 1 (1992): 173-179.

35. See chapter 12 below. See also George W. Knight, *Commentary on the Pastoral Epistles,* New International Greek Testament Commentary (Carlisle, U.K.: Paternoster/Grand Rapids, Mich.: Eerdmans, 1992), 173: "the home is the proving ground of fidelity for all officers."

36. In 2002 there were more than five million unmarried couples living together, and more than half of all marriages involved couples who had cohabited prior to marriage. Moreover, statistics show that cohabiting couples who marry are *more likely* to divorce than their non-cohabiting counterparts (Karen S. Peterson, "Cohabiting is not the Same as Commitment," *USA Today* [July 8, 2002]).

37. Cf. Monford Harris, "Pre-Marital Experience: A Covenantal Critique," *Judaism* 19 (1970): 134-144.

38. Cf., e.g., Deuteronomy 22:20-24; *Jubilees* 20:4; 33:20. See Craig S. Keener, "Adultery, Divorce," in *Dictionary of New Testament Background,* 10, who notes that this penalty was not enforced in New Testament times.

39. See the discussion of the betrothal view in chapter 11.

40. It is important to note that in 1 Corinthians 6:15-17 Paul does not say that intercourse with a prostitute means that one is married to her. Rather, he says that it results in a one-flesh relationship. It is important to make this distinction, for marriage is much more than sexual intercourse. Indeed, in the 1 Corinthians 6:15-17 passage Paul is not teaching on marriage per se, but rather on sexual immorality and its effect upon one's spiritual relationship with God. In this passage Paul notes that it is the Christ/Church relationship that is threatened by the illicit believer/prostitute union, not the marriage relationship. Furthermore, Paul writes that it is on account of the Christ/Church spiritual relationship, not the marriage relationship, that the believer is to abstain from sexual intercourse with a harlot.

41. As David Clyde Jones, *Biblical Christian Ethics* (Grand Rapids, Mich.: Baker, 1994), 158, notes, "The essential moral problem with nonmarital sexual intercourse is that it performs a life-uniting act without a life-uniting intent, thus violating its intrinsic meaning." Paul Ramsey, *One Flesh: A Christian View of Sex Within, Outside, and Before Marriage,* Grove Booklets on Ethics 8 (Bramcote, U.K.: Grove, 1975), 13, points out along similar lines that "[e]xtramarital acts of sexual love are . . . attempts to put asunder what God joined together . . ." Cf. Richard J. Foster, "Sexuality and Singleness," in David K. Clark and Robert V. Rakestraw, eds., *Readings in Christian Ethics,* vol. 2, *Issues and Applications* (Grand Rapids, Mich.: Baker, 1996), 157. Contra the unconvincing attempt by John F. Dedek, "Premarital Petting and Coitus," *Chicago Studies* 9 (1970): 227-242, to argue that there is no biblical condemnation of premarital sex. According to Dedek, *porneia* in Matthew 5:32 and 19:9 means adultery; in 1 Corinthians 5:1 it means incest; in 1 Corinthians 6:12-20 (cf. 1 Thess. 4:3-4) it means union with a prostitute; in Galatians 5:19-20 and Ephesians 5:5 it might mean adultery; in 1 Corinthians 6:9 it probably means prostitution and promiscuous sexual relations; and in Acts 15:20, 29 it refers to irregular marriages listed in Leviticus 18 such as incestuous unions. Deuteronomy 22:1-29 condemns a woman's deceiving her husband prior to marriage into thinking she is a virgin when she is not; rape; and sleeping with a woman already engaged to be married to another man. However, Dedek's attempt to determine Scripture's stance toward premarital sex exclusively by a study of *porneia* is misguided, first and foremost because he unduly ignores the foundational Old Testament passage on marriage, Genesis 2:23-24, and its covenant character. Moreover, even on Dedek's own terms, it clearly follows that if *porneia* means sexual immorality—which is everywhere forbidden in Scripture—and the only venue in which sexual relations are considered moral in

Scripture is within the marriage covenant, sex without, outside, and before marriage are equally beyond the pale of biblical morality.

42. Ramsey, *One Flesh*, 18.

43. Cf. Judith Treas and Deirdre Giesen, "Sexual Infidelity Among Married and Cohabiting Americans," *Journal of Marriage and the Family* 62 (2000): 48-60.

44. Matthew 5:28; Ephesians 5:3-4; 1 Timothy 4:12; 2 Timothy 2:22.

45. On modesty, see 1 Timothy 2:9-10; 1 Peter 3:3-6. On self-control, see 1 Timothy 2:9, 15; 3:2; Titus 1:8; 2:2, 5, 6. For a list of virtues to be cultivated by younger women, see the section on older women mentoring younger women in chapter 5, above. Other relevant passages for younger men are 1 Peter 5:5 and 1 John 2:13b, 14b (see further below). For relevant literature on modesty see especially Wendy Shalit, *A Return to Modesty: Discovering the Lost Virtue* (New York: Free Press, 1999); Jeff Pollard, *Christian Modesty and the Public Undressing of America* (San Antonio: The Vision Forum, 2003); Mary K. Mohler, "Modeling Modesty" (Louisville: The Southern Baptist Theological Seminary, n.d.), posted at www.albertmohler.com/Modeling Modesty.pdf; Nancy Leigh DeMoss, *The Look: Does God Really Care What I Wear?* (Buchanan, Mich.: Revive Our Hearts, n.d.). Scripture does not seem to address modesty with regard to men.

46. On betrothal customs in the ancient world, see the following essays in *Marriage and Family in the Biblical World*: Matthews, "Marriage and Family in the Ancient Near East," 7-14; Block, "Marriage and Family in Ancient Israel," 54-58; Baugh, "Marriage and Family in Ancient Greek Society," 109-110; Susan Treggiari, "Marriage and Family in Roman Society," 151-153; and Chapman, "Marriage and Family in Second Temple Judaism," 185-188.

47. See the sources mentioned in the previous note.

48. The question arises whether or not ancient betrothal practices and customs (such as marriages being arranged by parents, the payment of a dowry, and so on) are normative for believers today as well. Most would affirm that they are not. See, e.g., Joshua Harris, *I Kissed Dating Goodbye* (Sisters, Ore.: Multnomah, 1997); idem, *Boy Meets Girl: Say Hello to Courtship* (Sisters, Ore.: Multnomah, 2000); Jeff and Danielle Myers, *Of Knights and Fair Maidens: A Radical New Way to Develop Old-fashioned Relationships* (Dayton, Tenn.: Heartland Educational Consultants, 1996); and Michael Phillips and Judy Phillips, *Best Friends for Life* (Minneapolis: Bethany, 1997). For arguments in favor of continuing ancient betrothal practices today, see Wayne Israel, "Betrothal: Should We Kiss Courtship Goodbye?" *Home School Digest* 11, no. 2 (Spring 2000): 21-22; Jonathan Lindvall, "The Dangers of Dating: Scriptural Romance (parts 1 and 2)," at http://www.boldchristianliving.com/ site/articles/romance1.php and http://www.boldchristianliving.com/site/articles/ romance2.php (see also the comparison chart of dating, courtship, and betrothal at the same website); and Michael Pearl, "To Betroth or Not to Betroth? That Is the Question," *No Greater Joy* (January/February 2000): 1-11, 13-15.

49. See the previous section.

50. Cf. the incident involving Amnon and Tamar in 1 Samuel 13, where it is said that Amnon "fell in love" with his beautiful half-sister Tamar (1 Sam. 13:1; cf. v. 4) and subsequently raped her (1 Sam. 13:11-14).

51. See the resources, both pro-courtship and pro-betrothal, listed in note 48, above. It does seem reasonable to conclude that at least certain aspects of ancient betrothal customs, such as the payment of a dowry or the prearranging of marriages by the spouses' parents, are cultural rather than of abiding and normative relevance. At the same time, it does seem appropriate to be cautious and conservative in this area, to guard one's heart in all purity, and to trust the Lord to lead in his time and in his way. The fact that neither Jesus nor Paul directly comment on the subject seems to

suggest that there is a certain degree of latitude and Christian freedom on the subject, which would appear to caution against dogmatism in this area.

52. Of course, it is not only young single men who struggle in this area, but married men as well. Young unmarried men ought not to think that marriage by itself will eliminate these kinds of struggles. Taking appropriate steps prior to marriage is essential for experiencing a biblical, pure marriage later on. For help with pornography, see http://www.pureintimacy.org (a ministry by Focus on the Family) as well as http://www.settingcaptivesfree.com. Three practical books on accountability in this area are Stephen Arterburn and Fred Stoeker, *Every Man's Battle: Winning the War on Sexual Temptation One Victory at a Time* (Colorado Springs: WaterBrook, 2000); Stephen Arterburn, Fred Stoeker, and Mike Yorkey, *Every Man's Battle Guide: Weapons for the War Against Sexual Temptation* (Colorado Springs: WaterBrook, 2003); and Joshua Harris, *Not Even a Hint* (Sisters, Ore.: Multnomah, 2003).

53. While there is no direct biblical prohibition of masturbation, solitary self-stimulated sex should still be considered morally wrong because, as Daniel R. Heimbach (*True Sexual Morality: Biblical Standards for a Culture in Crisis* [Wheaton, Ill.: Crossway, forthcoming, 2004]) notes, it "opposes every positive moral characteristic revealed to be essential in God's design for sex": (1) sex is part of a personal relationship with another person—masturbation is non-relational; (2) sex is to be exclusive—masturbation typically involves sexually impure thoughts; (3) sex is to be special and intimate—masturbation is frequent and shallow; (4) sex is to be fruitful (productive)—masturbation treats sex like a commodity to be consumed; (5) sex is to operate within the context of selfless love—masturbation is designed to satisfy oneself; (6) sex is multi-dimensional—masturbation separates the physical from everything else; (7) sex is to be complementary—solitary self-stimulation is non-unitive (i.e., not designed to produce sexual union between two individuals).

54. For a discussion on young *married* women (especially in Titus 2) see chapter 5, above.

55. See already the comments on widows in Old Testament teaching above. See also the helpful and practical comments on widows in John MacArthur, Jr., *Different By Design: Discovering God's Will for Today's Man and Woman* (Wheaton, Ill.: Victor, 1994), 90-98, including the following characteristics drawn from 1 Timothy 5: a mature woman, a devoted wife, a devoted mother, hospitable, humble, unselfish, and kind (94-96).

56. Steven M. Baugh, "1–2 Timothy, Titus," in Clinton E. Arnold, ed., *Zondervan Illustrated Bible Backgrounds Commentary,* vol. 3 (Grand Rapids, Mich.: Zondervan, 2002), 467; cf. Jerome D. Quinn and William C. Wacker, *The First and Second Letters to Timothy,* Eerdmans Critical Commentary (Grand Rapids, Mich.: Eerdmans, 2000), 412-449.

57. This is borne out amply by Old Testament teaching regarding widows (Ex. 22:22-23; Deut. 10:8; 14:29; 24:17-21; 26:12, 14; 27:19; etc.).

58. This matches Paul's self-description as praying night and day (2 Tim. 1:3; cf. Eph. 6:18; Phil. 1:4) and his exhortation in 1 Thessalonians 5:17. For a New Testament example, see Anna the prophetess, who "had lived with her husband seven years after her marriage, and then was a widow until she was eighty-four. She never left the temple but worshiped night and day, fasting and praying" (Luke 2:36-37).

59. On single parenthood, see already our comments in chapter 8, above.

60. This, of course, does not affect our comments in chapter 11 below on biblically legitimate or illegitimate divorce and the scriptural teaching on remarriage. Specifically, single parents who are the guilty party in a divorce should not be encouraged to remarry but to be reconciled to their former spouse.

61. Cf. David P. Gushee, *Getting Marriage Right: Realistic Counsel for Saving and Strengthening Relationships* (Grand Rapids, Mich.: Baker, 2004), 57-83.

62. One ministry devoted to divorcees is DivorceCare, regarding which information can be accessed at http://www.divorcecare.com. For a very helpful resource for churches interested in starting a divorce recovery ministry see also Bill Flanagan, *Developing A Divorce Recovery Ministry: A How-To Manual* (Colorado Springs: NavPress, 1991).

63. See also the helpful discussion by MacArthur, *Different by Design*, 98-106, whose discussion includes headings such as Celebrating Singleness, The Difficulty of Being Single, The Gift of Singleness, What If You Don't Think You Have the Gift? and The Advantages of Being Single. Under the final rubric, MacArthur distills the following advantages from 1 Corinthians 7:25-40: (1) less pressure from the system; (2) fewer problems of the flesh; (3) more detachment from this passing world; (4) freedom from the preoccupations of marriage; and (5) not being bound to a lifelong relationship.

64. Cf. Judith M. Gundry-Volf, "The Least and the Greatest," in Marcia J. Bunge, ed., *The Child in Christian Thought* (Grand Rapids, Mich.: Eerdmans, 2001), 53, who points to the similarity of "Paul's and Jesus' restraint concerning procreation—which contrasts with conventional Jewish stress on marriage and sex for procreation—derived from their *shared outlook of eschatological expectation*" (emphasis added).

CHAPTER 10:
ABANDONING NATURAL RELATIONS:
THE BIBLICAL VERDICT ON HOMOSEXUALITY

1. Homosexuality had been classified as a mental disorder in all of the editions of the *Diagnostic and Statistical Manual of Mental Disorders* (known as the "DSM") since its inception in 1952. It was in the sixth printing of the second edition of the DSM in 1973 that homosexuality was reclassified as acceptable behavior.

2. John Jefferson Davis, *Evangelical Ethics: Issues Facing the Church Today*, 2d ed. (Phillipsburg, N.J.: Presbyterian & Reformed, 1993), 95-97.

3. This includes biblical scholarship on homosexuality. As Robert A. J. Gagnon, *The Bible and Homosexual Practice: Texts and Hermeneutics* (Nashville: Abingdon, 2001), 38-39, n. 5, notes, in each of four recent collections of essays on the subject, scholars opposed to same-sex intercourse are in a distinct minority: 4 or 5 out of 13 of the contributors in Jeffrey S. Siker, ed., *Homosexuality in the Church: Both Sides of the Debate* (Louisville: Westminster/John Knox, 1994) are opponents of homosexuality; 2 out of 9 in Robert L. Brawley, ed., *Biblical Ethics and Homosexuality: Listening to Scripture* (Louisville: Westminster/John Knox, 1996); 3 or 4 out of 13 in Choon-Leong Seow, ed., *Homosexuality and Christian Community* (Louisville: Westminster/John Knox, 1996); and 4 out of 11 in David L. Balch, *Homosexuality, Science, and the "Plain Sense" of Scripture* (Grand Rapids, Mich.: Eerdmans, 2000). This amounts to a two-thirds representation of scholars advocating a tolerant attitude toward homosexuality in these four volumes.

4. The Episcopal Church USA. Cf. David W. Jones's article on homosexuality in which he traces the connection between the acceptance of homosexuality and the endorsement of feminism in many of the mainline Christian denominations (David W. Jones, "Egalitarianism and Homosexuality: Connected or Autonomous Ideologies," *Journal for Biblical Manhood and Womanhood* 8, no. 2 [Fall 2003]: 5-19).

5. E.g., the Southern Baptist Convention, the Presbyterian Church in America, and the Lutheran Church-Missouri Synod.

6. For a discussion of Genesis 1–3 and homosexuality see Gagnon, *Bible and Homosexual Practice*, 56-62.

7. Cf. ibid., 169-176.

8. It is interesting to note, however, that although same-sex couples cannot participate in God's complementary design for gender roles in marriage, one partner almost always adopts the leadership role (assigned by God to the husband), while the other adopts that of the helper assigned by God to the wife (this may be reflected in the existence of two separate words for homosexuality in the New Testament, *arsenokoitēs* [1 Tim. 1:10] and *malakos* ["soft"; both terms are used in 1 Cor. 6:9-10]; cf. Johannes P. Louw and Eugene A. Nida, *Greek-English Lexicon of the New Testament Based on Semantic Domains* [2d ed.; New York: United Bible Societies, 1989], 1.772, who suggest that the former term may designate the active and the latter term the passive male partner in homosexual intercourse). This distorted manifestation of gender roles within a homosexual relationship is a testimony to the Creator's design of complementarity that is an integrated component, not only of the biblical model of marriage and the family, but also of other societal relationships such as parent/child (Eph. 6:1-4), employer/employee (Eph. 6:5-9), government/citizen (Rom. 13:1-7), and pastor/church member relationships (Heb. 13:17). Homosexual couples, however, while they may attempt to mimic the complementarity that is integral to God's design for marriage and the family, are inherently incapable of manifesting the true reciprocity of roles assigned by God to the differing genders within the context of a husband/wife relationship.

9. Cf. Gagnon, *Bible and Homosexual Practice,* 164-169, who also cites excess passion and animal heterosexuality as minor arguments for the unnaturalness of same-sex intercourse (176-180).

10. Procreation within a heterosexual context is discernible also in the Lord's description of marriage as a "one flesh" relationship (Gen. 2:24), which seems to presuppose male-female sexual intercourse, and may be implied in the account of God's creation of the living creatures "according to their kinds" (Gen. 1:21, 24, 25)—that is, separate in gender with the ability to procreate.

11. The argument is sometimes made that certain people are "born" homosexuals, just as they are born black or white, male or female (cf. D. F. Swaab and M. A. Hoffman, "An Enlarged Suprachiasmatic Nucleus in Homosexual Men," *Brain Research* 537 [1990]: 141-148; Simon LeVay, "A Difference in Hypothalamic Structure Between Heterosexual and Homosexual Men," *Science* 235 [August 30, 1991]: 1034-1037; J. Michael Bailey and Richard C. Pillard, "A Genetic Study of Male Sexual Orientation," *Archives of General Psychiatry* 48 [December 1991]: 1089-1096; and J. Michael Bailey and Deana S. Benishay, "Familial Aggregation of Female Sexual Orientation," *American Journal of Psychiatry* 150, no. 2 [1993]: 272-277). Hence, homosexuality ought to be viewed as moral behavior, for those who inherit "gay genes" must be allowed to embrace their inborn sexual orientation.

    However, even *if* homosexuality could be proven to be genetic, this would still not make it morally acceptable, for a genetic predisposition toward an act or a behavior can never be the proper basis for determining its moral legitimacy. To give but one example, a male with a genetic glandular condition resulting in the production of too much testosterone, and thus a higher-than-normal sex drive, could not appeal to his genetic condition to validate the morality of rape, incest, or pedophilia (for additional information on homosexual advocates' arguments from genetic determinism and a biblical response, see Sherwood O. Cole, "Biology, Homosexuality, and the Biblical Doctrine of Sin," *Bibliotheca Sacra* 157, no. 627 [July–September 2000]: 348-361; cf. Jeffrey Satinover, "The Gay Gene?" posted at http://www.cbmw.org).

    Another argument that is occasionally made is that homosexuality is linked to hormonal imbalances. If homosexuality were caused by a hormonal imbalance, one would assume that hormonal treatment would be highly successful. However, as Feinberg and Feinberg write, "Some have suggested that homosexuality is traceable to an imbalance in sex hormones. . . . Male homosexuality, however, has been treated with the injection of male hormones with very limited success" (John S. Feinberg and Paul D. Feinberg, *Ethics for a Brave New World* [Wheaton, Ill.: Crossway, 1993], 188), with reference to Garfield Tourney, "Hormones and Homosexuality," *Homosexual Behavior: A Modern Reappraisal* [ed. Judd Marmor; New York: Basic Books, 1980]).

12. For example, various surveys have reported that the average homosexual male has somewhere between 50 and 500 sexual partners in a lifetime, with some having well over 1000 (cf. Robert T. Michael, *Sex in America: A Definitive Study* [Boston: Little, Brown, 1994]; Richard A. Kaslow et al., "The Multicenter AIDS Cohort Study: Rationale, Organization, and Selected Characteristics of Participants," *American Journal of Epidemiology* 126, no. 2 [August 1987]: 310-318; Alan P. Bell and Martin S. Weinberg, *Homosexualities: A Study of Diversity Among Men and Women* [New York: Simon and Schuster, 1978], 308-309; one study reported that only seven of the 156 homosexual couples they studied were monogamous. Cf. David P. McWhirter and Andrew M. Mattison, *The Male Couple: How Relationships Develop* [Englewood Cliffs, N.J.: Prentice Hall, 1984], 3; also note that while surveys indicate that the average lesbian has multiple sexual partners, the total number of partners in a lifetime was far fewer than for male homosexuals). This is very different from the monogamy and fidelity prescribed by the biblical/traditional model of marriage and the family. Moreover, although exact numbers are difficult to determine on account of the novelty of homosexual marriage, the promiscuity that is often part of the homosexual lifestyle leads to the logical conclusion that homosexual marriages (or civil unions) will not be durable (cf. Russ Smith, *Baltimore City Paper Online*: "It's likely that half of homosexual marriages will end in divorce" ["Right Field," at http://www.citypaper.com/2004-01-28/right.html]).

13. Those who favor homosexuality sometimes agree that promiscuity is a problem among homosexuals but insist that the promiscuity, not homosexuality itself, is the real problem. They argue, further, that monogamous homosexual relationships are discouraged by a society that shuns homosexuality as a deviant lifestyle. Their solution is that if we legalize gay marriages, homosexuals will abandon their promiscuity. There are at least two problems with this argument, however: first, it assumes that society is to blame for not accepting homosexuality; and second, this argument overlooks the fact that regardless of society's acceptance of homosexuality—whether promiscuous or monogamous—homosexuality is nonetheless morally unacceptable according to Scripture.

14. Cf. Romans 1:21-28, 32, on which see further the discussion below. It should be noted that Romans 1:26 is the only explicit reference to lesbianism in the New Testament. While it falls under the same general prohibition as homosexuality, lesbianism does not appear to have been sufficiently prominent to warrant separate treatment.

15. The following presentation does not adopt a neutral stance toward homosexuality, nor is it primarily directed toward homosexual advocates themselves. Rather, in what follows we will discuss some of the major efforts at reinterpreting scriptural passages on homosexuality in order to equip readers to interact with proponents of homosexuality. For a helpful resource comparing the two major positions on homosexuality see Robert A. J. Gagnon and Dan O. Via, *Homosexuality and the Bible: Two Views* (Minneapolis: Fortress, 2003).

16. Genesis 9:20-27; 19:4-11; Leviticus 18:22; 20:13; Deuteronomy 23:17-18; Judges 19:22-25; 1 Kings 14:24; 15:12; 22:46; 2 Kings 23:7; Job 36:14; Ezekiel 16:50 (perhaps also Ezek. 18:12; 33:26); Romans 1:26-27; 1 Corinthians 6:9-10; 1 Timothy 1:9-10; 2 Peter 2:6; Jude 7; Revelation 21:8; 22:15. Cf. Gagnon, *Bible and Homosexual Practice*, 432.

17. In addition to these passages, some advocates of homosexuality claim close personal

relationships between members of the same sex (such as Jonathan and David or Ruth and Naomi) as examples of homosexual relationships in Scripture (see, e.g., Tom Horner, *Jonathan Loved David: Homosexuality in Biblical Times* [Philadelphia: Westminster, 1978], especially chapters 2–3; but see M. H. Pope, "Homosexuality," *The Interpreter's Dictionary of the Bible: Supplementary Volume* [Nashville: Abingdon, 1976], 416-417; M. Bonnington and B. Fyall, *Homosexuality and the Bible* [Cambridge: Grove, 1996], 9; and especially Gagnon, *Bible and Homosexual Practice,* 146-154 [citing as the "definitive refutation of a homophile reading of the text" Markus Zehnder, "Exegetische Beobachtungen zu den David-Jonathan-Geschichten," *Biblica* 79 (1998): 153-179]). However, since it is transparently fallacious and unwarranted to infer homosexuality from close same-sex relationships in the Bible, we will not deal with this argument in the discussion below.

18. See Isaiah 1:9, 10; 3:9; 13:19; 23:14; 49:18; 50:40; Lamentations 4:6; Ezekiel 16:46, 48, 49, 53, 55, 56; Amos 4:11; Zephaniah 2:9; Matthew 10:15; 11:23, 24; Luke 10:12; 17:29; Romans 9:29 (quoting Isa. 1:9); 2 Peter 2:6; Jude 7; Revelation 11:8.

19. For a discussion and refutation of various pro-homosexual interpretations of the Sodom and Gomorrah narrative see James R. White and Jeffrey D. Niell, *The Same Sex Controversy: Defending and Clarifying the Bible's Message About Homosexuality* (Minneapolis: Bethany, 2002), 27-52; and especially Gagnon, *Bible and Homosexual Practice,* 71-91, who also discusses Ham's act and Noah's curse in Genesis 9:20-27 (ibid., 63-71) and the rape of the Levite's concubine in Judges 19:22-25 (ibid., 91-97).

20. Walter Barnett, *Homosexuality and the Bible: An Interpretation* (Wallingford, Pa.: Pendle Hill Publications, 1979), 8-9.

21. Ibid.

22. Letha Scanzoni and Virginia Ramey Mollenkott, *Is the Homosexual My Neighbor? Another Christian View* (San Francisco: Harper & Row, 1978), 57-58.

23. D. Sherwin Bailey, *Homosexuality and the Western Christian Tradition* (London: Longmans, Green, 1955), 4.

24. Harry A. Woggon, "A Biblical and Historical Study of Homosexuality," *Journal of Religion and Health* 20, no. 2 (Summer 1981): 158.

25. John J. McNeill, "Homosexuality: Challenging the Church to Grow," *Christian Century* 104, no. 8 (March 11, 1987): 244. See also John J. McNeill, *The Church and the Homosexual* (Kansas City, Mo.: Sheed, Andrews, & McMeel, 1976), 42-50.

26. John Boswell, *Christianity, Social Tolerance, and Homosexuality: Gay People in Western Europe from the Beginning of the Christian Era to the Fourteenth Century* (Chicago: University of Chicago Press, 1980), 93.

27. James B. Nelson, "Homosexuality and the Church," *St. Luke's Journal of Theology* 22, no. 3 (June 1979): 199. See also Barnett, *Homosexuality and the Bible,* 7-10. The reference to Sodom being "haughty" and committing "an abomination" before the Lord in Ezekiel 16:50 is often (unconvincingly) cited in support of this view.

28. See also Allan N. Moseley, *Thinking Against the Grain* (Grand Rapids, Mich.: Kregel, 2003), 189-190.

29. The ESV renderings, "know" and "have not known," in Genesis 19:5, 8, while not technically inaccurate, unfortunately do not make this adequately clear in our contemporary English-speaking setting, since clearly what was at issue in these passages was more than merely making someone else's acquaintance in the sense of "getting to know" them (the common meaning of "know" in modern English), namely having sexual relations with them.

30. For a discussion and refutation of various pro-homosexual interpretations of the

Levitical Holiness Code see White and Niell, *Same Sex Controversy*, 53-108; and especially Gagnon, *Bible and Homosexual Practice*, 111-146.

31. Some interpreters have questioned the applicability of Leviticus 18:22 and 20:13 on the basis that no Old Testament laws apply to Christians today (cf. Scanzoni and Mollenkott, *Is the Homosexual My Neighbor?* 60-61, 112-115). However, this argument in its extreme form is indefensible, and the issue calls for greater nuancing. See, e.g., William J. Webb, *Slaves, Women, and Homosexuals: Exploring the Hermeneutics of Cultural Analysis* (Downers Grove, Ill.: InterVarsity Press, 2001), 28-29, 81-82, 87-90, 102-104, 108-110, 131-133, 155-157, 161, 177-178, 181-183, 196-200, 204-206, 216-220, 231-234, 250-252, who concludes after an extensive analysis that "the biblical prohibitions regarding homosexuality . . . should be maintained today" (250; this does not imply endorsement of Webb's "redemptive-movement hermeneutic" nor his views on the role of women in the church). On the relationship between the Old and the New Testament, see also John Feinberg, ed., *Continuity and Discontinuity: Perspectives on the Relationship Between the Old and New Testaments* (Wheaton, Ill.: Crossway, 1988); and Wayne G. Strickland, ed., *Five Views on Law and Gospel* (Grand Rapids, Mich.: Zondervan, 1993).

32. Barnett, *Homosexuality and the Bible*, 12.

33. Boswell, *Christianity, Social Tolerance, and Homosexuality*, 101-102.

34. Scanzoni and Mollenkott, *Is the Homosexual My Neighbor?* 60.

35. See Webb, *Slaves, Women, and Homosexuals*, whose conclusion is that "[v]irtually all of the criteria applicable to the issue suggest to varying degrees that the biblical prohibitions regarding homosexuality, even within a covenant form, should be maintained today. There is no significant dissonance within the biblical data" (250).

36. This is not to deny the existence of homosexual cult prostitution in ancient Israel, on which see Gagnon, *Bible and Homosexual Practice*, 100-110.

37. We have no record of Jesus commenting on the subject, which suggests that this was not a controversial issue in first-century Palestinian Judaism (though see chapter 3, "The Witness of Jesus," in Gagnon, *Bible and Homosexual Practice*; among other things, Gagnon contends that Jesus' reference to *porneiai* in Mark 7:21-23 implies a condemnation of homosexuality [191]).

38. The following discussion of homosexuality is adapted from Andreas J. Köstenberger's forthcoming commentary on the Pastoral Epistles in the New Expositor's Bible Commentary (Grand Rapids, Mich.: Zondervan). For a helpful treatment, see Thomas E. Schmidt, *Straight and Narrow? Compassion and Clarity in the Homosexuality Debate* (Leicester, U.K./Downers Grove, Ill.: InterVarsity Press, 1995). For an interaction and refutation of revisionist interpretations of Romans 1 see Moseley, *Thinking Against the Grain*, 193-194. See also the thorough treatment in Gagnon, *Bible and Homosexual Practice*, 229-303.

39. For a discussion and refutation of various pro-homosexual interpretations of Romans 1:26-27 see White and Niell, *Same Sex Controversy*, 109-140.

40. James E. Miller, "The Practices of Romans 1:26: Homosexual or Heterosexual?" *Novum Testamentum* 37 (1996): 1-11 claims that Romans 1:26 refers to unnatural heterosexual practice rather than homosexuality, but this is rendered unlikely by the close parallel in Romans 1:27. See further the critique by Thomas R. Schreiner, *Romans*, Baker Exegetical Commentary on the New Testament (Grand Rapids, Mich.: Baker, 1998), 94, n. 5.

41. Cf. Everett Ferguson, *Backgrounds of Early Christianity*, 2d ed. (Grand Rapids, Mich.: Eerdmans, 1993), 63-74, especially 63: "Paul's judgment on Gentile morality in Romans 1:18-32 finds considerable confirmation in other sources of the time." Ferguson proceeds to discuss Greco-Roman views on and practices of homosexuality and prostitution.

42. For a possible pre-Christian use of the term see *Sibylline Oracles* 2:73 ("Do not practice homosexuality"). James B. De Young, "The Source and NT Meaning of 'Αρσενοκοίται with Implications for Christian Ethics and Ministry," *The Master's Seminary Journal* 3 (1992): 211-215, argues that Paul coined the term *arsenokoitēs*.

43. For a brief discussion and refutation of various pro-homosexual interpretations of 1 Corinthians 6:9-10 and 1 Timothy 1:9-10 see White and Niell, *Same Sex Controversy*, 141-161.

44. It is often noted that "to Corinthianize" (*korinthiazō*, coined by the Greek writer Aristophanes [c. 450–385 B.C.]) served as a shorthand for sexual immorality and "Corinthian girl" referred to a prostitute (but see the discussion in David E. Garland, *1 Corinthians*, Baker Exegetical Commentary on the New Testament [Grand Rapids, Mich.: Baker, 2003], 240-241, who notes that these epithets were coined with a view toward Greek, not Roman Corinth but acknowledges the prominence of Aphrodite, the Greek goddess of erotic love, in the city). See also Gordon D. Fee, *The First Epistle to the Corinthians*, New International Commentary on the New Testament (Grand Rapids, Mich.: Eerdmans, 1987), 2-3, who says that "Paul's Corinth was at once the New York, Los Angeles, and Las Vegas of the ancient world" (3).

45. The renderings "males who are penetrated sexually by males" and "males who sexually penetrate males" are chosen by Garland, *1 Corinthians*, 214, with reference to Hans Lietzmann, *Die Briefe des Apostels Paulus: An die Korinther I, II*, 5th ed., ed. Werner G. Kümmel, Handbuch zum Neuen Testament 9 (Tübingen: Mohr, 1949), 27; C. K. Barrett, *The First Epistle to the Corinthians*, Harper's New Testament Commentaries (New York: Harper & Row, 1968), 140; Charles H. Talbert, *Reading Corinthians: A Literary and Theological Commentary on 1 and 2 Corinthians* (New York: Crossroad, 1987), 23; and Gagnon, *Bible and Homosexual Practice*, 306-332. See further the discussion below.

46. Some of the subsequent analysis is indebted to Fee, *First Epistle to the Corinthians*, 242-245.

47. Pederasty (Greek: *paidophthoria*), that is, homosexual intercourse between an adult male and a young boy, was a common form of homosexuality in the Greco-Roman world (see further discussion below). As the following discussion will show, however, this does not mean that Paul's condemnation of homosexuality is limited to pederasty. Cf. BDAG 135, which glosses *arsenokoitai* in 1 Corinthians 6:9 as "a male who engages in sexual activity w. a pers. of his own sex, *pederast*, of one who assumes the dominant role in same-sex activity, opp. μαλακός." BDAG proceeds to note that "Paul's strictures against same-sex activity cannot be satisfactorily explained on the basis of alleged temple prostitution . . . , or limited to contract w. boys for homoerotic service." It also refers to Evangelinus Apostolides Sophocles' *Greek Lexicon of the Roman and Byzantine Periods (from B. C. 146 to A. D. 1100)* (New York: Scribner's, 1900; reprint Elibron Classics, 2003), 1.253, which glosses *arsenokoitēs* as *ho meta arsenos koimōmenos koitēn gynaikeian* = "one who has intercourse with a man as with a woman." See also Gagnon, *Bible and Homosexual Practice*, 306-312, who likewise concludes that *malakos* in 1 Corinthians 6:9 refers to the passive partner in homosexual intercourse (312).

48. Fee, *First Epistle to the Corinthians*, 244. See further the discussion below.

49. For a competent summary and adjudication of the recent discussion see Garland, *1 Corinthians*, 212-215 (see also the additional note on 217-218), to which some of the discussion below is indebted. See also Gagnon, *Bible and Homosexual Practice*, 312-332 (following D. Wright, 315; see note 50, below).

50. Boswell, *Christianity, Social Tolerance, and Homosexuality*, 106-107, 335-353, decisively refuted by David F. Wright, "Homosexuals or Prostitutes? The Meaning of 'Αρσενοκοίται (1 Cor. 6:9; 1 Tim. 1:10)," *Vigiliae Christianae* 38 (1984): 125-153; see also idem, "Translating 'Αρσενοκοίται (1 Cor. 6:9; 1 Tim. 1:10)," *Vigiliae*

Christianae 41 (1987): 397; idem, "Homosexuality: The Relevance of the Bible," *Evangelical Quarterly* 61 (1989): 291-300; J. Robert Wright, "Boswell on Homosexuality: A Case Undemonstrated," *Anglical Theological Review Supplement* 66 (1984): 79-94; William L. Petersen, "Can 'Αρσενοκοίται Be Translated by 'Homosexuals'? (1 Cor 6.9; 1 Tim 1.10)," *Vigiliae Christianae* 40 (1986): 187-191; Richard B. Hays, "Relations Natural and Unnatural: A Response to John Boswell's Exegesis of Romans 1," *Journal of Religious Ethics* 14, no. 1 (1986): 210-211; David E. Malick, "The Condemnation of Homosexuality in 1 Corinthians 6:9," *Bibliotheca Sacra* 150 (1993): 479-492; Bruce W. Winter, "Homosexual Terminology in 1 Corinthians 6:9: The Roman Context and the Greek Loan-Word," *Interpreting the Bible: Essays in Honour of David Wright* (Leicester, U.K.: Inter-Varsity Press, 1997), 275-279; and McNeill, *Church and the Homosexual,* 53.

51. Boswell, *Christianity, Social Tolerance, and Homosexuality,* 140-141.

52. Ibid., 108.

53. Robin Scroggs, *The New Testament and Homosexuality* (Philadelphia: Fortress, 1983), 106-108; see also Graydon F. Snyder, *First Corinthians: A Faith Community Commentary* (Atlanta: Mercer University Press, 1992), 72-73; but see the critique in Hays, "Relations Natural and Unnatural," 210-211; and Jerome D. Quinn and William C. Wacker, *The First and Second Letters to Timothy,* Eerdmans Critical Commentary (Grand Rapids, Mich.: Eerdmans, 2000), 88; see also the helpful summary and refutation of Boswell, Scroggs, and Petersen (on whom see below) by De Young, "Source and NT Meaning of 'Αρσενοκοίται," 191-215 (apparently unaware of Wright, "Translating 'Αρσενοκοίται"). See also idem, *Homosexuality: Contemporary Claims Examined in the Light of the Bible and Other Ancient Literature and Law* (Grand Rapids, Mich.: Kregel, 2000).

54. Cf. Bailey, *Homosexuality and the Western Christian Tradition,* who argues that the term refers exclusively to a sex act with someone of the same sex.

55. Scanzoni and Mollenkott, *Is the Homosexual My Neighbor?* 61-65; McNeill, *Church and the Homosexual,* 53-56.

56. Dale B. Martin, "*Arsenokoitēs* and *Malakos*: Meaning and Consequences," in *Biblical Ethics and Homosexuality,* 129-130. But see the critique of Martin's views in Schreiner, *Romans,* 95, n. 7.

57. Petersen, "Can 'Αρσενοκοίται Be Translated By 'Homosexuals'?" 187-191 (the quote is from 189).

58. See the chart in Garland, *1 Corinthians,* 212-213. Cf. P. D. M. Turner, "Biblical Texts Relevant to Homosexual Orientation and Practice: Notes on Philology and Interpretation," *Christian Scholar's Review* 26 (1997): 435-445; D. Wright, "Homosexuals or Prostitutes?" 129; and Quinn and Wacker, *First and Second Letters to Timothy,* 88 and 101.

59. This is brought out by the NIV rendering "homosexual offenders" in 1 Corinthians 6:9 and perhaps even better in the TNIV's "practicing homosexuals."

60. Gordon J. Wenham, "The Old Testament Attitude to Homosexuality," *Expository Times* 102 (1991): 362.

61. Cf. Garland, *1 Corinthians,* 213.

62. Cf. De Young, "Source and NT Meaning of 'Αρσενοκοίται," 199-200, with reference to D. Wright, "Homosexuals or Prostitutes?"

63. See the long list of references cited in Garland, *1 Corinthians,* 213, n. 31.

64. Cf. De Young, "Source and NT Meaning of 'Αρσενοκοίται," 206. See also the reference to 1 Corinthians 6:11, above.

65. Cf. David F. Wright, "Homosexuality," in Gerald F. Hawthorne, Ralph P. Martin, and Daniel G. Reid, eds., *Dictionary of Paul and His Letters* (Leicester, U.K./Downers

Grove, Ill.: InterVarsity Press, 1993), 413-414, who notes that "unnatural" does not simply mean "contrary to accepted practice" but "the flouting of sexual distinctions basic to God's creative design" (413).

66. Wenham, "Old Testament Attitude to Homosexuality," 363; Craig S. Keener, "Adultery, Divorce," in Craig A. Evans and Stanley E. Porter, eds., *Dictionary of New Testament Background* (Downers Grove, Ill.: InterVarsity Press, 2000), 15, who comments that ancient Jews "usually viewed homosexual behavior as a pervasively and uniquely Gentile sin" and "regarded homosexual behavior as meriting death," noting also that "some Jewish people regarded homosexual intercourse as unnatural . . . , probably in part because it could not contribute to procreation." Similarly, Wright, who calls homosexuality "that homoerotic vice which Jewish writers like Philo, Josephus, Paul and Ps-Phocylides regarded as a signal token of pagan Greek depravity" ("Homosexuals or Prostitutes?" 145). See also D. Wright, "Homosexuality: The Relevance of the Bible," 291-300; and Hays, "Relations Natural and Unnatural," 184-215.

67. Gagnon, *Bible and Homosexual Practice,* 182.

68. Cf. Paul's argument from "nature" later in the same letter (1 Corinthians 11, especially v. 14). For Greco-Roman views on homosexuality, see the bibliographic references cited in Gagnon, *Bible and Homosexual Practice,* 159-160, n. 1.

69. Wolfgang Stegemann, "Paul and the Sexual Mentality of His World," *Biblical Theology Bulletin* 23 (1993): 161-168. We are indebted for the reference to Stegemann and the following reference in Philo to Garland, *1 Corinthians,* 214.

70. See especially David M. Halperin, "Homosexuality," in *Oxford Classical Dictionary,* 3d ed.; ed. Simon Hornblower and Antony Spawforth (Oxford/New York: Oxford University Press, 1996), 720-723.

71. Stegemann, "Paul and the Sexual Mentality of His World," 164 (cited in Garland, *1 Corinthians,* 218).

72. The quote is from Garland, *1 Corinthians,* 218.

73. See James Dobson, *Marriage Under Fire: Why We Must Win This Battle* (Sisters, Ore.: Multnomah, 2004); Erwin W. Lutzer, *The Truth About Same-Sex Marriage: Six Things You Need to Know About What's Really at Stake* (Chicago: Moody, 2004); Mathew D. Staver, *Same-Sex Marriage: Putting Every Household at Risk* (Nashville: Broadman & Holman, 2004); White and Niell, *Same-Sex Controversy;* and Glenn T. Stanton and Bill Maier, *Marriage on Trial: The Case Against Same-Sex Marriage and Parenting* (Downers Grove, Ill.: InterVarsity Press, 2004). For websites with information on same-sex marriage see CitizenLink (http://www.family.org/cforum/fosi/marriage/ssuap), Family Research Council (http://www.frc.org), The Alliance for Marriage (http://www.allianceformarriage.org), and American Family Association (http://www.afa.net).

74. Garland, *1 Corinthians,* 218 (emphasis added).

75. See the extensive refutation of Petersen on both historical and linguistic grounds by De Young, "Source and NT Meaning of Ἀρσενοκοῖται," 202-211; and the response by David Wright, "Translating Ἀρσενοκοῖται (1 Cor. 6:9; 1 Tim. 1:10)," 396-398.

76. Fee, *First Epistle to the Corinthians,* 245, n. 29, notes how often in this letter Paul concludes a discussion on a positive note, citing 1 Corinthians 3:22-23; 4:14-17; 5:7; 6:20; 10:13; 11:32.

77. For a discussion of the vice list in 1 Timothy 1:9-10 see Gagnon, *Bible and Homosexual Practice,* 332-336, who provides an extensive refutation of Scroggs (though Gagnon is very tentative as to the Pauline authorship of the letter).

78. Quinn and Wacker, *First and Second Letters to Timothy,* 95, following Neil J. McEleney, "The Vice Lists of the Pastoral Epistles," *Catholic Biblical Quarterly* 36

(1974): 204-210, see here four pairs connected with "and" plus six single terms, composing an unholy "Decalogue."

79. There is no need to revisit the issue of the meaning of the term *arsenokoitai* here. The issue has been adequately adjudicated in our discussion of 1 Corinthians 6:9-10, which features both expressions *malakoi* and *arsenokoitai*. It should be pointed out that the NIV rendering "pervert" in 1 Timothy 1:10 unduly dilutes the homosexual nature of the perversion addressed there (though note the commendable change to "those practicing homosexuality" in the TNIV).

80. Cf. the chart in I. Howard Marshall, *The Pastoral Epistles,* International Critical Commentary (Edinburgh: T. & T. Clark, 1999), 378-379, who says that the correspondence is clearest for commandments 5–9 and notes the general correlation between the present list and the dishonoring of God in the first four commandments.

81. For a thorough discussion and refutation of common contemporary objections to the biblical teaching on homosexuality see Gagnon, *Bible and Homosexual Practice,* 347-486, who deals with the following arguments: (1) the Bible condemns only exploitative, pederastic forms of homosexuality (e.g., Scroggs, *New Testament and Homosexuality*); (2) the Bible primarily condemns homosexuality because of its threat to male dominance (e.g., Bernadette Brooten, *Love Between Women: Early Christian Responses to Female Homoeroticism* [Chicago: University of Chicago Press, 1996]); (3) the Bible has no category for "homosexuals" with an exclusively same-sex orientation; same-sex passion was thought to originate in over-sexed heterosexuals (e.g., Dale B. Martin, "Heterosexism and the Interpretation of Romans 1:18-32," *Biblical Interpretation* 3 [1995]: 332-355; and Victor P. Furnish, *The Moral Teaching of Paul: Selected Issues,* 2d ed. [Nashville: Abingdon, 1985]); (4) homosexuality has a genetic component that the writers of the Bible did not realize (see the bibliographic references on 396, n. 83); (5) there are only a few biblical texts that speak directly to homosexuality; (6) we do not follow all the injunctions in the Bible now, so why should those against homosexual conduct be binding? (including an excursus on slavery and circumcision); and (7) since we are all sinners anyway, why single out the sin of same-sex intercourse?

82. Gagnon, *Bible and Homosexual Practice,* 25-30, lists several personal risks likely to be incurred by those who oppose homosexuality on biblical grounds; these may include being labeled homophobic, intolerant, inclusive, or uncritical, and being charged with following an outmoded morality, endowing the debate with unmerited importance, or promoting violence against homosexuals.

83. For organizations helping recovering homosexuals, see the websites of the following: Exodus Global Alliance (http://www.exodusglobalalliance.org); Desert Stream Ministries (http://www.desertstream.org); innerACTS (http://www.inneracts.org); Living Hope Ministries (http://www.livehope.org); Cross Ministry (http://www.cross ministry.org); and Love Won Out (http://www.lovewonout.org, featuring the one-day Love Won Out conferences organized by Focus on the Family [http://www.family.org]; see also http://www.pureintimacy.org/gr/homosexuality). See also the research posted at http://wwww.narth.com/menus/interfaith.html (NARTH, the National Association for Research and Therapy of Homosexuality, is a professional organization for counselors and therapists who believe change from homosexual orientation is possible); the website of the Institute for Marriage and Public Policy, http://www.marriagedebate.com; and Larry Burtoff, "Setting the Record Straight" (published by Focus on the Family). See also Joe Dallas, *Desires in Conflict: Hope for Men Who Struggle with Sexual Identity* (Eugene, Ore.: Harvest, 2003) and *A Strong Delusion: Confronting the "Gay Christian" Movement* (Eugene, Ore.: Harvest, 1996); Bob Davies and Lori Rentzel, *Coming Out of Homosexuality: New Freedom for Men and Women* (Downers Grove, Ill.: InterVarsity Press, 1994); Anne Paulk, *Restoring Sexual Identity: Hope for Women Who Struggle with Same-*

Sex Attraction (Eugene, Ore.: Harvest, 2003); and Anita Worthen and Bob Davies, *Someone I Love Is Gay: How Family and Friends Can Respond* (Downers Grove, Ill.: InterVarsity Press, 1996).

CHAPTER 11:
SEPARATING WHAT GOD HAS JOINED TOGETHER:
DIVORCE AND REMARRIAGE

1. The classic work is John Murray, *Divorce* (Grand Rapids, Mich.: Baker, 1961). For a range of evangelical views, see H. Wayne House, ed., *Divorce and Remarriage: Four Christian Views* (Leicester, U.K./Downers Grove, Ill.: InterVarsity Press, 1990), who presents the following four views: "No Divorce, No Remarriage" (J. Carl Laney); "Divorce, But No Remarriage" (William H. Heth; see also Gordon J. Wenham and William E. Heth, *Jesus and Divorce,* updated ed. [Carlisle, U.K.: Paternoster, 1997; orig. ed. 1984]; but see now Heth, "Jesus on Divorce: How My Mind Has Changed," *Southern Baptist Journal of Theology* 6, no. 1 [Spring 2002]: 4-29); "Divorce and Remarriage for Adultery and Desertion" (Thomas Edgar); and "Divorce and Remarriage Under a Variety of Circumstances" (Larry Richards). See also David Clyde Jones, *Biblical Christian Ethics* (Grand Rapids, Mich.: Baker, 1994), 177-204; John S. Feinberg and Paul D. Feinberg, *Ethics for a Brave New World* (Wheaton, Ill.: Crossway, 1993) 299-343; and the surveys by Raymond F. Collins, *Divorce in the New Testament* (Collegeville, Minn.: Liturgical Press, 1992); Pat E. Harrell, *Divorce and Remarriage in the Early Church: A History of Divorce and Remarriage in the Ante-Nicene Church* (Austin, Tex.: Sweet, 1967); and J. Glen Taylor, "The Bible and Homosexuality," *Themelios* 21, no. 1 (1995): 4-9. A helpful chart comparing the interpretation of the relevant passages by the proponents of five views (patristic, Erasmian, preteritive, betrothal, and consanguinity) is found in Paul Steele and Charles C. Ryrie, *Meant to Last* (Wheaton, Ill.: Victor, 1983), 96-97. See also David Instone-Brewer, *Divorce and Remarriage in the Bible: The Social and Literary Context* (Grand Rapids, Mich.: Eerdmans, 2002), who contends that (1) both Jesus and Paul condemned illegitimate divorce and discouraged divorce even on valid grounds; (2) both Jesus and Paul affirmed the Old Testament grounds for divorce, which were adultery and neglect or abuse (but see the critique of the latter point in chapter 2, above); and (3) both Jesus and Paul condemned remarriage after an invalid, but not a valid, divorce (ix; see especially 133-212). See also the information gathered at this author's website, http://www.Instone-Brewer.com.

2. See the helpful survey of this passage in R. Stanton Norman, "Biblical, Theological, and Pastoral Reflections on Divorce, Remarriage, and the Seminary Professor," *Journal for Baptist Theology and Ministry* 1, no. 1 (Spring 2003): 80-82.

3. See Gordon J. Wenham, "Gospel Definitions of Adultery and Women's Rights," *Expository Times* 95, no. 11 (August 1984): 330.

4. On the "betrothal view," see further below.

5. But not *vice versa*. For a general comparison between the schools of Shammai and Hillel, see Günter Stemberger, *Introduction to the Talmud and Midrash,* 2d ed., trans. and ed. Markus Bockmuehl (Edinburgh: T & T Clark, 1996), 66 (with further bibliographic information); and Emil Schürer, *The history of the Jewish People in the Age of Jesus Christ,* vol. 2, rev. and ed. Geza Vermes, Fergus Millar and Matthew Black (Edinburgh: T & T Clark, 1979), 363-367. For a comparison between Jesus and Hillel, see James H. Charlesworth and Loren L. Johns, eds., *Hillel and Jesus: Comparisons of Two Major Religious Leaders* (Minneapolis: Fortress, 1997).

6. Whether or not this death penalty was regularly administered is another question. Cf. Henry McKeating, "Sanctions Against Adultery in Ancient Israelite Society," *Journal for the Study of the Old Testament* 11 (1979): 57-72.

7. So Feinberg and Feinberg, *Ethics for a Brave New World,* 312. Norman, "Biblical, Theological, and Pastoral Reflections," 81, believes that the phrase refers to "[a]ny kind of deviant sexual behavior short of intercourse."

8. Cf. D. A. Carson, *Matthew,* Expositor's Bible Commentary (Grand Rapids, Mich.: Zondervan, 1984), 413.

9. Daniel I. Block, "Marriage and Family in Ancient Israel," in Ken M. Campbell, ed., *Marriage and Family in the Biblical World* (Downers Grove, Ill.: InterVarsity Press, 2003), 49-50, citing Leviticus 15:14, following John Walton, "The Place of the *hutqaṭṭēl* within the D-stem Group and Its Implications in Deuteronomy 24:4," *Hebrew Studies* 32 (1991): 14-15.

10. See Feinberg and Feinberg, *Ethics for a Brave New World,* 313.

11. Cf. Joachim Jeremias, *Jerusalem in the Time of Jesus* (Philadelphia: Fortress, 1969), 370-371.

12. Note that the traditional rendering of Malachi 2:16, which has God saying, in an unqualified fashion, "I hate divorce" (e.g., KJV, ASV, RSV, NASB, NIV, NRSV, NLT, TNIV), requires an emendation of the Hebrew text. However, two recent translations (the ESV and the HCSB) take the phrase as, not referring to God hating divorce, but to the person who "hates and divorces" and thus perpetrates injustice. For a defense of the reading adopted by the ESV and HCSB, see chapter 3, "Malachi 2:16 and Divorce," in Gordon P. Hugenberger, *Marriage as a Covenant: Biblical Law and Ethics as Developed from Malachi* (Grand Rapids, Mich.: Baker, 1998), 49-83. See also Thomas E. McComiskey, ed., *The Minor Prophets: An Exegetical and Expository Commentary,* vol. 3: *Zephaniah, Haggai, Zechariah, and Malachi* (Grand Rapids, Mich.: Baker, 1992), 1339, which translates, "If one hates and divorces (Yahweh, Israel's God, said), he covers his clothes with crime (Yahweh of the Armies said)" (see also 1341-1344, with further reference to van Hoonacker and Glazier-McDonald). See also M. A. Shields, "Syncretism and Divorce in Malachi 2,10-16," *Zeitschrift für die alttestamentliche Wissenschaft* 111 (1999): 81-85; and Block, "Marriage and Family in Ancient Israel," 51 (with further bibliographic references).

13. Note that Jesus' reference to Genesis 1:27 in Matthew 19:4/Mark 10:6 indicates that he defined marriage as a *heterosexual* rather than same-sex union (see chapter 9). Regarding Jesus' response to the Pharisees' question in Matthew 19:3 par. Mark 10:2 by citing two Old Testament passages, Genesis 1:27 and Genesis 2:24, that were part of a standard proof for monogamy, see Instone-Brewer, *Divorce and Remarriage in the Bible,* 133-141. Linking two biblical passages in support of a rabbi's argument was a common device known as *gezerah shawah.*

14. See note 13, above.

15. Carson, *Matthew,* 412, contra David Atkinson, *To Have and to Hold: The Marriage Covenant and the Discipline of Divorce* (Grand Rapids, Mich.: Eerdmans, 1979) especially pages 114ff.

16. The Markan parallel only says that "in the house the disciples asked him again about this matter" (Mark 10:10, ESV). The ESV rendering implies that the disciples had already asked Jesus once and now ask him again. The NIV, by contrast, translates, "When they were in the house again, the disciples asked Jesus about this," suggesting that the disciples waited to ask Jesus until they had gone back into the house.

17. Carson, *Matthew,* 416, citing Quentin Quesnell, "'Made Themselves Eunuchs for the Kingdom of Heaven' (Mt 19, 12)," *Catholic Biblical Quarterly* 30 (1968): 335-358, refers to a pattern which "is *not* to have Jesus agree with his misunderstanding disciples but to reemphasize the point just made."

18. E.g., Paul Ramsey, *Basic Christian Ethics* (Louisville: Westminster/John Knox, 1993 [1950]), 71.

19. See, e.g., W. D. Davies and Dale C. Allison, *The Gospel According to Saint Matthew,*

vol. 3, International Critical Commentary (Edinburgh: T & T Clark, 1997), 9, who
state that the Hillelite, "more liberal," position, was "presumably dominant" in Jesus'
day; and Jeremias, *Jerusalem in the Time of Jesus,* 370 (citing Philo, *Special Laws*
3.30 and Josephus, *Antiquities* 4.253 [viii.23], as only knowing the Hillelite point of
view), who says that "it appears that [Hillel's] position must have been the prevailing
view in the first half of the first century AD."

20. Compare Instone-Brewer, *Divorce and Remarriage in the Bible,* 168, who argues that
the disciples' answer most likely indicates that they held a Hillel-type "any matter"
view.

21. This is suggested by Heth, "Jesus on Divorce," 16. See also Feinberg and Feinberg,
Ethics for a Brave New World, 335-336 and the discussion below.

22. The NLT glosses, "unless his wife has been unfaithful." The Message paraphrases,
"I make an exception in cases where the spouse has committed adultery." The NRSV
has "unchastity," the KJV "fornication." The NASB and the NET Bible simply render
the phrase as "immorality."

23. E.g., Robert H. Gundry, *Matthew: A Commentary on His Handbook for a Mixed
Church Under Persecution,* 2d ed. (Grand Rapids, Mich.: Eerdmans, 1994), 90, who
states categorically, "The exceptive phrase . . . comes from Matthew, not from Jesus,
as an editorial insertion to conform Jesus' words to God's Word in the OT"; Donald
A. Hagner, *Matthew 14–28,* Word Biblical Commentary (Dallas: Word, 1995), 549:
"The evangelist adds the exception clauses for the sake of the moral sensitivities of
his Jewish-Christian readers"; Robert H. Stein, "Is It Lawful for a Man to Divorce
His Wife?" *Journal of the Evangelical Theological Society* 22 (1979): 116-120; and,
more recently, "Divorce," in Joel B. Green, Scot McKnight and I. Howard Marshall,
eds. *Dictionary of Jesus and the Gospels* (Downers Grove, Ill.: InterVarsity Press,
1992), 196, where Stein contends that "the exception clause is best understood as a
Matthean interpretative addition to help show his Jewish-Christian readers that Jesus
was not seeking in his divorce statement 'to abolish the Law' (Mt 5:17)"; and Richard
B. Hays, *The Moral Vision of the New Testament: A Contemporary Introduction to
New Testament Ethics* (San Francisco: Harper, 1996), 363, who says the
understanding may have constituted a tradition in the "Matthean community."

24. Some argue that the view that Matthew added the "exception clause" is incompatible
with inerrancy (e.g., Norman, "Biblical, Theological, and Pastoral Reflections," 82).
Feinberg and Feinberg, *Ethics for a Brave New World,* 324, also express concerns in
this regard, though they add the important clarification that "Matthew need not
quote Jesus *verbatim* in order to uphold inerrancy, but Jesus must have uttered the
sense of the exception." Others, such as Charles H. H. Scobie (*The Ways of Our God:
An Approach to Biblical Theology* [Grand Rapids, Mich./Cambridge: Eerdmans,
2003]) see in the biblical teaching on divorce "a striking example of diversity, if not
of contradiction within Scripture," pitting Mark 10:2-12 against Matthew 19:9.
Scobie concludes that it is "best to recognize the existence of two traditions in tension
with one another." The absolute statement is "the basic principle, seen in terms of
visionary ethics," while the other tradition "reflects the pragmatic side of NT ethics."
It is doubtful, however, that Scobie's view falls within the bounds of an inerrancy
view of Scriptrue.

25. Such as the proponents of the "betrothal view"; see the discussion below.

26. The only views that deny the existence of an exception altogether are the inclusivist
view (which translates the word usually rendered "except" as "not even"), the "no
comment" view (according to which Jesus refuses to even comment on the issue), and
the "clarification of the offense" view (which claims Jesus' point is that a woman
divorced for adultery cannot be *made* an adulteress by the divorce because she already
is one). These views are adequately refuted by Feinberg and Feinberg, *Ethics for a
Brave New World,* 325-327.

27. Though one of these views argues that Jesus allowed only for divorce (in exceptional circumstances), but not remarriage (see note 1, above). Moreover, even this "divorce, no remarriage" view is critical of the "no divorce, no remarriage" position. See, e.g., Wenham and Heth, *Jesus and Divorce,* 184, who contend that both the "unlawful marriages view" and the "betrothal view" "unnecessarily restrict the meaning of the broad term *porneia.*"

28. Regarding trends in recent evangelical scholarship on the present issue, see Heth, "Jesus on Divorce," 4. Those holding to alternatives to the majority viewpoint are cited on 23-24, n. 7.

29. The qualifying phrase "for any cause" is missing from the parallel in Mark 10:2.

30. John W. Shepard, *The Christ of the Gospels* (Grand Rapids, Mich.: Eerdmans, 1946 [1939]), 452, and many later interpreters (e.g., Carson, *Matthew,* 411; William L. Lane, *The Gospel According to Mark,* New International Commentary on the New Testament [Grand Rapids, Mich.: Eerdmans, 1974, 354], who notes the import of the phrase "tempting him" in Mark 10:2) suggest as a possible motive that the Jews sought to get Jesus in trouble with Herod Antipas, just as John the Baptist had suffered for his denunciation of Herod's illicit union with Herodias, his brother Philip's wife. Historically, this is indeed very plausible (see especially Mark 10:2-12; cf. Mark 6:14-29; see further below). It appears that Mark focuses more on the political dimension of the interchange, while Matthew emphasizes the rabbinic legal issue (see Gundry, *Matthew,* 377). Note the occurrence of the word "lawful" (*exestin*) in both Matthew 14:4 and 19:3.

31. The passage continues, "R. Akiba [c. A.D. 135] says, Even if he found another fairer than she, for it is written, 'And it shall be if she finds no favor in his eyes . . .'" See also Sir. 25:26: "If she does not go as you direct, separate her from yourself" (lit., "cut her off from your flesh," that is, divorce her: Deut. 24:1; up to this point they had been "one flesh": Gen. 2:24).

32. See further below. Some might object that this is an argument from cultural tradition, not Scripture. This is true, but it should be recognized that the interaction between Jesus and the Pharisees recorded in Matthew 19:3-12 did not take place in a vacuum, nor should one expect that first-century Jewish assumptions common to Jesus and the Pharisees as well Matthew and (the majority of) his readers would necessarily be made explicit. It seems therefore legitimate to utilize our knowledge regarding common first-century Jewish beliefs and practices in the area of divorce in our attempt to understand the thrust of Jesus' teaching in the present passage.

33. The question arises, if Jesus and his Jewish contemporaries did in fact assume the legitimacy of divorce for adultery, why Matthew included the reference to *porneia* at all. The most straightforward explanation is that Jesus in fact uttered the "exception clause," and Matthew recorded Jesus' statement the way it was spoken. Why Jesus referred explicitly to divorce in case of *porneia* (not only in Matthew 19, but already in Matt. 5:32), no one can know for sure, but Jesus may simply have acknowledged what everyone already knew so that his opponents could not accuse him of ignorance of what was common practice. See John R. W. Stott, "Marriage and Divorce," in *Involvement: Social and Sexual Relationships in the Modern World,* vol. 2. (Old Tappan, N.J.: Revell, 1984), 169-170, who defends the authenticity of the exception clause and suggests that Matthew may have included this for his Jewish audience while Mark and Luke, both writing primarily to Gentile readers, did not have the same concern. Contra Stein, "Divorce," 197, who claims that "its authenticity [i.e., the exception clause in Matthew] is doubtful" and proposes that "Matthew has added an exception clause to Jesus' teaching." On adultery, see especially Craig S. Keener, "Adultery, Divorce," in Craig A. Evans and Stanley E. Porter, eds., *Dictionary of New Testament Background* (Downers Grove, Ill.: InterVarsity Press, 2000), 7-10.

34. Norman, "Biblical, Theological, and Pastoral Reflections," 83, appropriately cites Carson, *Matthew*, 414, as saying that *porneia* "should not be restricted unless the entire context requires it," but the fact is, as the below examples show, that the context often *does* require it. General references are typically found in vice lists (e.g., Mark 7:21; Gal. 5:19; Eph. 5:3; Col. 3:5; see also 1 Thess. 4:3; Rev. 9:21). Instances where *porneia* is qualified by the context include references to prostitution (Matt. 21:31-32; Luke 15:30; 1 Cor. 6:13-18), incest (Acts 15:20, 29; 21:25; 1 Cor. 5:1), homosexuality (cf. Lev. 18:22: *arsenos . . . koitēn*), fornication (John 8:41), and adultery (cf. Jer. 3:9, LXX; and Hos. 2:4 LXX, on which see the discussion below; figuratively, Rev. 14:8; 17:2, 4; 18:3, 9). Cf. Joseph Jensen, "Does *Porneia* Mean Fornication? A Critique of Bruce Malina," *Novum Testamentum* 20 (1980): 161-184, especially 180-183; Donald A. Hagner, *Matthew 1–13*, Word Biblical Commentary (Dallas: Word, 1993), 125, who points out that *porneia* is a broad term that can also be used to refer to adultery (citing Sir. 23:23; and G. Kittel and G. Friedrich, eds., G. W. Bromiley, trans., *Theological Dictionary of the New Testament*, 10 vols. [Grand Rapids, Mich.: Eerdmans, 1964-1976], 6:592); and BDAG 854: "Of the sexual unfaithfulness of a married woman."

35. Hence the translation "marital unfaithfulness" in the NIV; the NLT's "unless his wife has been unfaithful"; and the rendering "sexual immorality" in most other versions. The lack of further qualification is noted by Stott, "Marriage and Divorce," 171, who concludes: "It seems, then, that he [Jesus] abrogated the death penalty for sexual infidelity, and made this the only legitimate ground for dissolving the marriage bond, by divorce not death, and then only as a permission" (173). Regarding the meaning of *porneia* in Matthew 19, see also the thorough discussion of the philological evidence in Instone-Brewer, *Divorce and Remarriage in the Bible*, 156-159, who contends that the phrase is here used because it was judged to be the best translation of the phrase in Deuteronomy 24:1. Instone-Brewer sums up Jesus' teaching on divorce as follows: (1) marriage should be monogamous and lifelong; (2) divorce is never compulsory and should be avoided unless the erring partner stubbornly refuses to repent; (3) marriage is optional; and (4) Hillelite "any matter" divorces are invalid (187).

36. Stein, "Divorce," 194 (emphasis added). Stein also points out that while Matthew elsewhere uses a more narrow term, *moicheia* (or the verb *moicheuō*), for adultery (5:27, 28, 32; 15:19; 19:18), and while elsewhere *moicheia* and *porneia* are distinguished (Mark 7:21-22 par. Matt. 15:19; 1 Cor. 6:9; Heb. 13:4), *porneia* is a broader term that nonetheless includes *moicheia* (195). See also the very thorough discussion in Carson, *Matthew*, 412-419, who discusses seven major interpretations of the Matthean "exception clause" and notes that "there is no reason to adopt [the betrothal view] if *porneia* is being squeezed into too narrow a semantic range" (414). Gundry, *Matthew*, 91, contends that "the specific word for adultery, *moicheia*, does not appear in the exceptive phrase simply because a general expression occurs in Deuteronomy."

37. For this reason the claim (regularly cited in support of their position by the "no divorce, no remarriage" view) by Abel Isaksson, *Marriage and Ministry in the New Temple: A Study with Special Reference to Mt. 19.13 [sic]-12 and 1. Cor. 11.3-16*, trans. Neil Tomkinson and Jean Gray, Acta Seminarii Neotestamentici Upsaliensis 24 (Lund, Sweden: Gleerup, 1965), 134-135, that the distinction between *porneia* and *moicheia* "was very strictly maintained in pre-Christian Jewish literature and in the N.T." and that "we can find no unequivocal examples of the use of this word [*porneia*] to denote a wife's adultery" misses the mark. If the above cited passages, Jeremiah 3:8-10 and Hosea 2:2-5a, are classified as "pre-Christian Jewish literature" (which they, of course, are), then Isaksson's claim stands refuted that the distinction between *porneia* and *moicheia* was "very strictly maintained" there, since those two expressions are, to the contrary, used in typical Hebrew-style parallelism and in essential continuity with one another. And even if there were no unequivocal

examples of *porneia by itself* denoting adultery (it is unclear why Isaksson limits the scope to "a wife's" adultery here), the fact is that *porneia* is not used *by itself* in Matthew 19:9 but occurs in conjunction with the expressions *moicheuō* ("commit adultery") and *gameō* ("[re]marry").

38. Another interesting suggestion as to why the term *porneia* rather than *moicheia* is used in Matthew 19:9 is made by Johannes P. Louw and Eugene A. Nida, *Greek-English Lexicon of the New Testament Based on Semantic Domains*, 2d ed. (New York: United Bible Societies, 1989), 772. Since adultery in New Testament times was normally defined in terms of the married status of the *woman* involved in any such act, sexual intercourse of a married *man* with an unmarried woman would usually have been regarded as *porneia*, while sexual intercourse of either an unmarried or a married man with someone else's wife was regarded as adultery, both on the part of the man as well as the woman. If this is accurate, and if Jesus (and Matthew) wanted to include *both* types of sexual immorality in Matthew 19:9, this would explain the use of *porneia*.

39. See the reference to Feinberg and Feinberg, *Ethics for a Brave New World*, 324, in the discussion above.

40. So rightly Hagner, *Matthew 14–28*, 549 (without endorsing his view that the "exception clause" was added by Matthew and without condoning his pitting the comments in Matt. 19:6-8 and 11-12 against the evangelist's alleged insertion of the "exception clause" in verse 9). See also Instone-Brewer, *Divorce and Remarriage in the Bible*, 173, who contends that "Matthew's version reflects a real rabbinic debate." For a similar dynamic, see Matthew 22:15-22; Mark 12:13-17; Luke 20:20-26.

41. Cf. Heth, "Jesus on Divorce," 11 and 16. See also Carson, *Matthew*, 411, who points out that, "On any understanding of what Jesus says . . . he agrees with neither Shammai nor Hillel; for even though the school of Shammai was stricter than Hillel, it permitted remarriage when the divorce was not in accordance with its own Halakah (rules of conduct) (M *Eduyoth* 4:7-10), and if Jesus restricts grounds for divorce to sexual indecency . . . , then he differs fundamentally from Shammai. Jesus cuts his own swath in these verses . . . , and he does so in an age when in many Pharisaic circles 'the frequency of divorce was an open scandal'" (citing David Hill, *The Gospel of Matthew*, New Century Bible [London: Marshall, Morgan & Scott, 1972], 280).

42. Cf. Hill, *Gospel of Matthew*, 280: "The form of argument was acceptable in Jewish exegesis: 'the more original, the weightier': an appeal to God's intention in creation outweighs (but does not therefore annul) the ordinances of Moses." Similarly, Carson, *Matthew*, 412.

43. Cf. Keener, "Adultery, Divorce," 6, who notes that Jesus "probably accepts but radicalizes the Shammaite position."

44. This, incidentally, does not necessarily imply that Jesus taught the indissolubility of marriage, as is held by the Roman Catholic Church and others (e.g., Wenham, "Gospel Definitions of Adultery and Women's Rights," 330-332; see the response by M. J. Down, "The Sayings of Jesus About Marriage and Divorce," *Expository Times* 95, no. 11 [August 1984]: 332-334).

45. So rightly Wenham, "Gospel Definitions of Adultery and Women's Rights," 331. Some advocates of the "betrothal view" have objected to the "divorce for adultery or sexual immorality" position on the basis that in light of Jesus' words in Matthew 5:28, the exception in Matthew 19:9 would need to include not only adulterous acts but also adulterous thoughts, which would render the exception virtually absurd. However, Judaism did make a distinction between sinful thoughts on the one hand and resulting sinful actions. Also, Jesus did not say in Matthew 5:28 that a married man who lusts after a woman other than his wife commits *adultery* but that he commits adultery *in his heart*, thus qualifying his statement.

46. So Stott, "Marriage and Divorce," 170, quoted in Jones, *Biblical Christian Ethics,* 202; and Hill, *Gospel of Matthew,* 281, who writes, "An adulterous relationship violated the order of creation, with its monogamous ideal. Therefore if Jesus upheld the indissolubility of marriage on the basis of Genesis, he must have permitted divorce for that, and that alone, which necessarily contravened the created order."

47. Note that Jesus extends the scope of adultery even to a man's heart attitude (Matt. 5:27-28; though see the note commenting on these verses above). At the same time, if the tradition underlying John 7:53–8:11 is authentic, Jesus also recasts the issue of proper punishment for adultery: "If any one of you is without sin, let him be the first to throw a stone at her" (John 8:7). See also Joseph considering divorce when suspecting his fiancée Mary of sexual infidelity (Matt. 1:19; see further below).

48. Cf. Edgar, "Divorce and Remarriage for Adultery and Desertion," in House, ed., *Divorce and Remarriage: Four Christian Views,* 151-152, who argues that the view he presents is the position most naturally derived from Scripture "if we do not presuppose a sacramental view of marriage or its equivalent (marriage is indissoluble)."

49. See chapter 2. See also the important discussion in Heth, "Jesus on Divorce," 16-20, who changed his mind and moved from a "no divorce, no remarriage" to a "divorce and remarriage in the case of adultery or sexual immorality" position after reconsidering his position on the nature of covenant in general and the marriage covenant in particular. Particularly influential in Heth's thinking was Hugenberger, *Marriage as a Covenant.* See also Craig L. Blomberg, *Matthew,* New American Commentary (Nashville: Broadman & Holman, 1992), 290, n. 6 (cited in Heth, "Jesus on Divorce," 27, n. 70); and the arguments for indissolubility and dissolubility discussed in Feinberg and Feinberg, *Ethics for a Brave New World,* 303-305.

50. For a similar list and discussion see Feinberg and Feinberg, *Ethics for a Brave New World,* 334-337.

51. Some may object that Jesus originally spoke Aramaic, so that Aramaic, not Greek, should be the primary point of reference. In response, it should be noted that the final text of the New Testament is in Greek, not Aramaic, so that Greek, not Aramaic, should be the ultimate focus of interpretation.

52. In any case, Jesus' statement in Matthew 5:17, "Do not think that I have come to abolish the Law or the Prophets; I have not come to abolish them but to fulfill them," is not primarily concerned with the way in which Jesus may annul or intensify certain aspects of the Mosaic Law but with presenting Jesus in his own person as the fulfillment of Old Testament prophecy and thus as the Old Testament's sole authoritative interpreter (see especially Carson, *Matthew,* 141-145). That Jesus in Matthew 5:18 did in fact advance Old Testament teaching is strongly suggested by the repeated cadence in the remainder of the chapter, "You have heard that it was said . . . But I say to you . . ."

53. See Feinberg and Feinberg, *Ethics for a Brave New World,* 334-335, who note that "[s]ome think exceptions negate the rule, but that misunderstands the logic of exceptions to universal rules. Exceptions negate the rule *only in exceptional cases, not in all cases.* Once one understands how exceptions modify rules, the apparent contradiction between verses 6 and 9 disappears." See also the above-cited contrast drawn between Jesus and Shammai in Carson, *Matthew,* 411.

54. See Heth, "Jesus on Divorce," 17-20, with reference to Hugenberger, *Marriage as a Covenant,* 3, n. 25, who writes that "in terms of Hebrew usage covenants may be both violated and dissolved," citing Genesis 17:14; Leviticus 26:44; Deuteronomy 31:20; 1 Kings 15:19; Isaiah 24:5; 33:8; Jeremiah 11:10; 14:21; 31:32; 33:20-21; Ezekiel 16:59; 17:15-18; 44:7; and Zechariah 11:10-11. Heth adds that "sexual infidelity is a particularly grave violation of the marriage covenant, a sin against both the covenant partner and against God, and if covenants can be violated and dissolved,

this sin strikes at the marriage covenant in a unique way" (19, citing Hugenberger, *Marriage as a Covenant*, 281-294). Regarding the argument that marriage is patterned after the covenant between Christ and the church, it should be noted that this notion is anachronistic, since the institution of marriage historically precedes the new covenant by several thousand years. More likely, marriage serves as an illustration for the intimate union between Christ and the church (see Andreas J. Köstenberger, "The Mystery of Christ and the Church: Head and Body, 'One Flesh,'" *Trinity Journal* 12 n.s. [1991]: 79-94; note also that the word "covenant" is not actually used in Eph. 5:21-33).

55. See the discussion and critique of these views in Feinberg and Feinberg, *Ethics for a Brave New World*, 306-307 and 327-339, who also list the "mixed marriage view" (cf. Ezra 9–10; Deut. 7:3). Incest is the view held especially by a growing number of Roman Catholic scholars, such as Joseph A. Fitzmyer, "The Matthean Divorce Texts and Some Palestinian Evidence," *Theological* Studies 37 (1976): 197-226, especially 208-211 (for a list of others holding this view, see Hagner, *Matthew 1–13*, 124, who also cites Guelich and Witherington). Premarital sexual unfaithfulness is advocated by Mark Geldard, "Jesus' Teaching on Divorce," *Churchman* 92 (1978): 134-143; Isaksson, *Marriage and Ministry in the New Temple*, especially 135, and John Piper (see below). Other (less credible) views include the "inclusivist" view (see the critique by Carson, *Matthew*, 414-415); the "preteritive or no comment" view (see Bruce Vawter, "Divorce and the New Testament," *Catholic Biblical Quarterly* 39 [1977]: 528-548); and the "clarification" view (see the critique by Feinberg and Feinberg, *Ethics for a Brave New World*, 327).

56. See, e.g., Carson, *Matthew*, 414.

57. So rightly Hagner, *Matthew 1–13*, 124-125. For a treatment and critique of the "unlawful marriages view," see Wenham and Heth, *Jesus and Divorce*, 153-168, 205-209. Heth, "Jesus on Divorce," 5, says that this view "is no longer a viable interpretive option." The view was held by Charles Ryrie, "Biblical Teaching on Divorce and Remarriage," *Grace Theological Journal* 3, no. 2 (1982): 177-192, especially 188-189, who also cites F. F. Bruce (188, n. 42).

58. Cf. Matthew 1:18-20, where Joseph and Mary, as betrothed, are called "husband" and "wife," the dissolution of whose relationship requires a "divorce." On the Jewish practice of betrothal see, e.g., George Foot Moore, *Judaism in the First Centuries of the Christian Era* (Cambridge, Mass.: Harvard University Press, 1962), 2.121: "Betrothal was a formal act by which the woman became legally the man's wife; unfaithfulness of her part was adultery and punishable as such; if the relation was dissolved a bill of divorce was required"; and Jeremias, *Jerusalem in the Time of Jesus*, 367-368: "Betrothal, which was preceded by courtship and the drawing up of the marriage contract, signified the 'acquisition' (*qinyān*) of the woman by the man, and thus the valid settlement of the marriage. The betrothed woman is called 'wife', can become a widow, be put away by divorce and punished with death for adultery. . . . But it is only with the *marriage* itself, which ordinarily took place one year after betrothal (M. Ket. V.2), that the girl definitely passed from her father's power to her husband's."

59. Isaksson, *Marriage and Ministry in the New Temple*; John Piper, "Divorce and Remarriage: A Position Paper," posted at http://www.desiringgod.org/library/topics/divorce_remarriage/div_rem_paper.html and "Divorce and Remarriage in the Event of Adultery," at http://www.desiringgod.org/library/topics/divorce_remarriage/dr_adultery.html. See also Stephen D. Giese, http://www.geocities.com/sdgiesedts2001/DivorceTP.htm, who defends the position that "the only legitimate conclusion concerning divorce is that the marital covenant is binding until the death of a spouse" and espouses a betrothal view on the basis of the conviction that the

marriage covenant is indissoluble. For a list of others holding this view see Wenham and Heth, *Jesus and Divorce,* 279, n. 7.

60.   Cf. Genesis 29:21; Deuteronomy 22:23-24; 2 Samuel 3:14; Matthew 1:18-25. See Carson, *Matthew,* 75, citing Numbers 5:11-31; *m. Soṭah* 1:1-5; David Hill, "A Note on Matthew 1.19," *Expository Times* 76 (1964–65): 133-134; Angelo Tosato, "Joseph, Being a Just Man (Matt 1:19)," *Catholic Biblical Quarterly* 41 (1979): 547-551. Craig S. Keener, *A Commentary on the Gospel of Matthew* (Grand Rapids, Mich.: Eerdmans, 1999), 91, whose entire treatment of Matthew 1:19 on 87-95 repays careful study, cites *m. Giṭṭin* 6:2; *Ketubbot* 1:2; 4:2; *m. Yebamot* 2:6; *b. Giṭṭin* 26b.

61.   The word "divorce" is put in quotation marks here to indicate that today the term "divorce" is not applied to severing an engagement.

62.   See the summary of this view in Wenham and Heth, *Jesus and Divorce,* 169-171.

63.   It should be noted, however, that Matthew does not use the word *porneia* to describe Mary's suspected offense in Matthew 1:18-25 (see Wenham and Heth, *Jesus and Divorce,* 173). Piper also believes that in Luke 16:18 Jesus excludes remarriage in the case of divorce and so interprets Matthew 5:32 accordingly.

64.   See also Feinberg and Feinberg, *Ethics for a Brave New World,* 328, who lodge three primary criticisms against the "betrothal view": (1) the illegitimate restriction of the meaning of *porneia* to sex during the betrothal period; (2) the fact that Deuteronomy 24 does not address sex during the betrothal period, because this subject had already been dealt with in Deuteronomy 22; (3) the lack of reference to betrothal in Matthew 19.

65.   Cf. Instone-Brewer, *Divorce and Remarriage in the Bible,* 161-167.

66.   Ibid., 185.

67.   Carson, *Matthew,* 417.

68.   Ibid., 418, citing James B. Hurley, *Man and Woman in Biblical Perspective* (Leicester, U.K.: Inter-Varsity Press, 1981), 104; and Murray, *Divorce,* 51ff.

69.   See the thorough treatment by Instone-Brewer, *Divorce and Remarriage in the Bible,* 189-212.

70.   For a thorough discussion of 1 Corinthians 7:12-14 see Judith M. Gundry-Volf, "The Least and the Greatest," in Marcia J. Bunge, ed., *The Child in Christian Thought* (Grand Rapids, Mich.: Eerdmans, 2001), 48-53.

71.   On the entire section, see especially the excellent treatment by Gordon D. Fee, *The First Epistle to the Corinthians,* New International Commentary on the New Testament (Grand Rapids, Mich.: Eerdmans, 1987), 290-306. On the phrase "God has called us to peace," see Instone-Brewer, *Divorce and Remarriage in the Bible,* 203, with reference to his earlier work, *Techniques and Assumptions in Jewish Exegesis Before 70 CE* (Texte und Studien zum antiken Judentum 30; Tübingen: Mohr-Siebeck, 1992), 21, 37, 82, 144-145, in which the author shows that "for the sake of peace" constitutes rabbinic legal terminology for what might be called "pragmatism" as opposed to a strict application of the law.

72.   See especially Will Deming, *Paul on Marriage and Celibacy: The Hellenistic Background of 1 Corinthians 7,* 2d ed. (Grand Rapids, Mich.: Eerdmans, 2004), who contends that the hermeneutical key to understanding the present passage lies in the Stoic-Cynic debate about the relative merits and demerits of marriage. Deming contends that Paul's position, properly understood, is not ascetic but that the apostle accentuates the advantages of celibacy in light of current circumstances that made it imperative that believers carefully weigh the pros and cons of entering into marriage.

73.   As Norman, "Biblical, Theological, and Pastoral Reflections," 87, rightly notes, *chorizō* here means divorce, not merely separation. This is borne out by contemporary Greek usage; the contrast between the same Greek word and "what God has joined

together" in Matthew 19:6; and the parallel use of the *chorizō* and *aphiēmi* (which also means "divorce") in the present context.

74. So rightly Instone-Brewer, *Divorce and Remarriage in the Bible,* 201-203.

75. Cf. Fee, *First Epistle to the Corinthians,* 296.

76. To this some have added other extreme circumstances (such as persistent spousal abuse) when confronted through the process laid out in Matthew 18:15-17, though great caution would need to be exercised in this regard in order not to undermine the high scriptural view of marriage. Cf. Hawthorne, "Marriage and Divorce," in Gerald F. Hawthorne, Ralph P. Martin, and Daniel G. Reid, eds., *Dictionary of Paul and His Letters* (Leicester, U.K./Downers Grove, Ill.: InterVarsity Press, 1993), 599, who asks, "Is it possible to extrapolate from this that other such marital travesties, although not identical to these (e.g., cruelty, desertion, physical abuse, the systematic psychological destruction of one's marriage partner, and the like), might also have been included as exceptions to the ideal . . . ?" and urges that "any plan to divorce must not be made independently of the community of faith or apart from the advice and support of the authorized leaders of the church." See also Norman, "Biblical, Theological, and Pastoral Reflections," 88-89. Others, such as Instone-Brewer, *Divorce and Remarriage in the Bible,* passim, postulate the permissibility of divorce more broadly for material and emotional neglect. Instone-Brewer maintains that Jesus' silence on this point in Matthew 19 should be construed as tacit agreement with universal Jewish practice in this regard on the basis of Exodus 21:10-11 (166, 181-182, 185) and contends that Paul alludes to the same passage in 1 Corinthians 7:3 (193-194; see chapters 2 and 3, above). But see the critique in chapter 2, above.

77. Beyond this, it is also possible that Herod Antipas's relationship with Herodias (denounced by John the Baptist) is in view as well (see above and further on Mark below).

78. See, e.g., Gundry, *Matthew,* 90-91; Wenham and Heth, *Jesus and Divorce,* 113-116, Edgar, "No Divorce and No Remarriage," in House, ed., *Divorce and Remarriage: Four Christian Views,* 37-38.

79. So rightly Hagner, *Matthew 1-13,* 125.

80. The following survey is indebted to Heth, "Jesus on Divorce," 12. Among those who interpret 1 Corinthians 7:15 as calling the believer to peace, but as not granting freedom to remarry, is Paige Patterson, *The Troubled Triumphant Church: An Exposition of First Corinthians* (Nashville: Thomas Nelson, 1983), 120-121.

81. Stein, "Divorce," 194.

82. Jones, *Biblical Christian Ethics,* 201, n. 81, suggests that in 1 Corinthians 7:27-28 Paul may "possibly" be saying that those who were legtimately divorced and proceed to remarry have "not sinned," but this is a rather unlikely reading of the text. Cf. Norman, "Biblical, Theological, and Pastoral Reflections," 88, with reference to John Jefferson Davis, *Evangelical Ethics: Issues Facing the Church Today,* 2d ed. (Phillipsburg, N.J.: Presbyterian & Reformed, 1993), 101-102.

83. See especially Craig S. Keener, *. . . And Marries Another: Divorce and Remarriage in the Teaching of the New Testament* (Peabody, Mass.: Hendrickson, 1991), 61-66. Contra Wenham and Heth, *Jesus and Divorce;* William E. Heth, "Divorce and Remarriage: The Search for an Evangelical Hermeneutic," *Trinity Journal* 16 (1995): 63-100. Note the critique of the Wenham/Heth position by Stott, "Marriage and Divorce," 171, who calls this view "extreme" and "not conclusive" (though "plausibly argued"; the reference is to a series of three articles by Wenham on "The Biblical View of Marriage and Divorce" published in *Third Way,* vol. 1, nos. 20-22 [October and November 1977]). See also House, ed., *Divorce and Remarriage: Four Christian Views.*

84. See, e.g., Stein, "Divorce," 192-193: "'Divorce' therefore in our texts should be

understood as assuming the right to remarry"; Jones, *Biblical Christian Ethics*, 199: "Where divorce is justified there is freedom to remarry"; and Craig L. Blomberg, "Marriage, Divorce, Remarriage, and Celibacy," *Trinity Journal* 11 (1990): 196: "Divorce in biblical times virtually always carried with it the right to remarry; no NT text rescinds this permission."

85. As Keener, "Adultery, Divorce," 6, notes, "The very term for legal divorce meant freedom to remarry."

86. "Divorce and remarry" are paired in Mark 10:11-12 (cf. v. 9). As Stein, "Divorce," 195, observes, the link is also assumed in Deuteronomy 24:1-4.

87. Originally part of an illustration in a different context, the verse states that a woman may remarry if her husband has died. As Douglas J. Moo, *The Epistle to the Romans*, New International Commentary on the New Testament (Grand Rapids, Mich.: Eerdmans, 1996), 413, n. 24, rightly notes, "These verses are sometimes cited to prove that remarriage on any basis other than the death of one's spouse is adulterous. Whether this is the biblical teaching or not, these verses at any rate are probably not relevant to the issue. Paul is not teaching about remarriage but citing a simple example to prove a point."

88. So rightly Norman, "Biblical, Theological, and Pastoral Reflections," 86.

89. The label is used by Wenham and Heth, *Jesus and Divorce* (though note the criticism by Jones, *Biblical Christian Ethics*, 181, who calls the label "misleading and pejorative"; similarly, Norman, "Biblical, Theological, and Pastoral Reflections," 79, n. 2).

90. On Erasmus, see V. Norskov Olson, *The New Testament Logia on Divorce: A Study of Their Interpretation from Erasmus to Milton*, Beiträge zur Geschichte biblischer Exegese 10 (Tübingen: Mohr Siebeck, 1971). Cf. Blomberg, *Matthew* and "Marriage, Divorce, Remarriage, and Celibacy"; Carson, *Matthew*; Feinberg and Feinberg, *Ethics for a Brave New World*; Hugenberger, *Marriage as a Covenant*; Jones, *Biblical Christian Ethics*; John MacArthur, *The Fulfilled Family* (Chicago: Moody, 1987) and http://www.gracechurch.org/divorce.asp; Murray, *Divorce*; Stein, "Divorce"; Stott, "Marriage and Divorce"; and Heth, "Jesus on Divorce." See also Thomas Edgar, "Divorce and Remarriage for Adultery and Desertion," in House, ed., *Divorce and Remarriage*.

91. Wenham and Heth, *Jesus and Divorce*; Heth, "Divorce, But No Remarriage," in House, ed., *Divorce and Remarriage*; Gundry, *Matthew*; Hagner, *Matthew 14–28*; Andrew Cornes, *Divorce and Remarriage: Biblical Principles and Pastoral Practice* (Grand Rapids, Mich.: Eerdmans, 1993); Jacques Dupont, *Mariage et divorce dans l'évangile: Matthieu 19, 3–12 et parallèles* (Abbaye de Saint-André: Desclee de Brouwer, 1959).

92. Piper has posted his views on his website (see references above); see also Isaksson, *Marriage and Ministry in the New Temple*; James Montgomery Boice, *The Sermon on the Mount* (Grand Rapids, Mich.: Zondervan, 1972) and "The Biblical View of Divorce," *Eternity* (December 1970): 19-21; Dwight Pentecost, *The Words and Works of Jesus Christ: A Study of the Life of Christ* (Grand Rapids, Mich.: Zondervan, 1981). Proponents of the incest view also fall under this rubric: see J. Carl Laney, *The Divorce Myth* (Minneapolis: Bethany, 1981) and "No Divorce, No Remarriage," in House, ed., *Divorce and Remarriage: Four Views*; F. F. Bruce, *New Testament History* (Garden City, N.Y.: Doubleday, 1980); and Charles Ryrie, "Biblical Teaching on Divorce and Remarriage," *Grace Theological Journal* 3, no. 2 (Fall 1982): 177-192.

93. The four positions discussed here are the major positions on the issue. Beyond this, individual interpreters hold other combinations of views. One example is Scobie, *Ways of Our God*, 840, who acknowledges the exception for adultery made by Jesus in Matthew 19:9 but who believes that while Paul does recognize separation as a

possibility in 1 Corinthians 7, there is no possibility of remarriage. Others, such as Robert A. J. Gagnon (*The Bible and Homosexual Practice: Texts and Hermeneutics* [Nashville: Abingdon, 2001], 201, n. 21: "I am not sure what the solution is") are not sure how to reconcile the various biblical injunctions on divorce.

94. Daniel R. Heimbach, *True Sexual Morality: Biblical Standards for a Culture in Crisis* (Wheaton, Ill.: Crossway, 2004). Note that this position is not represented in the volume edited by Wayne House.

95. We are aware that some will deny that any person is ever completely "innocent" when divorce occurs. In our view, however, there are demonstrably cases where one person's adultery or abandonment does not implicate the other spouse in complicity or guilt. Clearly, a marriage between two partners does not obliterate the fact that each person bears responsibility for his or her own actions, so that it seems to be entirely appropriate to refer to the person whose partner has committed sexual unfaithfulness as the victim and the adulterer as the perpetrator of sexual unfaithfulness.

96. So rightly Keener, . . . *And Marries Another*, 109. See also Norman, "Biblical, Theological, and Pastoral Reflections," 89-92 (Norman also discusses divorce and remarriage and the seminary professor, 92-100).

CHAPTER 12:
FAITHFUL HUSBANDS: QUALIFICATIONS FOR CHURCH LEADERSHIP

1. The following discussion will be limited strictly to those qualifications for church leaders that relate to his marriage and family. Other qualifications are beyond the scope of our present study and will not be treated here. For an investigation of these other qualifications see Andreas Köstenberger, *Pastoral Epistles*, New Expositor's Bible Commentary (Grand Rapids, Mich.: Zondervan, forthcoming).

2. See Vern S. Poythress, "The Church as Family: Why Male Leadership in the Family Requires Male Leadership in the Church," in John Piper and Wayne Grudem, eds., *Recovering Biblical Manhood and Womanhood: A Response to Evangelical Feminism* (Wheaton, Ill.: Crossway, 1991), 233-247. See also Malcolm B. Yarnell, III, "*Oikos theou*: A Theologically Neglected but Important Ecclesiological Metaphor," *Midwestern Journal of Theology* 2, no. 1 (Fall 2003): 53-65; and the brief survey by Judith M. Gundry-Volf, "The Least and the Greatest," in Marcia J. Bunge, ed., *The Child in Christian Thought* (Grand Rapids, Mich.: Eerdmans, 2001), 58-59.

3. The terms "pastor," "overseer," and "elder" are largely used interchangeably in the New Testament (cf., e.g., Acts 20:17, 28; Titus 1:5-7; 1 Pet. 5:1-3). On the issue of church government, see Andreas J. Köstenberger, "Hermeneutical and Exegetical Challenges in Interpreting the Pastoral Epistles," *Southern Baptist Journal of Theology* 7, no. 3 (Fall 2003): 10-13. See also Benjamin L. Merkle, "Hierarchy in the Church? Instruction from the Pastoral Epistles Concerning Elders and Overseers," in ibid., 32-43.

4. The following treatment is indebted to Köstenberger, *Pastoral Epistles* (forthcoming). On the history of interpretation, see Peter Gorday, ed., *Ancient Christian Commentary on Scripture: New Testament*, vol. 9, *Colossians, 1–2 Thessalonians, 1–2 Timothy, Titus, Philemon* (Downers Grove, Ill.: InterVarsity Press, 2000), 170-171 and 286-287. See also the survey in Ed Glasscock, "'The Husband of One Wife' Requirement in 1 Timothy 3:2," *Bibliotheca Sacra* 140 (1983): 244-249 and 253-256. The range of translations spans the following: "the husband of one wife" (KJV, NKJV, NASB, HCSB, NET, ESV [footnote: Or *a man of one woman*]), which leaves the question of interpretation open; "husband of but one wife" (NIV), which suggests a prohibition against polygamy; "married only once" (NRSV [footnote: Or *the husband of one wife*]), a prohibition against remarriage after being widowed, the prevailing

view of the church fathers; and "faithful to his wife" (NLT, TNIV), "faithful to his one wife" (NEB); "devoted to [lit. *a man of*] one woman" (ISV), "committed to his wife" (THE MESSAGE), which takes the expression as an idiom for marital faithfulness.

5. Cf. Glasscock, "'Husband of One Wife' Requirement," 244-258, who notes that the third and fourth views (excluding remarried widowers, opposing polygamy) were commonly held among the church fathers. The most common views today are the second and fifth views (excluding divorcees, requiring faithfulness in marriage). The first view (excluding unmarried candidates) is held by few.

6. Most biblical references are to widows, not widowers, remarrying, since it was far more common for women to lose their spouses than husbands their wives (cf., e.g., Rom. 7:2-3; 1 Cor. 7:39; 1 Tim. 5:14), but there is no good reason why Paul's encouragement for widows (especially younger ones) to remarry should not be applied to widowers as well.

7. See the NIV rendering, "husband of *but* one wife" (note that there is no equivalent for "but" in the original; but see the change to "faithful to his wife" in the TNIV). See also John Calvin, *1 and 2 Timothy and Titus* (Wheaton, Ill./Nottingham, U.K.: Crossway, 1998; original ed. 1556, 1549), 54.

8. See, e.g., William D. Mounce, *The Pastoral Epistles,* Word Biblical Commentary (Nashville: Thomas Nelson, 2000), 171.

9. Cf. Steven M. Baugh, "1–2 Timothy, Titus," in Clinton E. Arnold, ed., *Zondervan Illustrated Bible Backgrounds Commentary,* vol. 3. (Grand Rapids, Mich.: Zondervan, 2002), 501-502.

10. See especially Sidney Page, "Marital Expectations of Church Leaders in the Pastoral Epistles," *Journal for the Study of the New Testament* 50 (1993): 105-120, especially 108-109 and 114, n. 27. For a discussion of the biblical teaching on marriage (including the husband's role), see chapters 2 and 3, above.

11. See Page, "Marital Expectations," 112; contra Gordon D. Fee, "Reflections on Church Order in the Pastoral Epistles, with Further Reflection on the Hermeneutics of *Ad Hoc* Documents," *Journal of the Evangelical Theological Society* 28 (1985): 150, who contends that the present passage "probably prohibits remarriage of widows/widowers."

12. The present requirement contrasts with the Gnostic extremes of asceticism and sexual licentiousness. Marital fidelity was also held in high regard in the Greco-Roman world, so that this quality would have commended a Christian office-holder to his pagan surroundings (cf. Page, "Marital Expectations," 117-118).

13. David Instone-Brewer, *Divorce and Remarriage in the Bible: The Social and Literary Context* (Grand Rapids, Mich.: Eerdmans, 2002), 227-228, concurs and notes that the phrase is equivalent to our phrase "having eyes for only one woman" (see also 313). Note that in all its occurrences, the expression "of one wife" or "of one husband" is put first in the original for emphasis (cf. 1 Tim. 3:2, 12; 5:9).

14. Cf. Majorie Lightman and William Zeisel, "Univira: An Example of Continuity and Change in Roman Society," *Church History* 46 (1977): 19-32. "Uni" is Latin for "one," "vir" means "husband," and the female suffix "a" refers to a woman or wife, hence the meaning "one-husband-type-of woman or wife."

15. Catullus, *The Poems of Catullus* 111, trans. F. W. Cornish, in *Catullus, Tibullus, Pervigilium Veneris,* Loeb Classical Library, 2d ed. rev. G. P. Goold (Cambridge, Mass.: Harvard University Press, 1995), 179.

16. *Corpus Inscriptionum Latinarum* 6.5162.

17. Cited in Lightman and Zeisel, "Univira: An Example of Continuity and Change in Roman Society," 25.

18. See the discussion above.

19. See the treatment of Matthew 19:9 (marital unfaithfulness), 1 Corinthians 7:15 (desertion by unbeliever), and Romans 7:2-3 (death of a spouse) above. Regarding the question of whether or not men who underwent a biblically legitimate divorce could also be considered for church leadership positions if the divorce has taken place in the distant past (especially if the person was not a believer at the time) and if the man's present pattern (and proven track record) is that of marital faithfulness, see Page, "Marital Expectations," 103-113.

20. There is little biblical support for the type of sacramental model advocated in the Roman Catholic Church which roots its celibacy requirement for the priestly office in the unmarried state of Jesus Christ himself during his incarnate ministry. See "Singleness and Ministry" in chapter 8, above.

21. Cf. George W. Knight, *Commentary on the Pastoral Epistles*, New International Greek Testament Commentary (Carlisle, U.K.: Paternoster/Grand Rapids, Mich.: Eerdmans, 1992), 290; followed by Peter Balla, *The Child-Parent Relationship in the New Testament and Its Environment*, Wissenschaftliche Untersuchungen zum Neuen Testament 155 (Tübingen: Mohr Siebeck, 2003), 181.

22. For a discussion of the biblical teaching on children and parenting see chapter 4 and 5, above.

23. Calvin, *1 and 2 Timothy and Titus*, 54.

24. See discussion above. See also Chrysostom, *Homilies on 1 Timothy* 10.

25. See chapter 8, above.

Author Index

PRE-MODERN AUTHORS AND PERSONS

SUBJECT INDEX

Scripture Index

Extrabiblical References Index